"These fine studies on various aspects of Baptist fundamentalism in Canada fill a great need. . . . This book is also necessary reading for understanding the status and identity of Canadian Evangelicalism at the present. For like it or not, many modern-day Evangelicals in Canada are the spiritual and theological children and grandchildren of the believers discussed in these pages. Well conceived and superbly executed!"

—**Michael A. G. Haykin**
The Southern Baptist Theological Seminary

"Murray and Wilson have done yeoman's work for those interested in a more nuanced and scholarly view of fundamentalism in Canada. This edited volume is well researched, deftly edited, and a must-read for those interested in a much-maligned though highly influential movement among Canadian Baptists."

—**Gordon L. Heath**
McMaster Divinity College

"This book offers a carefully researched, well-argued, and accessible account of Canadian Baptists during a tumultuous century. For this American reader, it succeeds especially in showing the many ways in which Canadian Baptists resembled American fundamentalists, but also significant areas where being a Canadian made a difference. For pushing back against stereotypes and making good use of first-order research, editors Murray and Wilson have made a significant contribution to historical knowledge and theological understanding."

—**Mark Noll**
Author of *A History of Christianity in the United States and Canada*

"Understanding the role of fundamentalism among Canadian Baptists explains much about their life, ministry, and fragmentation in the twentieth century. This significant volume adds new perspectives on those who thought they were defending indispensable doctrines and demonstrates how Baptist congregational autonomy allowed them to have such a wide impact."

—**Robert S. Wilson**
Acadia Divinity College, emeritus

"The fundamentalist Baptists of Canada were not a small coterie of militant obscurantists but a varied set of conservative Protestants with diverse institutions and shifting priorities. In a volume that covers the whole of Canada and extends over an eventful century, eight authors ably portray the contours of a movement with strong but changing Christian convictions."

—**David Bebbington**
University of Stirling, emeritus

Canadian Baptist Fundamentalism, 1878–1978

McMaster Divinity College Press
McMaster General Studies Series, Volume 14
Canadian Baptist Historical Society Series 4

Other Volumes in the Canadian Baptist Historical Society Series:
- Heath, Gordon L., and Paul Wilson, eds. *Baptists and Public Life in Canada*. CBHS Series 1 (2012).
- Heath, Gordon L., and Michael A. G. Haykin, eds. *Baptists and War*. CBHS Series 2 (2014).
- Bowler, Sharon M., ed. *Canadian Baptist Women*. CBHS Series 3 (2016).

Canadian Baptist Fundamentalism, 1878–1978

edited by
TAYLOR MURRAY AND PAUL R. WILSON

☙PICKWICK *Publications* • Eugene, Oregon

CANADIAN BAPTIST FUNDAMENTALISM, 1878–1978

McMaster General Studies Series, Volume 14
McMaster Divinity College Press
Canadian Baptist Historical Society Series 4

Copyright © 2022 Wipf and Stock Publishers. All rights reserved. Except for brief quotations in critical publications or reviews, no part of this book may be reproduced in any manner without prior written permission from the publisher. Write: Permissions, Wipf and Stock Publishers, 199 W. 8th Ave., Suite 3, Eugene, OR 97401.

Pickwick Publications
An Imprint of Wipf and Stock Publishers
199 W. 8th Ave., Suite 3
Eugene, OR 97401

McMaster Divinity College Press
1280 Main Street West
Hamilton, ON, Canada L8S 4K1

www.wipfandstock.com

PAPERBACK ISBN: 978-1-7252-6071-9
HARDCOVER ISBN: 978-1-7252-6072-6
EBOOK ISBN: 978-1-7252-6073-3

McMaster General Studies Series
ISSN 2564-4408 (Print)
ISSN 2564-4416 (Ebook)

Cataloguing-in-Publication data:

Names: Murray, Taylor, editor. | Wilson, Paul R., editor.

Title: Canadian Baptist Fundamentalism, 1878–1978 / edited by Taylor Murray and Paul R. Wilson

Description: Eugene, OR: Pickwick Publications, 2022 | McMaster General Studies Series 14 | Canadian Baptist Historical Society Series 4 | Includes bibliographical references and index.

Identifiers: ISBN 978-1-7252-6071-9 (paperback). | ISBN 978-1-7252-6072-6 (hardcover) | ISBN 978-1-7252-6073-3 (ebook).

Subjects: LCSH: Baptists—Canada—Doctrines—History.

Classification: BX6251 .M87 2022 (print). | BX6251 (ebook).

VERSION NUMBER 04/19/22

Cover Photo: Jarvis Street Baptist Church, Toronto, ON. Photographed by Taylor Murray, 2017

We lovingly dedicate this volume to two conservative Baptists who would have been deeply interested in the contents of this book:

Rev. Robert Weldon Wilson, ThM
and
Rev. Stuart Eldon Murray, DMin, DD

Contents

Contributors | ix
Preface | xiii

Context and Contours: An Introduction to Canadian Baptist Fundamentalism—*Paul R. Wilson and Taylor Murray* | 1

1   Identity and Ideology: An Overview of Canadian Baptist Fundamentalism, 1878–1978—*Paul R. Wilson* | 17

2   Joshua Denovan: A Prototypical Militant Fundamentalist, 1829–1901—*Paul R. Wilson* | 49

3   The Quiet Fundamentalist—Edward John Stobo, Jr. —*C. Mark Steinacher* | 93

4   "The Great Contention": Ontario Baptists and the Fundamentalist-Modernist Struggle for McMaster University, 1919–1927 —*Doug Adams* | 119

5   Brandon College and the Regular Baptists of British Columbia —*Robert Burkinshaw* | 157

6   From United Baptist to Independent Baptist: Fundamentalism and Baptist Identity in the Maritime Provinces of Canada in the 1930s—*Taylor Murray* | 179

7   Prairie Preachers and Educators: William "Bible Bill" Aberhart, L. E. Maxwell, and Baptist Fundamentalism in Alberta, 1922–1970—*Brian Froese* | 205

8   Imports and Exports: Cross-Border Fundamentalism
    in the Early Twentieth Century—*Jeffrey P. Straub* | 235

9   "Wider Than This One Church": The Fellowship of Evangelical
    Baptist Churches in Canada, 1953–1970—*Ian Hugh Clary* | 265

    Canadian Baptist Fundamentalism Since 1978:
    An Epilogue—*Taylor Murray and Paul R. Wilson* | 292

    Index of Names | 301
    Index of Subjects | 305

Contributors

EDITORS AND CONTRIBUTORS

Taylor Murray is an Instructor of the History of Christianity and Creative Producer of Distributed Learning at Tyndale University in Toronto. He is co-author of *Baptists in Canada: Their History and Polity* (Pickwick, 2020) and co-editor of *Atlantic Baptists and Their World: A Festschrift in Honour of Dr. Robert S. Wilson* (Baptist Heritage in Atlantic Canada, 2020). He serves as Assistant Editor of *Post-Christendom Studies*, the McMaster Divinity College Centre for Post-Christendom Studies' academic journal.

Paul R. Wilson is a former professor and pastor, and he is currently the President of the Canadian Baptist Historical Society. He holds a PhD in History from the University of Western Ontario. Dr. Wilson has a long-standing interest in Canadian Baptist history. His PhD dissertation examined the relationship between "Baptists and Business." He has also co-edited with Gordon Heath a volume on *Baptists and Public Life in Canada* (Pickwick, 2012) and published articles, conference papers, and chapters in books about the rich history of Canadian Baptists.

OTHER CONTRIBUTORS

Doug Adams (MDiv, Toronto Baptist Seminary; PhD, Western University) is currently employed at Western University, London, Ontario. He studied at Toronto Baptist Seminary and graduated in 1977. He went on to serve as an associate pastor at Briscoe Street Baptist Church, London, Ontario, and later as pastor of East Williams Baptist Church, a position he occupied for 20 years. Doug also served as professor of church history at Toronto Baptist

Seminary for nearly twenty years. During those years and subsequently, Doug pursued further education at the University of Western Ontario and in 2015 earned his PhD in history. His dissertation was a biographical account of Dr. Thomas T. Shields, entitled: "The War of the Worlds: The Militant Fundamentalism of Dr. Thomas Todhunter Shields and the Paradox of Modernity."

Robert (Bob) Burkinshaw served as a member of Trinity Western University's Department of History between 1984 and 2020 and as Dean of Humanities and Social Sciences between 1998 and 2015. His research is in the area of evangelicalism in western Canada. In 2015 he moved to Ontario, dividing his time between developing a farm with his family and teaching for TWU online and at its Laurentian Leadership Centre in Ottawa. He officially retired in 2020 but still is busy with farming and a little online teaching.

Ian Hugh Clary (PhD, University of the Free State) is Assistant Professor of Historical Theology at Colorado Christian University, Lakewood, CO. He is the author of *Reformed Evangelicalism and the Search for a Usable Past: The Historiography of Arnold Dallimore, Pastor-Historian* (Vandenhoeck & Ruprecht, 2020) and *God Crown His Own Gifts: Augustine, Grace, and the Monks of Hadrumetum* (H&E Publishing, 2021). He and his family are members of Calvary Redeeming Grace Church in Lakewood.

Brian Froese is Professor of History at Canadian Mennonite University. He is the author of the book, *California Mennonites* (Johns Hopkins, 2015), and is currently finishing a book on Mennonite and transnational evangelical missions in British Columbia called, *Supernatural British Columbia: Mennonites*, and another project on conservative evangelicalism, transnationalism, and politics in the prairies called, "Northern Errand."

C. Mark Steinacher is a Baptist pastor who has served in Alberta and Ontario. A graduate of the University of Toronto (BA, MDiv, ThM, ThD), he is currently a member of the faculty at Tyndale Seminary, where he created and launched the Seminary's online program. He has taught at McMaster Divinity College, where he also was Acting Director of the Canadian Baptist Archives. A former President of the Canadian Baptist Historical Society, he is currently Vice President. He is the author of numerous book chapters, encyclopedia articles, and dictionary entries.

CONTRIBUTORS

Jeffrey P. Straub earned his PhD from Southern Baptist Theological Seminary. He spent sixteen years teaching Historical Theology at Central Baptist Theological Seminary in Minneapolis. He is the author of *The Making of a Battle Royal: The Rise of Liberalism in Northern Baptist Life, 1870–1920* (Pickwick, 2018). Now semi-retired, he continues to write, speak, and teach internationally.

Preface

This is not the final word on Canadian Baptist fundamentalism; it is, however, a helpful starting point. Each of the chapters in this volume tells a different piece of the story, and together they provide a sketch of the birth, growth, and evolution of the movement in the various regions of Canada. We hope we have done its retelling justice. While we are nearly a century removed from the fundamentalist-modernist debates, many Canadian Baptists continue to feel the after-effects of these events even today. We hope, therefore, that pastors and interested laypeople, as well as scholars, will engage with the contents of this book.

We have incurred many debts working on this project. Thanks first and foremost to the contributing authors, each of whom exceeded our already-high expectations. We are grateful to the editorial committee of the Canadian Baptist Historical Society Series for giving this project the greenlight. Robert S. Wilson and Adam D. Rudy each provided helpful feedback that improved this collection. Thanks, also, to David J. Fuller, Managing Editor of McMaster Divinity College Press, who helped us bring this project to life (and was gracious with us when we missed our deadline—twice).

We received a significant amount of personal support behind the scenes. Our wives, Leanne (Taylor) and Yvonne (Paul), deserve significant recognition, for they had the unenviable task of listening to us talk about this project for years.

—*Taylor Murray and Paul R. Wilson*
Easter 2021

Context and Contours

An Introduction to Canadian Baptist Fundamentalism

PAUL R. WILSON AND TAYLOR MURRAY

INTRODUCTION

HISTORIAN JOHN STACKHOUSE HAS observed that in Canada today "the most common term for frightening people is 'fundamentalist.'"[1] In a similar vein, sociologists Sam Reimer and Michael Wilkinson have captured how Canadians use the label "fundamentalism" and view those who fall into that social category: "'Fundamentalist' is a derogatory label for most Canadians, referring to those who are dogmatic, intolerant, and argumentative: in short, fundamentalists are un-Canadian."[2] With so much antipathy and anxiety present in the Canadian court of public opinion, why would anyone want to examine the history and theology of the Canadian Baptist fundamentalist movement?[3]

---

1. Stackhouse, "Evangelicalism and Fundamentalism," 1.
2. Reimer and Wilkinson, *A Culture of Faith*, 131.
3. Historians and theologians sometimes use "Canadian Baptists" to identify the convention Baptists, namely, those Baptists who are associated with the Canadian Baptist Ministries (i.e., Canadian Baptists of Atlantic Canada, the Canadian Baptists of Ontario and Quebec, the Canadian Baptists of Western Canada, and L'Union d'Églises Baptistes Francophones du Canada). This volume, however, employs the term broadly simply to designate the Canadian focus of the study.

Canadian Baptist Fundamentalism, 1878–1978

As scholars who focus on the history and theology of Canadian Baptists, the current aversion to fundamentalism within what Brian Clarke and Stuart Macdonald have argued is "Canada's post-Christian society," stimulates our intellectual curiosity and motivates us to investigate and deepen our knowledge and understanding of this controversial subject.[4] In our view, there are many historical patterns yet to be discerned, turning-points in need of analysis, and lessons still to be learned from the fundamentalist movement and its expressions within the Canadian Baptist experience. We readily admit that there are many risks in undertaking such a venture. But for us the potential rewards—namely a more nuanced, textured, and comprehensive understanding of Canadian Baptist fundamentalism—outweigh the risks. We invite our readers to resist the temptation to pre-judge this endeavour and engage the material offered here with an inquisitive and investigative mindset.

This book presents scholarship that addresses a serious gap in the historiography of Canadian Protestant fundamentalism. While multidisciplinary scholarship on fundamentalism has grown exponentially worldwide since the Iran hostage crisis of 1979 and the events of 9/11, and a few individual studies have advanced our historical and theological understanding of Canadian Baptist fundamentalism, there is no single volume that has presented a national picture that more fully explores Canadian Baptist engagement with the fundamentalist movement in the late-nineteenth and twentieth centuries.[5] From the historical and theological perspectives, this project partially fills this gap by exploring old themes in new ways and expanding the scope of the ongoing discussions and debates about Canadian Protestant fundamentalism through the presentation of new topics.

DEFINING TERMS

One challenge for any scholar engaged in the study of Canada's religious history is that one cannot assume that today's reader comes to a collection of articles about Baptist fundamentalism with a working knowledge

---

4. Clarke and Macdonald, *Leaving Christianity*, 232–45.

5. The selection of 1978 as the end date for this book was based on the increased worldwide awareness of fundamentalism that began with the Iran hostage crisis in 1979. As historians Martin Marty and R. Scott Appleby have noted, there are many forms of fundamentalism in various religious traditions worldwide. For a detailed analysis of these manifestations of fundamentalism see Marty and Appleby, *Fundamentalisms Observed*.

of Baptists, fundamentalists and fundamentalism, or their history and theology. In response to this reality, this introduction provides a few definitions and lays out the historical/theological context for this book's detailed discussion and analysis of fundamentalism within the Canadian Baptist religious subculture.

What (or Who) is a Baptist?

In broad terms, the Baptist religious character was and is individualistic, experiential, activist, and voluntary. Historically these characteristics found expression in beliefs and practices that were both shared with those in other Protestant denominations, such as some Anglicans, Methodists, Presbyterians, and Congregationalists, and also distinct from other Protestant religious groups.[6]

On the shared side, Baptists are Evangelicals. David Bebbington has argued that "four qualities" characterize evangelicals: "*conversionism*, the belief that lives need to be changed; *activism*, the expression of the gospel in effort; *biblicism*, a particular regard for the Bible; and . . . *crucicentrism*, a stress on the sacrifice of Christ on the cross."[7] Together these "special marks" of "Evangelical religion" constituted "a quadrilateral of priorities" that were and remain "the basis of Evangelicalism."[8] In the period covered by this book, many (but not all) Canadian Baptists held these views in common with evangelicals in other Canadian Protestant denominations.

On the distinct side, the list of beliefs and practices that shaped Baptist identity and distinguished Baptists from other Christian religious groups is considerable and complex. Careful and thoughtful study is required to fully grasp the scope and shape of the Baptist milieu. Baptists share an identity, but they are often not identical. For example, while historically many Baptists have been Calvinistic in their theology, Freewill Baptists are Arminian theologically. Also, based on their belief in the priesthood of all believers, Baptists have traditionally held to the view that the independence of a local Baptist church is paramount in matters of faith, polity, and practice.[9] One needs to keep in mind that although Baptists may generally have the same

---

6. For a discussion on what Baptists (and Baptists in Canada in particular) share with other Christians, see the extended discussion in Heath et al., *Baptists in Canada*.

7. Bebbington, *Evangelicalism*, 2–3. Emphasis in original.

8. Bebbington, *Evangelicalism*, 3.

9. E.g., Canadian Baptists of Ontario and Quebec, *Why Baptist?* 11.

distinctive beliefs and practices, there are also Baptists who, in one way or another, vary from the norm.

In the Canadian context, historian George Rawlyk has argued that by the late nineteenth and early twentieth centuries, four Baptist identities were evident: fundamentalists, modernists, liberal evangelicals, and conservative evangelicals. Around 1900, some "disconcerted Baptists" raised the alarm about "destructive" influences and ideas that, in their view, undermined "the theological and ideological underpinnings of their church and their society."[10] In particular, these fundamentalists were distressed by the development of "theological modernism" with its acceptance of "Darwinian scientific progress" and the hermeneutics of German higher criticism and its abandonment of traditional evangelical beliefs and practices. In response, these Baptists fought to preserve the theological and moral purity of their faith and, with "a remarkable degree of 'violence in thought and language,'" denounced all who displayed any modernist tendency.[11] At the other end of "the Baptist theological spectrum" were the modernists who rejected the erection of any barriers to new theological ideas and methods. Arrogant and self-assured, these Baptists sought to bring their church into the modern age both theologically and culturally.[12] To achieve their ends, modernist Baptists sought the support of wealthy and powerful liberal evangelical Baptists who "became the 'intellectual priests' of the emerging Central Canadian Baptist commercial elite."[13] Characterized by an "accommodationist spirit" that sought to "keep a foot in both camps" the liberal evangelicals maintained a commitment to both "biblical faith" and "a modern outlook."[14] In the "mainstream" of Canadian Baptist identity were the conservative evangelicals. While "sympathetic to the theological underpinnings of fundamentalism" and willing to erect some barriers to protect the purity of their faith, these Baptists were also "careful" to allow for the flow of new ideas and some accommodation of modernity.[15] These diverse Baptist identities lay at the heart of Baptist life and thought in the period covered by this book.

---

10. Rawlyk, "A. L. McCrimmon," 38–39. For another taxonomy, see also Rawlyk, *Champions of the Truth*, 70.

11. Rawlyk, "A. L. McCrimmon," 38.

12. Rawlyk, "A. L. McCrimmon," 38–39.

13. Rawlyk, "A. L. McCrimmon," 39.

14. Rawlyk, "A. L. McCrimmon," 39.

15. Rawlyk, "A. L. McCrimmon," 38–39.

Core Baptist principles, of course, also played a pivotal role in the ongoing exchanges between these identities. Scholars, denominational publications, and church leaders have covered these "Baptist distinctives" in detail,[16] so this introduction provides only a brief summary of the major theological perspectives that historically have defined Canadian Baptists. A basic knowledge of Canadian Baptists requires some understanding of five principles.

First is the Baptist view of salvation. Baptists hold that one is saved by faith in Jesus Christ and the efficacy of his sacrificial death and miraculous resurrection. Salvation is bestowed by the grace of God on the one who believes. Salvation is also an individual decision and experience. As Rex Mason noted, "We stress that no one is born a Christian, and no one becomes a Christian by the faith of someone else. We must face God one by one."[17] This view stands in contrast to some other Christian groups who believe that saving grace is conferred through sacraments, such as baptism, confirmation, the eucharist, penance, extreme unction, orders, and marriage. Although some elements of sacramental thought are not unknown among Baptists, such a view has not predominated within the Canadian Baptist experience.[18]

Second, instead of sacraments, Baptists have instituted two ordinances: baptism and the Lord's Supper (also called communion). Historically, Baptists in Canada have understood these practices symbolically. Believers' baptism by immersion is perhaps the best-known Baptist practice. Through the act of baptism, one gives public witness to a personal faith. And the immersion of the participant symbolizes the death and resurrection of Jesus and testifies to the salvation of the believer and their desire to walk in newness of life. This understanding and practice of baptism stands in contrast to other Christian groups that baptize infants as a means of conferring God's saving grace on an individual. It should also be noted that Baptists often make baptism a prerequisite for church membership, and a

---

16. Each of the major Baptist bodies in Canada have statements of faith accessible on their websites. For more detailed studies, see Heath et al., *Baptists in Canada*; Jones, *What Canadian Baptists Believe*; and Brackney, *The Baptists*.

17. Mason, "'Keynote' Lecture," 4.

18. For Canadian Baptist scholarship that argues that baptismal sacramentalism has also been present within the Baptist tradition, see Fowler, *More Than a Symbol* and *Rethinking Baptism*.

lively discussion and debate about the nature and purpose of baptism is currently ongoing among Baptist theologians.[19]

The other ordinance is the Lord's Supper. In this time of remembrance and reflection, Baptists give thanks to God for Christ's sacrifice on the cross. The bread is a symbol of Christ's body and the wine a symbol of his shed blood. These elements are given to each individual and often taken together as a congregation. Again, this practice is viewed as an act of discipleship, not as a sacramental act that imparts salvation. The question of who is eligible to partake of the Lord's Supper has prompted controversy among Baptists. Many Baptists practice close communion, which restricts participation to those who are church members. Other Baptists have favoured open communion. This practice permits access to anyone who has experienced salvation as the Baptists define salvation.

Third, Baptists believe that the Bible alone is the supreme authority in all matters of faith and practice. Traditionally, Baptists have held that the Bible is inspired by God. It should be noted here that biblical inerrancy (that the Bible is free of error) would become a cornerstone of Baptist fundamentalism.[20] Each person has the liberty to read and interpret the biblical text for themselves. Traditions, creeds, and the writings of church fathers are neither inspired nor authoritative. This view of biblical authority stands in contrast to some other Christian groups that accept traditional church teaching and creeds as authoritative.

Fourth, Baptists have a distinct perspective on the church. Church membership is voluntary. One must request membership in a Baptist church. The essential prerequisites to membership include the experience of salvation and believer's baptism. With the exception of pastors and other paid staff, service in the church is also voluntary. Also, traditional Baptist church polity is congregational. Each Baptist church is independent. A congregation must decide for itself what beliefs it holds and what actions it

---

19. The Baptism discussion and debate is a prime example of the fact that Baptist theology is not static. Canadian Baptist theologians Stan Fowler and Stanley Porter, and British Baptist historical theologian Anthony Cross have played leading roles in the ongoing discussion and debate about this issue. This debate shows that some Baptist theologians are not afraid to reconsider their theology and practice. For a sense of the discussion and debate, see, for example, Fowler, *More Than a Symbol*; Fowler, *Rethinking Baptism*; Porter and Cross, eds., *Dimensions of Baptism*; Porter and Cross, eds., *Baptism, the New Testament and The Church*; Cross, *Baptism and the Baptists*; Cross, *Recovering the Evangelical Sacrament*.

20. For an explanation and history of this doctrine from a Baptist source, see Graham, "The Inerrancy of Scripture," 1–15.

must take. Congregational polity, however, does not mean that Canadian Baptists have avoided or eschewed association with other Baptist churches or other forms of polity. For example, Stuart Ivison and Fred Rosser noted that "Before 1820, there was no such thing in Upper or Lower Canada as an 'unassociated' Baptist church."[21] Over time, some Baptist churches have adopted a "board rule" polity where organizational and/or operational decisions are made by a board of deacons or elders instead of the congregation.[22] Still, in the traditional Baptist context the individual congregation is paramount.

Baptists also believe in a hard separation between church and state. Baptists oppose state religion, state interference in religion, and prize the individual's right and freedom to follow his or her convictions and conscience in matters of faith and practice. Atlantic Baptists have clearly expressed this position: "There should not be a church-controlled state, nor a state-controlled church. God has given legitimate roles to both, but neither is to encroach upon the rights or obligations of the other. They are, however, under obligation to recognize and reinforce each other as each seeks to fulfil its divine function."[23]

Finally, Baptists are activists who share the good news of salvation through Christ with the world. Canadian Baptists have engaged in mission enterprises at home and around the globe.[24] They have also made efforts to bring about moral and social reform. For example, Canada's healthcare system owes its existence to the efforts of Tommy Douglas, a Baptist pastor turned politician from Saskatchewan.[25]

While the principles listed above provide a basic overview of what Baptists believe, two further strands of Baptist theology that do not normally appear in the list of Baptist distinctives are highly relevant in any discussion of Baptist fundamentalism: separation and eschatology. In the late nineteenth and early twentieth centuries, as part of their progressive view of sanctification, Canadian Baptists consistently emphasized the biblical teaching concerning separation between a Christian and the "world."

21. Ivison and Rosser, *The Baptists in Upper and Lower Canada*, 164.

22. For a contemporary Canadian Baptist example see the By-Laws of New Life Community Baptist Church, Duncan, British Columbia. Available at www.newlifechurch.ca.

23. Canadian Baptists of Atlantic Canada, "Baptist Distinctives," 2.

24. E.g., see Wilson, "A Mission Transformed"; and Elisha, "Canadian Baptist Mission Work Among Women in Andhra," 42–54

25. Beardsall, "One Here Will Constant Be," 157–62.

While many Baptists agreed that adherence to core Baptist beliefs and the practice of a strict morality and a circumspect lifestyle were marks of a separated Baptist, some liberal evangelical and modernist Baptists accepted and accommodated a more open and modern theology and a less restrictive and legalistic view of morality and lifestyle. These Baptists often sought respectability, sociocultural integration and their place in the middle and upper middle classes.[26] In response to these "modernists," fundamentalist Baptists extended separation to a second degree. They now sought not just separation from the "world," but separation also from their more liberal brethren. As we shall see, such views had profound implications for Canadian Baptists.

Eschatology—beliefs about the end of life, the age, the world, God's judgement, and Christ's return and kingdom—was also a key theological theme for fundamentalists. Many, but certainly not all, fundamentalists adopted the premillennial dispensationalist eschatological position as the means to explain the end of all things. Notable Canadian Baptists who accepted this view included Joshua Denovan, Pastor of Alexander Street Baptist Church in Toronto, from 1878–1893, and William Aberhart, Pastor of Westbourne Baptist Church in Calgary, 1915–1929.[27]

What (or Who) is a Fundamentalist?

How one defines fundamentalism is a hotly debated topic these days. The burgeoning literature on fundamentalism in multiple academic disciplines and in both religious and secular contexts has produced multiple definitions that can be confusing and difficult to navigate. Is fundamentalism a mental illness or disorder, a radical religious belief system, an orthodox religious belief system, a heretical religious belief system, a historical and theological religious movement, or one, none, some, or all of the above? One can find support for every one of these perspectives and plenty more besides.[28] This reality often leaves one in a quagmire.

---

26. For an extensive analysis, see Wilson, "Baptists and Business"; and Wilson, "Caring for Their Community," 219–62.

27. For a summary of Denovan's dispensational views see Sawatsky, "Looking for that Blessed Hope," 69–71. For a brief summary of Aberhart's dispensationalism see Ellis, "Baptists and Radical Politics," 168–73.

28. E.g., see Ross, "Losing Faith in Fundamentalist Christianity"; Strozier et al., *The Fundamentalist Mindset*; Larsen, *The Fundamentalist Mind*; Taylor, *The Brain Supremacy*, 5, 47–48, 110–15; Zhong et al., "Biological and Cognitive Underpinnings of Religious Fundamentalism," 18–25; and Abbott, "Religious Fundamentalism and Mental Illness,"

Our interest in this volume is on Canadian Baptist fundamentalism as a historical and theological movement. Consequently, the definitions of fundamentalism offered in this book are grounded in the work of historians and historical theologians. That being the case, it is necessary to briefly explore the origins of the term "fundamentalism" and how historians have defined such a contentious term. Curtis Lee Laws, an American Baptist pastor and editor of the *Watchman-Examiner*, is credited with first coining the term "fundamentalism" in 1920. Stackhouse has noted that "originally it was a positive term for those who maintained the essential 'fundamentals of the faith' against modern attacks from liberal or modernist theology."[29] As American historian John Fea has rightly pointed out "fundamentalism [both as term and a movement] is neither static nor monolithic."[30] Even with our specific focus, this makes arriving at a fixed definition challenging. Nevertheless, the definitions used in this volume are those that enable the authors to conduct a contextualized and nuanced historical and theological analysis.

The eminent historian of fundamentalism, George Marsden, offered a popular definition of an American Christian fundamentalist: "A Fundamentalist is an Evangelical who is angry about something."[31] Marsden went on to offer a more specific and precise academic definition: "an American fundamentalist is an evangelical who is militant in opposition to liberal theology in the churches or changes in cultural values or mores, such as those associated with 'secular humanism.'"[32] The list of key elements that define a fundamentalist offered by American scholars includes purity of doctrine and lifestyle, biblical inerrancy, separation, and a dispensational eschatology.[33]

In this book, we allow each author the freedom to define fundamentalism writ large or some aspects of fundamentalism in ways best-suited for their particular topic. This introduction and the opening chapter each employ a taxonomy of *militant fundamentalism/fundamentalist*, *moderate fundamentalism/fundamentalist*, and *rebels* in order to distinguish between

47–61.

29. Stackhouse, "Evangelicalism and Fundamentalism," 11.
30. Fea, "Understanding the Changing Façade," 198.
31. Marsden, *Understanding Fundamentalism*, 1.
32. Marsden, *Understanding Fundamentalism*, 1.
33. E.g., see Beale, *In Pursuit of Purity*; Pickering, *Biblical Separation*; and Bauder and Delnay, *One in Hope and Doctrine*.

post-WWII Canadian Baptist groups that sometimes agreed and disagreed with one another. One will note, however, that even within these groups there were differences in degree, theology, and perspective.

Generally, militant Canadian Baptist fundamentalism was characterized by its commitment to theological absolutism and orthodoxy, authoritarian structure and leadership, strident language and demeanor, its legalistic interpretation and application of biblical teaching, and its emphasis on entire separation from the world. Militant fundamentalists were often publicly critical of those Baptists who disagreed with its theological and cultural perspectives. And militants favoured division over dialogue or tolerance of those who held different views of theology and culture.

Moderate Canadian Baptist fundamentalism maintained the commitment to theological orthodoxy but was less authoritarian and legalistic. These Baptist fundamentalists were open to engagement with like-minded Baptists and evangelicals. Moderates believed that the militants went too far in their legalistic interpretation of separation, their fear-mongering, negativity, and exclusivity, their claims of theological infallibility, and their never-ending attacks on fellow Baptists and evangelicals. Instead, moderates chose to emphasize and share the "good news" offered in the Christian message. Also, without compromising their core beliefs, many moderate fundamentalists engaged in dialogue with other Christians and the culture at large.

A third Baptist group, sometimes labeled as "rebels," became evident within some Baptist communities by the late 1960s. These Baptists, who had fundamentalist roots, called for a reunification of Canadian Baptists, left behind the dogmatism, legalism, and separatism of fundamentalism, and were open to new theological movements, such as the Charismatic movement. The presence of these three Canadian Baptist groups by 1970 illustrates how profoundly the fundamentalist-modernist controversies reshaped Canadian Baptist identity.

When speaking about fundamentalism, the renowned and prolific religious studies scholar Huston Smith once said, "all isms end up in schisms."[34] That has certainly been true for Canadian Baptists. Fundamentalism has divided and separated Baptists and spawned new perspectives, movements, and institutions.[35] This reality raises many questions. Was there a distinctly

---

34. For this quotation see Larsen, *The Fundamentalist Mind*, xv.

35. For a recent publication that examines the schism within Ontario fundamentalism in 1948–49, see Wilson, "Torn Asunder." For a wider discussion on a new movement

Canadian version (or versions) of Protestant fundamentalism or did Canadian Protestant fundamentalists simply follow the lead of their American co-religionists? More specifically, did Canadian Baptists have a version (or versions) of fundamentalism that distinguished them from each other and their American brethren or were Canadian Baptists in lockstep with one another and like-minded American Baptists? One scholar that has wrestled with the matter of American fundamentalist influence on one Canadian Baptist is Tim Callaway in his analysis of Leslie E. Maxwell and the Prairie Bible Institute (PBI). Essentially, Callaway argues that the fundamentalism of PBI was not "a carbon copy of the American fundamentalist paradigm or any component or institution thereof."[36] Furthermore, Callaway contends that when American fundamentalism divided into two camps in the 1940s, "PBI attempted to steer a somewhat middle course between the two factions."[37] Whether or not a similar strategy was adopted by other Canadian Baptists remains to be seen. While this book will not provide complete answers to the questions posed above, it will offer some deeper insight into the factors, both foreign and domestic, that shaped the Canadian Baptist fundamentalist identity and experience.

OUTLINE OF THE BOOK

In the first chapter, Paul Wilson provides a roadmap for the remainder of the book by identifying three primary "phases" in Canadian Baptist fundamentalism that span a century—from 1878 to 1978. He identifies the first of these phases as the "Formative Phase" (1878–1918), during which fundamentalism found its footing among Baptists in Canada, especially in the central region. The second is the "Fight and Fragmentation Phase" (1919–1945), which includes the majority of events that historians have traditionally identified as the fundamentalist-modernist controversies. The third and final phase that Wilson highlights is what he calls the "Decline and New Forms Phase" (1946–1978), during which time militant fundamentalists were pushed to the edges of their own movement and a more moderate form of fundamentalism won the day.

In the next chapter, Wilson profiles Joshua Denovan, the Pastor of Alexander Street Baptist Church in Toronto, and argues that this influential

---

created out of these divisions, namely the Fellowship of Evangelical Baptist Churches of Canada, see Haykin and Lockey, eds., *A Glorious Fellowship of Churches*.

36. Callaway, *Training Disciplined Soldiers for Christ*, xv.

37. Callaway, *Training Disciplined Soldiers for Christ*, xv.

pastor's career clearly demonstrates that the militant breed of fundamentalism was present among Canadian Baptists in the late nineteenth century. Denovan, he argues, is a clear example of a Canadian Baptist proto-fundamentalist and a progenitor of the kind of militancy that characterized the career of another Toronto fundamentalist: T. T. Shields.

Exploring the career of yet another Canadian Baptist proto-fundamentalist, C. Mark Steinacher introduces us to E. J. Stobo, a Canadian contributor to the famous booklet series, *The Fundamentals*, and an atypical fundamentalist. Indeed, unlike others who adopted the title "fundamentalist," Stobo had a comparatively irenic demeanour and exhibited a very different kind of fundamentalism. According to Steinacher, while he was a keen proponent of biblical truth, he refused to "dehumanize, ridicule or argue unfairly against those with whom he differed."

Next, Doug Adams explores the events and key figures involved in the fundamentalist-modernist controversy over McMaster University in the early twentieth century. Adams provides an argument and additional evidence that gives more substance to the long-held assumption and claim that Shields was the primary fundamentalist instigator and driver of this controversy. He deepens our understanding of the tactics and machinations used by Shields and his fundamentalist allies to both defend and advance their cause.

Turning our attention westward, Robert Burkinshaw explores the reasons behind the fundamentalist schism within the Baptist Convention of British Columbia in the 1920s. As the first organizational division over fundamentalism among Baptists in North America, the events in British Columbia merit close consideration. He notes that a mixture of factors caused Baptists in British Columbia, especially in Vancouver, to be particularly receptive to the fundamentalist criticisms of Brandon College and the Baptist Union of Western Canada. Among them, he argues that a poignant evangelistic campaign under French E. Oliver in 1917 served as an indictment of liberalism in Vancouver and galvanized conservative Baptists in the region. Moreover, proximity to the Vancouver Bible Training School, which opened the year following Oliver's campaign, effectively supplemented these criticisms and helped solidify the theologically-conservative orientation of many Baptists in the city. Burkinshaw argues that these factors, among others, provided a fertile bed for Baptist fundamentalism in British Columbia.

In his chapter on Baptist fundamentalism in the Maritime Provinces, Taylor Murray shows the pivotal place that differences of opinion on Baptist polity played in both the attempted schism within the United Baptist Convention of the Maritime Provinces in 1934 and the significant internal schism within the Baptist fundamentalist movement in the region in 1939. In addition to his coverage of the movement's major protagonists, J. J. Sidey and J. B. Daggett, he looks at the contributions made by lesser-known regional Baptist fundamentalists—particularly T. A. Meister and his associates, Maxwell Bolser and Douglass M. Fraser. These latter insights shed more light on the activities and different perspectives of Maritime Baptist fundamentalists.

In his study of William Aberhart and L. E. Maxwell, Brian Froese reveals the surprising diversity that existed within Baptist fundamentalism in Alberta in the early twentieth century. His comparison of these two "Prairie Preachers" convincingly shows that although they shared opinions on the importance of biblical education and radio outreach, they differed wildly in their theological interpretations and approaches to ministry. In any event, despite their differences, Froese notes that together these two fundamentalists made "Alberta an internationally recognized centre of fundamentalist Christianity."

Jeffrey P. Straub takes a deeper look at cross-border influences, especially in central Canada. In particular, Straub's analysis explores the exchanges between some key American fundamentalists and T. T. Shields. His findings show that for a short time as President of the Baptist Bible Union from 1922–1929, Shields exerted considerable influence within the North American fundamentalist circles. The rift between Shields and William B. Riley that followed the debacle at Des Moines University in 1929 illustrates how severe cross-border tensions between fundamentalists were at times.

In the final chapter, Ian Clary traces the evolution of Canadian Baptist fundamentalism as exhibited in the formation of the Fellowship of Evangelical Baptist Churches in Canada. As he shows, the creation of this new body in 1953 was emblematic of the shift away from the more pronounced militant fundamentalism of the early twentieth century toward a much more moderate fundamentalism that was more in line with the North American evangelical movement. Indeed, he writes, the new national denominational body prioritized cooperation over division in order to more effectively evangelize coast-to-coast.

Canadian Baptist Fundamentalism, 1878–1978

There are many unanswered questions about the history of fundamentalism in Canada generally and more particularly the fundamentalist Canadian Baptist experience. This single volume does not attempt or claim to fill all of the existing gaps in our knowledge of Canadian Baptist fundamentalism. For example, we acknowledge that this book focuses primarily on male Baptist fundamentalist leaders and not the views of the Baptist laity generally. Various sections of this book provide brief glimpses into the female responses to the fundamentalist-modernist controversy; however, a separate volume is needed to fully explore what women and the laity thought and did as the disruption and division created by internal controversy and conflict between Baptist fundamentalists and their Baptist brethren took hold in many Baptist churches and some Baptist denominations. What this book does, however, is establish a starting-point on which future scholarship can build. Our hope is that this book will stimulate further discussion and debate about the role that fundamentalism played in reshaping the contours of Baptist belief and practice within the Canadian Baptist and wider Protestant contexts.

BIBLIOGRAPHY

Abbott, Roselyn M. "Religious Fundamentalism and Mental Illness: A Group Analytic Exploration." *Group Analysis* 42.1 (2009) 47–61.

Bauder, Kevin, and Robert Delnay. *One in Hope and Doctrine: Origins of Baptist Fundamentalism, 1870–1950*. Schaumburg: Regular Baptist Books, 2014.

Beardsall, Sandra. "'One Here Will Constant Be': The Christian Witness of T. C. 'Tommy' Douglas." In *Baptists and Public Life in Canada*, edited by Gordon L. Heath and Paul S. Wilson, 143–66. McMaster General Series 2. Canadian Baptist Historical Society Series 1. Eugene, OR: Pickwick, 2012.

Beale, David O. *In Pursuit of Purity: American Fundamentalism Since 1850*. Greenville, SC: Bob Jones University Press, 1986.

Bebbington, David. *Evangelicalism in Modern Britain: A History from the 1730s to the 1980s*. London: Routledge, 1988.

Brackney, William H. *The Baptists*. Westport, CT: Greenwood, 1994.

Callaway, Timothy Wray. *Training Disciplined Soldiers for Christ: The Influence of American Fundamentalism on Prairie Bible Institute*. Bloomington, IN: WestBow, 2013.

Canadian Baptists of Atlantic Canada, "Baptist Distinctives." N.p., Online: baptist-atlantic.ca

Canadian Baptists of Ontario and Quebec, *Why Baptist? A Tool for CBOQ Churches Exploring their Unique Baptist Identity in 21st Century Central Canada*. Etobicoke, ON: Canadian Baptists of Ontario and Quebec, n.d.

Clarke, Brian, and Stuart Macdonald. *Leaving Christianity: Changing Allegiances in Canada Since 1945*. Advancing Studies in Religion 2. Montreal and Kingston: McGill-Queen's University Press, 2017.

Cross, Anthony R. *Baptism and the Baptists: Theology and Practice in Twentieth-Century Britain*. Studies in Baptist History and Thought 3. Carlisle: Paternoster, 2000.

———. *Recovering the Evangelical Sacrament: Baptisma Semper Reformandum*. Eugene, OR: Pickwick, 2013.

Elisha, James. "Canadian Baptist Mission Work among Women in Andhra, India, 1874–1924." *Baptist History and Heritage* 41.1 (2006) 42–54.

Ellis, Walter E. "Baptists and Radical Politics in Western Canada, 1920–1950." In *Baptists in Canada: Search for Identity Amidst Diversity*, edited by Jarold K. Zeman, 161–82. Burlington, ON: Welch, 1980.

Fea, John. "Understanding the Changing Facade of Twentieth Century American Protestant Fundamentalism: Toward a Historical Definition." *Trinity Journal* 15.2 (1994) 181–99.

Fowler, Stanley K. *More than a Symbol: The British Baptist Recovery of Baptismal Sacramentalism*. Studies in Baptist History and Thought 2. Eugene, OR: Wipf and Stock, 2002.

———. *Rethinking Baptism: Some Baptist Reflections*. Eugene, OR: Wipf and Stock, 2015.

Graham, Michael. "The Inerrancy of Scripture: A Doctrine Under Fire." *Diligence* 1 (2016) 1–15.

Haykin, Michael A. G., and Robert B. Lockey, eds. *A Glorious Fellowship of Churches: Celebrating the History of the Fellowship of Evangelical Baptist Churches in Canada, 1953–2003*. Guelph, ON: The Fellowship of Evangelical Baptist Churches in Canada, 2003.

Heath, Gordon L., et al. *Baptists in Canada: Their History and Polity*. McMaster Ministry Studies Series 5. Eugene, OR: Pickwick, 2020.

Ivison, Stuart, and Fred Rosser. *The Baptists in Upper and Lower Canada before 1820*. Reprint, Toronto: University of Toronto Press, 1963.

Jones, William H. *What Canadian Baptists Believe*. Etobicoke, ON: ChiRho, 1980.

Larsen, Stephen. *The Fundamentalist Mind: How Polarized Thinking Imperils Us All*. Wheaton, IL: Quest, 2007.

Marty, Martin, and R. Scott Appleby, eds. *Fundamentalisms Observed*. Chicago: University of Chicago Press, 1991.

Marsden, George. *Understanding Fundamentalism and Evangelicalism*. Grand Rapids: Eerdmans, 1991.

Mason, Rex. "'Keynote' Lecture to Canadian Baptist History Conference, McMaster Divinity School." In *Canadian Baptist History and Polity: The McMaster Conference*, edited by Murray J. S. Ford, 1–9. Hamilton, ON: McMaster Divinity College, n.d.

Pickering, Ernest. *Biblical Separation: The Struggle for a Pure Church*. Schaumburg, IL: Regular Baptist Books, 2008.

Porter, Stanley E., and Anthony R. Cross, eds. *Baptism, the New Testament and The Church: Historical and Contemporary Studies in Honour of R. E. O. White*. London: Sheffield Academic, 1999.

———. *Dimensions of Baptism: Biblical and Theological Studies*. London: Sheffield Academic, 2002.

Rawlyk, G. A. "A. L. McCrimmon, H. P. Whidden, T. T. Shields, Christian Higher Education, and McMaster University." In *Canadian Baptists and Christian Higher Education*, edited by G. A. Rawlyk, 31–62. Kingston: McGill-Queen's University Press, 1988.

Reimer, Sam, and Michael Wilkinson. *A Culture of Faith: Evangelical Congregations in Canada*. Montreal: McGill-Queen's University Press, 2015.

Ross, Karen Heather. "Losing Faith in Fundamentalist Christianity: An Interpretative Phenomenological Analysis." MA Thesis, University of Toronto, 2009.

Sawatsky, Ronald. "'Looking for That Blessed Hope': The Roots of Fundamentalism in Canada 1878–1914." PhD diss., University of Toronto, 1985.

Stackhouse, John G., Jr. "Evangelicalism and Fundamentalism." *Church and Faith Trends* 2.2 (2009) 1–3.

Strozier, Charles B., et al. *The Fundamentalist Mindset: Psychological Perspectives on Religion, Violence, and History*. Oxford: Oxford University Press, 2010.

Taylor, Kathleen. *The Brain Supremacy: Notes from the Frontiers of Neuroscience*. Oxford: Oxford University Press, 2012.

Wilson, Paul R. "A Mission Transformed: Fellowship Baptist Outreach in Quebec, 1953–1986." In *Baptists and Mission: Papers from the Fourth International Conference on Baptist Studies*, edited by Ian M. Randall and Anthony R. Cross, 189–204. Studies in Baptist History and Thought 29. Eugene, OR: Wipf and Stock, 2007.

———. "Baptists and Business: Central Canadian Baptists and the Secularization of the Businessmen at Toronto's Jarvis Street Baptist Church, 1848–1921." PhD diss., University of Western Ontario, 1996.

———. "Caring for their Community: The Philanthropic and Moral Reform Efforts of Toronto's Baptists, 1834–1918." In *Baptists and Public Life in Canada*, edited by Gordon L. Heath and Paul R. Wilson, 219–62. McMaster General Series 2. Canadian Baptist Historical Society Series 1. Eugene, OR: Pickwick, 2012.

———. "Torn Asunder: T. T. Shields, W. Gordon Brown and the Schisms at Toronto Baptist Seminary and within the Union of Regular Baptist Churches of Ontario and Quebec, 1948–1949." *McMaster Journal of Theology and Ministry* 19 (2017–2018) 34–80.

Zhong, Wanting, et al. "Biological and Cognitive Underpinnings of Religious Fundamentalism." *Neuropsychologia* 100 (2017) 18–25.

1

Identity and Ideology

An Overview of Canadian Baptist Fundamentalism, 1878–1978

Paul R. Wilson

Canadian Baptists have sometimes represented their experience as a perilous journey. In his centennial history of the Baptist Convention of Ontario and Quebec (BCOQ), Murray J. S. Ford used the image of a ship on stormy seas to express this perspective: "The Baptists of Canada have rarely been able to sail their ship on smooth water. Most often the winds of controversy have whipped the waters to perilous heights and the ship has bobbed and tossed."[1] Without question the fundamentalist movement was a major contributor to the controversies that troubled the waters for Canadian Baptists.

This first chapter has one primary objective: It provides an overview of Canadian Baptist fundamentalism as a historical and theological movement from 1878–1978. This is no easy task. As the reader will soon discover, the Canadian Baptist fundamentalist movement was complex, full of ebbs and flows, both linear and circular, at times unified and at other times fragmented, sometimes in the limelight and often on the periphery, and driven by certainties and rerouted by contingencies. It is impossible to capture every change, challenge, controversy, expression, and nuance in this short chapter. Still, the account offered in the next few pages includes

---

1. Ford, *Convention Chronicles*, 48.

an historical analysis and key events, personalities, and developments that shaped the first one hundred years of the Canadian Baptist fundamentalist movement.

Absolute chronologies are always suspect, because social, cultural, and theological developments and movements do not always fit neatly into a rigid timeframe. Still, John Fea identifies four approximate phases in the development of American fundamentalism (1) an "irenic phase," which runs from approximately 1893–1919 and serves as a harbinger to fundamentalism "proper"; (2) a "militant phase," that runs from 1920–1936 and which encompasses the now famous "fundamentalist-modernist controversies"; (3) a "divisive phase" from 1941–1960, associated with the intramural fragmentation of fundamentalism into "evangelical" and "separatist" factions; and (4) a "separatist phase" from 1960 to the present, in which the term fundamentalism is applied to those Protestants who choose to remove themselves from the mainstream of American culture and religion.[2] These phases are certainly helpful for understanding in broad terms the development of American fundamentalism.

Another significant recent study of the origins and development of the American fundamentalist movement is provided by Kevin Bauder and Robert Delnay. This insider history offers a sympathetic perspective on the American Baptist fundamentalist movement.[3] Both men have a long history as participants, researchers, and observers. In their volume entitled, *One in Hope and Doctrine: Origins of Baptist Fundamentalism 1870–1950*, Bauder and Delnay provide a detailed chronological account of the emergence of fundamentalism in the Northern Baptist Convention and especially the theological controversies and schisms of the 1920s and 1930s. The contributions of Regular, Conservative, and Southern Baptists are also thoroughly examined. Among many other contentions and conclusions, Bauder and Delany argue that American fundamentalists were identified by five marks: "devotion to the Scripture," "the hope of an any-moment return of Christ," "separation, both from apostasy and the world," "an attitude of conviction, even militancy," and "a genuine devotion to Christ."[4] These marks, they argue, formed the core of the American Baptist fundamentalist identity.

2. Fea, "Understanding the Changing Façade," 182.

3. American Baptist in this context refers to the nation-wide fundamentalist movement not the American Baptist Association.

4. Bauder and Delnay, *One in Faith and Doctrine*, 385.

As useful as these American studies are, they do not specifically address the Canadian Baptist context. In this context three approximate phases in the first one hundred years of the Canadian Baptist fundamentalist movement are discernable: a Formative Phase, 1878–1918; a Fight and Fragmentation Phase, 1919–1945; and a Decline and New Forms Phase, 1946–1978.

FORMATIVE PHASE, 1878–1918

The work of Ronald Sawatsky provides valuable insight into how the movement began in central Canada. Although he did not provide an explicit definition of the term, in his doctoral dissertation entitled, "'Looking for that Blessed Hope': The Roots of Fundamentalism in Canada, 1878–1914," Sawatsky argued that "proto-fundamentalism" best described the first phase of the Canadian fundamentalist movement.[5] Essentially, he argued that "the success of the Canadian proto-fundamentalist movement in the late nineteenth century" was the result of a "powerful combination" of four "attributes."[6] These attributes were a network of social and business relationships, an unusually high level of interdenominational co-operation and interaction, constant "cooperation with the American side of the movement," and "the remarkable cooperation of both the clergy and the laity in setting the direction of the movement."[7]

For central Canadian Baptists, the Formative Phase from 1878–1918 unfolded in two stages. Initially, in the late nineteenth century, Canadian "proto-fundamentalist" Baptists, such as the renowned ultraconservative Baptist pastor Joshua Denovan, expressed their allegiance to "the fundamental doctrines of the faith."[8] Denovan associated with other proto-fundamentalist Baptists, including Elmore Harris, founder of the Toronto Bible Training School, and those in other denominations at numerous conferences and meetings where theological papers and lectures were presented

---

5. Sawatsky, "Looking for that Blessed Hope," i, 5–6, 23.

6. Sawatsky, "Looking for that Blessed Hope," 37.

7. Sawatsky, "Looking for that Blessed Hope," 36, 37.

8. The selection of 1878 as the starting point for Canadian Baptist fundamentalism is based on the militant proto-fundamentalist views and activities of Joshua Denovan. See Denovan's address given at a Toronto Conference in 1878, entitled, "The Believer in Christ and Christ in the Believer" in *Joshua Denovan*, 252. On page 253 in the same address Denovan declares his belief in "dispensations." Premillennial dispensationalism was a view of the end times that many proto-fundamentalists, including Denovan, would adopt.

and discussed in detail by those in attendance. For Baptists, the period until 1909 was characterized by a strong desire to preserve doctrinal orthodoxy and promote religious and social causes that strengthened evangelical expressions of the Protestant faith.[9]

With the arrival of the first major doctrinal controversy in 1909–1910, and the initial publication of *The Fundamentals* in 1910, the second part of this formative phase commenced. Some Canadian Baptists, particularly in central Canada, began an offensive against their brethren who supported or tolerated Baptist intellectuals who rejected traditional views of biblical inerrancy and inspiration and accepted elements of German higher criticism, Darwinian evolutionary theory, and/or a modernist view of society and culture. Many of these issues came to the fore in the 1909 controversy over the views held and expressed by McMaster University Professor I. G. Matthews. The charges put forward by pastor Elmore Harris, pastor of Walmer Street Baptist Church in Toronto, and McMaster Senators Charles J. Holman and Joseph N. Shenstone, reveal a growing unease in conservative Baptist quarters and discontent with McMaster's ethos of welcoming "truth from whatever quarter" in a "spirit of free inquiry" that allowed "students of the Sacred Scriptures the largest possible measure of freedom consistent with loyalty to the fundamentals of the Christian faith."[10] The exoneration of Matthews by the McMaster Senate did little to quell the rising tide of agitation. In fact, the Matthews affair put fundamentalist and like-minded conservative Baptists on high alert and helped to define more precisely an emerging fundamentalist identity and position. In addition, this event drew the battle lines for future controversies. Fundamentalist unease and discontent would continue to grow. However, preoccupation with the Great War kept fundamentalist rancour in central Canada on low boil until the BCOQ Convention of 1919.

Any discussion of the emergence of the western Baptist fundamentalist movement must keep in mind the late arrival of Baptists in this region. Baptist historians, such as Harry Renfree and Walter Ellis, have highlighted and lamented the slowness of Baptists to establish a meaningful western presence.[11] In addition, historians have not conducted studies that focus ex-

---

9. For a detailed discussion of the proto-fundamentalist activities of Denovan and Harris see Sawatsky, "Looking for that Blessed Hope," 69–72, 263–76.

10. Johnston, *McMaster University*, 1:105.

11. See Ellis, "Baptists and Radical Politics," 164 and Renfree, *Heritage and Horizon*, 171–78.

clusively on how the broader Baptist fundamentalist movement began and developed in the west. Of course, these realities limit what can be covered here.

Early signs of the emergence of a Baptist proto-fundamentalist perspective and the awareness of differences between conservative and liberal evangelicals in western Canada from 1878–1918, are evident in a few crucial events and the expressions and actions of some individuals. In his article entitled, "Conservative Protestantism and the Modernist Challenge in Vancouver, 1917–1927," Robert Burkinshaw has deftly drawn attention to the five-week-long campaign of evangelist French E. Oliver in 1917 as "the major catalytic event" in the British Columbia mainline conservative Protestant reaction to liberalism.[12] Effectively, as Burkinshaw has noted, Oliver's dogmatic conservative doctrinal declarations and vigorous protests against modernism shattered the comfortable and quiet coexistence between conservatives and liberals that had existed before 1917.[13] For British Columbia Baptists in particular, this event had profound consequences. It stimulated a decade long series of controversies between more theologically liberal and culturally-progressive Baptists and theologically fundamentalist and culturally-separatist Baptists.[14]

On the Prairies, with a few notable exceptions, the early signs of fundamentalism are largely unknown to us. The eccentric preaching and teaching endeavours of William Aberhart at Westbourne Baptist Church in Calgary, from 1916–1919, is perhaps the most noteworthy example. His efforts do reveal that some Albertans had an appetite for teaching about the end times. Clearly, some Alberta Baptists and other evangelicals were captivated by Aberhart's premillennial dispensational eschatology and his method of Bible study. After only a few years, his Sunday afternoon Bible classes at Westbourne on "Christian fundamentalism and Bible prophecy" had grown to over two thousand people and had to be relocated to the largest meeting hall in the city.[15] As Joseph Ban has noted, "At the urging of some men who sought a greater knowledge of his form of Bible study,

---

12. Burkinshaw, "Conservative Protestantism," 24.

13. Burkinshaw, "Conservative Protestantism," 27.

14. For a thorough analysis of these controversies see Burkinshaw, *Pilgrims in Lotus Land*, 76–99.

15. This information is taken from the accounts and analyses of Aberhart by Stackhouse, *Canadian Evangelicalism*, 37 and Ban, "T. C. Douglas and W. Aberhart," 72.

Aberhart organized the Calgary Prophetic Bible Conference in 1918."[16] Of course, the end times were often a focus of proto-fundamentalists.[17] Aberhart's fundamentalist views and methods were both eccentric and unconventional. But his charismatic personality, eloquence, determination, and conviction combined with his dispensational message to catch the imagination and attention of some Albertans and helped to lay a piece of the foundation for fundamentalism in Alberta and the other Prairie provinces.

The establishment of a Baptist fundamentalist presence in Alberta did not come about smoothly, easily, or without controversy. Aberhart's autocratic, demanding, and dictatorial leadership style alienated the majority of his Westbourne congregation, who withdrew to form Alberta's first Regular Baptist Church in 1929.[18] This group grew until 1942, when its Calgary Bible school that had been established in 1933, closed. By 1946, Regular Baptist membership in the Prairies numbered 430.[19] Meanwhile Aberhart's Calgary-based Prophetic Baptist Church and Institute reached their peak in 1935 with the Institute having 1,275 supporters and the church a membership of 500.[20] The church would soon experience hard times. By 1939, the membership would decline to 40.[21] Better times would return for both the church and the Institute in the 1940s after Aberhart's death in 1943 and Ernest Manning's revitalization of both the Institute and the church. By 1946, the church had 500 adherents and in 1947, the Institute could boast of 108 students.[22] A small independent Fundamental Baptist group would also develop and grow to 350 members by 1946.[23]

Baptist proto-fundamentalism in Manitoba and Saskatchewan remains largely in the shadows. Historians have focussed primarily, for good reason, on the impact of liberal and social gospel influences at Brandon College and the fits and starts that led to the creation of that institution in

---

16. Ban, "T. C. Douglas and W. Aberhart," 72.

17. For detailed analysis of William Aberhart's premillennial dispensationalism see Stackhouse, *Canadian Evangelicalism*, 37–38; Ban, "T. C. Douglas and W. Aberhart," 71–77; Elliott, "Three Faces," 173–74; Ellis, "Baptists and Radical Politics," 168–71.

18. Mann, *Sect, Cult and Church*, 23. To avoid confusion, I have purposely not adopted Mann's church and sect typology first defined and applied by Ernst Troeltsch.

19. Mann, *Sect, Cult and Church*, 23.

20. Mann, *Sect, Cult and Church*, 22.

21. Mann, *Sect, Cult and Church*, 23.

22. Mann, *Sect, Cult and Church*, 23, 83.

23. Mann, *Sect, Cult and Church*, 30.

1899.²⁴ Brandon would become a focus of the fundamentalist-modernist controversies on the 1920s. Walter Ellis has noted that politically for a half century after the death of Alexander Grant in 1897, "Baptist leadership" in this region, "reflected the decidedly liberal values and optimistic outlook of their eastern Canadian and American counterparts."²⁵ This perspective also shaped Baptist views of theology and education. Consequently, Baptists do not appear to have played a major role in the educational and religious institutions that were created in these provinces during the proto-fundamentalist phase. Instead, as Bruce Hindmarsh has revealed in his study of Winnipeg's fundamentalist network, Presbyterians, Methodists, Mennonites, and Pentecostals took the lead in the establishment of the trans-denominational Elim Chapel in 1910, the Winnipeg Bible Institute in 1925 and the Canadian Sunday School Mission in 1927.²⁶ As a result, the presence of fundamentalist views within the Manitoba and Saskatchewan Baptist constituencies did not figure prominently in later fundamentalist-modernist controversies.

Taylor Murray has pointed out that the Baptist fundamentalist movement in the Maritimes was "very different" from the experience of Canadian Baptists elsewhere.²⁷ Furthermore, Murray notes that "the fundamentalist element did not become significant within the United Baptist Convention of the Maritime Provinces until . . . the 1930s—and even then it produced only a tremor."²⁸ This reality means that one cannot really have a meaningful discussion about the presence and impact of Baptist fundamentalism in the Maritimes before the early 1920s.

This does not mean, however, that nothing happened in the Maritimes in the proto-fundamentalist phase. For example, the independent perspective, efforts, and experience of Neil Herman is an example of proto-fundamentalism in Nova Scotia. In 1911, Herman became the pastor of Immanuel Baptist Church in Truro, Nova Scotia. He soon set about the task of, in the words of one fundamentalist ally, "'ridding the church of some of its biggest drawbacks'" by putting a new by-law in to the church's charter that

---

24. For a history of Brandon College see, Ellis, "What the Times Demand," 63–88; Scott, "Brandon College," 139–59; McLeod, "'To Bestir Themselves,'" 22–31.

25. Ellis, "Baptists and Radical Politics," 164.

26. For a deeper understanding and analysis of these events see, Hindmarsh, "The Winnipeg Fundamentalist Network," 303–19.

27. Murray, "From Exodus to Exile," 1.

28. Murray, "From Exodus to Exile," 1.

made removal from church membership mandatory for those who missed a set number of communion services.[29] The result of this legalistic measure was the expulsion of the business element from the congregation. Murray notes that Herman's purge had dire consequences: "Those removed from fellowship contended that this had damaged their reputation and subsequently took the church to court, where they were awarded approximately $1,000 from Immanuel Baptist. As a result, during Herman's time as pastor, a number of Immanuel Baptist's congregants left the church and began to attend First Baptist Church, also in Truro."[30] Herman would become a militant fundamentalist who would continue to sow discord and division in his pastorates in the Maritimes and elsewhere well into the 1920s. Herman's experience makes it clear that although proto-fundamentalism was present in Eastern Canada, its influence before 1920 was confined to the occasional individual pastor and church.

For Canadian Baptists the proto-fundamentalist phase from 1878–1918 was most evident in Ontario. Although some early signs of a Baptist fundamentalist movement were present in British Columbia, Alberta, and Nova Scotia, the larger number of fundamentalist Ontario Baptists and their earlier engagement in theological discussions about biblical inerrancy and dispensationalism put them at the forefront in the proto-fundamentalist phase.

FIGHT AND FRAGMENTATION PHASE, 1919–1945

The fight and fragmentation phase of the Canadian Baptist fundamentalist movement carried forward the desire to preserve the purity of the faith but added an aggressive militancy, a legalistic insistence on the practice of a strict morality and traditional Baptist orthodoxy, and entire separation from and censure of those Baptists who refused to accept and follow fundamentalist positions.[31] This period was characterized by constant controversy, growing discontent, rancour, and schism. It was also in this period where a more defined fundamentalist theological and sociocultural identity became a reality. This did not mean that Canadian Baptist fundamentalists always agreed with each other. A strong tendency to favour independence was a consistent characteristic of the Canadian Baptist fundamentalist

29. Murray, "From Exodus to Exile," 47.
30. Murray, "From Exodus to Exile," 47.
31. For a historical and theological analysis of entire separation from an American Regular Baptist perspective, see, Pickering, *Biblical Separation*.

movement. But fundamentalists did adhere to certain core beliefs, such as biblical inerrancy, and a common disdain for all forms of modernism.

In central Canada a series of key events unfolded that both shaped and expressed Baptist fundamentalism. Only a brief overview of the key events is provided here, and T. T. Shields, the pastor of Jarvis Street Baptist Church in Toronto, is cast as a central figure in these events. According to John G. Stackhouse, Jr., however one may define fundamentalism, it is Shields who stands "squarely in the middle of anyone's definition" as "Canada's best known and most influential fundamentalist."[32] In October 1919, *The Canadian Baptist* published two editorials about the inspiration and authority of Scripture.[33] Some fundamentalists, such as the abovementioned Shields and C. J. Holman, a lawyer from Jarvis Street, vehemently expressed their disagreement with the views put forward in these editorials. An ongoing debate ensued. The culmination of this furor was the deliberations about the editorials at the 1919 Ottawa BCOQ annual gathering.

One example of how divisive this issue had become was found in the responses of the delegates from Jarvis Street. Shields and Holman called for return to the orthodox view of Biblical inspiration and authority "to which the Convention declared its adherence in 1910."[34] In contrast, prominent lawyer, McMaster Trustee, and Jarvis Street member, D. E. Thomson supported the editorials in the lead up to the convention and called for compromise, unity, and peace. At the convention itself, James Ryrie, a prominent Toronto businessman and Jarvis Street deacon, put forward an amendment that extended and challenged the resolution in support of the Bible as "the inspired word of God" offered by Shields. Ryrie's amendment effectively demanded an end to the controversy driven by Shields when it noted that "the Convention strongly deprecates controversy at this time as to the interpretation in detail of our distinctive beliefs . . . when we ought to be presenting a unified front in grasping the opportunity of the hour."[35] After a heated debate the amendment was defeated while the original motion was passed. This convention controversy signaled the growing division

32. Stackhouse, *Canadian Evangelicalism*, 23.

33. For analysis of the impact of these editorials see Johnston, *McMaster University*, 1:156–57; Renfree, *Heritage and Horizon*, 217–18.

34. Wilson, "Baptists and Business," 321.

35. For a detailed analysis of the issues and debate before, during, and after the 1919 Convention, see Adams, "The War of the Worlds," 143–56. For other brief overviews that also present a perspective on Shields' response, see Tarr, *Shields of Canada*, 64–71; Tarr, "Another Perspective," 211; Stackhouse, *Canadian Evangelicalism*, 25–26.

among Baptists on the question of whether doctrinal issues or other priorities should dominate the Baptist agenda.

The animosity and acrimony of the Ottawa convention was carried back to Jarvis Street Baptist Church. Shields challenged his deacons and the members at large. In his sermons he waged war against modernist perspectives on Biblical inspiration and authority. On matters of lifestyle and morality Shields was equally dogmatic. On 13 February 1921, he preached a sermon entitled, "The Christian Attitude Towards Amusements." In this message he directly challenged any deacon who engaged in amusements such as dancing, card-playing, or the theatre "to resign either his pleasure or his office."[36] On 14 February 1921, deacon Quartus B. Henderson, president of the Davis & Henderson printing firm, resigned.[37] The year and half battle for control of Jarvis Street intensified. After another eight months of rancour and controversy, schism was the result. Three-hundred and forty members departed from Jarvis Street to found what would become Park Road (today Yorkminster Park) Baptist Church. This new church, known originally as Central Baptist Church, was officially organized with 350 members on 28 June 1922.[38]

Until the end of his life in 1955, Shields vigorously pursued and prosecuted his fundamentalist agenda and his war on modernism. He actively recruited and enlisted other Baptists across the country to support his war effort.[39] In 1922, he founded *The Gospel Witness* as an alternative to *The Canadian Baptist*. In 1923, Shields helped to found the Baptist Bible Union, and he served as its first president. Shields was candid in his comments about the purpose of this body:

---

36. T. T. Shields, "The Christian Attitude Toward Amusements," *Gospel Witness* (hereafter *GW*), 19 August 1922, 7.

37. Wilson, "Baptists and Business," 320–26. For this sermon see Shields, "The Christian Attitude Toward Amusements," *GW*, 19 August 1922, 1–7.

38. For more detail and discussion of this schism see Stackhouse, *Canadian Evangelicalism*, 27; Tarr, *Shields of Canada*, 72–84; Wilson, "Baptist and Business," 331–95. For Shields' accounts of these events see Shields, *The Inside of the Cup* and *The Plot That Failed*.

39. The list of those with whom Shields corresponded is extensive. The best primary source is Shields' *Correspondence Files* housed in the Jarvis Street Baptist Church, Toronto. For examples of recent scholarship about some of Shields' recruits and allies, see the recently published articles on pastor John R. Boyd, a Shields lieutenant in northern Ontario, Holcomb, "John R. Boyd," 441–73, and pastor J. B. Rowell, a Shields ally in Victoria, British Columba, Dunlop, "James B. Rowell," 417–39.

> What then can be our answer to Modernism's declaration of war? There can be but one answer. The Baptist Bible Union is designed to mobilize the Conservative Baptist forces of the continent, for the express purpose of declaring and waging relentless and uncompromising war on Modernism on all fronts. We are resolved that we will not surrender the faith once for all delivered to the saints.[40]

As Doug Adams has so poignantly noted, "Shields now viewed himself as a heroic warrior, set for the defence of the faith."[41]

Shields continued his war on modernism on many fronts. He waged, for example, campaigns against McMaster University in 1924, after the University bestowed an honorary degree on W. H. P. Faunce, President of Brown University who defended the well-known liberal preacher Harry Emerson Fosdick. Shields also vehemently opposed McMaster's appointment of L. H. Marshall to fill the post of Professor of Practical Theology late in the same year. He accused Marshall of holding liberal views on core doctrines, such as biblical inerrancy, the atonement, the resurrection, and total depravity.[42] Eventually, Marshall was appointed despite Shields' objections.

With his sights firmly set on any manifestation of modernism, Shields railed against his fellow Baptists in every quarter of North America who supported modernism in any way or refused to condemn modernist theology or lifestyle.[43] By 1926, many central Canadian Baptists had grown weary of incessant controversy and Shields' relentless attacks on his Baptist

---

40. Shields, "A Holy War," *GW*, 21 June 1923, 5.

41. Adams, "War of the Worlds," 209. For a history of the Baptist Bible Union see Tarr, *Shields of Canada*, 101–7.

42. Russell, "Thomas Todhunter Shields," 269–70. For additional information about Faunce and Marshall see Pinnock, "The Modernist Impulse," 200–203 and Johnston, *McMaster University*, 1:182–86.

43. The list of targets who were the objects of Shields' attacks in the 1920s is lengthy. The attack on McMaster University is the best-known example. For a discussion of Shields' criticisms of McMaster see Priest, "T. T. Shields the Fundamentalist," 72–81 and Johnston, *McMaster University*, 1:153–55, 172–75, 193–94. For attacks on modernism in organizations see, for example, Shields, "McMaster University and 'The Student Christian Movement,'" *GW*, 8 May 1924, 7–8; Shields, "More About the Student Christian Movement," *GW*, 29 May 1924, 9. For attacks on Baptist individuals and institutions see, Shields, "A Religious Devil," *GW*, 10 April 1924, 3–4. In this sermon Shields calls out Matthews, Fosdick, Faunce, Cross, and others. See also, Shields, "British Columbia Baptists and Brandon College," *GW*, 27 March 1924, 7–9. For the impact of the controversy on The Women's Baptist Home Missionary Society of Ontario West see Cullen, "Debating and Dividing."

brethren.⁴⁴ The convention of 1926 censured Shields for his attacks, demanded his resignation from McMaster's Board of Governors, and barred him from future conventions.⁴⁵ The ultimate culmination of the protracted conflict among central Canadian Baptists came with the decision to expel Jarvis Street Church from the convention on 14 October 1927.⁴⁶ Twelve other churches were also expelled. And within a year 65 other churches would leave the Baptist Convention. In November 1928, the Union of Regular Baptist Churches of Ontario and Quebec was formed with 77 churches represented and Jarvis Street as its epicentre.⁴⁷

Shields also created the Toronto Baptist Seminary in 1927 as a fundamentalist alternative for theological training.⁴⁸ One key initiative that was undertaken by Toronto Baptist Seminary and the Union beginning in 1930 was the sending of Baptist fundamentalist missionaries to Quebec. The mission began as an English-speaking effort but by the 1940s became bilingual, then in the 1950s francophone and multicultural. The mission and the churches that were established retained much of their original fundamentalist character.⁴⁹

In the 1930s and 1940s, Shields would focus his attacks on Catholics, politicians, ecumenical organizations and efforts, and wayward Baptists. In 1934-35, for example, Shields publicly denounced Ontario Liberal Premier Mitchell Hepburn for his alcohol policy which arbitrarily loosened liquor controls and facilitated an increase in the availability of alcohol though the issuance of more liquor licenses. In 1935, Shields challenged Hepburn's proposal to amend the *Assessment Act* so public funding could be redirected to support Catholic schools in districts with a large Catholic population.⁵⁰

---

44. See, for example, Shields, "The Tragic Story of McMaster's Drift Toward Modernism," *GW*, 14 October 1926, 1-36.

45. For an analysis of this event see Adams, "The War of the Worlds," 223. For Shields' response see Shields, "Ichabod," *GW*, 4 November 1926, 8-13. See also, Carder, "Controversy," 79-82.

46. For events connected to expulsion see Tarr, *Shields of Canada*, 91-100; Renfree, *Heritage and Horizon*, 222-23; Adams, "The War of the Worlds," 430-95; Haykin, "'Jesus, Wondrous Saviour,'" 137-38; Carder, "Controversy," 79-82. For the social, cultural, and religious factors that led to this schism in 1927 see, Ellis, "Gilboa to Ichabod," 109-26 and Wilson, "Cultural Factors," 61-81.

47. Haykin, "'Jesus, Wondrous Saviour,'" 137.

48. For a history of Toronto Baptist Seminary see, Adams, *By His Grace*; Tarr, *Shields of Canada*, 108-20.

49. For a history of this mission see Wilson, "A Mission Transformed," 189-204.

50. Adams, "Fighting Fire," 62-78. Smale, "'The Voice,'" 5-28.

Shields insisted that an unholy alliance and a secret agreement existed between the Catholic hierarchy and Hepburn's government: "Surely one can only conclude that Mr. Hepburn and his party were under some sort of compact to the Roman Catholic Church to deliver the goods—and this, remember, is only the first installment."[51] The Conservative opposition certainly used Shields' claims to stir up public concern and gain political advantage. Ultimately, Hepburn accepted a motion from Conservative opposition member George Henry to repeal the separate school bill.[52]

In May 1940, Shields commenced a five-year-long series of attacks on Prime Minister Mackenzie King's handling of the war effort. Shields chided King for failing to prosecute the war with enough vigour, and Shields condemned King for selling out to Catholicism and Quebec politicians, such as M. Ernest Lapointe, on the conscription issue.[53] In response, King stated, "I wish to say that I have utter contempt for Dr. Shields and his unworthy utterances."[54] King's response was met with three addresses and a forty-eight page diatribe filled with *ad hominem* arguments.[55] These words and actions were the penultimate expression of militant central Canadian Baptist fundamentalism in the public domain.

Those within Shields' own Regular Baptist circle did not escape unscathed. In fact, in 1931–1933, Shields provoked a controversy between the Union and its own Fundamentalist Baptist Young People's Association (hereafter FBYPA) and The Women's Missionary Society of Regular Baptists of Canada (hereafter WMSRBC). Shields and the Union Executive accused the FBYPA of being "openly antagonistic to the interests of the Union" and a "menace to Baptist principles and policy."[56] In a similar fashion, the WMSRBC was charged with holding to principles that "are contrary to the principles of New Testament church polity, and therefore opposed to the polity of Regular Baptist churches as historically practised."[57] Furthermore, the WMSRBC was guilty of showing "a steadily diminishing support of the

51. Shields, "Hepburn's Betrayal," 26. See also, Adams, "Fighting Fire," 69–78.

52. Adams, "Fighting Fire," 73–75.

53. Adams, "Fighting Fire," 78–100. For a useful analysis Shields' anti-Catholic perspective see, Smale, "'The Voice.'"

54. Adams, "Fighting Fire," 94.

55. See Shields, "A Challenging Answer," in *Three Addresses*, 3–34; Shields, "*The Gospel Witness* and Its Parliamentary Critics," *GW*, 25 February 1943, 2; Adams, "Fighting Fire," 95.

56. See "Report of the Special Convention," *GW*, 16 July 1931, 7.

57. "Report of the Special Convention," *GW*, 16 July 1931, 6.

Mission objects of the Union" and admitting to its membership "any woman who will sign the Statement of Faith, provided she is a member of what is called a Regular Baptist Church—in the old or any other Convention."[58] These practices and policies were cast as compromise with the modernists. Eventually, these controversies prompted some churches to leave the Union. In 1931, the Union had reached the all-time high of 90 churches. By 1933, that number had dropped to 60.[59] In that same year 27 former Union churches and independent Baptist churches joined together to form the fundamentalist Fellowship of Independent Baptist Churches of Canada. This group would grow to 125 churches by 1950.[60]

In some ways the fundamentalist movement in western Canada showed parallels with developments in central Canada. In both regions, Baptist institutions of higher learning were a focal point for controversy in the 1920s. The most notable example was the controversy at Brandon College. In 1922–23, the school and its President, Howard P. Whidden, faced a serious challenge after former student and fundamentalist pastor John Linton and the Vancouver Baptist Ministerial charged that Professors Carl H. Lager and Harris Lachlan MacNeill were guilty of holding and teaching modernist theology. The Brandon College Commission found that Lager was orthodox. MacNeill's views were a different matter altogether. His open questioning of the virgin birth, the penal substitutionary view of the atonement, and eschatology made him an easy target for fundamentalist ire and an ongoing source of controversy.[61] As Walter Ellis and Robert Burkinshaw have noted, in 1927 the result of constant controversy and conflict over the theology of Brandon's professors resulted in schism within the Baptist Convention of British Columbia. In that same year, the fundamentalist-conservative Convention of Regular Baptists of British Columbia was formed.[62]

In British Columbia, a series of divisions continued to plague the Convention of Regular Baptists. In 1928, for example, as Burkinshaw notes, "half of the congregation of the new denomination's largest church, Mount Pleasant Baptist, left to form the independent Metropolitan Tabernacle. This highly militant and separatistic church soon began attracting

58. "Report of the Special Convention," *GW*, 16 July 1931, 6.
59. Haykin, "'Jesus, Wondrous Saviour,'" 139.
60. Haykin, "'Jesus, Wondrous Saviour,'" 139; Tarr, *This Dominion*, 113.
61. Ellis, "What the Times Demand," 77.
62. Burkinshaw, *Pilgrims*, 99; Ellis, "What the Times Demand," 77.

congregations of more than a thousand."[63] Another split took place in 1935–36. According to Burkinshaw, these schisms "eventually formed the basis of several additional streams of Baptists" within the province.[64] Instead of hindering Baptist growth, the schisms that produced these new independent fundamentalist offshoots that stimulated growth for British Columbia Baptists well into the 1940s.[65] Within the Baptist Union of Western Canada the response to schism was often renewed resolve and increased giving. As Callum Jones has noted, "When the Baptist Convention of British Columbia lost one quarter of their membership in 1927 over accusations of modernist teaching at Brandon College, women loyal to the Convention gave $6,081.00—the largest amount in their history to date-and an additional $1,500.00 to mark the fiftieth anniversary of their first circle."[66] Such evidence challenges the claim that the results of the fundamentalist-modernists battles and divisions were always negative.

The factors in the 1928 creation of the Metropolitan Tabernacle and its separation from the Regular Baptists are particularly noteworthy and deserve comment. In this case, there was no "'difference of opinion on the great doctrines of the faith.'"[67] Instead, the more culturally-focused doctrine of separation from the world and disagreement over what constituted worldliness were the key drivers of the controversy. This example illustrates that Baptist responses to cultural change played a key role in the development of the fundamentalist movement in this period and the fragmentation of the Baptist community in western Canada.

Of course, not all Baptists in western Canada participated in the fundamentalist-modernist controversies. The General Conference of German Baptist Churches in North America (North American Baptist Conference as of 1944), for example, chose to stay out the conflicts and focus instead on growth and development. Cindy Wesley has noted the role that ethnicity and pietistic theology played in the German Baptist perspective and actions. "The Fundamentalist-Modernist controversy," Wesley concludes, "gave credence to the German Baptist claims that the English-speaking

---

63. Burkinshaw, *Pilgrims*, 122.
64. Burkinshaw, *Pilgrims*, 122.
65. Burkinshaw, *Pilgrims*, 134–35.
66. Jones, "'Our Women,'" 143.
67. Burkinshaw, *Pilgrims*, 125.

churches held unbiblical views."[68] Furthermore, Wesley captures well the German Baptist perspective:

> Rather than jumping into the fray, the German Baptists withdrew further into their own group. There was general agreement on the authority of the Bible, which had sympathy with the position of Fundamentalism. Since the biblicism of the pastors and churches in the Conference was generally the same, there was no need to become involved in the strife. Instead, they continued with their work and questioned the spiritual and biblical character of their English-speaking brethren.[69]

In a similar vein David Priestley observed that "During the years 1920 to 1950 when modernist-fundamentalist controversies split the American Baptists and two regional units of Canadian Baptists, the ethnic churches found it convenient to foster the institutions and ministries which bound them ethnically rather than to become partisans in political battles where their few numbers would have been ineffective."[70] This response to the fundamentalist-modernist controversies underscores the fact that western Canadian Baptists were far from uniform or universal in their reactions to such fractious and turbulent disputes.

In eastern Canada the fundamentalist movement gained a foothold in the 1920s and 1930s throughout the Maritimes. While the fundamentalist presence was never large, it was certainly more active, organized, and vocal than it had ever been before this period. In *Champions of the Truth: Fundamentalism, Modernism and the Maritime Baptists*, George Rawlyk provided a detailed account and analysis of the religious influences and movements in the region from the late eighteenth century to the end of the 1930s. Rawlyk focuses on the enduring impact of revivalism first introduced by Henry Alline and Freeborn Garrettson in the last quarter of the eighteenth century.[71] He also highlights the emergence of the "Evangelical social gospel consensus" that Maritime United Baptists affirmed and reaffirmed throughout the 1920s and 1930s.[72] These influences helped to define and shape the Baptist identity and ethos of the region.

68. Wesley, "The Pietist Theology," 192–93.
69. Wesley, "The Pietist Theology," 194.
70. Priestley, "North American Baptist Conference," 381.
71. Rawlyk, *Champions*, 5–23.
72. Evidence of this consensus is found in the 1921 social gospel platform and the declaration of 1936. See Rawlyk, *Champions*, 35–36.

In his dialectical treatment of the fundamentalist movement and the fundamentalist-modernist controversies of the 1920s and 1930s, Rawlyk presents the key causes, personalities, and events that defined and dominated this era. According to Rawlyk's analysis, the key causes of tension between fundamentalists and modernists included acceptance in 1921, of a "nineteen point progressive, social gospel 'platform'" by the United Baptist Convention of the Maritime Provinces, the rise of a "'New Paganism'" that accepted consumerism, cultural accommodation, and unorthodox theology, and the tolerance of a "'modernist impulse'" within some quarters of the convention, and most particularly, the "liberal-modernist stronghold" at Acadia University.[73] Rawlyk also emphasizes the role of John James Sidey, "who became the most outspoken [fundamentalist] critic of the [United Baptist] convention leadership," John Bolton Daggett, who was Sidey's co-pastor in Kingston, Nova Scotia, and failed attempts by T. T. Shields to steer events in the region, such as during the Kingston Parsonage Case of 1935.[74] Finally, Rawlyk highlights the contributions of key events. The rapid rise and fall of the Maritime Christian Fundamentalist Association in 1925–26, the bestowal of an honorary Doctorate on University of Chicago Professor of Divinity, Shirley Case, by Acadia University in 1928, the creation of the fundamentalist Kingston Bible College in 1930, the confrontation between the convention and the Sideyites in 1933 and after, and the Kingston Baptist Parsonage Case were the key defining events of this era in the Maritimes.[75]

Taylor Murray's analysis of Sidey and his close associates in the Baptist fundamentalist movement, deepens and widens our understanding of that movement. Essentially, Murray argues and demonstrates that the "influence in the region" of J. J. Sidey and "his 'lieutenants,' including J. B. Daggett, Neil Herman, J. W. Hill, and T. A. Meister," was "largely ineffective."[76] In the end, Murray concludes, "Only a hand-full [sic] of churches followed them in their crusade, the majority of which had split from them by 1939."[77] In short, fundamentalist attempts to bring the United Baptist Convention in line with a fundamentalist theological and cultural agenda in this period, failed.

---

73. For a fuller analysis of these events see Rawlyk, *Champions*, 35–36, 53–56, 58.
74. Rawlyk, *Champions*, 42, 43–49, 49–50, 56–67.
75. Rawlyk, *Champions*, 50–75.
76. Murray, "From Exodus to Exile," vi.
77. Murray, "From Exodus to Exile," vi.

The fight and fragmentation phase of the Baptist fundamentalist movement from 1919–1945 represented the high point of militant influence within the movement. Baptist fundamentalists also came to a stronger sense of their own identity and pushed forward, with varying degrees of success, their agenda of renewal through the rejection of modernism in all of its forms and a return to traditional Baptist theological orthodoxy and orthopraxy. The resulting schisms, particularly in Ontario and British Columbia, had profound consequences for Baptists across the country including a desire, within the fundamentalist movement itself, to move beyond endless controversy to new forms of fellowship and ministry.

DECLINE AND NEW FORMS PHASE, 1946–1978

In the third phase of the Canadian Baptist fundamentalist movement, the militant fundamentalist tendency to fight, legislate, and separate would continue. These actions would stimulate two diverse outcomes: the continuing erosion of militant fundamentalism and the development of some alliances between more moderate fundamentalists within the Canadian Baptist fold.

Fundamentalist Baptists were not immune or isolated from the exuberance, optimism, conservatism, and growth that took hold in Canada's churches in the immediate aftermath of World War II.[78] In central Canada, some Baptist fundamentalists, who were solidly committed to the "fundamentals of the faith," grew tired of endless controversy, "wrangling" and the "fighting fundamentalist" posture maintained by militant fundamentalists within the Union of Regular Baptist Churches.[79] The deterioration of T. T. Shields' relationship with his long-time Baptist fundamentalist ally, W. Gordon Brown, and the ensuing conflicts and schisms at Toronto Baptist Seminary in 1948 and within the Union of Regular Baptist churches in 1949, are compelling examples of the strife and division that some Baptist fundamentalists resented.[80] Essentially, these events demonstrated that central Canadian Baptist fundamentalists held different views of leadership,

---

78. The post-war upsurge in church growth and the return to conservatism has received considerable attention from historians. See, for example, Grant, *The Church in the Canadian Era*, 177–79, 196–201, 237.

79. Some of these quotations are from Jack Scott, a leading Independent Fellowship Baptist pastor. See Haykin, "'Jesus, Wondrous Saviour,'" 142.

80. For a detailed analysis of this relationship breakdown and these events see, Wilson, "Torn Asunder," 34–80.

ecclesiology, methodology, and vision. The subsequent creation of the Canadian Baptist Seminary (later Central Baptist Seminary) early in 1949, and the Fellowship of Evangelical Baptists in 1953, would signal the arrival of a new moderate form of central Canadian Baptist fundamentalism.

Instead of endless fighting, these moderate fundamentalists longed to focus on evangelization, progress, cooperation, and unity. As Kenneth Davis noted, "After World War II there was a significant move towards wider fellowships, and more effective cooperation with other Baptists of like theological convictions, including a greater willingness to set aside minor differences for the sake of unity."[81] Leslie Tarr in his history of the Fellowship Baptists also noted this trend: "By 1950, there was a growing conviction that the evangelical Baptist cause would be better served by closer cooperation and planning."[82] In 1949, J. F. Holliday, the editor of *The Fellowship Evangel* stated the matter plainly to his independent Baptist constituency: "In recent years there has been a steadily growing spirit of cooperation between Fellowship and Union churches."[83] This "spirit" not only continued, but also expanded. A Liaison Committee was established in 1951 to facilitate serious preliminary discussions and produce reports about a possible merger.

By 1952, the Fellowship and Union pastors were ready to meet informally for prayer, fellowship, and discussion. On 11 March 1952, 90 pastors met at High Park Baptist Church in Toronto. These pastors gave unanimous approval for a seven-point Liaison Committee report that offered a path to amalgamation.[84] As Tarr observed in his history of the Fellowship in this period, from this point "The movement toward a merger precede at a rapid rate."[85] At a Pastors' Conference in September of 1952, held at Benton Street Baptist Church in Kitchener, Ontario, another "resounding expression" of support for merger came from the 125 pastors in attendance. Arnold Dallimore, editor of *The Union Baptist*, expressed the spirit of those present and the impact on those who participated:

> Anyone present at this two-day conclave could not fail to be impressed by the unity of spirit that characterized the whole assembly. . . . The effect of the conference was such as to cause all

---

81. Davis, "The Struggle," 238.
82. Tarr, *This Dominion*, 127.
83. Tarr, *This Dominion*, 127.
84. Tarr, *This Dominion*, 128.
85. Tarr, *This Dominion*, 129.

to see the future as a time of untied action on the part of all of us, with all divisions of spirit long since destroyed, and finally in oneness in doctrine, practice, and organization, going forward for the Lord.[86]

Following the Pastors' Conference both the Union and the Fellowship voted to accept the proposal to move forward toward a merger. In the spring of 1953, both groups held special conventions at which their respective executives were empowered to make union a reality. In October of 1953, the two groups held separate conventions and then on the evening of 21 October messengers from 51 Union churches and 81 Fellowship churches met for the first session of the founding convention. This convention unanimously approved the resolution that officially the new Baptist fundamentalist entity be called the Fellowship of Evangelical Baptist Churches in Canada (FEBCC).[87] This less vitriolic version of Canadian Baptist fundamentalism would grow quickly. But as we will see, this new expression of fundamentalism would have its share of internal struggles and challenges.

It should be noted that not all central Canadian Union and Independent Baptist churches joined the newly constituted Baptist Fellowship. Some Union Baptists in central Canada denounced the new Fellowship even as the process of amalgamation was underway. T. T. Shields decried this new form of fundamentalism on numerous grounds. Three major criticisms stand out. First of all, the name Fellowship of *Evangelical* Baptist Churches in Canada was problematic. Shields argued that "omitting the word 'Regular' omits entirely the statement of the doctrine, on which, as Baptists we should stand."[88] "We say advisedly," Shields declared, "the word 'Evangelical' in no way safeguards the Baptist position."[89] Second, the new Fellowship would undermine the autonomy of the local church:

> The proposed amalgamation therefore does not permit the individual Churches to decide whether they shall enter this amalgamation. It simply declares that all the members of either Union or Fellowship are automatically in it when the proposed Constitution for Amalgamation passes the two separate bodies.[90]

86. Tarr, *This Dominion*, 130.
87. Tarr, *This Dominion*, 130–34.
88. Shields, "More About Amalgamation," *GW*, 1 October 1953, 13.
89. Shields, "More About Amalgamation," *GW*, 1 October 1953, 13.
90. Shields, "More About Amalgamation," *GW*, 1 October 1953, 13.

Finally, the new Fellowship was inconsistent in its practice of the ordinances. For Shields, and militant fundamentalists like him, this was betrayal of Baptist principle and practice: "To unite in one body those who desire to obey the commands of Christ concerning the order, of the Ordinances, with those who will not accept that New Testament command of Christ in practice, is to deny Christ's Lordship."[91] This scathing criticism was used to sustain the view that new Fellowship was both theologically and culturally compromised.

Regular Baptists in western Canada also kept a close eye on developments in central Canada. Pastor D. W. Reed shared the impression of many in an issue of *Western Regular Baptist* in 1953: "'As a Convention we have watched with keen interest developments . . . among our Eastern brethren something for which our heart has cried out to God for many, many months—the effecting of a united front of all fundamental Baptists across our Dominion.'"[92] Meanwhile, many leaders in the new Fellowship "were dreaming of a trans-Canada movement that would re-establish on a national basis the work which the Baptist pioneers had initiated in Canada."[93] But despite this sense of shared vision, much goodwill, and many good intentions, union between Regular Baptists in the east and west was not easily achieved. Kenneth Davis has provided a detailed account of the twelve-year struggle to achieve "a Canada-wide Fellowship of Evangelical Baptist Churches."[94] The leaders of three Baptist groups, British Columbia Regular Baptists, the Prairie Fellowship, and the FEBCC had to overcome challenges from American Baptist groups, including the Southern Baptists and the General Association of Regular Baptist Churches, internal resistance in Ontario to the proposed structure of the new organization, and the fear and resistance of the British Columbia Regular Baptists following the absorption of the Prairie Fellowship into the FEBCC in 1963. Eventually, in 1965, "an uneasy, inconsistent compromise" was achieved.[95] This agreement made the inclusion of the British Columbia Regular Baptists and a more national FEBCC a reality. In the years that followed, the Fellowship would hold together and grow, even as it struggled to find its identity and

91. Shields, "More About Amalgamation," *GW*, 1 October 1953, 13.
92. Tarr, *This Dominion*, 132.
93. Tarr, *This Dominion*, 132,
94. Davis, "The Struggle," 258.
95. Davis, "The Struggle," 258.

discussions and debates about the fundamentalist response to new theological and cultural challenges continued.

In the period from 1966–1978, Fellowship Baptists in central Canada wrestled with numerous theological and cultural issues. Only a few of these matters are mentioned in the next few pages. Before one begins, however, some definition of Fellowship Baptist group identity is required. In this period, three loosely-knit Fellowship Baptist identities are discernable. Militant fundamentalists retained the fighting spirit, hyper-separatist posture, strict morality, and negative outlook of the Regular Baptists. Moderate fundamentalists retained the central tenets of fundamentalist theology, but rejected the negativity, legalism, and hyper-separatism of the militants. Instead, moderate fundamentalists adopted a positive, liberty-oriented, and cooperative approach to the Christian life. The "Rebels," who were by far the smallest in number but often rivaled the militants as the most vocal, challenged the *status quo* both theologically and practically. They were open to new theological trends, such as the Charismatic movement and social welfare endeavours, often associated with more liberal-minded Baptists. They also wanted to set aside differences and restore Baptist unity. In the late 1960s and 1970s, these identities characterized the life and work of the FEBCC.

Historians have sometimes overlooked the debates over legalism and how one makes lifestyle decisions that began in the late 1960s. Militant fundamentalists maintained that in order to be separate from the world one was obliged to follow a list of lifestyle rules. The list of taboos often included not watching television on Sunday, going to a movie theatre, dancing, taking a social drink of alcohol, swimming in mixed company, or card-playing. Moderate fundamentalists viewed such legalism as a "joyless distortion of New Testament Christianity."[96] In a paper entitled "Legalism, Liberty or License" that was presented to the Evangelical Theological Society on 26 May 1969, Fellowship Baptist pastor Robert W. Wilson of Wortley Baptist Church in London, Ontario, argued that "Unfortunately, Fundamentalism is doing an excellent job of producing pharisaical Christians in appalling numbers."[97] Furthermore, Wilson claimed that "having escaped the error of legalism in the realm of justification, Fundamentalism has been ensnarled

---

96. Wilson, "Legalism," 1. A copy of this paper is in the possession of this chapter's author. For a brief autobiography of Robert W. Wilson see Vaughan, *Trailblazers 1*, 393–400.

97. Wilson, "Legalism," 1.

with it in the sphere of sanctification."[98] Wilson presented an exposition of Rom 14:1—15:7 and Gal 5:13–15 to make the biblical case for the principle and practice of liberty and the rejection of legalism and license.[99] Wilson concluded that the biblical view was clear: "The Christian is to stand fast in his liberty in Christ refusing to be entangled again with the yoke of bondage, which is legalism (Gal. 5:1), and being careful not to use his liberty as an occasion to flesh, which is license (Gal. 5:13)."[100] Wilson subsequently presented his paper to Fellowship Baptist pastors in Winnipeg. Not surprisingly, a firestorm of criticism came from those militant fundamentalist pastors who remained committed to legalism. Wilson was branded as a compromiser who was "soft on sin," and his church was given the nickname of "worldly Wortley" by more strict and strident fundamentalist Fellowship Baptist pastors.[101]

Wilson's views were indicative of a group of moderate fundamentalist Fellowship pastors who were true to the basic theological tenets of fundamentalism but were sceptical about the biblical accuracy of some militant views and the efficacy of militant methods. Reformers, like Wilson, rejected the militant fundamentalists' tendency to fight with their fellow Baptists, and their determination to legislate, regulate, condemn, and control to a minute degree the conduct and behaviour of church members. Furthermore, as Michael Haykin has noted, the militant fundamentalist perspective contributed to the practice of defining the identity of the Fellowship "not so much in terms of what it is as what it is not."[102] Wilson and his fellow moderates held to a much more positive, joyful, and hopeful view of the Christian life: "Let us remember," said Wilson, "that the Christian life is essentially positive not negative."[103]

Of course, legalism was not the only issue that caused vigorous debate and discussion. Questions about acceptable biblical translations, the Charismatic movement, biblical inerrancy, the role of women in the church, eschatology, and many other issues caught the attention of the Fellowship in the 1960s and 1970s. Often these issues would be brought forward by way of a resolution at the annual convention long after the issue had stirred

98. Wilson, "Legalism," 2.
99. Wilson, "Legalism," 4–9.
100. Wilson, "Legalism," 8.
101. Wilson, "Legalism," 1.
102. Haykin, "'Jesus, Wondrous Saviour,'" 145.
103. Wilson, "Legalism," 9.

up controversy. The issue would be discussed, and a vote would be taken on the resolution. While this process had its merits, the tardiness of the process and tendency to define its identity in negative terms often "put the Fellowship on the backside of the swell, unable to 'make the wave' and more often than not, paddling madly to catch up."[104] Despite these characteristics the Fellowship continued to flourish.

It would be remiss not to note the shift back to conservative evangelicalism that took place in the 1970s within the BCOQ. The appointment of Clark Pinnock to the faculty of McMaster Divinity College in 1977 is but one of many examples that reflected this change.[105] No published comprehensive historical analysis of the causes and reasons for this shift within the BCOQ exists. But this change was significant for Baptist fundamentalists in central Canada. It would eventually prompt a call in 1983, by the "rebel" Fellowship Baptist pastor Bruce Woods, for the FEBCC and the BCOQ to move from "our present frozen hostility" to "spiritual oneness; love among the brethren; justice in our treatment of one another; and greater effectiveness in mission."[106] Woods' bold challenge would receive a standing ovation at the 1983 Fellowship convention, disapproval from the Fellowship leadership, and mixed responses from the BCOQ.[107] Ultimately, the unity Woods and others desired would not materialize.

The Baptist fundamentalist mission to Quebec that began under the Regular Baptists in the 1930s experienced a temporary lull from 1953–1958 until the new FEBCC could decide what to do about outreach in Quebec. Finally, on 28 November 1958 the Executive Council declared its intentions: "This is to announce the formation of a French Missions Committee by the Executive Council."[108] Effectively, this action established the Fellowships' commitment to support and move forward with the former Regular Baptist Quebec mission.

Progress in Quebec was painfully slow. In 1970, after thirty-two years of fundamentalist evangelistic effort the total provincial attendance was

---

104. Haykin, "'Jesus, Wondrous Saviour,'" 145.

105. Beverley, "Tensions," 222.

106. Beverley, "Tensions," 223–24. Woods eventually published his call for cooperation. See Woods, "Theological Direction and Cooperation," 178–85. For a biographical sketch of Woods, see Lockey and Haykin, "'Polemic, Polity and Piety,'" 152–54.

107. Beverley, "Tensions," 224–27.

108. Wilson, "A Mission Transformed," 197.

542.[109] Beginning in 1971, the mission experienced unprecedented rapid growth. Fellowship Association records show that church membership grew from 371 in 1970 to 4,279 by 1990.[110] The missionaries were both overjoyed and overwhelmed by this amount of numerical growth. In addition, numerous new initiatives were undertaken to strengthen ministry and outreach in the province. These efforts included a shift in focus from rural areas to large urban centres, numerous church plants, summer camps for children, radio and television broadcasts, the establishment of the *Séminaire Baptiste Évangélique du Québec* (Evangelical Baptist Seminary of Quebec) in 1974, and the creation of various youth outreach ministries, and the establishment of a formal campus ministry in 1975.[111] By 1978, the fundamentalist Baptist presence was growing and thriving in Quebec.

In the Maritimes, a few fundamentalist strongholds, particularly in New Brunswick persisted, and controversies bubbled to the surface at various times for various reasons in the period from 1946–1978. Outside influences, such as the central Canadian Fellowship Baptists desire to establish a significant presence in the region, certainly created fear that exacerbated tensions.[112] To date there are few studies that have examined in detail the fundamentalist experience in this era.

The best examinations of fundamentalist views and influence from the late 1940s to 1970, are found in studies by Robert S. Wilson. In his analysis of the events and perspectives that led to the founding of the United Baptist Bible Training School (UBBTS; today Crandall University), Wilson highlights the influx of new students at Acadia University after World War II, the investigations into the quality, quantity, and identity of Christian higher education in the region, what education students wanted, and where they were going to get that education. Wilson notes that at the behest of the United Baptist Institute, pastor A. G. Crowe was tasked with producing a study. Crowe's findings in 1946 indicated that the New Brunswick Bible Institute, founded in 1944, was the institution of choice for Baptist

---

109. Wilson, "A Mission Transformed," 200.

110. Wilson, "A Mission Transformed," 20

111. Wilson, "A Mission Transformed," 199–203.

112. It should be noted that despite their intentions and efforts, the FEBCC never really established a significant presence in the Maritimes. A few churches were established in the early years after 1953, but the breadth and depth of Fellowship Baptist influence in the region was minimal. In 2003, Gordon Rendle noted that "Today there are 20 Fellowship Baptist Churches in the Atlantic provinces." See Lockey, "Fishing For Men," 60, 33–60.

fundamentalist students.[113] "It was strongly fundamentalist and dispensational," Wilson states, "and the students that attended it usually went into independent Baptist churches."[114] Essentially, the creation of the UBBTS, which opened on 7 September 1949, was driven by conservative Baptists from New Brunswick who were suspicious of Acadia's theological leanings and desirous of having a conservative Baptist evangelical educational institution that they could support.[115]

Wilson's detailed examination of UBBTS in its early years, 1949–1960, provides deeper insight into fundamentalism as a "disruptive force" within "Maritime Baptist life."[116] Wilson argues that the creation of the UBBTS and its use of the Bible school model was "a compromise between two theological extremes" fundamentalism and liberal evangelicalism. The desire of the conservative Baptist majority was to "allow fundamentalists to have their own school and yet remain within the Convention."[117] Despite protestations from those on the left, this strategy worked. There was no major split in the United Baptist Convention of Maritime Provinces. Vigorous debates between fundamentalists and liberals, however, would persist well into the 1970s.

In another study of Atlantic Baptists in the 1960s, Wilson makes a number of important observations about fundamentalist and conservative Baptists in the 1950s and 1960s. One important development was the move by a new generation of pastors, a number of whom were fundamentalists, to organize the Evangelical Fellowship in 1953 and later in the 1960s the Concerned Pastors. These fundamentalist groups pushed on many fronts, including education and denominational leadership, for a return to their definition of "orthodoxy" and "Christian."[118] The height of their success was achieved in 1971, when the Concerned Pastors were able to persuade a majority within the United Baptist Convention of the Atlantic Provinces (hereafter UBCAP) to adopt two significant changes: (1) Withdrawal from the Canadian Council of Churches (CCC); (2) Require believer's baptism

---

113. Wilson, "Evangelical, Missionary," 134.

114. Wilson, "Evangelical, Missionary," 134.

115. Wilson, "Evangelical, Missionary," 143–44.

116. Wilson, "Conservative," 133.

117. Wilson, "Conservative," 148. For a recent biographical article about Stuart E. Murray, who personified this perspective in his role as Principal of the United Baptist Bible Training School see, Murray, "Stuart E. Murray," 500–33.

118. Wilson, "Atlantic Baptists Confront," 150–57.

by immersion of all convention delegates.[119] Wilson notes that "The passage of these two motions sparked an immediate reaction by those opposed."[120] A group known as the Atlantic Baptist Fellowship (today the Canadian Association for Baptist Freedoms) was formed in October 1971 with the expressed purposes of sustaining "ecumenical contact, independence of the local congregation, preservation of religious liberty, and the unity of the Convention."[121] On the fundamentalist side the Association of Evangelical Baptists and the Concerned Pastors banded together to press forward with their agenda.[122] In response to the efforts of these "pressure groups" a "broad spectrum" of pastors "produced the Wentworth Statement" in November of 1971.[123] As Wilson astutely notes, "This was an attempt to recall the pastors and people to a commitment to unity within the denomination and to the reaffirmation . . . of church government practised by the UBCAP."[124] Most significantly, according to Wilson, "the 1971 Convention and the UBCAP withdrawal from the CCC mark the turning point for Atlantic Baptists."[125] From here forward the UBCAP would chart and adopt a middle course that would be in Wilson's words, "Conservative but not Contentious."[126]

The Canadian Baptist fundamentalist movement simultaneously matured, reformed, grew, and declined in the period from 1946–1978. Militant fundamentalists continued their fights for theological and moral purity, the preservation of Protestantism, and the primacy of their own political and cultural agendas. Moderate fundamentalists chose to overlook some doctrinal differences, such as differing eschatological views, and pursue unity and cooperation. They also showed a willingness to revisit the militant fundamentalist view of sanctification and separation that was highly legalistic and judgemental. The Canadian Baptist fundamentalist movement developed new forms, such as the FEBCC, in this period that flourished in central Canada and the west but did not establish a significant

---

119. Wilson, "Atlantic Baptists Confront," 167.
120. Wilson, "Atlantic Baptists Confront," 167.
121. Wilson, "Atlantic Baptists Confront," 167.
122. Wilson, "Atlantic Baptists Confront," 167.
123. Wilson, "Atlantic Baptists Confront," 168.
124. Wilson, "Atlantic Baptists Confront," 168.
125. Wilson, "Atlantic Baptists Confront," 168.
126. Wilson, "Conservative," 133. Wilson used this phase as part of the title for his article on the development of United Baptist Bible Training School. It is an apt description of the identity that would eventually characterize the majority within the UBCAP.

presence in the Maritimes. Meanwhile, despite attempts to rally, the Regular Baptist presence and influence showed signs of decline. Independent Baptist fundamentalists were scattered, small in number, and increasingly on the periphery of the movement. Overall, the state of the movement by the late 1970s was a mix of strength and weakness.

CONCLUSION

This brief overview has presented factors, figures, and developments that shaped and defined the Canadian Baptist fundamentalist movement between 1878 and 1978. It has also provided a historical chronology and narrative that explains three approximate phases in the Baptist fundamentalist story. It is apparent that there were significant regional differences in how Baptist fundamentalism developed and was expressed within our country. It is also evident that the Canadian Baptist fundamentalist movement was neither static nor monolithic. While Canadian Baptist fundamentalists shared an identity, they were seldom in every respect identical. There were, in fact, diverse forms of Canadian Baptist fundamentalism that were part of the broader Canadian fundamentalist movement. This reality underscores the complexity of a movement that is often stereotyped as universally militant, rigid, and irrelevant. As this chapter and the rest of this book demonstrates, when it comes to the Canadian Baptist fundamentalist movement, one must resist the temptation to adopt or accept unfounded stereotypical or oversimplified conclusions.

BIBLIOGRAPHY

Primary

NEWSPAPERS

Gospel Witness (Toronto), 1922–1924, 1926, 1931, 1943, 1953
Maclean's Magazine (Toronto), 1949

OTHER

Shields, T. T., "A Challenging Answer to Premier King and Other Parliamentary Critics." In *Three Addresses*, 3–34. Toronto: The Canadian Protestant League, 1943.

———. *The Hepburn Government's Betrayal of Its Public Trust by Diverting Public School Revenue to The Support of Roman Catholic Separate Schools*. Toronto: The Gospel Witness, 1936.

———. *The Inside of the Cup, An Address by T. T. Shields delivered October 14, 1921.* Toronto: Jarvis Street Baptist Church, 1921.

———. *The Plot that Failed*. Toronto: The Gospel Witness, 1937.

———. *Three Addresses*. Toronto: The Canadian Protestant League, 1943.

Wilson, Robert W. "Legalism, Liberty or License." Paper presented to the Evangelical Theological Society (Canada), 26 May 1969.

Secondary

Adams, Doug. "Fighting Fire with Fire: T. T. Shields and His Confrontations with Premier Mitchell Hepburn and Prime Minister Mackenzie King, 1934–1948." In *Baptists and Public Life in Canada*, edited by Gordon L. Heath and Paul R. Wilson, 53–106. McMaster General Series 2. Canadian Baptist Historical Society Series 1. Eugene, OR: Pickwick, 2012.

———. "The War of the Worlds: The Militant Fundamentalism of Dr. Thomas Todhunter Shields and the Paradox of Modernity." PhD diss., University of Western Ontario, 2015.

Adams, Geoffery A. *By His Grace to His Glory: Toronto Baptist Seminary and Bible College 1927–1987*. Toronto: Bryant, 1987.

Ban, Joseph D. "T. C. Douglas and W. Aberhart: A Comparison of their Theological Premises and Social Perspectives." In *Costly Vision: The Baptist Pilgrimage in Canada*, edited by Jarold K. Zeman, 69–84. Burlington: Welch, 1988.

Bauder, Kevin, and Robert Delnay. *One in Hope and Doctrine: Origins of Baptist Fundamentalism, 1870–1950*. Schaumburg, IL: Regular Baptist Books, 2014.

Beverly, James A. "Tensions in Canadian Baptist Theology, 1975–1987." In *Baptists in Canada: Search for Identity Amidst Diversity*, edited by Jarold K. Zeman, 217–40. Burlington: Welch, 1980.

Bowler, Sharon M., ed. *Canadian Baptist Women*. McMaster General Series 8. Canadian Baptist Historical Society Series 3. Eugene, OR: Pickwick, 2016.

Burkinshaw, Robert K. *Pilgrims in Lotus Land: Conservative Protestantism in British Columbia, 1917–1981*. Montreal: McGill-Queen's University Press, 1995.

Carder, W. G. "Controversy in the Baptist Convention of Ontario and Quebec, 1908–1929." BD thesis, McMaster University, 1950.

Cullen, Pamela. "Debating and Dividing: The Women's Baptist Home Missionary Society of Ontario West 1925–1927." *McMaster Journal of Theology and Ministry* 4 (2001) n.p.

Davis, Kenneth R. "The Struggle for a United Evangelical Baptist Fellowship, 1953–1965." In *Baptists in Canada: Search for Identity Amidst Diversity*, edited by Jarold K. Zeman, 237–66. Burlington: Welch, 1980.

Denovan, Joshua. "The Believer in Christ and Christ in the Believer." In *Joshua Denovan*, compiled and edited by O. C. S. Wallace, E. O. White and Editorial Committee, 244–96. Toronto: Standard Publishing Company, 1901.

Dunlop, Aaron. "James B. Rowell 1888–1973." In *A Noble Company 12: The Canadians*, edited by Michael A. G. Haykin and Terry Wolever, 417–39. Springfield, MO: Particular Baptist Press, 2019.

Elliott, David R. "Three Faces of Baptist Fundamentalism in Canada: Aberhart, Maxwell, and Shields." In *Memory and Hope: Strands of Canadian Baptist History*, edited by David T. Priestley, 171–82. Waterloo, ON: Wilfrid Laurier University Press, 1996.

Ellis, Walter E. "Baptists and Radical Politics in Western Canada, 1920-1950." In *Baptists in Canada: Search for Identity Amidst Diversity*, edited by Jarold K. Zeman, 161–82. Burlington: Welch, 1980.

———. "Gilboa to Ichabod: Social and Religious Factors in the Fundamentalist-Modernist Schisms Among Canadian Baptists, 1895-1934." *Foundations* 20.2 (1977) 109–26.

———. "What the Times Demand: Brandon College and Baptist Higher Education in Western Canada." In *Canadian Baptists and Christian Higher Education*, edited by George A. Rawlyk, 63–87. Montreal, QC: McGill-Queen's University Press, 1988.

Fea, John. "Understanding the Changing Facade of Twentieth Century American Protestant Fundamentalism: Toward a Historical Definition." *Trinity Journal* 15.2 (1994) 181–99.

Ford, J. S. Murray. *Convention Chronicles*. Mississauga: Baptist Convention of Ontario and Quebec, 1988.

Grant, John Webster. *The Church in the Canadian Era*. 2nd ed. Vancouver, BC: Regent College Publishing, 1988.

Haykin, Michael A. G. "'Jesus, Wondrous Saviour': Ontario Baptist Roots in the Nineteenth Century." In *A Glorious Fellowship of Churches: Celebrating the History of the Fellowship of Evangelical Baptist Churches in Canada, 1953-2003*, edited by Michael A. G. Haykin and Robert B. Lockey, 115–43. Guelph, ON: The Fellowship of Evangelical Baptist Churches in Canada, 2003.

Haykin, Michael A. G., and Robert B. Lockey, eds. *A Glorious Fellowship of Churches: Celebrating the History of the Fellowship of Evangelical Baptist Churches in Canada, 1953-2003*. Guelph, ON: The Fellowship of Evangelical Baptist Churches in Canada, 2003.

Haykin, Michael A. G., and Terry Wolever, eds. *A Noble Company 12: The Canadians*. Springfield. MO: Particular Baptist Press, 2019.

Heath, Gordon L., and Paul R. Wilson, eds. *Baptists and Public Life in Canada*. McMaster General Series 2. Canadian Baptist Historical Society Series 1. Eugene, OR: Pickwick, 2012.

Hindmarsh, D. Bruce. "The Winnipeg Fundamentalist Network, 1910–1940: The Roots of Transdenominational Evangelicalism in Manitoba and Saskatchewan." In *Aspects of the Canadian Evangelical Experience*, edited by George A. Rawlyk, 303–19. Montreal: McGill-Queen's University Press, 1997.

Holcomb, Douglas J. "John R. Boyd 1909–1994." In *A Noble Company 12: The Canadians*, edited by Michael A. G. Haykin and Terry Wolever, 441–73. Springfield, MO: Particular Baptist Press, 2019.

Jones, Callum Norman. "'Our Women Have Wrought Loyally': Baptist Women, Their Roles, Their Organization, and Their Contribution in Western Canada between 1907-1940." In *Canadian Baptist Women*, edited by Sharon M. Bowler, 135–54. McMaster General Series 8. Canadian Baptist Historical Society Series 3. Eugene, OR: Pickwick, 2016.

Johnston, Charles M. *McMaster University Vol. 1: The Toronto Years*. Toronto: University of Toronto Press, 1976.

Lockey, Robert B. "Fishing for Men: Fellowship Atlantic." In *A Glorious Fellowship of Churches: Celebrating the History of the Fellowship of Evangelical Baptist Churches in Canada, 1953-2003*, edited by Michael A. G. Haykin and Robert B. Lockey, 33–60. Guelph, ON: The Fellowship of Evangelical Baptist Churches in Canada, 2003.

Lockey, Robert B., and Michael A. G. Haykin. "Polemic, Polity, and Piety: Some Themes in the story of FEB CENTRAL." In *A Glorious Fellowship of Churches: Celebrating the History of the Fellowship of Evangelical Baptist Churches in Canada, 1953-2003*, edited by Michael A. G. Haykin and Robert B. Lockey, 145-73. Guelph, ON: The Fellowship of Evangelical Baptist Churches in Canada, 2003.

Mann, William E. *Sect, Cult and Church in Alberta*. Toronto: University of Toronto Press, 1955.

McLeod, Tommy. "'To Bestir Themselves:' Canadian Baptists and the Origins of Brandon College." *Manitoba History* 56 (2007) 22-31.

Murray, Taylor James. "From Exodus to Exile: The Early Fundamentalist Movement Among Maritime Baptists, 1930-1939." MA thesis, Acadia University, 2016.

———. "Stuart E. Murray 1919-1985." In *A Noble Company 12: The Canadians*, edited by Michael A. G. Haykin and Terry Wolever, 500-33. Springfield, MO: Particular Baptist Press, 2019.

Pickering, Ernest. *Biblical Separation*. Arlington Heights, IL: Regular Baptist Press, 2008.

Pinnock, Clark H. "The Modernist Impulse at McMaster University, 1887-1927." In *Costly Vision: The Baptist Pilgrimage in Canada*, edited by Jarold K. Zeman, 193-208. Burlington: Welch, 1988.

Priest, Gerald L. "T. T. Shields the Fundamentalist: Man of Controversy." *Detroit Baptist Seminary Journal* 10 (2005) 69-101

Priestly, David T., ed. *Memory and Hope: Strands of Canadian Baptist History*. Waterloo, ON: Wilfrid Laurier University Press, 1996.

———. "North American Baptist Conference." In *Baptists Around the World* edited by Albert Warden, 381. Nashville: Broadman, 1995.

Rawlyk, George A. *Aspects of the Canadian Evangelical Experience*. Montreal: McGill-Queen's University Press, 1997.

———. *Champions of the Truth: Fundamentalism, Modernism, and the Maritime Baptists*. Montreal: McGill-Queen's University Press, 1990.

Rawlyk, George A., ed. *Canadian Baptists and Christian Higher Education*. Montreal: McGill-Queen's University Press, 1988.

Renfree, Harry. *Heritage and Horizon: The Baptist Story in Canada*. Mississauga: Canadian Baptist Federation, 1988.

Russell, C. Allyn. "Thomas Todhunter Shields, Canadian Fundamentalist." *Ontario History* 70.4 (1978) 261-80.

Sawatsky, Ronald. "'Looking for That Blessed Hope': The Roots of Fundamentalism in Canada 1878-1914." PhD diss., University of Toronto, 1985.

Scott, J. Brian. "Brandon College and Social Christianity." In *Costly Vision: The Baptist Pilgrimage in Canada*, edited by Jarold K. Zeman, 139-66. Burlington: Welch, 1988.

Smale, Robert R. "'The Voice of One Crying in the Wilderness' or Verbal Bigotry—T. T. Shields, *The Gospel Witness* and Roman Catholicism, 1922-1942." *Historical Papers of the Canadian Society of Church History* (1997) 5-28.

Stackhouse Jr., John G. *Canadian Evangelicalism in the Twentieth Century*. Toronto: University of Toronto Press, 1993.

Tarr, Leslie K. "Another Perspective on T. T. Shields and Fundamentalism." In *Costly Vision: The Baptist Pilgrimage in Canada*, edited by Jarold K. Zeman, 209-224. Burlington: Welch, 1988.

———. *Shields of Canada*. Grand Rapids: Baker, 1967.

———. *This Dominion His Dominion*. Willowdale, ON: Fellowship of Evangelical Baptist Churches in Canada, 1968.

Vaughan, Fred A., ed. *Fellowship Baptist Trailblazers: Life Stories of Pastors and Missionaries—Book One*. Belleville, ON: Guardian, 2001.

Wallace, O. C. S., E. O. White and Editorial Committee. *Joshua Denovan*. Toronto: Standard Publishing Company, 1901.

Warden, Albert, ed. *Baptists Around the World*. Nashville: Broadman, 1995.

Wesley, Cindy K. "The Pietist theology and Ethnic Mission of the General Conference of German Baptists in North America, 1851–1920." PhD diss., McGill University, 2000.

Wilson, Paul R. "A Mission Transformed: Fellowship Baptist Outreach in Quebec, 1953–1986." In *Baptists and Mission: Papers from the Fourth International Conference on Baptist Studies*, edited by Ian M. Randall and Anthony R. Cross, 189–204. Studies in Baptist History and Thought 29. Eugene, OR: Wipf and Stock, 2007.

———. "Baptists and Business: Central Canadian Baptists and The Secularization of the Businessmen at Toronto's Jarvis Street Baptist Church, 1848–1921." PhD diss., University of Western Ontario, 1996.

———. "Central Canadian Baptists and the Role of Cultural Factors in the Fundamentalist-Modernist Schism of 1927." *Baptist History and Heritage* 36.1–2 (2001) 61–81.

———. "Torn Asunder: T. T. Shields, W. Gordon Brown and the Schisms at Toronto Baptist Seminary and within the Union of Regular Baptist Churches of Ontario and Quebec, 1948–1949." *McMaster Journal of Theology and Ministry* 19 (2017–2018) 34–80.

Wilson, Robert S. "Atlantic Baptists Confront the Turbulent Sixties." In *A Fragile Stability: Definition and Redefinition of Maritime Baptist Identity*, edited by David Priestley, 149–69. Baptist Heritage in Atlantic Canada 15. Hantsport, NS: Lancelot, 1994.

———. "'Conservative but Not Contentious': The Early Years of the United Baptist Bible Training School." In *Revivals, Baptists, and George Rawlyk*, edited by Daniel C. Goodwin, 133–52. Baptist Heritage in Atlantic Canada 17. Wolfville, NS: Acadia Divinity College, 2000.

———. "'Evangelical, Missionary, and Christ-Centred': The Founding of Atlantic Baptist College." In *A Fragile Stability: Definition and Redefinition of Maritime Baptist Identity*, edited by David Priestley, 131–48. Baptist Heritage in Atlantic Canada 15. Hantsport, NS: Lancelot, 1994.

Woods, Bruce A. "Theological Direction and Cooperation Among Baptists in Canada." In *Canadian Baptist History and Polity*, edited by Murray J. S. Ford, 178–85. Hamilton, ON: McMaster University Divinity College, 1983.

Zeman, Jarold K., ed. *Baptists in Canada: Search for Identity Amidst Diversity*. Burlington: Welch, 1980.

———. *Costly Vision: The Baptist Pilgrimage in Canada*. Burlington: Welch, 1988.

2

Joshua Denovan

A Prototypical Militant Fundamentalist, 1829–1901

Paul R. Wilson

THE ORIGINS OF THE Baptist fundamentalist movement in central Canada are still largely unknown. Few historians have examined in detail the beliefs, actions, and attitudes of nineteenth-century central Canadian Baptist proto-fundamentalists. This chapter is a small first step in addressing this gap in our knowledge and understanding.

Joshua Denovan is not usually a name that comes to mind when one thinks about militant Baptist fundamentalists in Canada. In fact, his many contributions to early fundamentalism, within central Canadian Baptist circles in the late nineteenth century, have received far less attention from historians and theologians than they deserve. In his 1981 unpublished study, Brent Reilly made an astute observation: "Though largely forgotten today, the Reverend Joshua Denovan, LLD, was a leading figure in Baptist life during the last quarter of the nineteenth century."[1] With the objective of gaining a better understanding of central Canadian Baptist fundamentalist roots, this chapter examines Denovan's beliefs, endeavours, expressions, and experiences.

---

1. Reilly, "The Reverend Joshua Denovan," 1. Please note: This chapter could not have been completed without the diligent and kind assistance of Adam McCulloch, Archivist at the Canadian Baptist Archives.

The central claim of this chapter is straightforward: The beliefs, actions, and attitudes of Joshua Denovan constituted a late-nineteenth century central Canadian Baptist prototype for what would become militant fundamentalism. To sustain this claim, this chapter examines his life and career, his theological and moral views, his attitudes and actions, and his controversies with his fellow Baptists in the period from 1871–1901. Some comparison and contrast between his views and that of his coreligionists is also presented to support the case offered here and provide some perspective on his fundamentalist legacy.

A BRIEF BIOGRAPHICAL SKETCH

Joshua Denovan's relative anonymity warrants a brief biography. Born on 27 December 1829, in Glasgow, Scotland, he grew up in Gouroch and Glasgow. As members of the Church of Scotland, his family was connected to the institutions of Kirk and parish school. He received education in the Gouroch parish school, the Academy at Greenoch, the High School at Glasgow, and the University of Glasgow. Denovan's family was intensely religious. Like many other Scots, the Denovan family was caught up in the "Great Disruption of 1843."[2] The Denovans sided with those in favour of establishing an evangelical Free Church.

On the personal religious level, this was a time of despair, decision, devotion, and discipleship for Joshua Denovan. After a period of hypocrisy and despair, he was drawn, in his late teens, to embark on a new life in Christ.[3] His new-found faith led him to diligently search the Scriptures. For the Bible "had been the one book in his father's house to which all others and all else had been subordinated."[4] According to his biographer, he decided "to devote all his attention and energies to the study of this

---

2. For examinations of the Great Disruption and its consequences see Moir, *Enduring Witness*, 101–27; Reid, *The Scottish Tradition*, 131–34; Brown and Fry, eds., *Scotland in the Age of Disruption*; Talbot, *The Search for a Common Identity*, 229–31.

3. Memorial Committee, *Denovan*, 18–19. The memorial volume entitled, *Joshua Denovan*, was arranged, authored, and edited by a Committee that included O. C. S. Wallace, Thomas Bengough, Samuel John Moore, H. P. Welton, W. W. Weeks, G. F. Ronald, Allan M. Denovan, Benjamin David Thomas, and E. O. White. Sir John Alexander Boyd and William Davies also authored chapters. Since multiple individuals authored and/or edited each chapter and who did what is not always clear, I have used Memorial Committee, *Denovan*, as the form of citation.

4. Memorial Committee, *Denovan*, 20.

book."[5] It should be noted that study became a life-long pursuit for Denovan. He read widely, and he did not hesitate to draw on his knowledge in his many discussions and debates with friends, foes, and colleagues.

After his conversion, Denovan took up the novel work of secretary and teacher in a Sunday School run by his father.[6] In addition to this endeavour, he felt compelled to preach in the open air to "a number of noisy idlers" who crowded Glasgow's streets. For him, this first sermon marked his call to ministry: "As in the event of my conversion, so in this event of my call, neither my wish nor my will was consulted. My own preferences, plans, and purposes were simply ignored and overborne. Against my will a dispensation of the gospel was committed unto me."[7] This calling set Denovan on a course of even more intense theological and biblical study. He also became more active in the Free Church where his father was now pastor. In fact, he "was appointed to the office of Helper to the Pastor."[8] By 1853, his courtship of Jane Macnab, the daughter of Alan Macnab, a well-known and highly respected Free Church elder, culminated in their marriage on 15 June 1853.[9] By all accounts the young couple was well-matched and well-supported by both sides of the family.

Another turning point in Denovan's beliefs came while he was teaching a Monday evening Bible class for young men. He used the Bible and the Shorter Catechism of the Church of Scotland as the basis for his classes. The Catechism contained a question concerning baptism: "To whom is baptism to be administered?"[10] This question sparked a lively debate that went on for weeks. Some argued against infant baptism; others argued for that practice. After considerable thought and study, Denovan concluded that believer's baptism by immersion, the position held by Baptists, was the correct biblical view. He, and some of his parishioners, subsequently left the Free Church and pursued Baptist church membership.

In the 1860s, Baptists in Scotland were few and divided by doctrinal disagreements. In fact, the union of Scottish Baptists would not happen until 1869, three years after Denovan's departure to Canada.[11] In his last

---

5. Memorial Committee, *Denovan*, 20.
6. Memorial Committee, *Denovan*, 22.
7. Memorial Committee, *Denovan*, 23–24.
8. Memorial Committee, *Denovan*, 24.
9. Memorial Committee, *Denovan*, 25.
10. Memorial Committee, *Denovan*, 29.
11. Talbot, *The Search for a Common Identity*, 307–12.

few years in Scotland, he conducted his church ministry with great success in Glasgow's local Halls. Unfortunately, the strain of ministry, a large family of seven children aged twelve and under, and other family tensions—especially a rift over religious views between himself and his father—took a toll on Denovan's health.[12] Seeking recovery and a new start, he made the decision to emigrate to Canada.

Carrying a letter of recommendation from Charles Haddon Spurgeon, the most renowned British Baptist preacher at this time and one who knew Denovan, the Denovan family arrived in Quebec on 5 September 1866.[13] They then headed for St. Mary's in Canada West with the intention of taking up farming.[14] However, Denovan was so ill that he almost died. He recovered and, hearing that there were mountains in the Eastern Townships south of Montreal that resembled those in Scotland, he purchased a farm near Abbott's Corner, Quebec and moved his family there.[15] It was not long before he began preaching in a Baptist Church, connected with the Baptists in Montreal, and was asked to become a missionary to churches in central Canada. He moved to Smith's Falls in November 1867, and served the Baptist churches at Smith's Falls, Almonte, and Carleton as pastor for two years.[16]

In 1869, the Stratford Baptist church called Denovan as pastor. After two years of successful ministry there, he moved back to Montreal in 1871 to become pastor of the Baptist church on St. Catherine Street.[17] As Brent Reilly has noted, "the move to Montreal marked the beginning of Denovan's involvement in denominational affairs."[18] In his six and half years of ministry in Montreal, two hundred people joined the church, and a new building was erected. In 1878, Alexander Street Baptist Church in Toronto called him as its pastor, and he welcomed the opportunity to take on this new role. In his reminiscence of Denovan, one former parishioner William Davies noted that, "Pastor Denovan's preaching was pungent, poignant, and

---

12. Memorial Committee, *Denovan*, 32–34.

13. Memorial Committee, *Denovan*, 34–35. Spurgeon's letter began with this statement: "Mr. J. Denovan is a man well known to me as an earnest preacher of the word, . . ." Excerpts from the letter are in Denovan's memorial volume on page 34.

14. Memorial Committee, *Denovan*, 35.

15. Memorial Committee, *Denovan*, 36.

16. Memorial Committee *Denovan*, 37.

17. Memorial Committee, *Denovan*, 37.

18. Reilly, "The Reverend Joshua Denovan," 12.

attractive to the studious and thoughtful."[19] Denovan served this church as pastor until ill-health forced him into retirement in 1889. Despite serious ailments, including the loss of his sight, he would continue to write and publish his views until at least 1899. According to Brent Reilly, "Denovan was one of the most published, most published, Baptist minister in nineteenth century Ontario."[20] After a bout of pneumonia, Joshua Denovan died on 5 January 1901. Death notices, eulogies, and obituaries noted his many accomplishments and contributions to the cause of Christ as expressed and practiced by central Canadian Baptists. A memorial service was held for him in Jarvis Street Baptist Church on 8 January 1901.

DENOVAN'S EARLY PROTO-FUNDAMENTALISM: BELIEFS, VIEWS, AND OBSERVATIONS, 1871–1877

Throughout his life, Denovan made attempts to persuade his fellow Baptists to accept his perspectives on doctrinal orthodoxy, polity, and strict morality. In letters to his friend and former parishioner James Hogg, he shared his deep-seated ultraconservative beliefs and his observations about the spiritual, moral, and doctrinal health of his fellow Baptists. In his letters, he underscored the need for doctrinal orthodoxy, the authority and supremacy of Scripture in all matters of faith and practice, the use of a literal hermeneutic, proper polity, and the requirement that Baptists adhere to a strict morality. He also expressed his dismay, displeasure, and discontent with the worldliness and lapses in polity that were, he feared, taking over the church.

In a letter to Hogg dated 13 October 1871, for example, Denovan offered a revealing statement about his desires and devotion to doctrinal orthodoxy: "I sometimes wish I had physical and mental strength to wander over broad Canada, preaching substitution, imputation and sanctification, and contradicting without mercy every thought to the contrary."[21] In addition to expressing his devotion to the core doctrines of salvation and sanctification, and his desire to stamp out error related to such views, he went on to share with Hogg his ardent support for evangelism and his utter distain for every expression and hint of Arminian doctrine: "My prayer to

---

19. Memorial Committee, *Denovan*, 82.

20. Reilly, "The Reverend Joshua Denovan," 8. All forms of emphasis used in this chapter, including underline, italics, and capital letters, are as they appear in the original documents.

21. Memorial Committee, *Denovan*, 169.

God is that he would send us a Whitfield for an evangelist and a Haldane for a theological professor,—men of power enough to beat the last breath out of Arminianism and see it buried a thousand fathoms deep before they leave it. *Salvation is all of grace.*"[22] Such dogmatic and violent statements reveal how devoted Denovan was to his own proto-fundamentalist views and how committed he was to doctrinal purity and orthodoxy.

As a strong Calvinist, Denovan was also deeply disturbed by false doctrine, doctrinal ignorance, and man's depravity. He cast himself as a flawed messenger of true and pure doctrine. Following his rant against doctrinal error, he engaged in deep introspection about his own sinfulness and unworthiness. He concluded this exercise with the following declaration of admiration and devotion: "And now I desire to record my admiration of divine grace in my salvation. Henceforth, far be it from me to make mention of any righteousness save God's alone. I see more plainly than ever that it will take the substitution of Jesus, and the invincible sanctification of the Holy Ghost to make me or anyone fit for heaven."[23] These were doctrinal positions often held by Baptist proto-fundamentalists. To his credit, Denovan recognized that having sound doctrine was not enough. Doctrine had to be applied and lived out in his own life first before he could preach to his flock about living a sanctified life.

For Denovan, the pervasiveness and pernicious influence of Arminian theology in Baptist circles was especially detrimental to the Baptist cause. This topic is a recurring theme in his letters to Hogg. In his letter of 25 January 1872, for example, he expressed his deep disappointment with the Arminian doctrinal position held by pastor William Cheetham of the First Baptist Church in Montreal:

> Mr. C[heetham], poor fellow, is at present confined to home with a bruised limb—occasioned by a fall on the ice. He and I don't agree doctrinally—his favorite commentator being Adam Clarke!!! In fact there is no religious sympathy between us, and I very much fear there never can be. This is a great loss to me, but to the cause of Christ it is a fearful calamity, considering the position he holds in the city. He is (as minister of the first and central church), our representative man.[24]

---

22. Memorial Committee, *Denovan*, 169.

23. Memorial Committee, *Denovan*, 170.

24. Memorial Committee, *Denovan*, 175. For informational about Cheetham see *The Canadian Baptist Register for 1872*, 81; Adam Clarke was a Methodist theologian who wrote a series of biblical commentaries between 1 May 1798 and 28 March 1825. He was

For Denovan, the division and damage caused by Arminian theology was personally and professionally profound. The impact on efforts to advance the gospel and the Baptist denomination was, in his view, equally devastating. Again, his aversion to Arminianism in any form and his strong commitment to Calvinist views of salvation and sanctification were often held by his fellow Baptist proto-fundamentalists.[25]

In his ongoing correspondence with Hogg, Denovan was quick to correct, admonish, and encourage brother Hogg when he devalued, misinterpreted, or misunderstood the Bible, or was tempted to not take full advantage of his opportunities for ministry. In his letter of 14 December 1871, for example, he underscored that authority of the Bible and challenged Hogg's understanding of Christ's ministry: "With reference to your remarks regarding Christ's personal ministry not being such a success in converting souls, I do not think his ministry was ever designed to be so successful in this respect as the ministry of the disciples on and after Pentecost. I need not tell you that many scriptures plainly indicate this."[26] After this correction, he admonished and encouraged Hogg to keep on doing the good work of spreading the gospel, engaging in Bible study, and furthering the Baptist cause:

> I am anxiously concerned that you should employ every opportunity of speaking the truth in love. The work of tract distribution, your S[unday] S[chool] Class, and the other two weekly meetings for the study of the Word, give you room for great usefulness. These opportunities, if used properly, with talents such as you have, will tell upon the Baptist Church and the society around you FOREVER.[27]

Such statements reveal that in his personal relationships, Denovan was committed to correcting perceived error, upholding biblical authority, and encouraging his Christian brother to be a good and faithful servant. Each of these traits were typical of early proto-fundamentalists like Denovan.

Of course, Denovan did not limit his criticism to his Baptist friends and colleagues. He was disgusted by divines in other denominations who

---

decidedly Arminian in his theology. For a brief biography of Clarke see Edwards, "Adam Clarke," 50–56.

25. See, for example, Alumni Association, *Memoir of Daniel Arthur McGregor* (hereafter Alumni Association, *Memoir of McGreagor*), 187–88, 198.

26. Memorial Committee, *Denovan*, 172.

27. Memorial Committee, *Denovan*, 173.

held a low view of biblical authority and shied away in public "undenominational" meetings from any reference to core doctrines. In his letter dated 25 January 1872, for example, he castigated both the meetings and the shallowness of his fellow clergymen: "Large, undenominational meetings gratify the flesh, while I suspect God is dishonoured in them by that care with which the speakers shun all reference to the distinctive doctrines of the gospel. Connected with this professional politeness and platform suavity, I fear there is what God esteems positive hypocrisy."[28] In the same letter, Denovan went on to quote the comments of some Presbyterian clergymen. One offered the following comment: "The day is past for the use of such antiquated terms as justification, predestination, and so forth, in a sermon."[29] Denovan's despairing response was telling: "Thus they talk, and I listen and—mourn. I can see little hope indeed of doing any good except by the old, slow process of patiently educating a few people."[30] Despite the tendency of some clergy to lower the standards of doctrinal literacy by eliminating doctrinal terms and content in their sermons, Denovan remained resolute in his commitment to educate his flock in the fundamental doctrines of the faith as found in the Bible.

In line with his ardent belief in the Bible as the sole and supreme inspired authority in all matters of faith and practice, Denovan brooded about the worldliness and moral laxity that were, in his view, eroding Baptist separation from the world and the strict morality that was supposed to characterize Baptist expressions of a sanctified life. One spiritual and moral issue that greatly disturbed Denovan was the "unequal yoke" of believer and unbeliever in marriage. In his letter of 5 March 1872, he shared his disapproval for such marriages: "The godless marriages of the sisters whose names you mention is very evil tidings. Since I came hither, I have had to refuse marrying a sister who sinned in the same way. The church must suffer in purity and strength by such unhallowed alliances."[31] He was also shocked and surprised by those of his fellow Baptist clergymen who seemed oblivious to the ill-effects of these marriages: "It amazes me," declared Denovan, "that the ministry do not all see this at a glance, as of this I am sure, the growing worldliness and corruption of many Baptist Churches

28. Memorial Committee, *Denovan*, 175.
29. Memorial Committee, *Denovan*, 176.
30. Memorial Committee, *Denovan*, 176.
31. Memorial Committee, *Denovan*, 179.

is mainly traceable to this one source."[32] For Denovan, Baptists were paying a high price for such ignorance, laxity, and lack of vigilance.

In his letter of 21 May 1872, Denovan was also disgusted by the "schemes and contrivances" used by churches from all denominations in their "competition" to attract the young. He was especially put out by their efforts to "vie with each other to give the raciest entertainment."[33] Such worldly behaviour by Protestant clergy provoked him exceedingly. It was everything he could do to hold his temper:

> To speak the truth, without the manifestation of personal feeling—without displaying a bad temper—is a most difficult task. To treat these ministers as ministers of Christ while they are doing everything in their power to accommodate the Church to the world and making the ruin of the coming generation as sure as they can, is nearly beyond my power.[34]

This evidence indicates that Denovan was convinced that worldliness and moral laxity were on the rise, and Baptists were certainly not immune from these evils. He was determined to do what he could to resist such trends, stay true to the doctrines of separation and sanctification, and challenge his fellow Baptists to do the same.

By the late 1870s, Denovan had expressed, in no uncertain terms, his devotion to certain core doctrinal and moral antecedents of what would become militant Baptist fundamentalism. Using strident language and a dogmatic and hypercritical tone, he left no doubt about his Calvinist belief in salvation, sanctification, and separation, the supremacy of Scriptures in all matters of faith and practice, the need to provide the Baptist laity with education in pure (Calvinist) doctrine, and his aversion and strong opposition to Arminianism, moral laxity, and worldliness. With his move to Toronto in 1878, to take on the pastorate of Alexander Street Baptist Church, Denovan was poised to take a more active and prominent public role in voicing his concerns, expressing his proto-fundamentalist doctrinal views, and contending as a warrior for the Baptist faith. His efforts would soon reverberate throughout central Canada.

---

32. Memorial Committee, *Denovan*, 180.
33. Memorial Committee, *Denovan*, 184.
34. Memorial Committee, *Denovan*, 185.

DENOVAN'S MOVE TO ALEXANDER STREET AND HIS PROTO-FUNDAMENTALIST ACTIVISM, 1878–1879

It is challenging to establish with absolute certainty when one can classify Denovan as a fundamentalist. He was always on the ultra-conservative end of the Baptist theological and moral spectrum, and he was unquestionably a key figure in the formative phase of Baptist fundamentalism and an early adopter of, and active participant in, the Canadian proto-fundamentalist movement; however, based on the available evidence, the year 1878 was a turning point for Denovan. His new charge in the heart of Toronto put him at the epicentre of both the Canadian proto-fundamentalist movement and central Canadian Baptist life. Ronald Sawatsky has noted that "Canadian proto-fundamentalists lived primarily in Toronto" in the late nineteenth century, and "Toronto appears to have been the unofficial headquarters for the [proto-fundamentalist] movement."[35] Denovan fit the ethnic make-up of these proto-fundamentalists perfectly. "The vast majority of the proto-fundamentalists," Sawatsky notes, "were Anglo-Saxon, Celtic, or Scottish in origin."[36] Toronto Baptist fortunes were also on the rise. From a low of 2.9 per cent of the city's populace in 1861, the number of Toronto Baptists grew to 3.1 per cent by 1871 and 4.2 per cent by 1881.[37] For Denovan, his relocation to Toronto was both fitting and fortuitous.

Given this environment and these conditions, it is not surprising that Denovan quickly became more outspoken about his proto-fundamentalist views, and more active and prominent in local, denominational, and proto-fundamentalist affairs. In two addresses to fellow proto-fundamentalists and central Canadian Baptists he left no doubt about his doctrinal perspective.

Anyone who was aware of the history of Alexander Street Baptist Church would have found the selection of Denovan as pastor in 1878 to be entirely in keeping with the ultraconservative and feisty ethos of this church. Alexander Street (as of 1888, Immanuel Baptist Church) had a long history of maintaining a strict moral line and an unwavering commitment to orthodox Baptist theology. Alexander Street was created in 1857, by about twenty disgruntled members of Bond Street Baptist Church, after a church controversy caused by a business dispute between two members, Francis T. Parson, a commission merchant, and William Davies, a provision

---

35. Sawatsky, "Looking for That Blessed Hope," 134.
36. Sawatsky, "Looking for That Blessed Hope," 136.
37. See Wilson, "Baptists and Business," 4; and Grant, *A Profusion of Spires*, 224.

dealer.[38] The disagreement between Parson and Davies created a power struggle for control of Bond Street between William Davies and William McMaster, a dry goods merchant, later banker and Senator, who supported Parson.[39] Eventually, a church split occurred at Bond Street. Davies and his supporters left to form Alexander Street Baptist Church. This schism had a deleterious effect on relationships within Toronto's Baptist community and frustrated Baptist attempts to make headway in the city. For years, the efforts of Alexander Street were actively opposed by the supporters of William McMaster, including Robert Alexander Fyfe, one of the nineteenth century's most influential Canadian Baptists. Members of Alexander Street were also ostracised and shunned by their Bond Street brethren.[40]

Longstanding friction, anger, resentment, and suspicion about Bond Street's (as of 1875, Jarvis Street's) motives within the Alexander Street congregation was never far from the surface. In his letter to Carrey Tyso of 15 June 1876, for example, Davies was scathing in his assessment of the actions and attitude of the McMasters and the new Jarvis Street Baptist Church. In particular, he expressed his dislike for the spirit and motives that lay behind the new Baptist "cathedral" located on Jarvis Street: "There appears to have been a spirit of centralization & aggrandisement ab[ou]t it which is hateful."[41] Such statements illustrate that the animosity and rivalry between Alexander Street and Jarvis Street were still alive and well in the minds of some only a couple of years before Denovan's arrival.

It was into this context that Denovan in March 1878—after two "Sabbaths" of candidacy, a unanimous recommendation of Pulpit Committee, and a unanimous "standing vote" of the Alexander Street congregation—was invited to become pastor.[42] The 15 March 1878, edition of the *Christian Helper* published a "verbatim report" of Denovan's remarks that were based on 1 Cor 12. His address was telling in its candour and clarity about his purpose for coming to Alexander Street: "I come among you with a purpose,—a purpose confirmed by experience,—to live as close to Christ as I can, and to act in relation to you as the Head shall dictate. You can expect

---

38. See Wilson, "Baptists and Business," 183–89.
39. Wilson, "Baptists and Business," 183–89.
40. Wilson, "Baptists and Business," 188.
41. Fox, ed., *Letters of William Davies*, 135. See also Wilson, "Baptists and Business," 172–74.
42. *Alexander Street Baptist Church Minutes*, (hereafter *ASBC Minutes*), 330.

nothing less."[43] He also provided what could have been easily interpreted by his audience as a critique of Jarvis Street Baptist Church. His remarks countered and criticized the business-like and industrial view of the church that some of his fellow-Baptists were adopting: "But I come among you not to do your work. Mark what I say: I don't come to run the machine. I don't believe that the church of Christ is a machine at all," he thundered, "I don't believe that any body runs it but the Holy Ghost."[44] Then Denovan offered his view of role and responsibility of the pastor and the people:

> I come distinctly, brethren and sisters, to work with you, and to do no more; to work with you,—not to work against you,—not to work instead of you. And I come on the express understanding that in the name of God and the strength of the Spirit, and according to the 12th chap[ter] [of] 1st Corinthians, you will do your part of the work.[45]

So Denovan's ministry at Alexander Street began.

Denovan's Paper on the Millennium, October 1878

Denovan wasted no time in making his proto-fundamentalist views known within the wider circle of Ontario Baptists. On 15 October 1878, he read a paper entitled, "The Scriptural Doctrine of the Millennium" to the Baptist Ministerial Conference held in Brantford, Ontario. He clearly sensed that his topic was both a curiosity and a sensation, and he felt compelled to signal caution from the start. "Perhaps no other biblical subject has been the occasion of greater variety of opinion," he noted, "or has given scope to more fanciful interpretations, and wing to wider speculations than this one."[46] He claimed that he had "avoided making the 'Second Advent' a specialty" and consequently, he offered "no well defined Millennial theory" that included a "scheme of events and dates corresponding with prophetic figures and predictions."[47] Instead, Denovan proposed to focus on what he had "learned" from "twenty-five years" of reading "the Bible." For him the

---

43. The published version of this report was pasted into the *ASBC Minutes*, 331.
44. *ASBC Minutes*, 331.
45. *ASBC Minutes*, 331.
46. Memorial Committee, *Denovan*, 197.
47. Memorial Committee, *Denovan*, 197.

Bible clearly taught that "the Messiah and his saints shall reign on earth."[48] And it was this millennial kingdom doctrine that he would present.

Using passages from both the Old and New Testaments, Denovan demonstrated that the Bible contained extensive references to a millennial kingdom where Christ would reign on earth. His hermeneutical approach to biblical prophecy was in keeping with the literal method of interpretation supported and practiced by proto-fundamentalists. In his closing remarks about Old Testament prophecy, he made his hermeneutical stance clear: "With regard to the entire subject of Old Testament prophecy, I think it would remove many serious difficulties out of the way of easy and correct interpretation were we to take the words as nearly as possible in their literal sense; God's Word is a *revelation*, not a mystification."[49] This statement is telling on many levels. It certainly put Denovan squarely in the proto-fundamentalist frame as a defender of the Bible as the only divinely-inspired source of absolute truth. It also underscored his belief that the Bible could only be rightly understood if one adopted and applied a literal hermeneutic. The heart of his view of the millennium and Christ's second coming is found in his summary statement about what the Bible teaches: "I think Scripture plainly teaches that the Lord Jesus Christ shall himself personally inaugurate and rule the Millennial kingdom on earth: in other words, that Christ's second coming shall be pre-mille[n]nial."[50] Here is the evidence that Denovan's eschatology, as Sawatsky claimed, "was vintage dispensational premillennialism."[51]

In the last section of his paper, Denovan discussed a number of "difficulties and objections" to "Christ's pre-millennial advent."[52] Specifically, he addressed two main troublesome points. He noted that "several passages" appear "to teach us to expect that the righteous and the wicked shall rise from the grave simultaneously 'at the last trump.'"[53] He acknowledged that "Daniel, as well as the Lord and his apostles, do use language that fairly interpreted can be regarded as conveying this meaning."[54] In response, he argued that "the prophetic Scriptures very often fail to indicate the intervals

---

48. Memorial Committee, *Denovan*, 197.
49. Memorial Committee, *Denovan*, 206.
50. Memorial Committee, *Denovan*, 218.
51. Sawatsky, "Looking for That Blessed Hope," 70.
52. Memorial Committee, *Denovan*, 224.
53. Memorial Committee, *Denovan*, 224.
54. Memorial Committee, *Denovan*, 224.

of time between events predicted." "The prophetic picture," claimed Denovan, "delineates only the more prominent hills and heights, leaving us to imagine the intervening plains and hollows." In his view, the apostle Paul's assertion in 1 Thess 4:16 that "the dead in Christ shall *rise first*" and three other passages, including Rev 5:20, which notes that "The *rest of the dead* lived not again till the thousand years were fulfilled" sustain a "secondary meaning" that "the dead in Christ *shall precede* in resurrection all the other dead."[55]

After making the case that the resurrection of the righteous and the wicked are separate events, Denovan turned his attention to the difficulties associated with "the *mode*" of Christ's appearing. He opposed the view held by "some premillennial friends" who argued "that Jesus will first come quietly and without observation, secretly and noiselessly 'like a thief in the night.'"[56] In his assessment, this line of argument "is decidedly fanciful."[57] Instead, Christ will come "with power and great glory." The redeemed "who are caught up in the air . . . to welcome Him" will then "escort Him back to dwell Him here."[58]

Having laid out his basic eschatological position, Denovan presented "scriptural outlines of the millennium" and his assessment of the timing for Christ's return in a section about "The Period of Christ's Second Advent." In his conclusion, he provided a threefold biblical answer to the question of "How can we hasten the coming of the Lord?" First, believers must "*Pray for it*." Second, "*Let us purify ourselves for it*." And finally, "*Work for it*." For "the end shall come not until the gospel has been proclaimed for a witness to all nations."[59] The editor of Denovan's memorial volume, where this paper was published, offered an account of the reactions to Denovan's premillennial dispensationalist views. "This paper caused much comment and criticism," the editor noted, "and aroused an interest in the doctrine of the second coming that is still felt."[60] Clearly, this paper not only broke new ground for Canadian Baptists, but also, it put Denovan on the record as one who held a key tenet of proto-fundamentalism, dispensational premillennialism. Of course, this was not his only proto-fundamentalist doctrinal position. In

---

55. Memorial Committee, *Denovan*, 226.
56. Memorial Committee, *Denovan*, 227. Here Denovan is citing 1 Thess 5:2.
57. Memorial Committee, *Denovan*, 227.
58. Memorial Committee, *Denovan*, 228.
59. Memorial Committee, *Denovan*, 243.
60. Memorial Committee, *Denovan*, 243.

fact, in the Alexander Street Minutes of 30 June 1878, there was a published list of sixteen "Fundamental Doctrines" pasted into the Minute Book.[61] His stance on many of these doctrines would soon become apparent to all.

Denovan's Address to the First Canadian Christian Conference, October 1878

At the "First Canadian Christian Conference" held in the YMCA's Shaftesbury Hall, Toronto on 21–25 October 1878, Denovan delivered a similarly provocative address entitled, "The Believer in Christ and Christ in the Believer." As Sawatsky has noted, this interdenominational evangelical conference was an effort "to duplicate" similar events in the Britain and the United States. Furthermore, its purpose was "to deepen the spiritual life of believers and bring about more fully consecrated service to 'our Lord.'"[62] Denovan's address fit this purpose well. For he took this opportunity to call his listeners to recommit themselves to the fundamentals of their faith.

In the first section of his address Denovan offered his audience an account of the "great fundamental doctrines" of the Christian faith. He began by answering the question of "What *is* living faith?" After examining and rejecting the popular notions that faith is "a moral influence on the mind," "a *feeling* you are saved," or "consists of a strong *mental effort* to believe," he asserted that "true saving faith is simply our resting on the testimony—the

---

61. *ASBC Minutes*, 355–56. Here is my brief summary list of these doctrines: 1. There is one God in three persons. 2. All men are sinners who are under condemnation and destined for misery and death both temporal and eternal. 3. There is only one way of salvation through the death of Christ and regeneration by the Holy Spirit. 4. Jesus was God in the flesh, and he alone justifies us. 5. Only the special work of the Holy Spirit can bring about a saving change in the heart of man. 6. All saved sinners are elect according to the foreknowledge of God. 7. The final perseverance of all true believers is certain. 8. Baptism and the Lord's Supper are the ordinances, and they are the duty of every believer. Baptism precedes the Lord's Supper. 9. Baptism was instituted by Jesus, and it is scripturally administered only when the whole body is immersed in water. 10. The Lord's Supper was instituted by Jesus, and worth receivers are by faith made partakers of this ordinance.11. Believers should devote the first day of the week to religious work and worship. 12. Christ is the end of the law, but Christ's body should keep all the moral law as a rule of life. 13.It is our duty to support those who labour in word and doctrine, relieve those in distress, and do good to all men. 14. It is our duty to watch over our members and not suffer sin upon a brother. 15. It is the duty of all who hear or read the Gospel to repent and believe it. 16. There will be the resurrection and a final judgement after which the wicked will go into everlasting punishment and the righteous into eternal life. Specific Rules of Order for Alexander Street were also included.

62. Sawatsky, "Looking for That Blessed Hope," 144.

record of God concerning His Son."⁶³ In the end, "Our faith rests down into quiet recumbency on the solid veracity of God's Word," said Denovan. To avoid the error of believing that one's faith was the source of personal salvation, he made the relationship between faith and salvation clear: "It is not faith that saves us, but Christ; faith does nothing more than realize, appropriate and enjoy that salvation of Christ; faith, far from being *the cause* of our salvation, is, strictly speaking, the *immediate result* of our knowing on divine authority that He took away our sins by the sacrifice of Himself."⁶⁴

Having established what true faith was, in his second main point Denovan addressed the matter of "*What then is meant by* 'THE BELIEVER'S BEING IN CHRIST?'" His first subpoint examined when and how the union between Christ and the believer took place. Using Eph 1:3–5 as his source, he argued that "the cause of this union" between God and believer "was the choice of God."⁶⁵ Furthermore, this choice was made "*Before the foundation of the world*" and "that is *when* the union between Jesus Christ and believers really began." This did not happen by chance or accident but was in actuality "a grand deliberate purpose predestined in the perfect calm of the by-past eternity."⁶⁶

Having offered his view of salvation and predestination, Denovan argued, in his second subpoint, that "Believers having been thus *chosen in Christ*, are . . . PONTIFICALLY AND REPRESENTATIVELY."⁶⁷ According to Denovan, Christ is the believer's "High Priest," "Mediator," and "Vicar."⁶⁸ And Christ is also every believer's "one sacrificial Substitute" and everything Christ did "He did *vicariously* on their behalf and in their stead."⁶⁹ He noted further that "the entire apostolic epistle to the Hebrews (not to mention many other large portions of holy writ) elaborates these great fundamental doctrines. Suffice it now to state that there was never any saving or sanctifying efficacy in any other priestly offering of mediation."⁷⁰ He also claimed that "down through all dispensations and all ages has Jesus Christ represented his people *pontifically*." Such statements reveal many

63. Memorial Committee, *Denovan*, 245–46.
64. Memorial Committee, *Denovan*, 246–47.
65. Memorial Committee, *Denovan*, 248.
66. Memorial Committee, *Denovan*, 248–49.
67. Memorial Committee, *Denovan*, 251.
68. Memorial Committee, *Denovan*, 251.
69. Memorial Committee, *Denovan*, 251.
70. Memorial Committee, *Denovan*, 252.

proto-fundamentalist hallmarks including the persistent reliance on and appeal to the Bible to support a clear and cogent case for the "fundamental doctrines" that sustained a Calvinist Baptist view of salvation and sanctification.

Denovan moved on in his third subpoint to argue that "*Believers are in Christ* FORENSICALLY, that is, He is their legal surety before God."[71] After laying out support for this teaching from the books of Philemon and Isaiah, he concluded this section of his address with the assurance that believers "were secured *in Him*, and he was Surety for them."[72]

In his fourth subpoint Denovan claimed that "*Believers are in Christ by* Marriage Settlement and Relation." Using Old Testament texts, such as, Ps 45 and New Testament passages including Rom 7:1–5 and Eph 5:22–33, He argued that "throughout the New Testament we have the symbol of marriage introduced once and again for the express purpose of explaining the union of Christ and His church."[73] To illustrate this point, he drew a comparison between the patriarchal understanding and practice of marriage and the biblical view of the relationship between Christ, the bridegroom and his bride, the church. "Now, we all know," declared Denovan,

> that in matrimonial relationship the husband is, legally as well as socially, the head and representative of his wife. If this illustration, so frequently used by the Holy Spirit . . . teach anything at all, it assuredly teaches that Jesus Christ is the full representative of His church in such a sense that she loses her separate individuality and singularity in Him, she becoming one with Him in His life and fortune and name, and He one with her by legally absorbing her personality in His.[74]

He concluded this section of his address with the claim that "All this, I feel bold to assert, exemplifies fairly the relation believers sustain to Christ, and its necessary and legal results."[75] This point revealed his belief that just as Christ was the head of his bride, the church, so in an earthly marriage a husband was the head of his wife. As we shall see below, this highly patriarchal view of male-female relations would become a source of controversy.

---

71. Memorial Committee, *Denovan*, 254.
72. Memorial Committee, *Denovan*, 257.
73. Memorial Committee, *Denovan*, 259.
74. Memorial Committee, *Denovan*, 259–60.
75. Memorial Committee, *Denovan*, 261.

Denovan ended his presentation about believers in Christ with a fifth and final subpoint: "*Believers are* IN CHRIST CORPOREALLY—ORGANICALLY." "I do not mean in the material," said Denovan, "but in the spiritual and mystical sense. He and they compose one spiritual organization called in Scripture 'the body of Christ,' as it is written, 'we are members of his body;' He is the Head and believers are the members in particular of this body."[76] He directed his hearers to 1 Cor 12 and John 17. After he presented a comparison between the union of believers with Christ and the union between God the Father and God the Son "which is mysteriously incorporated into the divine hypostasis," he offered his own dogmatic and certain position: "There is no doubt in my mind that the Holy Spirit of inspiration intends us to believe that Jesus and believers are as closely, as permanently, as indissolubly one as the first and second persons of the Deity."[77]

Having established that believers are one with Christ, Denovan presented four consequences of being "in Him." "Thus Jesus Christ 'of God,' states Denovan, 'is made unto us wisdom and righteousness and sanctification and redemption.'" On the matter of sanctification, he presented the progressive view traditionally held by Baptists: "There is a gradual process of personal sanctification wrought by the Holy Spirit in the actual experience of every believer."[78] He developed each of the other points in detail and then concluded with the following statement: "These things being so, it is evident that the function of faith is not to make our salvation either more complete or more sure, but simply to realize and enjoy this, our blessed condition *in Christ*."[79]

From what Denovan shared with his audience in the first two sections of his address, his views were in alignment with the core doctrines that his fellow proto-fundamentalists held dear. For Denovan, as a Baptist proto-fundamentalist, these beliefs included the supreme authority of the Bible in all matters of faith and practice, a literal method of biblical interpretation, the inspiration and infallibility of the Bible, the hypostatic union within the Godhead, between Christ and his church, and between the human and the divine in Christ's incarnation, the predestined choice by God of his chosen people, salvation through the substitutionary and vicarious sacrifice

76. Memorial Committee, *Denovan*, 261.
77. Memorial Committee, *Denovan*, 262.
78. Memorial Committee, *Denovan*, 267–68.
79. Memorial Committee, *Denovan*, 270.

of Christ, progressive sanctification, and premillennial dispensationalism, which is only briefly mentioned in this treatise.

After his examination of the believer in Christ, Denovan turned his attention to "'CHRIST IN THE BELIEVER.'" Essentially, he covered two main topics in this section: Christ in the individual believer and Christ in the church universal and local. According to Denovan, the text that "epitomizes" the "great doctrine" of Christ in the believer is Phil 1:21: "'*To me to live is Christ.*'"[80] An "instructive illustration of His dwelling in believers" is found in Christ's "parable of the 'true vine' and its branches."[81] Believers in Christ have "His vital virtue" in them, and the "operation of their new Christ-nature" brings forth "much fruit." "This fruit," said Denovan, "is proof positive that Christ dwells in them."[82] Based on this understanding of the biblical teaching concerning the Christian life, he expressed his view of how the truth of Christ's indwelling operates in daily life: "Every word and deed of our Christ-life ought to be Christ-like. True Christianity is nothing more," declared Denovan, "than common, every day life lived out '*In the name of the Lord Jesus.*'"[83] For Denovan, and his fellow proto-fundamentalists, this was the reasonable expectation of every true believer in Christ.

Denovan then shifted his focus to answering the question of "What should the Church of Christ be?" His answer was simple: "One *mighty agent.*" He lamented the "shame and weakness" of the church. In his view the church was "so divided and sub-divided into sectional fragments as to present to the world the spectacle of elements in a state of mutual repulsion."[84] Furthermore, "the modern church presents to the world such variety and diversity that no person can suppose" that the church has come close to achieving the oneness Jesus spoke of in John 17.[85] While "every sincere Christian heart must deplore" the current state of disunity that characterized the universal church, "every such heart must draw comfort and hope" from those occasional "indications of oneness that are visible."[86] For example, he cited the "noble work through the Bible Society." In this

80. Memorial Committee, *Denovan*, 271.
81. Memorial Committee, *Denovan*, 272.
82. Memorial Committee, *Denovan*, 272.
83. Memorial Committee, *Denovan*, 275.
84. Memorial Committee, *Denovan*, 276.
85. Memorial Committee, *Denovan*, 276.
86. Memorial Committee, Denovan, 277.

organization at least the universal church "appears to be one in sentiment, aim, and honest effort."[87] In this "honoured organization, the Presbyterian and the Methodist, the Episcopalian and the Baptist hand out one and the same volume, and they hand it out to every person under heaven as the very best gift they can bestow."[88]

After this critique and celebration of the universal church, Denovan used Rev 14:6 as an "expressive and impressive illustration of what the Christian Church should be and do."[89] He first examined the commission, place, and work of the church. Both the individual Christian and the church are commissioned "to be a witness for God, a messenger of mercy, a minister of grace amongst the lost."[90] The place of the church is "in the midst of heaven."[91] According to Denovan, "the Church ought always to occupy a region above the level of mere worldly life—a region in which she shall be free from earthly obstacles. In the world she should not be *of* it, but live *above* it—living, so to speak, on the wing of holy desire and activity."[92] Finally, the work of the church was "the preaching or *proclamation* of 'the everlasting gospel.'"[93]

Next Denovan examined more closely the "ANGEL-CHURCH'S MINISTRY" of "THE EVERLASTING GOSPEL." As one would expect, he emphasized the church's responsibility to true to the gospel. In his customary strident tone, he stressed the need for everyone to have access to the Bible, and he called out those who held heretical views, abandoned the teachings of the faith once delivered to the saints, and showed open disrespect for all that is sacred:

> I for one feel sure that the circulation of *the entire Bible* is absolutely demanded in these our days, if never before. In these days of unblushing and blatant heresy, when professed ministers of the gospel can subscribe creeds with mental reservation, when scientific atheism and rationalistic scepticism dare to arraign both God and nature at their bar and to assert anything feasible or plausible in tones whose presumption is amazing, when, without either

---

87. Memorial Committee, *Denovan*, 277.
88. Memorial Committee, *Denovan*, 277.
89. Memorial Committee, *Denovan*, 276.
90. Memorial Committee, *Denovan*, 279.
91. Memorial Committee, *Denovan*, 280.
92. Memorial Committee, *Denovan*, 280.
93. Memorial Committee, *Denovan*, 283.

scruple or apology, men can lay the rudest and most familiar grasp on everything sacred and find public and respectable support while they do so.[94]

After his diatribe against those who have strayed from proclaiming the true everlasting gospel, Denovan called his listeners and the church to return to God's Word as the sole basis for truth, to fulfill the church's mission of maintaining orthodoxy, and to turn their backs on the teachings of men:

> In short, the whole world needs to be brought back to, and brought up to, this old Word of God, as the one and unchangeable standard of morals, faith, worship and life; and the great mission of the one true Church . . . is to keep us all to this Word as the everlasting verity, and to tolerate no deviation from it according to the commandments, tradition and theories of men.[95]

Having articulated the reforms that his hearers and the church at large needed to adopt, he concluded his address by turning his attention to "THE AREA OVER WHICH THIS 'ANGEL'S'—THE CHURCH'S COMMISSION EXTENDS: 'EVERY NATION, AND KINDRED, AND TINGUE, AND PEOPLE.'" According to Denovan, "to proclaim . . . 'the wonderful works of God,'—'the everlasting Gospel'" was the "great work" of "the Church of Christ."[96] While "some of our denomination schemes" were characterized by "the impurity and ambiguity and frailty of human organization," that was not so for all evangelistic endeavours.[97] "In this holy crusade of the British and Foreign Bible Society," declared Denovan, "we may fearlessly invest money, work and prayer."[98] After this point, he brought his address to a close.

Without question, Denovan's address to the First Canadian Christian Conference was a comprehensive expression of proto-fundamentalist doctrine and a critique designed to advance an agenda of proto-fundamentalist doctrinal reform. His aim was to call his audience to follow biblical truth, to challenge his hearers (and later readers) to examine their faith for signs of doctrinal error, correct these errors, and return to the truth. Denovan also earnestly contended for the true and everlasting gospel, in what he

---

94. Memorial Committee, *Denovan*, 285–86.
95. Memorial Committee, *Denovan*, 285–87.
96. Memorial Committee, *Denovan*, 294.
97. Memorial Committee, *Denovan*, 295.
98. Memorial Committee, *Denovan*, 295.

perceived, as a time of individual and church compromise with the world and theological drift away from "the faith which was once delivered unto the saints" (Jude 1:3). After one reads this address, there can be no doubt about where he stood. He was zealously committed to preserving and proclaiming fundamental doctrines and opposing all who sought to do otherwise. Denovan's proto-fundamentalist perspective would soon produce a protest, provoke controversy, and bring to the surface deep divisions within the central Canadian Baptist fold.

DENOVAN'S PROTO-FUNDAMENTALIST "PROTEST": THE WILLIAM BROOKMAN CONTROVERSY OF 1880

By 1879, Denovan was convinced that Baptist doctrinal and moral drift had taken Canadian Baptists to a crossroads. Would Baptists stay true to orthodoxy, their polity, and their strict morality or adopt modern theological views, a more relaxed approach to polity, and the ways of the world? As he pondered these questions, he was on the lookout for any action, attitude, or viewpoint that would further threaten or destroy the spiritual and moral well-being of God's people. He was also fearful that central Canadian Baptists were on the precipice of a crisis.

Denovan's reaction to the news that his friend and ally George Richardson, pastor of the First Baptist Church in Port Hope, intended to accept a call to a church in Texas is a case in point. In an affectionate, humorous, and strongly worded letter to Richardson dated 2 October 1879, he shared his insights, thoughts, and feelings about Richardson's plans. From a denominational perspective, Denovan believed that Richardson's impending departure would be a set-back to the Baptist proto-fundamentalist cause and could not be more ill-timed: "You know very well we cannot want you here without suffering. Our present critical condition of denominational transition is itself reason more than strong enough why you should remain."[99] After threatening in jest to legally prohibit Richardson's departure, he pleaded with Richardson to reconsider his decision to leave: "Seriously, if it be possible to reconsider this question please do so in the light of our necessities. But if you must go, may the God of old Abraham go with you forever!"[100] For Denovan the potential loss of a friend and ally like Richardson was personally painful and denominationally harmful. In his

99. Denovan File. "Letter to Brother Richardson, 1879."
100. Denovan File. "Letter to Brother Richardson, 1879."

view, central Canadian Baptists needed pastors like Richardson to remain if the denomination's "critical condition" was going to be navigated successfully and Baptist orthodoxy was to prevail.

Evidently, despite Denovan's best efforts to persuade him otherwise, Richardson decided to accept the call to Texas. At the Baptist Convention, held in St. Catharines that began on 14 October 1879, Richardson was commended for having "laboured successfully with us during the past twenty years, serving during that time with many tokens of the Master's favour."[101] Denovan was left without Richardson's support when, less than a year later, he was confronted with a serious and difficult circumstance: the "recognition" as pastor by Toronto's Yorkville Baptist Church in 1880, of former Anglican minister, William Brookman.

On 3 June 1880, *The Canadian Baptist* published an announcement about an important event the following week at Toronto's Yorkville Baptist Church:

> Pastoral Recognition:
>
> On Thursday the 10th of June next at 8 o'clock p.m. (D.V.) the public recognition of the Rev. Wm. Brookman, M.A., as pastor of the Yorkville Baptist church, will take place. . . The Yorkville church extend an invitation to the churches in the city and neighbourhood to meet with them. It is an occasion of interest, not only to the Yorkville church, but also to the denomination at large, to give a hearty recognition and welcome to Mr. Brookman as a minister of the Baptist church. Mr. Brookman resigned his position as a clergyman in the church of England and all the advantages that his connection with that church gave him, and united himself with the Baptist church, from a thorough conviction of duty.[102]

This announcement was unusual and irregular. Only Toronto churches were invited to attend instead of those throughout the province. Also, this was a "recognition" instead of the customary "ordination" that was normally required when a minister from another denomination chose to join the Baptists.[103]

---

101. *Canadian Baptist*, hereafter *CB*, 23 October 1879, 5.

102. *CB*, 3 June 1880, 5.

103. For a typical ordination service and process see the one related to the Lobo Baptist church for H. C. Speller. *CB*, 10 June 1880, 5, 8.

Nevertheless, the following week on 10 June, the event to welcome Brookman took place. Brookman was examined by a "large" council of eminent Baptist brethren from Toronto and found fit for his ministry at Yorkville. A service of welcome followed Brookman's examination and the council's approval of him. On the surface, all seemed to be well. The day following the event, however, Denovan wrote a letter of protest to William Muir, editor of *The Canadian Baptist*, published a week later, on 17 June 1880, under the heading of "Explanation and Protest." His protest letter reported on his council role and registered his objections to Brookman's heretical doctrinal views and the council's approval of him:

Rev. Wm. Muir;

DEAR BROTHER: By special request last Thursday I took part in the recognition of the Rev. Wm. Brookman as pastor of the Yorkville Baptist church, in a short address to the church. But it is due to the church of Jesus Christ in Toronto, and to myself, as a minister of the Gospel, that my position in this matter be perfectly understood by the community. I opposed the action of the council, because in the examination of Mr. Brookman it appears that he denies

1. The obligation to the Decalogue upon the unbelieving Gentile world and the believer;
2. The moral obligation of the sanctification of the weekly Sabbath;
3. The natural and inherent immortality of man;
4. The eternity of the future conscious punishment of the wicked.

The council, which was a large one, professed to "recognize" Mr. Brookman because

1. His position in regards to these points of orthodoxy was apparently more negative than positive;
2. He was a good man and transparently honest;
3. The Baptist body could not afford to drive him away to another denomination;
4. A number of the council (all *regular* Baptists) indulged his views especially on the 3rd and 4th points.

> From all I have seen and heard of Mr. Brookman I entertain him for both esteem and affection; notwithstanding I must be permitted to protest solemnly in this case.[104]

Denovan's "protest" sparked a serious controversy that had profound consequences for the denomination in central Canada, the Toronto Association, Alexander Street Baptist Church, Yorkville Baptist Church, and Denovan himself.

Over the summer of 1880, *The Canadian Baptist* published responses, both for and against Denovan's letter, the actions of Yorkville, the process, and the decision of the council. The first response to Denovan's protest came from a council member who signed his letter, published in the 24 June edition of *The Canadian Baptist*, as "L." The writer claimed that "the published protest of Mr. D. is much stronger and more extensive than his utterances to the council at the time of deliberation." When the council was in session, Denovan's "statements were confined to the 3rd and 4th points which he names." Furthermore, Denovan's protest at the time "was not very energetic" and if he was so opposed "Why not enter the formal protest then and there!" The writer also accused Denovan of misrepresenting the case. "The reasons given why the council professed to recognize Mr. Brookman," "L." asserted, "are not fairly stated, because of what is omitted." The writer was also angered by Denovan's "assertion" that "The Baptist body could not afford to drive him away to another denomination." In fact, the writer claimed, "that no such reason had any weight with the council." Instead, "The recognition was decided upon from much higher considerations than that and the others Mr. Denovan names."[105]

If "L." hoped to dispel any concern, his letter had the opposite effect of provoking more interest and eliciting strong responses from Denovan and others. Denovan responded with a letter written on 26 June 1880 and published in the 1 July 1880, edition of *The Canadian Baptist*. He first offered an apology for "any false or distorted representation of the council." But he quickly countered the notion that any distortion had occurred by noting that "what I stated in my 'protest' was written down *the morning immediately after the council and* in the hope of making my statement correct." Denovan also responded to "L.'s" claims that his representation of the council's "grounds" for recognition were false and that there were "much higher considerations." At this point, he made his position clear: "I never

---

104. *CB*, 17 June 1880, 4.
105. All of the quotations in this paragraph are taken from *CB*, 24 June 1880, 5.

heard any such 'considerations' *mentioned*. The very highest considerations *I heard* advanced in the council were those I have named." Denovan concluded his letter with a declaration of his own convictions and conclusions on the matter: "After reviewing the pages of memory with some care I must, with all respect due to my fellow councillors, adhere to my original statement."[106]

Another letter to the editor from the same issue of *The Canadian Baptist*, from Archibald P. McDiarmid, pastor of First Baptist Church, Port Hope, Ontario, and eventually in 1899, Principal of Brandon College, expressed what was on his mind and the minds of "many" other Baptists: "Many of your readers were waiting anxiously for this week's issue of your paper for the refutation or confirmation of Bro. Denovan's statement of Rev. W. Brookman's denial of the four doctrines referred to. They have been disappointed." McDiarmid criticized "L." for creating "a great deal of dust" and "obscuring the real point at issue." He also characterized the discussion about "the course pursued by Brother D." as "a side issue." "There is an earnest desire to know the facts in regard to Mr. B's doctrinal views," noted McDiarmid, "so as to put the denomination in a position to endorse or protest against the action of the Council."[107] McDiarmid particularly asked for clarification on the doctrinal points about the immortality of man and the punishment of the wicked.

The council members responded in the same 8 July 1880, issue of *The Canadian Baptist*. John Harvard Castle, chair of the council and pastor of Jarvis Street, offered what he claimed was "a fuller statement of the facts" surrounding Mr. Brookman's recognition. Claiming that he had no "wish to vindicate the Council, or explain its action, or to justify its resolutions," and an earnest desire to "carefully avoid questions which simply gender strife and divisions, and minister nothing to our Christian or denominational power," Castle offered unequivocal support for the recognition of Brookman and listed five reasons that he felt justified it. First, the Yorkville church had "called Brookman as pastor" and "his ministration of the word" at the church "was greatly enjoyed." Second, Brookman "had for many years been a successful minister in the Church of England." Third, Brookman had come to the conviction "of the unscripturalness of infant baptism" and "the immersion of a believer as the only valid baptism." Based on this conviction, "he united with the Tabernacle Baptist Church in Branford." Fourth,

---

106. All of the quotations in this paragraph are taken from *CB*, 1 July 1880, 5.

107. All of the quotations in this paragraph are taken from *CB*, 1 July 1880, 5.

in the course of what Castle claimed was a "searching and protracted examination," Brookman provided the council with "no uncertain evidence of having had a rich experience of the grace of God, and a decided and unequivocal call to preach the Gospel." Finally, and perhaps most importantly for many Baptists, "in the statement of his doctrinal views," Castle claimed, "he [Brookman] gave the most satisfactory evidence of earnest thought and profound study of the Word of God, and was candid and outspoken in all his utterances." Castle acknowledged Denovan's doctrinal concerns, but he believed that Brookman's views were beyond satisfactory: "With the exception of the points to which attention has been called in the protest of Mr. Denovan, his [Brookman's] views of divine truth were not only satisfactory to the entire Council, but in the highest degree edifying."[108]

Upon offering the rationale for Brookman's recognition, Castle turned his attention to the four doctrinal points raised in Denovan's protest. After reprinting Denovan's points, Castle responded with sarcastic humour: "Well, this is indeed a ghastly skeleton!" Then Castle did his best to dampen the severity of Denovan's claims by raising doubt about the validity of such claims: "But it is only a skeleton of a very small portion of Mr. Brookman's views. And this skeleton might have a very different appearance when filled out by Mr. Brookman himself." Castle noted that he asked Brookman to provide "a condensed statement of his views as expressed to the Council." Castle provided Brookman's views on each of Denovan's four points with a commentary and conclusions after points one, two, and four. On the matter of "the obligation of the Decalogue upon the unbelieving Gentile world and the believer," Brookman used relevant biblical passages to support four arguments. First of all, "the Gentiles were never under the law of Israel—Rom. ii. 14." Second, the law "recognizes no mercy" and "only condemns the short-comer—Heb. X. 28., Gal. iii. 10." Third, the "ministration" of the law "is called one of death—2 Cor. iii, 6,7." Finally, "now the Christian is under law to Christ, and it constrained by a higher power, even love, to all holy obedience to God's will, as Paul clearly shows—2 Cor. v. 14.15., Rom. vii. 4."[109] Castle's response was a shot aimed squarely at Denovan and any other Brookman critics. "Now, Mr. Editor, would you reject a man from the Baptist ministry for such a heresy as this![?]" For Castle and others on the council who shared his view of Brookman, the obvious answer to this rhetorical question was decidedly "No!"

---

108. All of the quotations in this paragraph are taken from *CB*, 8 July 1880, 4.

109. All of the quotations in this paragraph are taken from *CB*, 8 July 1880, 4.

On Denovan's second point about "the moral obligation of the sanctification of the Sabbath," Brookman argued "That the Sabbath is distinct from the Lord's Day, which is the *first* day of the week . . . and we have no right to confound the two days and thus mingle law and gospel." "In my estimation," Brookman exclaimed, "the Christian is bound by all the powerful ties of love and gratitude to honour the Lord's Day . . . and he cannot honour it too highly in sacred joy and holiness."[110]

Castle again used the similarity of Brookman's view to other Baptist pastors and sarcasm to make Denovan's heresy charge on this point look ridiculous. "There are many Baptist ministers," Castle retorted, "who are equally careful with Mr. Brookman to designate the day of rest and worship, the Lord's Day, and not the Sabbath. But perhaps their heresy should depose them from the sacred office."[111] Clearly, Castle believed that Denovan's charge of heresy was unfounded for the first two doctrinal points. But points three and four were an entirely different matter.

On the subject of "the natural and inherent immortality of man" Brookman flatly denied the existence of such immortality: "I cannot find in the word of God," he declared, "that man is possessed of an immortal life or soul." Furthermore, the claim that "every man . . . by nature possesses eternal life" was "utterly contrary to the declarations of Holy Writ which maintains that life, eternal life is only possessed by the believer in Christ, as witnessed by Gen. 3:22–24, Jno. 6:47, 1 Jno. 5:12, *et al*." After this statement, which was clearly—from a Regular Baptist perspective—doctrinally unorthodox, Castle made no comment. Instead, he moved on to the fourth and last point about "the eternity of future conscious punishment." On this subject Brookman put forward an annihilationist view of future punishment. Using Rev 19 and 20 as the basis for his views, Brookman argued that "the word of God, *while revealing awful wrath and punishment to come*, does not warrant me in maintaining or averring that the second death is everlasting life in misery and sin, so much as eventual everlasting destraction [sic]."[112]

In his final comments and assessment, Castle made the case for recognizing Brookman clear. Brookman's views, "in regard to the duration of future punishment," argued Castle, "met no acceptance in the Council" and "there was a general expression of regret" that Brookman held such views

---

110. *CB*, 8 July 1880, 4–5.
111. *CB*, 8 July 1880, 5.
112. *CB*, 8 July 1880, 5. "Destraction" should read as "destruction."

"and the regret was deep." However, Castle contended that he and the council were convinced that Brookman's "divergence from the orthodox faith on this single point (for points 3 and 4 involve each other)" was insufficient grounds to "disqualify him" from preaching "salvation." Furthermore, Brookman was not "a materialist" nor was he "in the least rationalistic." In Castle's view the rationale for recognizing Brookman, far outweighed Denovan's after-the-fact objections to Brookman's recognition. Castle also maintained that had other Baptists heard Brookman, the outcome would have been the same. "I am persuaded," Castle stated, "that if the Yorkville Council had consisted of all the Baptists in Canada, and they had listened to his [Brookman's] general views, and felt his truth-loving spirit, the result would have been the same. He would have been most cordially recognized as a Baptist minister."[113]

To sustain and cement a final capstone on his position that council's actions were entirely justified, Castle implied that Denovan's protest was at best contradictory and at worst hypocritical. To prove his point Castle used Denovan's public comments, in which he expressed words of welcome and support for Brookman, as evidence that Denovan's claims were indefensible: "Certainly no very serious mistake has been made," Castle concluded,

> or Mr. Denovan himself would not have said to the church at the public services, . . . though he and Mr. Brookman did not see eye to eye in every particular point, yet, he felt satisfied that the new pastor . . . is a man of unfeigned and unquestioned piety, an excellent Biblical scholar,—that he has a profound love for God's word and God's work and God's people. When he said that he meant all he did say. He would not say that of every one of our Baptist ministers,—but he said that about Mr. Brookman.[114]

At this point, it was left to the Baptist community to express its verdict on the Brookman affair.

Published alongside Castle's defense was another letter of defense written by Samuel A. Dyke, then pastor of College Street Baptist Church in Toronto, to the editor of *The Canadian Baptist* dated 3 July 1880. The letter was signed by Dyke and eight delegates of the Yorkville Council who voted with the majority for Brookman's recognition. This letter proposed "to narrate what seemed to the majority of the Council to be the facts of the case," and it provided an overview of the council's proceedings and

113. All of the quotations in this paragraph are taken from *CB*, 8 July 1880, 5.
114. *CB*, 8 July 1880, 5.

findings. Brookman's "examination" before the council took almost three hours. Brookman's "Christian experience and call to the ministry," were "eminently satisfactory." His doctrinal views were "up to a certain point equally so." However, when Brookman was asked to present his views on "the Sabbath, the immortality of the soul and the punishment of the wicked" his non-Baptist views became apparent. In fact, according to Dyke, "it was evident that there was a divergence from our standards as expressed in our articles of faith."[115] As Castle had done, Dyke offered a summary of Brookman's views. Unlike Castle's account, on some points the traditional Baptist view of these doctrines was also presented in Dyke's letter.

The most striking content in this letter, however, was its unvarnished condemnation of Denovan's actions and behaviour. Dyke argued that

> if Bro. Denovan did, indeed, believe while in the council, . . . that Mr. Brookman held the heresies he now charges him with . . . his conduct was inexcusable, for he did not vote against his recognition, nor enter his protest, nor say that he was ineligible for the pastorate of a Baptist church. On the contrary, he sanctioned the recognition by his presence and his words.[116]

Like Castle, Dyke then quoted Denovan's remarks about Brookman. Dyke's letter concluded with another charge against Denovan. According to Dyke, he had publicly "betrayed our trust" and if Denovan "after sober second thought" had arrived at "the conclusion we had made a mistake he ought to have said so without charging his brethren with betraying their trust." The eight other signatories to the letter declared, "we very cheerfully and fully endorse the above."[117] This letter and Castle's account set off another round in the controversy.

Of course, in the 15 July 1880, issue of *The Canadian Baptist*, Denovan responded to his critics. Instead of being chastened, he was unmoved. In his view, his position was sustained not countered by the words of Castle and Dyke. In his opening statement he employed sarcastic humour in an attempt to deflect criticism and claim victory:

> Under the Broad shadow of our benevolent Castle and protected by the outstretched aegis of our heroic Dyke, supported by "eight good men and true," Mr. Brookman has sallied forth to the fray;— and now my statements are incontrovertible, the four corners of

115. CB, 8 July 1880, 5.
116. CB, 8 July 1880, 5.
117. CB, 8 July 1880, 5.

my original position are fortified, and the "ghastly skeleton" still stands unburied grinning at the Council.[118]

Interestingly, Denovan used primarily Presbyterian examples and sources to show that each of Brookman's four aberrant doctrinal views were judged as heretical. In his assessment of Castle and Dyke's letters, he argued that they were essentially "a circumstantial and expository apology for Mr. Bookman's doctrinal peculiarities."[119] He expressed his deep sorrow and disappointment over the positions taken by Castle and Dyke. And he closed his letter with a reiteration of his position. "My opinion is now," stated Denovan, "just what it was at the outset."[120] To make his stance absolutely clear he summarized his conclusions about Brookman on the four doctrinal points at issue: "Mr. Brookman's doctrines are not *what is commonly called evangelical or orthodox*—are not *the historical doctrines of the Baptist denominations*: that is all."[121] This statement may have settled the matter in Denovan's mind, but the controversy and its consequences were far from over.

Disturbance and Division

At this point, in mid-July 1880, the fissures and fractures caused by the Brookman controversy became apparent. Opposing viewpoints were quickly hardening into opposing factions. Individual Baptists, both laypeople and clergy, and Baptist Associations weighed in with letters of support for one side or the other and raised concerns about Regular Baptist polity, process, and practice.

Not everyone immediately took sides, however. Alarmed by the contents of Denovan's protest, the East Ontario Association passed a resolution that called for an explanation that would alleviate their anxiety: "*Resolved That we respectfully request the brethren who composed that council [at Yorkville] to give an explanation of their action, with a view to the removal of our fears.*"[122]

Dyke was outraged. And one did not have to look far to read Dyke's feelings and thoughts about the East Ontario Association's resolution. In

118. *CB*, 15 July 1880, 4.
119. *CB*, 15 July 1880, 4.
120. *CB*, 15 July 1880, 4.
121. *CB*, 15 July 1880, 4.
122. *CB*, 8 July 1880, 4.

his letter that appeared in *The Canadian Baptist* defending the action of the council, Dyke chastised the East Ontario Association for passing such a resolution:

> Time alone will tell whether they [the Yorkville Council] were right or wrong, and whether it is right for brethren at a distance [the East Ontario Association] to hastily pass censorious judgement before they have the other side, and upon men who have done more that most others to extend Baptist principles in this city and elsewhere. I enter my indignant protest against such conduct.[123]

Dyke's "protest" was not received well by Baptists who longed for definitive answers to nagging questions about Brookman's views and the Yorkville Council's process, practices, and decision.

For example, Daniel Arthur McGregor, then serving as pastor of small Baptist churches in Brooklin and Whitby, Ontario, a future principal of Toronto Baptist College and one who would become an ally of Denovan, responded immediately to Dyke's attack on the East Ontario Association's action. Essentially, McGregor supported the East Ontario Association's call for further explanation and Denovan's right to protest. He also charged Dyke with misdemeanors of his own. In a letter to the editor of *The Canadian Baptist*, McGregor argued that since "the council is unanimous in its admission that there were serious divergences from orthodox faith." No one, including Dyke, should "censure the anxiety thereby awakened among those who are set for the defence of the gospel." Furthermore, it was "the duty of Christians to contend earnestly for the faith." Given the "present serious disagreement" over the Yorkville Council's "decision," McGregor called "for the truth's sake to see this this matter thoroughly investigated."[124]

Having expressed his overall perspective, McGregor turned his sights on Dyke's letter and his "protest" against the resolution of the East Ontario Association. McGregor began by noting that "an anxious discussion did take place at that gathering on this subject [the decision of the council]." He also noted that Mr. Dyke "was present" at the meeting, and when he was asked "to offer information, that might obviate the necessity of discussion, he refused to do so." Third, the resolution was subsequently passed "respectfully requesting explanation." After setting in place this context, McGregor set about dismantling Dyke's protest and position. Through a series of stated and implied questions, McGregor exposed the errors,

123. *CB*, 8 July 1880, 5.
124. All of the quotations in this paragraph are taken from *CB*, 15 July 1880, 5.

contradictions, and hypocrisy in Dyke's "protest." As one who despised "'proscription' even against false doctrines" did Mr. Dyke now "mean to deny liberty of speech to an Association of Baptist churches in a matter of denominational concern." In the light of protest by council members and Dyke's own admission that "Time alone will tell" if the council was "right or wrong," did he now "expect us to accept without inquiry, the decision of the Council as infallible." Furthermore, McGregor questioned the intent and legitimacy of Dyke's protest against "expressed anxiety for the integrity of the faith" because of "his strong faith in our principles." "Does history prove that principles of truth need not to be defended?" McGregor asked.[125] The implied answer to all these questions was "Surely not!"

McGregor also claimed that the resolution of the East Ontario Association was reasonable and unworthy of Dyke's chastisement. The Association's "request," McGregor noted, was presented "respectfully" and was entirely sensible. In fact, McGregor claimed, it was Dyke's "course" that was "more liable to the censure he pronounces." For McGregor, Dyke's singular "indignant protest" against a united Association's "respectful request" to a "divided Council" was at best contradictory, and at worst hypocritical. After a lengthy analysis of Dyke's and Castle's views, McGregor put forward his final conclusions:

> If then, the position taken by Mr. Dyke is wrong, no amount of signatures, however worthy, can make it right. And furthermore, a protest against expressed anxiety for the integrity of the faith can have but little weight with those who believe their Bibles and therefore know that they "should contend earnestly for the faith which was once delivered to the saints."[126]

McGregor's proto-fundamentalist perspective and his support for the East Ontario Association, and by implication Denovan, comes through loud and clear in his rebuttal of Dyke. Other Baptists would be even more direct and dogmatic than McGregor in their unequivocal censure of the Yorkville Council.

As one reads the pages of *The Canadian Baptist*, it is evident that some Baptists believed strongly that the time had come to register unequivocal and emphatic denunciation of the council's sanctioning of Brookman's views and its complete disregard for Regular Baptist polity and process. The Huron Association, for example, was the first body to pass a resolution that

125. All of the quotations in this paragraph are taken from *CB*, 15 July 1880, 5.
126. *CB*, 15 July 1880, 5.

openly and expressly opposed the actions of the council and Brookman's recognition. After a lengthy discussion about a resolution concerning the "Yorkville recognition" took place and the letters by Castle and Dyke "were read," the Huron Association passed the following resolution:

> *Resolved*—That we, as an Association, put upon the record (1) the expression of our intense sorrow at, and solemn protest against the action of said Council in recognizing a man with such views as a Regular Baptist minister; (2) Our kind but emphatic protest against recognizing or installing any person as a Regular Baptist minister and pastor who has never been ordained among us.[127]

This resolution captured and expressed opposition to Brookman's views and the process and practices that were used to recognize him.

Perhaps the Huron Association was prompted on the second point about ordination by the letter from "An Old Baptist" that was published in *The Canadian Baptist* on 8 July 1880. Without mentioning the Brookman case specifically, this letter raised questions about what the "Canadian Baptist" practice of ordination ought to be. The writer was particularly concerned about a possible trend away from the traditional Regular Baptist practice of "hands being laid on the brother" who was undergoing ordination. The writer noted that "in England the custom of laying on hands is almost abolished" and he questioned whether Canadian Baptists now considered an ordination without the laying on of hands to be "valid." The editor of *The Canadian Baptist* took the unusual step of responding immediately to this letter. While the editor was not prepared to go as far as declaring that an ordination with the laying on of hands was "invalid," he was of the view that it was "decidedly irregular." This provoked a lively discussion and debate about the "Regular Baptist" practice and process of ordination and whether proper practice was followed in the Brookman case. Other letters about ordination were sent to *The Canadian Baptist*.[128] Clearly, the Huron Association sided with those who opposed the "recognition" of Brookman.

---

127. *CB*, 15 July 1880, 4.

128. All of the quotations in this paragraph are taken from *CB*, 8 July 1880, 4. The "Old Baptist" was not alone in raising concerns about proper polity and process. See, for example, the letters from W. W. Willis, *CB*, 8 July 1880, 1, and A. Grant, *CB*, 15 July 1880, 5. The usual Regular Baptist practice was ordination by a council followed by a service of recognition held at the church that the newly ordained pastor was to serve.

Serious Consequences

Meanwhile, the controversy raged on, and among the many consequences of the Brookman affair were division and schism in some of Toronto's Baptist churches. In fact, Denovan faced discord within his own congregation at Alexander Street. For accountant and church member Frederick William Wellinger, for example, the Brookman controversy was the breaking-point. On 27 January 1881, he wrote a letter and sent it to the church Clerk: "Having for a very long time past lost all sympathy with the theology and practice of the Pastor of your church, I have to ask, with most sincere regret, that my name be dropped from the Church Roll."[129] Here was one casualty, but more were still to come. Thomas Lailey, a prominent businessman, long-time church member and former deacon at Alexander Street, and his family sided with Brookman and opposed Denovan. The division became so pronounced that that on 28 December 1881, all the members of the Lailey family, except Thomas Lailey, "were granted letters of dismission to the Yorkville church" and their names "were removed from the Membership Roll for wilful and persistent neglect of duty and privilege."[130] Alexander Street paid a heavy toll for Denovan's stand.

Similarly, in 1881, a report of the Brookman controversy, by the Scots Baptist James Lesslie, then living in the village of Eglinton, Ontario and formerly a prominent businessman and reformer in Toronto, was published in *The Rainbow*, a British religious publication. Lesslie noted that "through the intolerance of the Baptist denomination" the Brookman case "has given rise to thought and discussion to a remarkable extent." Lesslie was extraordinarily sympathetic to Brookman and critical of his fellow Baptists in their handling of the affair. At the time of writing his report, Lesslie was still waiting to hear from Brookman what his future path would be. Evidently, because he had "been in his [Brookman's] company a good deal of late" Lesslie had an inclination that Brookman was contemplating a new course of action.[131] Lesslie's suspicions were soon confirmed. In June of 1881, under the leadership of William Brookman "thirty members" from Yorkville "seceded" and "formed a new congregation, unattached to any

---

129. Alexander Street/Immanuel Records. "Letter from F.W. Wellinger to Alexander Street Baptist Church, 1881."

130. *ASBC Minutes*, 451. The denial of a letter of dismission for Thomas Lailey was a punishment intended to shun and shame him. Such action would also make it difficult for Lailey to join another Baptist Church.

131. Lesslie, "Notes" *The Rainbow*, Volume XVIII, 1881, 360–61.

sect."¹³² After 1882, Brookman would be associated with the first Jehovah's Witness group in Toronto.¹³³ Clearly, the Yorkville church also paid a heavy price for its support of Brookman.

To make matters worse, Baptist opponents used the Brookman controversy to discredit and disparage Baptist belief and practice. In his 1881 treatise against baptism by immersion, for example, the Presbyterian William Alexander McKay, then the pastor of Chalmer's Presbyterian Church in Woodstock, Ontario, cited the Brookman case and Denovan's protest as evidence of Baptist over-commitment to baptism by immersion and under-commitment to orthodoxy. "It would seem from late occurrences in this Province," McKay exclaimed, "that a man may hold very loose views indeed on vital Scripture truth and Christian morals, but if he takes to the water, he will be welcomed not merely as a member but as a pastor, within the Baptist fold." McKay also noted, "Mr. Brookman is sound on the 'dipping' question and that is enough to make him a good Baptist, even if he does deny the punishment of the wicked, and the immortality of the natural man, and repudiate the Sabbath and the law of God." As proof to sustain his claims, McKay cited and republished Denovan's protest letter in a long footnote.¹³⁴

At this point, the central Canadian Baptist community was reeling from the effects of the Brookman controversy. Two churches had suffered the pain of division and loss. Associations, leaders, and the laity were exercised, strained, and divided by the endless squabbling over Denovan's protest, the council's decision and responses, Brookman's views, the process and practice of ordination, and the legitimacy of Bookman's "recognition." Baptists in Ontario were also the subject of attack and ridicule by other Protestants, like McKay, who used the Brookman affair to discredit Baptist beliefs and tarnish the Baptist reputation. And if this was not enough, Baptist unity in Ontario was in tatters even as ongoing discussions about "Baptist Union" continued. Denovan responded by launching a nineteen-year long crusade to right and regularize the Baptist denomination in central Canada.

---

132. *History of Toronto and the County of York*, 1885, 318.
133. Sawatsky, "Looking for That Blessed Hope," 159.
134. All of the quotations in this paragraph are taken from McKay, *Immersion*, 14.

DENOVAN'S PROTO-FUNDAMENTALIST CRUSADE, 1880–1899

While the Brookman controversy was still fresh in the minds of central Canadian Baptists, Denovan initiated a proto-fundamentalist crusade against heresy and irregular Baptist practice. He fought this fight on many fronts.

In the fall of 1880, Denovan expressed his opposition to Baptist union on any terms and decried the tendency among some Baptists to redefine, ignore, or abandon long-held theological and polity positions. For example, in a 11 November 1880, *Canadian Baptist* article entitled, "Independency and Soul Liberty, What Are They?", he offered his scathing critique of Baptists who were abandoning traditional Regular Baptist orthodoxy and orthopraxy and adopting instead divergent beliefs and practices. Cognizant of the recent Brookman controversy and the current discussions about union, he used examples of doctrinal divergence from that controversy, Protestant denominational differences in belief and practice related to the ordinances of baptism and the Lord's Supper, and thoughts shared about independency and soul liberty at the recent Assembly on Baptist Union, to make the case that "no ecclesiastical union is possible except on the basis of harmony in doctrine." To prove that doctrinal drift among Baptists was already well underway, Denovan cited "Dr. [George] Broadman's book, 'The Creative Week,' where... he tells us for example that the first three chapters of Genesis are a 'divine parable.'" He then expressed his outrage: "This is Baptist theology corrected by modern geological research!" He went further to suggest that such unorthodoxy was widely accepted in Baptist circles under the guise of independency and soul liberty:

> All this sort of thing [Broadman's claims] I presume to pass unchallenged as Baptist orthodoxy, and no body of men or angels has any right to express authoritatively upon it—in the sacred name of "Independency" and "soul-liberty." No! Is not this the direction in which Baptists are drifting? Is this method of handling God's word "soul-liberty?"

Of course, Denovan hoped that the exposure to these views would motivate his fellow Baptists to join his crusade against unorthodoxy, but he feared that Canadian Baptists were, in fact, adopting such views: "What has our recent Ministerial Institute divulged? I think we are drifting in the direction so plainly indicated by the 'Creative Week,'" declared Denovan. "Of all the churches," he noted, "the Baptist church was the most carefully guarded in doctrinal fundamentals and in a membership avowedly committed to these fundamentals . . . it seems to me evident we have arrived at a stage in the history of Canadian Baptists when it both fair and necessary to ask the question, 'What is a Baptist Church?'"[135]

Denovan's question had already been addressed directly in a paper delivered by his proto-fundamentalist ally, Daniel Arthur McGregor, at the Toronto Ministerial Institute's meeting held at Jarvis Street Baptist Church on 23 October 1880. McGregor's paper entitled, "What Constitutes a Regular Baptist Church?" was printed in *The Canadian Baptist* directly after Denovan's article, and it had stimulated a "lively discussion" at the meeting.[136] Essentially, McGregor argued that there were five essential characteristics that together constituted a Regular Baptist church. First of all, there was "*the essential character of its membership.*"[137] A Regular Baptist church consisted of "regenerate persons" who had "submitted themselves to Christian baptism [by immersion], upon a profession of faith."[138] These were "indispensable prerequisites to church membership."[139] But for a church to exist such "believers" had to be "united in local organization." Second, there was "*the doctrinal basis of its unity.*" McGregor argued that "a definite form of doctrinal belief is requisite to Regular Baptist Church existence" and he further argued "that in Regular Baptist Churches doctrinal belief is regarded as an indispensable basis for church unity."[140] McGregor then covered the core doctrines of the Baptist faith. Third, there was "*the nature and number of its permanent offices.*" There were two offices, "the pastoral and the diaconal." And the church had "the power to elect persons to, or depose them from, these official positions, but it has no power to change the offices themselves."[141] Fourth, there was "*its form of government, which is that of congregational independency.*"[142] "Free from State aid and State legislation, . . . Individual churches are the highest executives of Christ on earth,"

---

135. All of the quotations in this paragraph are taken from *CB*, 11 November 1880, 1.

136. *CB*, 11 November 1880, 2.

137. The content cited in this paragraph is from the reprint of McGregor's paper found in the Alumni Association, *Memoir of McGregor*, 153.

138. Alumni Association, *Memoir of McGregor*, 155.

139. Alumni Association, *Memoir of McGregor*, 156.

140. Alumni Association, *Memoir of McGregor*, 157.

141. Alumni Association, *Memoir of McGregor*, 163.

142. Alumni Association, *Memoir of McGregor*, 164.

McGregor argued.[143] Finally, there was the "essential and distinctive principle" of "*absolute non-interference with divine institutions.*"[144] By this McGregor meant no interference with "the laws which Christ has instituted for the government of His Kingdom." "Christ is the sole legislator," McGregor argued, and "churches are called upon not to enact laws for self-government, but simply to observe all things whatsoever He has commanded."[145] In practice, this meant "that regeneration . . . precedes baptism, and baptism, . . . precedes church-fellowship."[146] Not only was McGregor's paper published in *The Canadian Baptist*, but also it was disseminated and discussed at denominational and church meetings throughout central Canada.

It should be noted that there is a high probability that Denovan's militant proto-fundamentalist crusade was supported by more than McGregor. The other papers presented at the Ministerial Institute on 23 October 1880, provide preliminary evidence that Denovan's crusade was well underway and perhaps gaining some traction before he published his article on independency and soul-liberty. Following McGregor's paper, Reverend J. P. McEwen offered a paper entitled, "What Constitutes a Regular Baptist Pastor?" Reverend William Stewart then presented his paper entitled, "Does Congregational Government involve Independency?" Taken together the papers by McGregor, McEwen, and Stewart, all Scots Baptists, addressed issues that were central in Denovan's crusade to regularize the denomination. This tantalizing but superficial evidence begs for a much deeper investigation into which other Baptists held militant proto-fundamentalist views and supported Denovan's crusade.

Of course, Denovan's multi-faceted crusade would continue. He addressed numerous doctrinal and socio-cultural issues that were of interest and importance to his fellow Baptists. On more than one occasion his crusade against heresy, worldliness, and moral laxity and his calls for the restoration of doctrinal orthodoxy and moral reform provoked a firestorm of controversy. For example, in 1889, Denovan attacked fellow Toronto pastor, Ira Smith of Beverly Street Baptist Church, for "taking a new departure, *a la* modern Wesleyanism in the form of a *Married Man's Social* and a Sunday *Flower Festival.*" For Denovan, Smith's support of such activities proved conclusively that "the baptized church of Jesus Christ" could not

---

143. Alumni Association, *Memoir of McGregor*, 164.
144. Alumni Association, *Memoir of McGregor*, 165.
145. Alumni Association, *Memoir of McGregor*, 165.
146. Alumni Association, *Memoir of McGregor*, 167.

"be content with apostolic truth and simplicity." Furthermore, Smith's lack of propriety was symptomatic of growing moral compromise. Pastors like Smith were "straining their wits to popularize their ministry." Their methods including "cookstove—ice cream—flower pot apostacies" were "in full blast." Denovan asked, "Can it be any great wonder that a gentleman of Mr. Smith's experience and aspirations should be tempted to try the attractive power of something extra scriptural?"[147] To Denovan the answer was obvious. Baptists like Smith were on the road to "apostasy" through the acceptance and use of such "vicious innovations." His charges brought a stern response from Ira Smith.[148] And Denovan responded in kind.[149] This conflict was indicative of Denovan's crusade.

Another example was Denovan's tirade against "Woman's rights." The 15 and 22 June 1893, issues of *The Canadian Baptist* carried a two-part article by Denovan about "Woman's Sphere and Work." In the first part, he declared that "The place and relation of woman" was "fixed immutably." He argued, on the basis of Gen 2:18-25 that, "God and nature do not lie. WOMAN IS THE COMPLIMENT AND HELPMEET OF MAN." Consequently, a woman must "submit to her husband's judgement and heartily work in co-operation with him." Moreover, Denovan used 1 Tim 5:14 and Titus 2:4-5 to demonstrate that a woman's "sphere" was the home and her "power" was found in "motherhood." In his view, Scripture supported no claim of "'equality'" between men and women. A woman must know her place and stay in it. If women entered "business," for example, their actions would "deprive young men of their place and living" and result in "the murder of matrimonial hope" and "the murder of Chivalry."[150] In the second part, Denovan expanded his condemnation of "economic competition between the sexes for a living" and those women who associated "ordinary domestic work" with "social degradation." Frustrated by women who felt mistreated or unappreciated and men who took a woman's work and contributions for granted, he took both women and men to task: "Why should wife or daughter deprecate or deplore the strife and condition in which honest domestic work puts them? Every person possessed of a modicum of

---

147. The quotations here are taken from *CB*, 18 July 1889, 4.

148. For Smith's response see, *CB*, 25 July 1889, 4.

149. For Denovan's rejoinder see, *CB*, 1 August 1889, 4.

150. The quotations used here from the first part of Denovan's tirade are found in *CB*, 15 June 1893, 1. For a brief discussion of gender and "separate spheres" see Wilson, "Caring for Their Community," 222–24.

brains understands and appreciates the situation, and honours the woman properly attired for the work divine providence has brought to her hand."[151]

Unsurprisingly, Denovan's views and vitriolic expressions stimulated another controversy. Alexander Campbell from St. Catharines, Ontario, for example, was taken aback by Denovan's views. Campbell's letter in response to Denovan appeared in the 29 June 1893, issue of *The Canadian Baptist*. He argued that instead of using Genesis to argue that "because woman was made *from* man, she is therefore inferior," it was not "any less logical to affirm that because she was taken from man's side to be his companion, she must be his equal." Campbell questioned Denovan's logic, and by inference he suggested that it was ludicrous for Denovan to "allow a woman, as inferior, to mould his [a man's] character, influences his opinions, etc." Furthermore, Campbell found Denovan's denial of "equality" and women's suffrage, illogical and unjust. "Why not allow her the privilege of voting . . . ?" After all, Campbell argued, "Over five-ninths of the Christians of to-day are deprived of the right . . . not because they are incapable, but because they happen to be women instead of men. Is not this an injustice? Is it not detrimental to the furtherance of Christ's Cause?" For Campbell, women's suffrage would benefit "mankind as a whole," and Donovan's arguments were "weak" and unjust.[152] The exchange between Denovan and Campbell over a woman's place and rights added another contentious doctrinal and socio-cultural issue to the long list of controversial issues that characterized Denovan's ongoing crusade.

As one who saw himself as a combatant for Christ, Denovan and his militant proto-fundamentalist allies used the Baptist pulpit and the press to wage an ongoing crusade from 1880–1899 against all forms of Baptist "apostacy" and laxity. His overarching aim was to bring about doctrinal and moral reform within his central Canadian Baptist community. Of course, Denovan challenged his fellow Baptists on many other topics beyond the few examples presented here.[153] His warrior stance, vitriolic and violent language, unrelenting attacks, unwavering commitment to absolute truth and his conviction that he possessed a superior knowledge of such truth,

---

151. The quotations used here from the second part of Denovan's tirade are found in *CB*, 22 June 1893, 1.

152. For the quotations from Campbell's letter see *CB*, 29 June 1893, 1.

153. The list of other topics is extensive. Only a couple of examples are provided here. See, for example, Denovan's condemnation of musical innovations in "Churchianity versus Genuine Christianity," *CB*, 12 October 1899, 4. For Denovan's response to science and evolutionary theory see, "Understanding as Grounded on Faith," *McMaster Monthly*, 1893–94, 299–309.

both spiritually and morally, represented a model of militant fundamentalism that Baptists of the succeeding generation would follow.

What was Joshua Denovan's legacy within the central Canadian Baptist community? Certainly he was among the first to adopt and propagate a militant proto-fundamentalist identity and prototype that other Baptists, like T. T. Shields, would later emulate. Whether Shields knew of Denovan or not is a matter that requires further investigation. Nevertheless, the parallels between the two men are striking. Both Denovan and Shields were of British origin and heavily influenced by religious trends and developments in Britain. Both were effective preachers. Both were influenced by Spurgeon, though the extent of that influence in Denovan's case is unknown and requires more exploration. They shared a commitment to the fundamental doctrinal tenets held by Calvinist Regular Baptists. They were also obsessed with upholding and protecting Baptist orthodoxy and orthopraxy. And both used pulpit and press to crusade against heresy, irregular polity, and worldliness.

CONCLUSION

Essentially, this chapter has argued that Joshua Denovan was a prototypical militant fundamentalist. Through his devotion to the verbal and plenary inspiration of the Bible, the Bible as the source of all truth in matters of faith and practice, and his literal biblical hermeneutic, he established the biblicism that would characterize militant fundamentalism in the early-twentieth century. Similarly, his positions on strict morality and his censure of worldliness in all its forms was a model that future militant Baptist fundamentalists would follow. His distrust of those who compromised Baptist polity in any way was also a hallmark that was adopted by others. His bombastic rhetoric, relentless criticism, and vitriolic attacks on those Baptists who opposed his militant proto-fundamentalist views and agenda were also the tactics and style that later militant fundamentalist Baptists would employ.

At best, this chapter has offered some insight on Joshua Denovan's militant Baptist proto-fundamentalism. But many questions remain unexplored and unanswered, and many topics require further investigation and analysis. Of course, a fuller and more textured exploration of Denovan's crusade needs to be undertaken. British connections and influences also require more extensive investigation. And other questions also need to be addressed: Were there other militant Baptist proto-fundamentalists in central Canada beyond Denovan and McGregor? If so, who were these Baptists? Did these militants support Denovan's crusade? And did these Baptists form informal or formal alliances to advance militant proto-fundamentalist reform agendas? Furthermore, what was the nature of the relationship between militants like Denovan and moderate proto-fundamentalists like Edward John Stobo and Elmore Harris? To fully understand the early expressions of fundamentalism in central Canada, much more study is needed. One hopes that this chapter is only the first study of many that are still to come.

BIBLIOGRAPHY

Primary Sources

Archival Sources

Alexander Street Baptist Church, Minutes 1866–1884. Canadian Baptist Archives, Hamilton, Ontario.
Alexander Street/Immanuel Baptist Church Records, 1866–1904. Box 1. "Letter from F.W. Wellinger, 27 January 1881. Canadian Baptist Archives, Hamilton, Ontario.
Joshua Denovan Files. "Letter from Brother Richardson." 2 October 1879. Canadian Baptist Archives, Hamilton, Ontario.

Memorial Volumes

Toronto Baptist College Alumni Association. *Memoir of Daniel Arthur McGregor, Late Principal of Toronto Baptist College.* Toronto: Dudley and Burns, 1891.
Memorial Committee. *Joshua Denovan.* Toronto: Standard Publishing Company, 1901.

Newspaper/Journals

Canadian Baptist (Toronto, ON), 1878–1899.
McMaster Monthly (Toronto, ON), 1893–1894.
The Rainbow (London, UK), 1881.

Printed Sources

Fox, William Sherwood, ed. *Letters of William Davies Toronto 1854–1861.* Toronto: University of Toronto Press, 1945.
History of Toronto and the County of York. Volume 1. Toronto: C. Blackett Robinson, 1885.
Lesslie, James. "Notes from the Dominion." In *The Rainbow*, Volume XVIII, 360–64.
McKay, W. A. *Immersion Proved To Be Not A Scriptural Mode Of Baptism But A Romish Invention; And Immersionists Shewn To Be Disregarding Divine Authority In Refusing Baptism To The Infant Children of Believers.* Toronto: James Campbell & Son, 1884.

Yearbooks

Canadian Baptist Register (Toronto, ON), 1872–1876.
Baptist Yearbook, Ontario, Quebec and Manitoba (Toronto, ON), 1882–1884.

Secondary Sources

Brown, Stewart J. and Fry, Michael, eds. *Scotland in the Age of the Disruption*. New York: Columbia University Press, 1993.
Edwards, Maldwyn L. "Adam Clarke, The Man." *Methodist History* (1971) 50–56.
Grant, John Webster. *A Profusion of Spires: Religion in Nineteenth Century Ontario.* Toronto: University of Toronto Press, 1988.
Moir, John S. *Enduring Witness: A History of the Presbyterian Church in Canada.* Burlington, ON: Eagle Press, 1987.
Reid, W. Stanford, ed. *The Scottish Tradition in Canada*. Toronto: McClelland and Stewart, 1976.
Reilly, Brent A. "The Reverend Joshua Denovan, LL.D.: A Forgotten Figure of Canadian Baptist History." Unpublished Graduate Paper for John S. Moir, 1981. Canadian Baptist Archives, Hamilton, Ontario
Sawatsky, Ronald George. "'Looking For That Blessed Hope': The Roots of Fundamentalism in Canada, 1878–1914." PhD diss., University of Toronto, 1985.
Talbot, Brian R. *The Search for a Common Identity: The Origins of the Baptist Union of Scotland* 1800–1870. Bletchley, Milton Keys, UK: Paternoster Press, 2003.
Wilson, Paul. "Baptists and Business: Central Canadian Baptists and The Secularization of the Businessmen at Toronto's Jarvis Street Baptist Church, 1848–1921." PhD diss., University of Western Ontario, 1996.
———. "Caring for Their Community: The Philanthropic and Moral Reform Efforts of Toronto's Baptists, 1834–1918." In *Baptists and Public Life in Canada*, edited by Gordon L. Heath and Paul R. Wilson, 219–62. McMaster General Series 8. Canadian Baptist Historical Society Series 1. Eugene, OR: Pickwick, 2012.

3

The Quiet Fundamentalist

Edward John Stobo, Jr.

C. Mark Steinacher

INTRODUCTION

In some ways, the description of Edward John Stobo, Jr. (1867–1922) as "the Quiet Fundamentalist" is apt, as he appears virtually unknown to many historians of the fundamentalist movement that arose before the outbreak of the First World War.[1] In other ways, it is ironic, as Stobo was a prominent figure in Canadian Baptist circles for much of his student life and ordained ministry. The title remains fitting because, above all else, he evinced an irenic spirit in an increasingly fractious situation, providing a quiet and steady hand through leadership. He embodied the polar opposite spirit to the bellicose ecclesiastical pugilism of a Thomas Todhunter Shields (1873–1955) or a John Frank Norris (1877–1952). This chapter seeks to redress this individual void of Stobo's life in the telling of the collective story of the Baptists of Ontario and Quebec. This chapter will unfold the general theological tenor of Stobo's era, his family background, his life first

---

1. Although this chapter looks at the formative period, it uses the term "fundamentalism" in place of "proto-fundamentalism." A version of this chapter was first delivered to the Canadian Baptist Historical Society, 28 April 2018, at McMaster Divinity College. For more on the "proto-fundamentalist" designation, see chapters one and two in this volume.

as a student, then as a minister and leader in the then Baptist Convention of Ontario and Quebec. This will be followed by a discussion of Stobo's contribution to *The Fundamentals*.[2] Although in later life Stobo was notably restricted by the impact of a 1916 stroke, he continued low-key work as a pastor and popular writer until his premature death at the age of 55.

GENERAL BACKGROUND TO STOBO'S LIFE AND MINISTRY

In the early twentieth century, conservatives rallied to create a series of twelve pamphlets, bearing the title *The Fundamentals*, dedicated to defending matters central to the conservatives' theology. Scientific advances (particularly the insights of Charles Darwin), biblical criticism, and comparative religion undermined conservative Protestantism in this era; moreover, according to George Rawlyk, consumerism proved to be equally corrosive, eating away at a long-standing sense of duty and self-sacrifice and replacing it instead with a quiet permission to self-indulge.[3] In this atmosphere, *The Fundamentals* addressed topics such as prophecy, the literal resurrection of Christ, internal evidence supporting the authenticity of the Gospel of John, and the Mosaic authorship of the Pentateuch, attempting to rebut perceived assaults on the sanctity of Scripture.

In all, eight Canadians contributed to *The Fundamentals*. They were Anglicans, Baptists, and Presbyterians, a reflection of the type of theologically-conservative Christian that would develop into an inclusive, transdenominational evangelicalism represented by organizations such as Inter-Varsity Christian Fellowship and the Evangelical Fellowship of Canada.[4] Often ignored by American scholars, except when excerpts from *The Fundamentals* helped them caricature fundamentalists as buffoons, the series was taken seriously by scholars in the Church of England. They did not wait for the last few volumes before engaging in careful debate in *Foundations* (1912).[5] Edited by Burnett Hillman Streeter (1874–1937), known

---

2. Stobo, "The Apologetic Value of Paul's Epistles," 89–96

3. Rawlyk, "A. L. McCrimmon, H. P. Whidden, T. T. Shields, Christian Education and McMaster University," 36–37.

4. Stackhouse, *Canadian Evangelicalism in the Twentieth Century*, 10.

5. Steinacher, "Fundamentalism," 1160–65, as well as Steinacher, "Evangelicalism," 1078–84. Burnett Hillman Streeter was allegedly excommunicated by Frank Weston, the Bishop of Zanzibar, for editing *Foundations*, although one source indicates it was the bishop who appointed Streeter in 1915 as a canon of Hereford Cathedral whom Weston disfellowshipped. Chapman, *Anglicanism*, 125.

for his concept of the Synoptic Gospel "Two Source Hypothesis," the book proved popular enough to merit several reprints.[6]

Among Anglicans, the Reverend Canon Dyson Hague (1857–1935) served as a node, a gathering point to whom all contributors related, even if there is no readily-available evidence that they had direct links with each other. William Henry Griffith Thomas (1861–1924), co-founder of Dallas Theological Seminary,[7] died before a clear-cut division between evangelicals and fundamentalists transpired, so his alignment with Anglicanism was never seriously challenged. The Reverend Canon George Osborne Troop (1854–1932), the final Anglican contributor, remained a committed theological conservative. Both Hague and Troop ministered at St. Paul's, Halifax, Nova Scotia, although about a decade apart.[8] Hague's biography of Troop, augmented by memories from Troop's daughter Mona Johnston (b.ca.1884), stresses his active and orthodox faith but does not refer at all to Troop's contribution to the increasingly controversial pamphlets.[9]

Hague also was a rallying figure for contributors from other denominations, notably the Canadian Presbyterian authors. There does not appear to have been a direct relationship between Hague and the late Principal William Caven (1830–1904) of Knox College, University of Toronto, but there is a strong likelihood the two had met at some point. Caven's article was published posthumously. There is no doubt, however, of Hague's notable friendship with long-serving Principal John McNicol (1869–1956) of the Toronto Bible Training School, later Toronto Bible College.[10] As Elmore Harris (1854–1911) was a key founder of the school, his connection with McNicol, who became principal in 1906, is self-evident. Hague's father, George Hague (1825–1915), a banker with lay preacher's license, was also

---

6. The copy in McMaster University's Mills Library is a later reprinting of the 1912 original edition. Streeter, ed., *Foundations*.

7. Another co-founder was Alex B. Winchester, called in 1901 to the pulpit of Knox (Spadina) Presbyterian Church, Toronto.

8. Troop was a curate from 1877–1880; Hague served from 1890–1897.

9. Hague, ed., *Prophet, Presbyter, and Servant of Mankind*. Principal McNicol's copy of Hague's book is in Tyndale's library collection; it contains a personal inscription from Hague to McNicol.

10. Toronto Bible College amalgamated in 1968 with London College of Bible and Missions to form the Ontario Bible College. The college and its 1976-founded seminary rebranded at Tyndale College & Seminary, later Tyndale University. Stackhouse, *Canadian Evangelicalism in the Twentieth Century*, 3, 121.

a member of the Board of Trustees of Toronto Bible Training School. The web of relationships among Canadian contributors was dense and rich.

Unquestionably the most prominent of the Canadian Baptists involved in *The Fundamentals* project was Elmore Harris.[11] Scion of a wealthy farm implement family, Harris took leading roles in the founding of the Toronto Bible Training School and Walmer Road Baptist Church, but is perhaps most famous for his attempt during the First Battle of McMaster University (1909–1910) to secure the dismissal of the liberal-leaning Professor Isaac George Matthews (1871–1959). Although Matthews survived the attempt, the hasty resignation of the unitarian-leaning John Nelson Dales (1863–1935) was serious collateral damage.[12] The 1911 appointment of Abraham Lincoln McCrimmon (1865–1935) as Chancellor allegedly displeased Harris, who feared McCrimmon might allow the university to continue to drift theologically.[13] Harris' death of smallpox in India on 18 December 1911 proved to be a massive set-back to Canadian fundamentalists. Harris' loss was particularly troublesome for theologically-conservative Baptists in central Canada, because he functioned as a node around whom other "fundamentalists" gathered.

Harris' varied and widespread connections extended beyond Baptists to include conservatives from various denominational backgrounds. William ("Bible Bill") Aberhart (1878–1943), for example, obliged Harris during a visit to Brantford (probably in 1903) by conducting a Bible study at the Massey-Harris factory.[14] No obvious successor to this role immediately emerged after Harris' demise. It is not impossible that his mantle might have fallen upon Stobo, had he not been himself sidelined by his stroke, emerging as the central person to the amorphous yet undeniable Canadian fundamentalist network. Stobo's intense participation in a broad range of activities and committees in the Baptist Convention of Ontario and Quebec, including the influential "State of Religion Committee" (for which he wrote the annual report several years) and election as First Vice-President suggest this as a plausible outcome.

---

11. The precise nature of Harris' involvement in *The Fundamentals* is unclear, since he did not author a chapter himself; however, it is clear that he was the person who linked personally the disparate Canadian characters.

12. Steinacher, "'Sheep Not of This Fold,'" 287–90.

13. Canadian Baptist Archives, Box MNJ/1: 1911–1912 correspondence.

14. Elliott, "Studies of Eight Canadian Fundamentalists," 174.

Oddly enough, despite Thomas Todhunter Shields' extensive participation in convention work and his eventual leadership of the more conservative elements of the Baptist Convention during the Second Battle of McMaster University (1927), he does not appear to have had personal links to the early cohort of Canadian "fundamentalists." An exhaustive search of Shields' preserved letters reveals absolutely no correspondence with any of the Canadian contributors to *The Fundamentals*.[15] Neither did he contribute an article to the series; it does not appear that he was invited to submit. During the period articles were being written and published, Shields was engrossed in adapting to his new pastoral setting, Jarvis Street Baptist Church, as well as the publication of a book of his own.[16] By the end of the series' publication in 1915, the Great War had erupted, a conflict that increasingly garnered Shields' attention, even obsession.[17] The only contributor to *The Fundamentals* with whom Shields is known to have been exposed to in any significant way was Stobo, the two men's paths crossing during the extensive Baptist Convention of Ontario and Quebec committee work into which both men threw themselves enthusiastically.[18] His subsequent prominence, notably his extensive publishing and radio broadcasting ministries,[19] served to diminish the luminance of Stobo's memory.

The third Canadian Baptist contributor was James Josiah Reeve (b. 1866).[20] That he has been overlooked is more understandable, as he allegedly eventually abandoned the idea of an infallible Bible.[21] Reeve, born and raised in the Guelph area, also attended McMaster, where he befriended classmate Stobo. After serving as Professor of Hebrew and Cognate Languages and Old Testament Theology at Southwestern Baptist Theological Seminary in Fort Worth, Texas, Reeve dropped out of the evangelical community. His entries in the 1915 *International Standard Bible Encyclopedia* remained, however, in a 1982 revised edition.[22]

---

15. A debt of gratitude is owed to Dr. Michael Haykin for obtaining permission to access the Shields' archive at Jarvis Street Baptist Church. Research took place in 2006.

16. Adams, "The War of the Worlds," 108, 115, 129, 131.

17. Adams, "The War of the Worlds," 109, 129, 139–40, 160, 170, 172, 186, 190.

18. Adams, "The War of the Worlds," 134–36.

19. Adams, "The War of the Worlds," 7.

20. Personal email to the author from James Lutzweiler, Southeastern Baptist Theological Seminary, 13 April 2018.

21. Personal email to the author from James Lutzweiler, Southeastern Baptist Theological Seminary, 3 December 2001.

22. Bromiley, ed., *The International Standard Bible Encyclopedia*, 2:x, 65, 449, 520,

STOBO'S FAMILY BACKGROUND

E. J. Stobo Jr. was a "PK"—a "preacher's kid"—the eldest of seven children and the first son of the Reverend Edward John Stobo Sr. (1838–1918). The elder had entered life into an unremarkable family in Glasgow, the son of a pay-sergeant with the Second Battalion of the Royal Scots Regiment.[23] As an adult, he was converted, became a Baptist and, although approved for missionary service in India, was forced by the economic climate to settle for evangelistic work in Scotland. He relocated to Kilmarnock, Ayrshire, Scotland in 1865, pioneering a Baptist congregation that formed the next year. That year he also married Elizabeth Stuart Lindsay (1837–1924) of Glasgow, the youngest of five children. At least the first four of the Stobos' children were born in Kilmarnock.[24]

Ordained in 1866,[25] E. J. Stobo Sr. took up work with the "Scottish National Orphan Homes" founded 1871 by William Quarrier (1829–1903). Quickly Stobo became involved in the Homes' child emigration program, leading seventy-six boys and girls to Canada. This led to the family's 1872 emigration to Canada; his last two children definitely being born in Canada. Relinquishing his settlement work in 1872, Stobo initially accepted a pastorate at Font Hill, Ontario, then in 1886 became the fourth pastor of Quebec Baptist Church, eventually resigning to accept the post of secretary of the Quebec Auxiliary of the British and Foreign Bible Society. Quebec Baptist Church formed in 1845; the elderly Stobo received the honour of laying the cornerstone for the new building started in 1918.[26] In 1901 he

---

525, 527, 609, 620–21, and 786.

23. Morgan, *Canadian Men and Women of the Time*, 972,c.2, 973,c.1

24. In addition to Edward John Stobo, Jr., John M. Stobo, Katie Stobo, and Annie Stobo were born in Kilmarnock. The following details on Stobo's family were gleaned from www.geni.com. John Morrison Stobo: 23 July 1868, Kilmarnock, Scotland; 29 July 1940 (72), Quebec City; married Annie McIntyre Stobo; no children. Catherine (Katie) Edwards Stobo: 14 December 1869, Kilmarnock; 1 March 1945 (75), Quebec City; never married. Annie Lindsay Stobo: 18 July 1871, Kilmarnock; 31 October 1961 (90), Quebec City; never married.

25. *The Baptist Yearbook 1891*, 176

26. History of Quebec Baptist Church, available online at www.quebecbaptistchurch.homestead.com. "The architects of the new building were Burke, Horwood and White of Toronto. The building of medieval-period influence was built in Gothic style architecture with Citadel Rustic Tapestry brick, Deschambault stone dressings and 'Colorblend' Asbestos shingling. The sanctuary has a seating capacity of two hundred people."

published a novel, *The O'erturn o'Botany Bay or Dipper folk idylls*.[27] He remained in Quebec City until his death in 1918.[28]

At least two other children of E. J. Stobo Sr. became involved in Christian work. Catherine ("Katie") Edwards Stobo (1869–1945), third child and eldest daughter, for many years beginning in 1895 was involved in educational work through the Grande Ligne Mission.[29] The youngest child was named in honour of the social-worker/resettlement entrepreneur William Quarrier. Beginning in 1914, he served for some years on the Advisory Board of the Grande Ligne Mission.[30] At the time of his father's death, W. Q. Stobo (1877–1956) was a deacon of the Quebec congregation.[31] He was awarded an honorary doctorate by McMaster University in 1948 for his collective services rendered.

AN OVERVIEW OF EDWARD JOHN STOBO JR'S LIFE

Sources for reconstructing Stobo's life and ministry include his correspondence with various figures at McMaster University, *McMaster Monthly*, Baptist yearbooks, "Who's Who"-type books, articles written for *The Canadian Baptist* and secular newspapers, as well as the highlights of those newspaper articles bundled into a compendium entitled *The Glory of His Robe*.

He was born on 28 January 1867 in Kilmarnock. Coming to faith in 1879 while living in Collingwood, Ontario, he was baptized the same year. Before sensing a call to ministry, Stobo worked a year as a shop clerk, three years in a law office, and an unspecified length of time as night-editor of the *Quebec Morning Chronicle*. This marked the beginning of his life-long interest in publishing. Licensed to preach in 1887, he spent the summer preaching at Dixville and Arnprior, before enrolling at the Baptists' Woodstock College that Fall.[32] In September 1896 he married May Macklem. His

---

27. Philadelphia: American Baptist Publication Society, 1901. Stobo Sr. may also have been the editor of *The Kilmarnock Pioneer*, E. J. Stobo. no. 1–8; London, 1870, 71. He is given that credit by "WorldCat" but the British Library's entry lists no editor.

28. *Canadian Baptist*, 5 December 1918, 4.

29. *McMaster Monthly*, Volume V, February 1896, 248. She had been working for a few months at the Grande Ligne-supervised school at Coaticook.

30. *The Baptist Yearbook 1914*, 159; *The Baptist Yearbook 1915*, 197.

31. *Canadian Baptist*, 12 August 1909, 5.

32. *McMaster Monthly*, Volume VI; June 1896, 18.

name is the sixth entry in the McMaster University Enrollment Book,[33] graduating in 1896 with a Bachelor of Theology, in 1899 with a Bachelor of Divinity, and awarded the Bachelor of Arts *Ad Eundem* in 1903. Later he graduated from the University of Western Ontario (BA, 1903) and Temple University in Philadelphia (DST [sic], 1907; *magna cum laude*). A thirst for knowledge and insight, Stobo began work in 1915 on a Master of Arts in Sociology at McMaster, for which he submitted a 17,500-word thesis in 1916.[34] An irenic figure, Stobo's strong social conscience is probably traceable to his father's work. While many evangelicals were "interested" in such work, his father actually emigrated as a result of his engagement in social action. He died on 22 March 1922 in Toronto.

STUDENT LIFE

McMaster University appears to have been highly unusual in empowering students in daily life. No faculty member or hired adult supervisor lived in the student-run residence. Students formed their own executive committee to manage affairs. Stobo and Reeve both served on this committee, together during the 1894–1895 academic year.[35] The following year Stobo was First Vice-President, serving with fellow conservative George Russell Welch (b. 1867), and the later liberal protagonist I. G. Matthews.[36] Stobo could be a social butterfly, someone to be counted on to make toasts at banquets and to pitch in to help make a community event a success.[37] Apparently a Renaissance man, Stobo, along with McMaster's Literary Society teammate William Wardley McMaster (1867–1959), took on the Literary Society of Victoria University on the topic: "Resolved that 'Municipal ownership and working of monopolistic services is practicable for the city of Toronto and would be in the interests of said city.'" The McMaster team held the negative, allegedly winning the debate.[38]

---

33. Canadian Baptist Archives, "Enrollment Book, 1890–1929," Accession #96-040.

34. Personal Correspondence with Chancellor McCrimmon, Canadian Baptist Archives, Box MML/13: 6 February 1915; Box MMM/13: 16 February 1915, 24 February 1915; Box MMM/43: 5 February 1916, 16 March 1916.

35. *McMaster Monthly*, Volume IV, November 1894, 40; January 1895, 187.

36. *McMaster Monthly*, Volume V, November 1895, 90.

37. *McMaster Monthly*, Volume IV, February 1895, 234; March 1895, 282; Volume V, January 1896, 186.

38. *McMaster Monthly*, Volume V, January 1896, 185; February 1896, 235–36.

Throughout his undergraduate years, Stobo was the "indefatigable" secretary of the student-run Fyfe Missionary Society.[39] Subjects covered in the annual reports included the names of those taking up foreign mission work and home mission work. A church plant in "Little York" was reported in 1891.[40] Students fanned out to seven provinces in 1892, often taking up difficult situations, including in "our benighted sister province" (i.e., Quebec).[41] In 1893, three churches were organized through student missionary efforts, with two buildings erected. At least three hundred and two baptisms were recorded that summer.[42] Amidst all of the activity, Stobo managed to shoehorn in a quick visit to the Danville Association's annual meeting, held in North Troy, Vermont, a mere mile across the international border. He reported to them the Eastern Association's appointment of "a day of humiliation, fasting and prayer" for "the conversion of souls," and being one of nine leaders leading a discussion of "Successful methods of work."[43] Stobo opined that "McMaster University exists primarily for the extension of the kingdom of Jesus Christ, and if she is to achieve this purpose, her students must have a right conception of the character, extent and progress of that kingdom, and the obligation under which they rest to give the gospel to the perishing."[44] His enthusiastic report masked the reality that Stobo had been forced to drop out of McMaster temporarily because of ill-health, a harbinger of his difficulties in later life.[45] Despite his temporary setback, Stobo remained an enthusiastic fan of the university, placing him at odds with Shields, who believed "McMaster men"

---

39. *McMaster Monthly*, Volume I, November 1891, 69; Volume II, November 1892, 100; Volume III, November 1893, 89; Volume V, February 1896, 237. The flattering adjective appeared in Volume III, December 1893, 137.

40. *McMaster Monthly*, Volume I, November 1891, 73. Any doubt as to Stobo's intended reference is dispelled in Stobo's paper on "French Colportage" by the Quebec Auxiliary Bible Society. "Our hearts were drawn out as never before to that part of Quebec where the blackness of Romanism is more dense, and we were impressed more forcibly with the responsibility resting upon us as a denomination so[sic] carry the Gospel to those 'who sit in darkness and in the shadow of death.'" *McMaster Monthly*, January 1892, 188, cf. *The Baptist Yearbook 1898–1899*, 75.

41. *McMaster Monthly*, Volume II, February 1893, 228.

42. *McMaster Monthly*, Volume III, January 1894, "Eleventh Annual Report of the Fyfe Missionary Society," 160–64.

43. *Minutes of the Vermont Baptist Anniversaries for the Year 1893*, 17, 19. The minutes incorrectly refer to him as "Rev E. J. Stobo, Jr."; he was not ordained until 1896.

44. *McMaster Monthly*, Volume III, January 1894, 161, 162.

45. *McMaster Monthly*, Volume VI, June 1896, 18.

epitomized what was wrong with the Baptist Convention of Ontario and Quebec.[46] The 1894 "Monthly Missionary Day" saw a resurgence in student interest in missions, including a report on that year's Inter-Collegiate Missionary Convention, held in Belleville. Reeve declared that Stobo's paper on "Mohammedanism" was *the* paper of the Convention [and] was greeted with prolonged applause."[47] In his final year, Stobo "prepared a very exhaustive report" on the comparative state of spirituality among American and Canadian university students.[48] His own student mission efforts included Second Baptist Church in Markham (1892),[49] Sarnia Township (1894),[50] and the self-supporting field in Tiverton, Ontario (1895).[51] Although no dates are provided, his graduation biography also refers to summer work in Papineauville, Belfountain, Second Markham, and Potton.[52]

Another salient feature of his heady undergraduate years was his writing. His peers acknowledged Stobo's particular gift with the pen, suggesting that while his loyalties lay with evangelism his talents better suited him for teaching. There is also a hint that he might have been stubborn in those days: "His pure Scotch[sic] parentage and early religious training will account largely for the stern uprightness," yet any pugnacity was also matched by the evident "sterling honesty of his character."[53] One early effort eloquently examined the spirit of the age, which Stobo summarized as "the age of doubt."[54] Standing for truth sets apart a preacher, he assured his readers, inviting abuse from those raising cries of "Bigotry!" Yet "the true child of God can be no more liberal than are the Scriptures," and while there is room for honest and enquiring doubt, much that passes for "broad mindedness is often but another name for shallowness."[55] The article con-

46. Adams, "The War of the Worlds," 111.

47. *McMaster Monthly*, Volume IV, January 1895, 190. Emphasis in the original.

48. *McMaster Monthly*, Volume I, February 1892, 234: "We are glad to announce that our fellow student, Mr. E. J. Stobo, Jr., has returned convalescent. We trust the coming summer may entirely restore him to vigor. Mr. Stobo is one of our best men."

49. *McMaster Monthly*, Volume II, June 1892, 44. The church had experienced a revival that netted more than one hundred new young people. Stobo's summer work primarily lay "along the line of training and building up the young converts."

50. *The Baptist Yearbook 1894-95*, 173.

51. *The Baptist Yearbook 1895-96*, 145.

52. *McMaster Monthly*, Volume VI; June 1896, 18–19.

53. *McMaster Monthly*, Volume VI; June 1896, 18.

54. *McMaster Monthly*, Volume II, November 1892, 79.

55. *McMaster Monthly*, Volume II, November 1892, 79–80.

tinued with discussion of the apparent contradiction of the thorny question of "Divine Sovereignty and Man's[sic] Free Agency."[56] A more mature entry reflected Stobo's musing on "Paul's Conception of a Gospel Minister," stressing Paul's own continued habit of study.[57] One's pulpit ministry must display "fearlessness" and the backbone to stand up to "errorists."[58] This requires ministers to be heroic, not allowing personal feelings to impede lovingly disciplining the one in error, no matter how close a friend. Even after graduation, Stobo continued to be involved with McMaster through the Alumni Association, of which he was elected First Vice-President in 1904.[59]

PASTORAL LIFE AND DENOMINATIONAL LEADERSHIP

Stobo's pastoral career began with a number of short-lived appointments, although that may not have been atypical for the time.[60] He was called unanimously to the North Bay church (Northern Association), although the logistical difficulties of convening an examination council there led to his 1896 ordination in Toronto.[61] He served three years (1895–1898), during which the lone Baptist church in the Nipissing District enjoyed a number of conversions and transfers from Baptist churches, although membership totals remained static as several members who worked for the railroads were transferred elsewhere. The church debt was reduced and a new congregation was planted in Widdifield.[62] July 1899 found him in Pop-

---

56. *McMaster Monthly*, Volume II, November 1892, 81.

57. *McMaster Monthly*, Volume V, February 1896, 257, 264.

58. *McMaster Monthly*, Volume V, February 1896, 269–70.

59. *Canadian Baptist*, 12 May 1904, 9. He may have been elected in other years but this is the sole reference in the author's notes. Stobo "reviewed Professor H. C. King's 'Reconstruction in Theology,'" which he discerned "on the whole destructive rather than constructive."

60. While in-depth analysis of pastoral longevity could be both interesting and useful, it falls far beyond the scope of this chapter. In the 1915 "State of Religion" report, admittedly a decade later, Stobo noted that the average tenure of the pastors who had resigned their congregations that year was 3.3 years. *The Baptist Yearbook 1915*, 53.

61. *McMaster Monthly*, Volume VI; June 1896, 18. The report declares that "he was ordained in the Jarvis St. and Bloor St. churches" although it is not clear if there were two services or if the examination were held in one and the ordination service in the other. North Bay was originally intended to be his summer ministry post. *The Baptist Yearbook 1896–97*, 172, 174, 196.

62. *The Baptist Yearbook 1898–1899*, 68, 202, 218; *The Baptist Yearbook 1899–1900*, 57. Widdifield was, at the time, a township near North Bay; currently it is a neighbourhood within North Bay.

lar Hill, a one hundred and thirty-seven member church in the Middlesex and Lambton Association.[63] After not quite four years he accepted a call to Port Burwell (Elgin Association), staying two years.[64] Then he was on to Mount Forest for a brief pair of years.[65]

As early as 1906, Stobo inquired concerning the possibility of a teaching appointment at McMaster, perhaps as a tutor in homiletics or in some theological topic that he had covered in his doctoral work.[66] His tenure at Logan Avenue Baptist Church, Winnipeg was both remarkably short (under a year) and fraught with difficulties.[67] Failing to secure work at McMaster, he accepted a call to First Baptist, Smiths Falls in Ontario, where his pastorate also experienced membership volatility, in his first year adding thirty-one but losing thirty-five, for a total of two hundred and one. Some of the losses were to "exclusion," presumably as the result of discipline.[68] At Smiths Falls, Stobo experienced the cruel blow of his wife's death in March 1913. Apparently cut from the same cloth as her husband, she was described as "most active . . . a benediction to many . . . a strong leader [who] held many positions of trust in religious and moral spheres."[69] One last time he moved, to Hespeler, Ontario in 1914, his final pastorate.

Leaving the logistics of Stobo's life, his interests and commitments will be examined, elucidating how he occupied his time during these years. As peripatetic as he was, Stobo demonstrated consistent concerns and action at the convention level. In North Bay, he was the Northern Association's representative for the Baptist Young People's Union in 1898–1899.[70] Both father and son were visibly involved in the annual conventions on 1900 and 1901, then again in 1908.[71] E. J. Stobo Jr. was one of four to address

---

63. *The Baptist Yearbook 1899–1900*, 194, 212.

64. *The Baptist Yearbook, 1903*, 211.

65. Canadian Baptist Archives, MMF/74: A letter dated 29 January 1906 from Stobo to Chancellor Alexander Charles McKay (1861–1945) is preserved in McKay's correspondence. Canadian Baptist Archives, MMF/71.

66. Personal correspondence, 14 August 1907, Canadian Baptist Archives, MMI/13.

67. Personal correspondence, 14 August 1907, Canadian Baptist Archives, MMI/13.

68. *The Baptist Yearbook 1908*, 278.

69. *The Baptist Yearbook 1913*, 37.

70. *The Baptist Yearbook 1898–1899*, 190.

71. *The Baptist Yearbook 1900*, 13, 21; *The Baptist Yearbook 1901*, 12, 18, 19, 20; *The Baptist Yearbook 1908*, 8, 10, 12, 14, 15, 17, 26, 27, 263, 277. It is possible that the Stobos met E. Y. Mullins, an American Fundamentalist contributor. *The Baptist Yearbook 1908*, 26. The two definitely met in 1915, when Stobo moved that Foreign Mission report be

the convention on "Church Problems."[72] Laying groundwork for advancement, Stobo conducted a continuing education seminar, aimed at promoting broader reading among those who had not been able to study at McMaster.[73] This period also saw him begin writing for *The Canadian Baptist* in 1910–11. Administrative duties also called as Stobo became secretary of the Canada Central Association.[74] Even the Obituaries Committee lured him in.[75] Of greatest importance, however, and another marker of Stobo's increasing stature within the convention, was his 1910 election as First Vice-President.[76] In that role he convened all but one of the sessions for the first three days, with President Charles J. Holman (1852–1928; a prominent member of Jarvis Street Baptist Church) in the chair for Saturday and Sunday.

His undergraduate dedication to foreign mission work also continued. For a number of years Stobo acted as association chair for the Board of Home Missions, first for Elgin Association, then Walkerton Association, followed by the Canada Central Association.[77] The colonialist and racist underbelly of central Canadian culture unfortunately revealed itself in the 1898–1899 Home Mission Board report, penned by Stobo.[78] Reports on a number of developments was summed up by claiming "the recital of these facts may impress neither mind nor heart beyond what would be experienced were we listening to a patriotic address on the Onward March of the Anglo-Saxon race to commercial supremacy." Less toxic, but still very much reflecting the era's spirituality of "muscular Christianity" was the Home Missions report's call to take up "the opportunity for building up a great Christian nationhood . . . absolutely unparalleled in all history . . . a genuine Christian patriotism."[79] In keeping with postmillennial eschatology espoused by leaders of many of the era's mainstream Protestant

---

interrupted to allow for the first of several addresses to the convention by E. Y. Mullins. *The Baptist Yearbook 1915*, 12, 16–17.

72. *The Baptist Yearbook 1906*, 14.
73. *The Baptist Yearbook 1908*, 17.
74. *The Baptist Yearbook 1908*, 277.
75. *The Baptist Yearbook 1915*, 30.
76. *The Baptist Yearbook 1910*, 6, 10.
77. *The Baptist Yearbook 1903*, 155; *The Baptist Yearbook 1904*, 105; *The Baptist Yearbook 1905*, 92; *The Baptist Yearbook 1906*, 34; *The Baptist Yearbook 1909*, 232.
78. *The Baptist Yearbook 1898–1899*, 49.
79. *The Baptist Yearbook 1906*, 37.

denominations, Stobo voiced the concern that Baptists must more thoroughly recognize that "education and evangelism must go hand in hand if God's Kingdom is to be established in these Provinces."[80] Work on the missions committee exposed Stobo earlier than many to the attitudes of I. G. Matthews, Home Missions chair in 1903. Matthews delivered the Educational Address in the controversial year 1908.[81] That same year Stobo provided an update on the missionary efforts in Bolivia.[82] This venue for service also found him rubbing shoulders with T. T. Shields.[83] He continued to serve on the committee until waylaid by health issues.[84]

One prong of this campaign to civilize the country was the "Moral Reform Committee" formed in 1905.[85] Such committees were also common in the early twentieth century among other denominations. Leaders were urged to set an example for lay people, whose collective behaviour will "promote the moral progress of our beloved country," particularly through taking a "stand for prohibition of the Liquor Traffic." Stobo threw himself with typical fervour into this crusade, being elected as the Walkerton Association's representative.[86] The group appears to have rebranded as the "Social Service Committee," again with Stobo massively involved.[87]

His strong family ties to Quebec, where his father was one of the Protestant pioneers, opened the door for Stobo's role as convention representative on the board of the Grande Ligne Mission.[88] He resisted a proposal to incorporate the mission entirely into the convention. He did support increased representation on the mission's board, given that fifty to sixty percent of its income derived from the convention.[89] Work for the board included attending board meetings and addressing students at the Feller

---

80. *The Baptist Yearbook 1914*, 57.
81. *The Baptist Yearbook 1908*, 23.
82. *The Baptist Yearbook 1908*, 14, 15, 263.
83. *The Baptist Yearbook 1911*, 211; *The Baptist Yearbook 1912*, 268.
84. *The Baptist Yearbook 1914*, 215.
85. *The Baptist Yearbook 1905*, 16–17.
86. *The Baptist Yearbook 1906*, 11, 165.
87. *The Baptist Yearbook 1912*, 21; *The Baptist Yearbook 1913*, 28.
88. *The Baptist Yearbook 1909*, 10, 180.
89. *The Baptist Yearbook 1910*, 20, 217–18.

Institute.⁹⁰ After presenting the mission's annual report in 1911, Stobo handed the torch to G. R. Welch.⁹¹

By 1908 Stobo had begun to set his sights higher, securing appointment to the State of Religion Committee.⁹² The State of Religion Committee produced an annual report that was an amalgam of statistics, events, observations and opinions.⁹³ At this time, Elmore Harris chaired the committee. With this advancement, Stobo placed himself firmly among the convention's circle of primary leaders. This setting is perhaps where Stobo attracted Harris' attention, leading to the invitation to contribute to *The Fundamentals*. Apparently Stobo did not share Harris' disquietude regarding McCrimmon's appointment, assuring the new chancellor "I am certain that your appointment will do much to still the unrest that has prevailed, and that you will have the hearty co-operation of the denomination."⁹⁴ As one bears in mind that this irenic statement was made around the time Stobo stepped into Harris' role on the State of Religion Committee, this attitude bode well for the denomination's future unity. He continued to be elected chair year-after-year.⁹⁵

The value of Baptists' dwelling together in unity, for Stobo, reached to the national level. At a time when the proposed creation of a "Baptist Union of Canada" was opposed by fifty-three percent of congregations and unequivocally approved by only one in six, Stobo seconded the 1909 motion to create the union, urging its adoption as a token of "the spirit of fraternity in the denomination."⁹⁶ Discussion the following year centred on unified efforts for foreign missions and Sunday School work. Dust from the First Battle of McMaster still clogged the air in 1910, as motions from Goderich Baptist Church and Centre Street Baptist Church, St. Thomas, urged caution in light of the disturbed theological climate.⁹⁷ The formation

---

90. *The Baptist Yearbook 1911*, 172–73.

91. *The Baptist Yearbook 1911*, 25; *The Baptist Yearbook 1912*, 23.

92. *The Baptist Yearbook 1908*, 8, 12; *The Baptist Yearbook 1909*, 53.

93. For examples, see *The Baptist Yearbook 1911*, 8, 14; *The Baptist Yearbook 1912*, 8, 14, 24, 66–69.

94. Personal correspondence of A. L. McCrimmon, 4 September 1911; Canadian Baptist Archives, Box MMK.

95. *The Baptist Yearbook 1913*, 8, 22, 23, 68; *The Baptist Yearbook 1914*, 8, 11, 14, 56; *The Baptist Yearbook 1915*, 8, 14, 15, 53, 54.

96. *The Baptist Yearbook 1909*, 12–13, 22.

97. *The Baptist Yearbook 1910*, 7.

of a national organization had to wait until the 1944 creation of the Baptist Federation of Canada.

Stobo perceived no threat by the academy to faith's integrity. His 1917 recommendation that Professor Peter Sinclair Campbell (1847–1930) be rewarded with an honorary doctorate took pains to note Campbell's conservative academic prowess was balanced with his profound spirituality. Stobo noted: "Many young men have been led to Christ thru his earnest personal work, others have received fresh inspiration to Christian service, and a good many have gone into the ministry because this good man took them off for a walk and presented the claims of the pulpit to them."[98] Although uneducated ministers continued to serve faithfully, Stobo noted and approved of the shift to college-trained pastors.[99] Desire in the convention for revival had increased, if anything, rather than abated over the years, suggesting Stobo held no dichotomy between piety and education.[100]

In this embrace of higher education, Stobo differed starkly from Shields, for whom a "McMaster man" was anathema.[101] Although the two served on many convention committees, Stobo loved McMaster as deeply as Shields loathed it. The Great War almost destroyed McMaster, as a painfully problematic proportion of pupils enlisted.[102] Had McMaster been another casualty before the Armistice was signed, Shields would not have shed a tear. Attention must also be drawn to the inverse trajectories of the two men's careers. Stobo, seriously unwell, could not maintain his salient contribution to convention work; Shields, having overcome internal dissention at Jarvis Street Baptist Church, saw his influence increase by the year.[103] Shields raised havoc over editorials in *The Canadian Baptist* that advocated a lesser view of inspiration, one that affirms "the spiritual content of the record and not necessarily with illuminating and inerrantly controlling the minds of the writers with reference to physical, scientific, or historical facts."[104] At the contentious 1919 assembly in Ottawa, Shields launched an

---

98. Personal correspondence of A. L. McCrimmon, 29 March 1917, Canadian Baptist Archives Box MMN/6.

99. *The Baptist Yearbook 1914*, 57–58.

100. *The Baptist Yearbook 1914*, 59.

101. Adams, "The War of the Worlds," 66, 138, 151, 259.

102. Rawlyk, "A. L. McCrimmon, H. P. Whidden, T. T. Shields, Christian Education and McMaster University," 49.

103. Adams, "The War of the Worlds," 158

104. Adams, "The War of the Worlds," 150–51.

all-out frontal assault by means of a proposed amendment to the report of the Publication Board.[105] The conciliatory voice of Stobo, the quiet fundamentalist, was increasingly drowned out by Shields', the bellicose pulpiteer. Had Stobo been in better health, perhaps Shields' rise to prominence would not have been as meteoric.

THE ARTICLE IN THE FUNDAMENTALS

The tenth volume of *The Fundamentals: A Testimony to the Truth*, contains Stobo's article: "The Apologetic Value of Paul's Epistles." Written while he ministered in Smiths Falls, this piece represents the zenith of his lexical agility. Although he continued writing short articles after his stroke until the time of his death, he laboured under great disability. A striking feature of his contribution to the pamphlets is its generally outward-looking view. He attempts not simply to argue from a conservative redoubt, lobbying intellectual squibs at straw-person opponents, delighting those who already agreed with him but merely annoying opponents. Whether he actually defeated his opponents, or even won some of them over to his position, is beyond the scope of this paper, but he certainly essayed valiantly to provide a useful apologetic that could be deployed by any faithful believer who might engage a searching skeptic in conversation. Once again, by adopting a respectful tone he displays his irenic and what would later become known as a "missional" approach, evincing not merely a desire to win but to lead folk to faith.

He began on the higher critics' home-turf, acknowledging that only four Pauline letters are unquestionably his.[106] Working from that basis, one explicitly rejected by his McMaster classmate Reeve,[107] Stobo first attempted to establish a case to justify his conclusion that the coherence of the Gospels and these particular Epistles by Paul allows one to trust the integrity, authority and authenticity of the rest of the New Testament. His goal was to demonstrate the four acknowledged missives' interconnectedness with the Gospels in particular. Basic to this point is his assertion that it is impossible to explain Paul's conversion solely in naturalistic terms; the story makes no sense without the involvement of the supernatural.[108] If the

---

105. Adams, "The War of the Worlds," 153.

106. Stobo, "The Apologetic Value of Paul's Epistles," 89–90.

107. Reeve, "My Personal Experience of Higher Criticism," 102. "There is no possible middle ground as I once fondly imagined there was."

108. Stobo, "The Apologetic Value of Paul's Epistles," 91.

supernatural be granted here there is no longer a fundamental objection to the claim that the content of Christianity and the Bible at its foundation are supernatural. Stobo's syllogism aligns with the core arguments of Dyson Hague, James Orr, and James Josiah Reeve.[109] The depth of Paul's conversion, that it was no trivial matter but a reorientation of his entire world, adds weight to Paul's testimony and thus the veracity of the claims he makes. Paul's letters corroborate his conversion story found in Acts; since Acts is the continuation of Luke, it follows (in Stobo's mind) that the Gospels are trustworthy.[110] Supernatural as the conversion was, Stobo took pains to affirm in the conclusion, it was "not due to extreme mysticism . . . [but] remarkably sane and logical."[111]

His second point may have distressed some conservatives at first reading, in light of Stobo's allowance that Paul's representation of Christ does not include Jesus' miracles.[112] Miracles are a particular subset of the supernatural phenomena recorded in the Bible. Whether the miracle be the virginal conception, the literal resurrection, or one of myriad healings Jesus performed, all were points of contention between liberal and conservative theological factions throughout the first half of the twentieth century.[113] The basic timeline of Jesus' life remains intact so, Stobo avers, Paul's work still affirms the Gospels. What might be lost on first reading is that Stobo proceeds to defend the veracity of the Resurrection as a palpable historical event, a position defended at greater length by Reuben Archer Torrey (1856–1928), an editor of *The Fundamentals*.[114] Stobo would not grant higher critics the ground that one might preach faithfully with a reading of the Gospels that allows for a merely narrative theology that fails to affirm the historicity of Jesus' life,[115] a position shared by Hague, although

---

109. Hague, "The History of Higher Criticism," 91; Orr, "Science and Christian Faith," 93, 96; and Reeve, "My Personal Experience with the Higher Criticism," 100, 103, 112.

110. Stobo, "The Apologetic Value of Paul's Epistles," 91–92.

111. Stobo, "The Apologetic Value of Paul's Epistles," 96.

112. Stobo, "The Apologetic Value of Paul's Epistles," 92.

113. Marsden, *Reforming Fundamentalism*, 4, 101–102, 292–93; Stackhouse, *Canadian Evangelicalism in the Twentieth Century*, 179.

114. Torrey, "The Certainty and Importance of the Bodily Resurrection of Jesus Christ from the Tomb," *passim*.

115. Stobo, "The Apologetic Value of Paul's Epistles," 92. It would be anachronistic to claim Stobo argued against both a narrative theology that takes the Evangelists' stories at fact value while not accepting their historicity, as well as Rudolph Bultmann's program of demythologization. It is likely, however, that Stobo would have opposed those concepts

the latter allowed for reverent criticism.[116] In an era when liberal scholars routinely sought to drive a wedge between the Jesus of the Gospels and the churchly, institutional vision attributed to Paul, Stobo drew a line in the sand. The faithful could never accept the notion that the Evangelists and Paul are at odds, representing two distinct and contradictory visions of Christianity, with the Pauline corruptions of the pristine vision winning out. Whether the ostensibly reverent *bon mot* by Alfred Firmin Loisy (1857–1940) that Jesus announced a kingdom but the world got the church instead,[117] or the more explicitly destructive approach embodied by Adolf von Harnack (1851–1930) that pitted the Lucan portrayal of Paul with the picture that emerges from the Epistles, Stobo flatly rejected such bifurcations. For him, Paul's Christology aligned immaculately with that extracted from the Gospels.[118]

The second half of the article is broken down into four sub-points, each examining a different aspect of Jesus' relation to reality: time; humans; the universe; God. Regarding time, Jesus' eternal existence is affirmed, yet (as the ancient creeds insist) He is also God's Son in a unique way, the physical descendant of the biblical King David.[119] An element of Jesus' relation to humans, although the precise term is not used, is the substitutionary atonement. From some inexplicable reason, Stobo ascribes to Jesus a description said first to be applied by William Wordsworth to John Milton: "His soul was like a star and dwelt apart."[120] Briefest is the section on Jesus' relation with the universe, a mere paragraph.[121] Despite its brevity, it is this point in which Stobo drifted beyond his self-imposed restriction on the four undisputed Epistles, citing Col 1's declaration that all that exists, visible and invisible, was created in, through, for and by Jesus. That an ardent *alumnus* of McMaster felt the need to include this verse—the university's motto—is more than understandable.[122] Reflections on Jesus' relation to God take up

once they entered theological parlance.

116. Hague, "The History of the Higher Criticism," 100.

117. Charles et al., "Alfred Firmin Loisy."

118. Stobo, "The Apologetic Value of Paul's Epistles," 93, 96.

119. Stobo, "The Apologetic Value of Paul's Epistles," 93.

120. Stobo, "The Apologetic Value of Paul's Epistles," 93. For the Wordsworth quotation, consult Hazlett, "Lectures on the Drama," 442.

121. Stobo, "The Apologetic Value of Paul's Epistles," 94.

122. For the uninitiated, the motto of McMaster University is τὰ πάντα ἐν αὐτῷ συνέστηκε from Col 1:17.

the lion's share of the article, almost two full pages out of the entire eight. He cites 1 Cor 15's affirmation of the historicity of the Resurrection, made as it was by Paul who was an eyewitness to the risen Jesus, as yet another indication of the trustworthiness of the Gospels.[123] A final flourish is the defence of Trinitarianism on the basis of the benediction at the end of 2 Corinthians.[124]

STOBO'S LATER AND LIMITED LIFE

Despite his physical limitations, the widower continued with the normal rounds of life. A happier occasion was the 1918 "quiet house wedding" of his daughter, Dorothy Macklem Stobo (b. 1897), to James Masson Hall.[125] He performed the ceremony. As he was able, he participated in a number of "secret societies," finding their teaching congenial and noble, even if some Christians objected to them. His main concern was that if people were pressed for time their church involvement would suffer before their attendance at lodge would.[126]

Much of his time was spent creating a regular column for the Toronto *Mail and Empire*. Many of these were reproduced in *The Canadian Baptist*. Others were collected and printed as an anthology under the title *The Glory of His Robe*. It is not clear if these stories were edited into a single volume by Stobo himself or after his death. In early 1916 he learned to type, easing the physical process of writing after he endured the stroke that crippled his remaining years.[127]

Ever vigilant for opportunities to share his faith, Stobo related in one of these stories a successful example of his personal evangelism.[128] He was also quick to note, though, he refused to demand that all Christians present highly similar stories of discovering Jesus' power in their lives. He disparaged "cheese-press" conversion, elsewhere noting that no two daisies look alike so why should all new Christians share the same precise process.[129] Once convinced of the authenticity of a person's conversion he refused to

123. Stobo, "The Apologetic Value of Paul's Epistles," 94–95.
124. Stobo, "The Apologetic Value of Paul's Epistles," 96.
125. *Toronto World*, 22 August 1918, 5.
126. *Canadian Baptist*, 28 February 1918, 11.
127. Letter of 16 March 1916 to A. L. McCrimmon in McCrimmons' correspondence. Canadian Baptist Archives Box MMM/43.
128. Stobo, *The Glory of His Robe*, 35–36.
129. Stobo, *The Glory of His Robe*, 36, cf. 12, 26.

worry about the precise details.[130] To illustrate his point, he compared and contrasted Quaker quietism with the Primitive Methodists' shouting.[131] His own conversion entailed no great emotional crisis but a firm and lasting decision based on his own quiet and crude prayer of submission. What was essential was the "soul's return to God," a reality easily lost in the rush to reduce faith to acceptance of propositions.[132]

He heartily endorsed the use of gentler stories when sharing the faith, rather than a more consumeristic approach, akin to the practices of door-to-door sales representatives.[133] The religious use of humour also struck him as an underutilized form of communication. One example he provided was a Scottish preacher in London, taking up Paul's "I am not ashamed of the gospel." The preacher suggested this was akin to the Scottish dialect's "I'm no sae bad," which actually means doing well, so Paul actually claimed he is proud of the gospel. "The preacher had captured them by the pawkiness of his humour."[134] Stobo urged readers to think of the humour inherent to Jesus' parable of the splinter in one eye and a log in another, or of figs growing on a thistle, images that he also noted stressed Jesus' humanness.[135] Humour also helps, he claimed, deal with life's vicissitudes, no small matter for a man debilitated by a stroke.[136]

The ethics of war, more than understandably, garnered Stobo's attention on a number of occasions throughout conflict. No pacifist, he shared a common view of those seeking exception from military service, those whom he termed "slackers."[137] They were hypocrites, he argued, for accepting the benefits of the rule of law but then baulking at defending that rule and their freedoms by claiming they were citizens of a heavenly country, answering only to the commands of their heavenly king, Jesus. As a result, they believed they owed "no duty towards Canada and the Empire."[138] Their true motivation for avoiding service, according to Stobo, was "to gather all the filthy lucre of the earthly [country] that they possibly can." Part of the

130. Stobo, *The Glory of His Robe*, 27.
131. Stobo, *The Glory of His Robe*, 25.
132. Stobo, *The Glory of His Robe*, 13, 25–26.
133. Stobo, *The Glory of His Robe*, 13.
134. Stobo, *The Glory of His Robe*, 30.
135. Stobo, *The Glory of His Robe*, 31.
136. Stobo, *The Glory of His Robe*, 33.
137. *Canadian Baptist*, 13 June 1918, 7.
138. *Canadian Baptist*, 13 June 1918, 7.

problem, as he understood it, was that a number "base their answers upon the conviction that the Second Advent of our Lord is nigh, and that we are in the midst of a falling away from the truth."[139]

In an article published in *Mail & Empire* and later in *The Canadian Baptist* entitled, "The Religion of the Soldier," Stobo asserted that by the time a soldier reaches enlistment age his faith is well-grounded, although it must adapt to the realities of soldierly suffering. As a result, it may not look like civilians' polite and ordered faith but it is real, nonetheless, faith trimmed to its basics, although it stresses justice and Judgment Day. Stobo worried the average soldier would draw too close a parallel between dying in combat and the Cross, as if salvation were "attained through giving his life on the battlefield."[140] That said, "Tommy has got a glimpse of the inner meaning of the Cross . . . [linking] in a new fashion to the Christ of the Cross," a more profound understanding than doctrinal statements can make.

Some articles included warnings that it was all too easy to neglect church during the war. Fuel shortages led for calls to close churches yet, as Stobo lamented, bars and other sources of amusement remained open. Lightening the mood with a humorous anecdote, Stobo then wryly suggested that perhaps a return to the Jewish observance of retiring at sundown might be in order.[141] Ever the optimist, Stobo averred "it would almost appear that the present financial stringency and the war with Germany combined are driving God's people to their knees, resulting in increased attendance in some urban congregations."[142] Not for him was moaning of the war's allegedly deleterious impact.

A mainstay of his posts was advice concerning how the laity could assist ministers to achieve the church's broad goals. This might turn on the question of the latest methods for teaching Sunday School, even if they differed from the modes handed down from the work of Robert Raikes (1736-1811). He recommended the use of Socratic questioning to draw the children in. He also opined that many ministers themselves had lost the art of teaching and needed to brush up on expository preaching.[143] Layfolk, for their part, could resurrect the old-time practice of shouting

---

139. *The Baptist Yearbook 1915*, 56.

140. *Canadian Baptist*, 1 August 1918, 7. The article originally appeared in the *Mail & Empire*, 19 July 1918. The jingoistic hymn "O Valiant Hearts" vindicates Stobo's concerns.

141. *Canadian Baptist*, 28 February 1918, 11.

142. *The Baptist Yearbook 1914*, 59; cf. *The Baptist Yearbook 1915*, 56-57.

143. *Canadian Baptist*, 31 January 1918, 3.

vocal interjections during the message, encouraging the preacher not to lose heart.[144]

His chapter "Come and Rest Awhile" in *The Glory of His Robe* developed a positive theology of work.[145] This aspect of theological anthropology, a common theme among the Puritan divines, was largely ignored in the twentieth century by Protestant and Roman Catholic alike until renewal of interest during the deliberations of the Second Vatican Council. Stobo took pains to distinguish between the sense of calling underpinning work and the wearisome toil that characterizes mere labour. Stobo specifically noted that few still "labor under the delusion that work is a curse. It is not. Read your Bible and you will discover" otherwise. It would appear he was no proponent of organized labour, as he averred: "The first strike transformed work into labour, injected bitterness into toil, and converted glorious achievement into mere drudgery . . . Just think over the difference between work and labour and you will understand. . . . It is not work that disheartens and kills. It is labour." Work is not among the "no mores" found at the close of the Book of Revelation. God's servants shall serve him: "Work will be the joy of heaven."

His opinion of the church's duty toward social concerns was nuanced. Apparently taking a swipe at the full-blown Social Gospel, he grumbled that some treat the pulpit as "the venue for demands to changes in 'social conditions' . . . [but] the local police office is established for that very purpose."[146] His point was not that the church should eschew all social concern. Indeed, Stobo's work as an "agent" with the Stratford Children's Aid Society included working with police "to compel shiftless, drunken fathers to care for their families, and [I] have dealt with some cases that could not be reached in any other way."[147] Rather, he feared preachers' potential withdrawal into their own little world in which words flowed from their crabbed spirits and vanished into the auditorium's air without results.[148] That, of course, is at the other end of the spectrum of gospel engagement from the career of someone like Shields. That Stobo's prime concern was the temptation for preachers to retreat from interaction with the world underlines that his worldview encompassed a moderate form of fundamentalism.

---

144. *Canadian Baptist*, 9 May 1918, 7.
145. All quotations in this paragraph are from *The Glory of His Robe*, 20–22.
146. *Canadian Baptist*, 17 October 1918, 4.
147. *Report of Superintendent of Neglected and Dependent Children of Ontario, 1913*, 80.
148. *Canadian Baptist*, 17 October 1918, 4.

It is all too easy, Stobo warned, for "the knocker" to excoriate others while missing the positive work of encouraging each other to stronger efforts for the marginalized.

The interface of faith and action also surfaces in an article on prayer.[149] Clearly committed to the expectation that God answers prayer supernaturally, Stobo lamented that some "remain confused as to what prayer does and does not accomplish." Because "prayer works miracles [there] has arisen the prayer-test proposition." That proposition entailed what he considered to be a pseudo-scientific process, praying for people in one hospital ward but not another and seeing who gets healed. The idea was wrong on so many levels, not the least of which is that it seems cruel not to pray for all. The critique of the pseudo-scientific process should not be interpreted as rejection of scholarly inquiry; Stobo explicitly valued science.[150] However God answered prayer, the journalist affirmed, "prayer operates with respect to physical forces . . . in accordance with physical laws."[151] Rather than chasing quixotically after some supposed scientific test that pitted intellect against faith, the reader needed to grasp that prayer is about "our yearning after God," developing an attitude that instinctively cries out to God. Stobo died before the so-called "Scopes Monkey Trial" unfolded, a technical win against the teaching of evolution in Tennessee schools but a major blow to the estimate of evangelicals' intellectual capacities in the court of public opinion. As a result, there is little to build a case for or against his attitude toward William Jennings Brian's forensic defence of creationism.

CONCLUSION

Within half a decade of E. J. Stobo Jr's death the Baptist Convention of Ontario and Quebec would be divided. It is not the concern of this chapter to examine the issues and personalities associated with this unfortunate breaking of fellowship, much less to assign either honour or blame to those involved. Nevertheless, scholars lack any solid grounds to speculate as to Stobo's reaction to the Second Battle of McMaster University in the later 1920s. What is known is that for most of his life, Stobo was a dedicated and energetic Christian minister who invested his prodigious energies into a dazzling array of causes. Core to his work was sharing the gospel, whether working with youth, evangelizing personally, preaching, or promoting the

---

149. *Canadian Baptist*, 21 November 1918, 7.

150. Stobo, *The Glory of His Robe*, 36.

151. *Canadian Baptist*, 21 November 1918, 7.

work of Baptist Home and Foreign Missions. It seems clear he was maturing into a position of leadership after Harris' death, only to be cut down himself by a stroke. One wonders if he might have avoided his incapacitation had he not worked so frenetically. After all, his siblings all lived to between seventy-two and ninety years; his father reached the ripe age of eighty and his mother eighty-six. One can only muse how the character of Canadian fundamentalism in general, and the Canadian Baptist community in particular, would have differed had Stobo's calm voice endured longer than it did. Like Stobo, the contributors to this Canadian Baptist Historical Society tome live and minister in a fractious and polarized theological climate. Perhaps one of the key facets of Edward John Stobo Jr.'s life to be grasped and emulated is his irenic spirit, standing resolutely for truth while refusing to dehumanize, ridicule, or argue unfairly against those with whom he differed.

BIBLIOGRAPHY

Primary Sources

Newspapers

Canadian Baptist (Toronto, ON), 1904, 1909, 1918.
McMaster Monthly (Toronto, ON), 1891–1896.
Toronto World (Toronto, ON), 1918.

Archives

Canadian Baptist Archives, Hamilton, Ontario.
Jarvis Street Baptist Church Archives, Toronto, Ontario; "Shields Correspondence."

Other

Baptist Yearbook (Baptist Convention of Ontario and Quebec) 1891–1915.
Hague, Dyson. "The History of the Higher Criticism." In *The Fundamentals: A Testimony to the Truth, Vol. I*, edited by Amzi Clarence Dixon et al., 87–122. Chicago: Testimony Publishing Company, n.d.
Hague, Dyson, ed. *Prophet, Presbyter, and Servant of Mankind: A Memoir of the Reverend Canon G. Osborne Troop, M.A., Containing 'Intimate Recollections' by Mona Johnston and a Selection of His Writings*. N.p.: n.d.
Minutes of the Vermont Baptist Anniversaries for the Year 1893. Rutland, VT: The Tuttle Publishing Company, 1893.
Morgan, Henry James. *Canadian Men and Women of the Time*. Toronto: William Briggs, 1898.
Orr, James. "Science and Christian Faith." In *The Fundamentals: A Testimony to the Truth, Vol. IV*, edited by Amzi Clarence Dixon et al., 91–104. Chicago: Testimony Publishing Company, n.d.

Reeve, J. J. "My Personal Experience with the Higher Criticism." In *The Fundamentals: A Testimony to the Truth, Vol. III*, edited by Amzi Clarence Dixon et al., 98–118. Chicago: Testimony Publishing Company, n.d.
Report of Superintendent of Neglected and Dependent Children of Ontario, 1913. Toronto: Department of Public Welfare. Children's Aid Branch, 1913.
Stobo, Edward John, Jr. "The Apologetic Value of Paul's Epistles." In *The Fundamentals: A Testimony to the Truth, Vol. X*, edited by Amzi Clarence Dixon et al., 89–96. Chicago: Testimony Publishing Company, n.d.
———. *The Glory of His Robe*, Toronto: McClelland and Stewart, 1922.
Streeter, Burnett Hillman, ed. *Foundations: A Statement of Christian Belief in Terms of Modern Thought: by Seven Oxford Men.* London: Macmillan and Co, 1918.
Torrey, Reuben Archer, "The Certainty and Importance of the Bodily Resurrection of Jesus Christ from the Tomb." In *The Fundamentals: A Testimony to the Truth, Vol. V*, edited by Amzi Clarence Dixon et al., 81–105. Chicago: Testimony Publishing Company, n.d.

Secondary

Adams, Douglas Allan. "The War of the Worlds: The Militant Fundamentalism of Thomas Todhunter Shields and the Paradox of Modernity." PhD diss., University of Western Ontario, 2015.
Bromiley, Geoffrey W., ed. *The International Standard Bible Encyclopedia.* Volume 2. Grand Rapids: Eerdmans, 1982.
Chapman, Mark. *Anglicanism: A Very Short Introduction.* Oxford: Oxford University Press, 2006.
Charles, Michelle, et al. "Alfred Firmin Loisy." In *Boston Collaborative Encyclopedia of Western Religion.* N.d., Online: http://people.bu.edu/wwildman/bce/loisy.htm.
Elliott, David R. "Studies of Eight Canadian Fundamentalists." PhD diss., University of British Columbia, 1989.
Hazlitt, William. "*Lectures on the Drama.*" *Edinburgh Review* 34 (1820) 438–49.
Marsden, George *Reforming Fundamentalism: Fuller Seminary and the New Evangelicalism.* Grand Rapids: Eerdmans, 1986.
Rawlyk, George. "A. L. McCrimmon, H. P. Whidden, T. T. Shields, Christian Education and McMaster University." In *Canadian Baptists and Christian Higher Education*, edited by George Rawlyk, 31–62. Montreal: McGill-Queens University Press, 1988.
Stackhouse, John G., Jr. *Canadian Evangelicalism in the Twentieth Century: An Introduction to Its Character.* Toronto: University of Toronto Press, 1993.
Steinacher, C. Mark. "Evangelicalism." In *Religions of the World: A Comprehensive Encyclopedia of Beliefs and Practices,* edited by J. Gordon Melton and Martin Baumann, 1078–84. 2nd ed. Santa Barbara: ABC-CLIO, 2010.
———. "Fundamentalism." In *Religions of the World: A Comprehensive Encyclopedia of Beliefs and Practices,* edited by J. Gordon Melton and Martin Baumann, 1160–65. 2nd ed. Santa Barbara: ABC-CLIO, 2010.
———. "'Sheep Not of This Fold': Case Studies of Non-Baptist Student Populations at McMaster University, 1890–1929." In *Baptists and Public Life in Canada*, edited by Gordon L. Heath and Paul R. Wilson, 263–303. McMaster General Series 2. Canadian Baptist Historical Society Series 1. Eugene, OR: Pickwick Publications, 2012.

4

"The Great Contention"

Ontario Baptists and the Fundamentalist-Modernist Struggle for McMaster University, 1919–1927[1]

Doug Adams

IN THE SUMMER OF 1952, an article entitled "The Tragedy of Schism" appeared in *The Maritime Baptist* discussing the McMaster controversy of the 1920s and its aftermath. Its author, Dr. T. B. McDormand, the General Secretary of the Baptist Convention of Ontario and Quebec, spoke of the "division in our ranks, engineered by Dr. T. T. Shields."[2] Bristling at McDormand's characterization of his role, Shields retaliated with a series of articles he quickly labelled "The Great Contention."[3] The series that was to appear in *The Gospel Witness* for "four to six months"[4] actually lasted for the next eleven months and ran to thirty-eight chapters. Vigorously denying that he was the aggressor, and pointing to the "Disruption Caused by Modernists,"[5] Shields went to great lengths to prove that he was completely

---

1. This title ("The Great Contention") is borrowed from Dr. Shields' own account of the McMaster controversy which culminated in the rupture of the Baptist Convention of Ontario and Quebec in 1927. T. T. Shields, "The Great Contention," chapter 2, *Gospel Witness and Protestant Advocate*, 27 November 1952, 8–14. *Gospel Witness and Protestant Advocate* are hereafter *GW&PA* and references to *Gospel Witness* are *GW*.
2. T. T. Shields, "I Am Become a Fool in Glorying," *GW&PA*, 20 November 1952, 1.
3. T. T. Shields, "The Great Contention," chapter 2, *GW&PA*, 27 November 1952, 1.
4. T. T. Shields, "I Am Become a Fool in Glorying," *GW&PA*, 20 November 1952, 1.
5. T. T. Shields, "The Great Contention," chapter 2, *GW&PA*, 27 November 1952, 12.

justified in contending "for the faith once for all delivered to the saints."⁶ Setting aside the question of who was at fault for the disruption within Ontario Baptist circles during the 1920s, there can be little question that the outspoken fundamentalist, Dr. Thomas Todhunter Shields, played a prominent role. This article will attempt to explore the tempest that surrounded Shields from his first attempt to champion evangelical orthodoxy among Ontario Baptists in the 1919 Ottawa convention to his eventual eviction from the convention in 1927. Significant to that story is a consideration of the legacy of the rupture in the Ontario Baptist ranks. Shields' defence of orthodoxy was critical to the survival of a faith based evangelical testimony in Ontario Baptist circles. However, his methodology was angry and unnecessarily divisive. The separatist impulse that so characterized the evangelical offshoot of the controversy was as much a result of Shields' methods and his consequent failure to convince the convention of the truth of his allegations as it was to the biblical mandate to "come out from among them and be . . . separate."⁷ The construct that emerged in the Union of Regular Baptist Churches everywhere bore Shields' fingerprints. The legacy of controversy was both positive and negative, but the radical militancy of his efforts would leave deep scars both within and without his new denomination.

HISTORICAL CONTEXT

While the full storm of the fundamentalist-modernist controversy did not burst upon Baptists in Ontario and Quebec until the Ottawa convention of 1919, distant rumblings had been heard for several years. In Ontario the fundamentalist-modernist controversy can be traced back to McMaster University and its appointment of professors who actively challenged traditional views of inspiration. The debate first surfaced with the appointment of I. G. Matthews to the Chair of Hebrew in 1904. The matter was "briefly discussed . . . at the convention held at Jarvis Street Church in October, 1904."⁸ The debate was rekindled in 1910 when Dr. Elmore Harris made "certain charges" against Matthews relative to the inspiration issue "in the Senate of McMaster University."⁹ The matter came before the convention

---

6. T. T. Shields, "I Am Become a Fool in Glorying," *GW&PA*, 20 November 1952, 8.
7. 2 Cor 6:17.
8. Shields, *The Plot that Failed*, 38.
9. Shields, *The Plot that Failed*, 39.

in Bloor Street church in October 1910 with the report of the committee appointed to investigate Harris' charges. This also marked Shields' first involvement in the controversy. Since he was now the pastor of Jarvis Street Baptist Church, the leading church in the convention, Shields was persuaded by Dr. John MacNeill to second a compromise motion. MacNeill's motion ended the debate by leaving the matter to McMaster's Board of Governors to oversee. Shields long regretted his complicity in the matter. He realized in hindsight that his course of action was taken in ignorance and naiveté. It did provide, however, an excuse to challenge the university when the issue arose again in 1919.

Though Shields was dragged into the debate in its early stages by virtue of the significance of the church he then pastored, the roots of the issue clearly predated Shields' involvement. In many ways the fundamentalist-modernist controversy in Ontario was a spill-over from events occurring south of the American border.[10]

The American Context

Augustus Hopkins Strong was "perhaps the most notable Baptist Theologian of the nineteenth and early-twentieth century" and his "magnum opus," *Systematic Theology* "embodied the best . . . reflection of Baptist theological thought prior to the . . . Fundamentalist/Modernist controversy."[11] In an address entitled "Our Denominational Outlook" delivered at the general denominational meeting 19 May 1904, for the American Baptist Missionary Union, the American Baptist Publication Society, and the American Baptist Home Mission Society, Strong observed that "laxity of belief, worldliness of life and indifference to missions" were among the "deeply working causes of decline."[12]

Robert George Delnay, in his "History of the Baptist Bible Union," observed that Baptist fortunes in the United States were on the decline particularly in urban centres. He noted that "Christianity had already become identified with business and had lost most of its appeal to the industrial classes."[13] Educated by his own struggle with business interests in Jarvis Street, Shields soon took a leading role in the Bible Baptist Union's challenge

---

10. For the best and most recent treatment of the rise of theological liberalism in the Northern Baptist Convention see Straub, *The Making of a Battle Royal*.
11. Richardson, "Augustus Hopkins Strong."
12. Strong, "Our Denominational Outlook," 7.
13. Delnay, "A History of the Baptist Bible Union," 4.

to the suffocating influence of the Rockefellers upon the Northern Baptist Convention.[14]

At the denominational level, the governing apparatus was infiltrated by modernists, and Baptist theological institutions were everywhere filled with rationalism and theological liberalism. Strong's *Systematic Theology* of 1906 was prefaced with expressions of his distress at the theological tendencies which threatened to be more serious than the Unitarian issue of the previous century.[15] Shields, in his 1921 exposure of modernism in Jarvis Street, quoted Strong noting: "Dr. A. H. Strong—that great Baptist and great theologian—has said: 'The unbelief in our seminary teaching is like a blinding mist settling down upon our Churches,' and our Churches are 'being honeycombed with doubt and indifference.' Already this is creeping into our Canadian Churches."[16]

Delnay identified some of the Baptist intellectuals who were leading the way. These were men such as Walter Rauschenbusch, a member of Strong's own faculty; William Newton Clarke whose rationalism was evident before 1880 in his *Sixty Years with the Bible*; Nathaniel Schmidt who was "expelled from the faculty of Hamilton Seminary for denying the Canon, inspiration, the supernatural, the miracles, the deity and resurrection of Christ, as well as the ordinances as practiced by Baptists"; and Shailer Mathews whose *New Faith for Old* suggested that the divinity school of the University of Chicago was openly liberal from its very inception.[17] He also noted that of all the Baptist seminaries of the North, "only Central and Northern were still making any serious claim to Biblical orthodoxy by 1920."[18] As Shields struggled at home with the liberal infestation of McMaster University, he discovered the source of the blight in prominent American seminaries. As he joined the fight he was fully awakened to the reality that nearly all the

14. See for instance: T. T. Shields, "Mr. John D. Rockefeller, Jr., and Dr. Fosdick," *GW*, 28 May 1925, 9. T. T. Shields, "Shall the Northern Baptist Convention Remain the Religious Department of the Standard Oil Co.? Modernism Shows its Teeth—Fierce Battle at Seattle. Report of Baptist Bible Union and Northern Baptist Convention at Seattle, Wash., June 24th to July 4th." *GW*, 9 July 1925, 1–17. For an outstanding discussion of the business interests in Jarvis Street Baptist Church from this period see Wilson, "Baptists and Business." See also Adams, "The War of the Worlds," cf. pp. 102–69; 254–82.

15. Strong, *Systematic Theology*, viii–xii.

16. Shields, *The Inside of the Cup*, 34.

17. Delnay, "A History of the Baptist Bible Union," 3.

18. Delnay, "A History of the Baptist Bible Union," 3. See also Riley, "Breaking the Bible School Defense Line," 16 (Also published as a separate pamphlet), "Shields' Correspondence," Jarvis Street Baptist Church Archives (hereafter JSBC), Toronto,

leading Baptist seminaries across the continent had been so infected.[19] The fundamentalists' response was to establish "a last line of defense" in the Bible Institute movement with their claim "The Bible Training School has been God's answer to the scepticism of theological seminaries."[20] Shields, who had begun his own Bible Institute by 1924, was more than ready to support the cause by travelling across the continent to help in the reorganization of the Bible Institute of Los Angeles in its hour of crisis.[21] In 1952, he would dedicate several chapters of "The Great Contention" to tracing the theological links between the American modernists, and the faculty of McMaster University.[22]

British Context and the Emergence of the "Canadian Spurgeon"

In the years leading up to the fundamentalist-modernist battle, Shields realized the life-long dream of preaching in the famous Metropolitan Tabernacle of Charles Haddon Spurgeon. A youthful boast of rising "to heights no McMaster man ever dreamed of" was finally realized.[23] His first visit was arranged by the friend he first met in Vancouver in 1908, Rev. T. I. Stockley, the pastor of West Croydon Tabernacle.[24] Four more times during the war years Shields made the arduous trip to England by ship to exchange pulpits with his friend A. C. Dixon, who was by this time the pastor of the

---

19. Note: Shields was actively involved in controversies surrounding other Canadian Baptist seminaries. He was fully cognizant of the situation in Brandon College and often published editorials on the matter in *The Gospel Witness*. One major concern there was the presidency of Dr. H. P. Whidden, who was a University of Chicago graduate. This would boil over into the Ontario situation when Whidden was made Chancellor of McMaster. For more on Whidden and Shields see Rawlyk, "Whidden, T. T. Shields, Christian Higher Education, and McMaster University"; and Ellis "What the Times Demand." Cf. T. T. Shields, "The Baptist Union of Western Canada and Brandon College," *GW*, 14 February 1924, 7; "More about Western Baptists and Brandon College," *GW*, 20 March 1924, 7-9; "British Columbia Baptists and Brandon College," *GW*, 27 March 1924, 7.

20. W. B. Riley, "Breaking the Bible School Defense Line," *The Christian Fundamentalist*, April 1928, 3.

21. "Bible Institute of Los Angeles," "Shields' Correspondence," JSBC.

22. See Shields' discussion of Professor George Burman Foster, Professor George Cross, Professor Ernest W. Parsons, and Professor I. G. Matthews in chapters viii–xii of "The Great Contention," *GW&PA*, 38, 39, 40, 41, 42. Cf. Pinnock, "The Modernist Impulse at McMaster University," 193–207.

23. Dallimore, *Thomas Todhunter Shields*, 14.

24. Shields, *The Plot That Failed*, 35; *Sermons Preached*, 1908; Shields, "Letter Diary," 21 July 1915.

famous London church. Shields' repeated visits led some observers to begin to compare him to Spurgeon himself, and eventually earned him the appellation, "The Canadian Spurgeon."[25] Even after the rupture of their relationship, Dr. W. B. Riley, a leading American fundamentalist, called Shields "The Spurgeon of the American Continent."[26]

Shields' first entanglement with McMaster began in 1919. This was the year that Shields proposed the appointment of an "Examining and Stationing Committee of the Home Mission Board" to examine summer students for their orthodoxy before funding them to send them to churches. This was a response to the complaint coming from many churches concerning the orthodoxy of McMaster students. The board adopted the proposal and Shields wrote its constitution. However, the action was "vigorously opposed by McMaster University."[27] In the same year Shields used the excuse of his involvement in the 1910 motion to raise the issue of a successor for Matthews. A letter was sent to the Board of Governors and a sympathiser provided financial means to make sufficient copies to make a circular mailing throughout the convention. The Board of Governors "as a measure of expediency"[28] bowed to the pressure and appointed an orthodox professor, Rev. H. S. Curr of Scotland.[29]

Perhaps as a retaliatory response to Curr's appointment, on 2 October 1919 an editorial appeared in *The Canadian Baptist*. At the time Shields strongly suspected it was written by a McMaster professor. The editorial entitled "Inspiration and Authority of Scripture" was a sharp censure on the "crude theological views" still held by those who believed the traditional view of inspiration.[30] In the evaluation of the ultimate origins of the controversy and hence the genesis of the fundamentalist movement as represented by the Shields' faction, it is interesting to note that both sides of the debate understood this as a continuation of a struggle that first erupted in Britain. The McMaster liberals saw the issue as a matter which had already

---

25. "Dr. Shields, Baptist Warrior," *Toronto Telegram*, 17 October 1927. L. K. Tarr credited the editor of the *British Weekly*. Sir W. R. Nicol's for the title "The Canadian Spurgeon."

26. Rev. R. W. Bennett to T. T. Shields, 22 June 1938, JSBC.

27. Shields, *The Plot That Failed*, 99.

28. Shields, *The Plot That Failed*, 122.

29. Shields, *The Plot That Failed*, 101.

30. Shields, *The Plot That Failed*, 128.

been settled in England. In the 2 October editorial the correspondent made the claim:

> Some fifteen or twenty years ago the question of the inspiration and authority of the Scriptures agitated the evangelical churches of Great Britain a great deal more than it does to-day. This agitation has now largely ceased in the old land because the leading men in whom these churches have large confidence have brought themselves and their people into clearer light. Occasional echoes of the old acrimonious disputations are still heard there, but in the main they have ceased to interest or influence intelligent Christian people.[31]

Shields and his conservative friends were quick to point out that the consequences were devastating to the health of British evangelicalism. One respondent to the editorial, C. J. Holman KC, a man who was closely affiliated for many years with Shields, noted:

> The decrease of membership in the evangelical churches of the United Kingdom in the ten years from 1906 to 1916 is as follows: Baptists, 27,712; Congregationalists, 9,300; Wesleyan Methodists, 49,053. And in the same period the scholars in the Sunday Schools have decreased as follows: Baptists, 59,026; Congregationalists, 104,554; Wesleyan Methodists, 103,409. From the foregoing figures it is apparent that, apart from the effect on the adults, the Bible teaching in the Sunday Schools in the light of 'Modern Scholarship' has 'ceased to interest' a large number of the rising generation.[32]

Shields noted that these sad results clearly validated C. H. Spurgeon's claims of decline. In a series of articles published in 1887, Spurgeon contended that the Baptist church in particular and evangelicalism at large were in the throes of a significant spiritual downgrade. David Bebbington rightly noted that "Spurgeon's protest against emerging liberal tendencies may not have carried many with him at the time, but the enduring esteem in which he was held in the whole Evangelical world ensured a wider hearing for conservative opinion in subsequent generations."[33] Shields, throughout his career, sought to capitalize on that esteem. Consciously borrowing Spurgeon's

---

31. Anon, "Inspiration and the Authority of Scripture," in Shields, *The Plot That Failed*, 128.

32. Shields, *The Plot That Failed*, 127.

33. Bebbington, *Evangelicalism in Modern Britain*, 146.

phrase, he labelled this the "Canadian Baptist 'down grade' movement."[34] So far as Shields was concerned, the roots of his fundamentalist protest were British and Spurgeonic.

Upon reading the 2 October editorial, Shields reacted with great indignation. His first response was to preach on the matter the following Sunday in Jarvis Street Baptist Church. The message contained a strong denunciation of the article and announced his intention to present a resolution at the Ottawa convention which was only three weeks away. He argued that the resolution "would afford opportunity for the Convention to declare itself for or against the principles of the editorial."[35] Shields' comments about his audience that morning was a significant commentary on how deeply intertwined the matters of church, denomination and university were:

> Just in front of me, slightly to the left, sat Dr. D. E. Thomson, K.C., Chairman of the Board of Governors of McMaster University; behind him, Mr. F. L. Ratcliff, ex-Chairman of the Publication Board; on the right, Mr. James Ryrie, chairman of the Home Mission Board; the Secretary of the Foreign Mission Board; Secretary of the Sunday School Board; and many others who were members of other Boards, including several who were members of the Board of Governors of McMaster University, were there.[36]

This sermon and the resulting storm surrounding the Ottawa convention marked the first step towards a significant split in Shields' own church, Jarvis Street, and in the convention itself. Years later, as he reflected on his decision to decline the honour of pastoring Spurgeon's Metropolitan Tabernacle, Shields divulged the measure of his commitment to the battle that was then shaping up. Despite his cherished goal of rising to the "most famous pulpit on earth," Shields readily sacrificed his own dreams abroad

---

34. In 1887 C. H. Spurgeon published in the *Sword and Trowel* a series of articles under the heading of "The Downgrade." The major issue was the question of the inerrancy or infallibility of scripture. The resulting "Downgrade Controversy" led to Spurgeon's withdrawal from the Baptist Union and a polarization of evangelical opinion. cf. T. T. Shields, "Why I am Not a Modernist, But Believe the Bible to be the Word of God," *GW&PA*, 13 July 1950, 12. Here Shields challenged some of Spurgeon's methods but clearly identified the Downgrade Controversy with the fundamentalist-modernist controversy of his own period. See also Erroll Hulse, "Charles Haddon Spurgeon and the Downgrade Controversy," 169–86.

35. Shields, *The Plot That Failed*, 123.

36. Shields, *The Plot That Failed*, 124.

to stand for the principles at stake in Canada.[37] Having thrown down the gauntlet at the Ottawa convention of 1919, he realized "that it would be utterly cowardly to retire from the field before the victory was won."[38] When Shields handily won the first round in that convention, his enemies mounted an insurgency in his own church, a revolt which he barely survived. Realizing that this personal assault had originated with the modernistic forces entrenched in McMaster University, Shields vigorously turned his attention to rousting his foes from their purloined stronghold. Over the course of the next six years, Shields became consumed with his passion to liberate McMaster from what he saw as its modernist overlords.

SHIELDS, THE BAPTIST BIBLE UNION, AND THE WAR ON MODERNISM

It is very significant that just as the battle was breaking out on the convention floor in the Baptist Convention of Ontario and Quebec, Shields was becoming actively involved in the fundamentalist struggles south of the border. Indeed, within months of launching his campaign against McMaster, he would be inducted as President of the Baptist Bible Union (BBU). This occurred at the organization's initial convention in Kansas City, 15 May 1923. In his inaugural address, "A Holy War," Shields immediately set his militant stamp upon the BBU with a declaration of war. In his mind, the "express purpose" of the organization was for "declaring and waging relentless and uncompromising war on Modernism on all fronts."[39] Almost immediately Shields appealed to a military service model and called up images of the Great War and the entire separation required of soldiers upon enlistment.

In this war on modernism, Shields demanded the same level of commitment. He decried the feeble allegiance of many Christians to the cause: "The New Testament standard for measuring recruits has been lowered, and people have been received into the church as though they were registering for attendance at a summer picnic, instead of enlisting for active service in a great war."[40] Shields' goal—which would require the expenditure of enormous personal energies over the next five years—was "to mobilize the

---

37. T. T. Shields, "This Shall be Written for the Generation to Come," *GW*, 25 September 1947, cited in Dallimore *Thomas Todhunter Shields*, 34.

38. T. T. Shields, "The Great Contention," chapter 34 *GW&PA*, 16 July 1953, 12.

39. T. T. Shields, "A Holy War," *GW*, 21 June 1923, 5.

40. T. T. Shields, "A Holy War," *GW*, 21 June 1923, 3.

conservative Baptist forces of the Continent."[41] He envisioned an intensive recruitment campaign in both Canada and United States uniting "in one great fellowship all Baptists who believe the Bible to be the Word of God."[42]

His recruitment standards were exacting. In light of the Northern Baptist Convention's rejection of a creed, Shields informed his audience that the BBU would require subscription to a confession of faith. This would be a seal of fidelity to the Baptist cause. The second standard was that they were to be committed fighters: "I desire to act this evening as a recruiting agent to call to the colours all men of might . . . who are men of war fit for the battle." Quoting a former American president, he noted "Your own Theodore Roosevelt once said: 'There may often be justification for not fighting at all. There can never be justification for fighting feebly.'"[43] The third recruitment standard was the commitment of entire separation unto Christ: "The Baptist Bible Union will fight side by side with anyone who is really separated unto Christ." For Shields, separation meant no toleration of, or compromise with modernism. He avowed "[we] will not be deceived and disarmed by a religious pacificism [sic] which is only disguised Modernism." Perhaps reflecting the prevailing disillusionment with the Fundamental Fellowship, he noted "Our greatest danger is the religious pacifist: the man who while professing to believe the principles of evangelical orthodoxy yet insists that it is wrong to contend for them."[44]

In his address the following Sunday entitled "Contending for the Faith," Shields stood in his own pulpit and made the announcement of his presidency, almost as an afterthought. At the very end of his message, he

---

41. T. T. Shields, "A Holy War," *GW*, 21 June 1923, 3.

42. T. T. Shields, "Editorial, The Baptist Bible Union," *GW*, 9 August 1923. Note: The BBU was built as a continent-wide organization. Shields actively campaigned in both Canada and United States to establish local branches of the BBU. He was particularly active in Western Canada. See for instance T. T. Shields, "The Editor Abroad; Further Observations on Conditions in the West," *GW*, 5 March 1925, 9. Cf. Burkinshaw, *Pilgrims in Lotus Land*, 96–99. He built significant contacts in the East as well. Under his inspiration J. J. Sidey and J. B. Daggett formed the Maritime Christian Fundamentalist Association. See Rawlyk, *Wrapped up in God*, 128–31. See also Rawlyk, *Champions of the Truth*. Though the situation at Brandon College generated significant attention, the primary focus of the BBU in Canada became the issue of McMaster University.

43. T. T. Shields, "A Holy War," *GW*, 21 June 1923, 6.

44. The quotations after footnote 43 are taken from T. T. Shields, "A Holy War," *GW*, 21 June 1923, 6. Note: The Fundamentalist Fellowship was an earlier and more moderate manifestation of fundamentalist response to the modernism encroaching upon the Northern Convention.

noted: "There is a little matter that I suppose I ought to tell you. It was against my judgment, but at that great meeting in Kansas City they insisted upon electing the pastor of this church as President of the Baptist Bible Union of America."[45] It was a telling statement of Jarvis Street's commitment to the cause that not a ripple of dissent was registered.

BOARD OF GOVERNORS DEBACLE

With a growing entanglement in the fundamentalist resistance to modernist gains in the Northern Baptist Convention south of the border, Shields was not prepared to ignore the tentacles of the same modernist threat spreading into his own backyard. In some ways the skirmishes with Shields' domestic foes were minor irritants in comparison with the larger conflict in which the BBU would be engaged. Nevertheless, because the Baptist Convention of Ontario and Quebec was his home turf, the local fight took on a deeply emotional character. It became the most virulent battle of them all.

In 1920, Shields had been appointed to the Board of Governors of McMaster University and he would hold that office until his ejection during the Toronto convention of 19 October 1926.[46] In one of the earliest editions of his fledgling enterprise, *The Gospel Witness*, Shields served notice of his intent to exercise his authority in watching for "doctrinal defection." He noted the great ideal that "education should go hand in hand with evangelism" and expressed his conviction that he felt it "worthwhile making great sacrifices to maintain a Baptist University." However, he was quick to point out that "the only legitimate claim a university, as a religious university, can have upon the special support of Baptists is that it is doing Baptist work." This work, he believed, included "producing Baptist preachers who will preach what Baptists believe; teachers who will teach the principles for which Baptists stand; and leaders in business, professional, and political life, who hold uncompromisingly the principles of 'the faith once for all delivered to the saints.'" However, he quickly warned that "doctrinal defection" would "inevitably force a reconsideration of the whole question of the wisdom of taxing the resources of the Denomination for the support of a

---

45. T. T. Shields, "Contending for the Faith," *GW*, 31 May 1923, 7.

46. "Proceedings," *Baptist Year Book*, 1926, 37–38. With a large majority Shields was by convention vote removed from his governorship. His eligibility to sit as a delegate to the following year's convention was also revoked. Shields refused to acquiesce to this judgment and returned the following year to sit as a delegate for Jarvis Street and his name was not removed from McMaster's list of governors until the following year.

university which would be Baptist only in name." In that case he argued it would be better to leave "university education to the state and concentrate the denominational energy upon the work of providing means of giving a sound thorough theological education to ministerial students." Though he professed his belief in the place of a "strong, independent, Baptist University, consecrated to the high and holy task of producing strong Baptist leaders for every walk of life," he made it clear that failure to serve traditional Baptist interests would be to forfeit Baptist support.[47]

As the 1922 convention approached, Shields opened his crusade against McMaster administrators with an announcement that he would be publishing a series of articles on denominational matters over the next few weeks. The articles that followed set the tone of the debate and established the methodology and trajectory of his campaign. The first two articles raised serious concerns about the viability of Woodstock and Moulton colleges, the continuance of the Arts department at McMaster University and how educational money was raised and spent within the denomination. Shields likely had little idea of the storm of protest that his next article would provoke. Published just eight days before the beginning of the annual convention, the matters addressed by the editorial "How to Improve McMaster" would be fresh on everyone's mind as the convention convened. This proved to be the most controversial of the series of articles leading up to the convention. Shields opened the article with a discussion of the Trust Deed to which the University was bound by virtue of its Act of Incorporation and the terms under which the "Honourable William McMaster" conveyed "the lands and premises" to the trustees of the university. For Shields, this would be the defining issue of the whole controversy.

The Trust Deed was distinctively Baptist and contained reference to the cardinal doctrines of the inspiration of Scripture, the Trinity, human depravity, election, effectual calling, the atonement, justification, preservation of the saints, sanctification, the resurrection of the dead, final judgment, and the eternal state. It was also clearly a *Regular* Baptist statement containing the provision that "parties so baptized [immersion in the name of the Father, Son, and the Holy Spirit] are alone entitled to Communion at the Lord's Table, and that a Gospel church is a body of baptized believers voluntarily associated together for the service of God."[48] Shields boasted

47. The quotations in this paragraph are taken from T. T. Shields, "A Great Opportunity," *GW*, 3 June 1926, 2.

48. T. T. Shields, "How to Improve McMaster," *GW*, 12 October 1922, 1. Note: A

that because of this document McMaster had largely been preserved from apostasy and "on the whole, stands today truer to the evangelical position than any other." However, he was quick to note that it had "a certain proneness to wander into unbaptistic paths." The guard against this drift, he argued, was the convention's determination to hold the university to the standards outlined in their incorporation documents. He also believed that "Academic or doctrinaire views of religion can be accurately appraised only when tested in the crucible of experience." Shields predicated that it was the common man, "be he layman or pastor . . . engaged in practical everyday ministry" who was best qualified to "judge of the value of academic religious pronouncements." Hence, McMaster was subject to "the collective judgment of the churches' practical Christian experience."[49]

By this line of reasoning Shields established his *modus operandi*. Since the university was subject to the convention, and since the convention was made up of its people, Shields determined to take his message to the common people of the denomination, its pastors and laymen. He would reach them largely by means of *The Gospel Witness* and whatever third party influence he could stir up. He would appeal to their judgment on the convention floor where he believed the majority of the Baptist populace would vote to hold McMaster accountable.

In his first appeal to the general constituency Shields seriously overstepped his bounds. In his mind this convention provided a critical opportunity to "Improve McMaster" by electing the right governors. Each year four of the sixteen governors retired and four were elected to fill the empty positions. It was common for a retiring governor to be re-elected to his office. What followed was an assessment of the potential candidates for the four retiring governors. Among those retiring this particular year and possibly seeking re-election were three men Shields viewed with deep suspicion. Seeing his opportunity to clean house once and for all, Shields went for the jugular. Trading on his own reputation, Shields seriously impugned the reputation of leading members of the Board of Governors. In the exchange, Shields came out the loser and seriously damaged whatever goodwill he had left in the denomination.

---

church was considered to be a Regular Baptist Church if it practiced closed communion.

49. The quotations after footnote 48 are from T. T. Shields, "How to Improve McMaster," *GW*, 12 October 1922, 2.

DR. W. H. P. FAUNCE AND THE 1924 LONDON CONVENTION

The real showdown between fundamentalism and modernism erupted in two separate issues. The first was the 1923–24 controversy surrounding the awarding of an honorary degree to an avowed modernist. The second was the 1925–27 controversy over the appointment of Dr. L. H. Marshall, a suspected modernist, to the faculty of McMaster. In the former affair, Shields was able to regain some ground, but in the latter controversy Shields soon found himself and his following outside of the convention altogether.

As the denomination looked forward to its annual convention in October of 1923, in Olivet Baptist Church, Montreal, Shields was heavily engaged at home reorganizing his church and Sunday-school. At the same time, he was busily involved in the affairs of the BBU, having just a few months earlier accepted its presidency. Perhaps his preoccupation with these tasks distracted him, but as the Baptist denomination headed into the 1923 convention things were relatively quiet. The convention passed amicably, but within weeks of its conclusion a new crisis rocked the denomination. The first public indication of trouble appeared in a *Gospel Witness* article entitled "A Regrettable Incident." The editorial largely consisted of Shields' recent correspondence with the Chancellor of McMaster University, Dr. H. P. Whidden.[50] This time the matter was of much more serious import and the publication of Shields' "protest" immediately stirred up a storm within the denomination.

The matter at hand related to the decision of the Senate to confer an honorary Doctor of Laws degree on a leading modernist, Dr. W. H. P. Faunce. Shields' first letter to Whidden offered an insincere apology for refusing to attend the convocation ceremony in which Whidden was installed as Chancellor. In one breath he was apologizing for the slight, but in the next he was informing Whidden that he had voted against his appointment "as Chancellor on account of the record of Brandon College under your Presidency." Having made his attitudes toward Whidden perfectly clear he indicated that Whidden's investiture was not the real reason for his absence. In celebration of Whidden's investiture, the Senate had decided to use the event as an occasion to confer an honorary degree on a renowned Baptist leader. Faunce, the man chosen, was the President of Brown University. Citing at some length a pamphlet of Faunce entitled "What are the Fundamentals?" Shields demonstrated Faunce's ridicule of the very doctrines that McMaster's Trust Deed enumerated and which the Board professed

---

50. T. T. Shields, "A Regrettable Incident," *GW*, 29 November 1923, 9.

to believe in their 1922 convention report. Almost as a taunt, Shields commented: "It must be known to yourself and to the Senate of the University that although called a Baptist, the principles of Dr. Faunce's teaching would absolutely destroy the foundations upon which McMaster University professes to stand." He concluded: "I frankly say that in my humble judgment the presence of Dr. Faunce on the McMaster platform is a dishonour to the University and an insult to the Denomination."[51] Later, in December, at a six-day conference of "Fundamentalists" held in Calvary Baptist Church, New York, Shields shocked his audience with an emotionally charged outburst denouncing Faunce as a heretic. "I refuse to stand on the same platform with one who would deny the divinity of Christ."[52]

Shields had no doubt that there was an insult implicit in the Senate's choice of Faunce. However, it was an insult to which Shields primarily would have been sensitive. Many within the Canadian context were largely oblivious to the role played by Brown University and its president in the fundamentalist-modernist conflicts south of the border.[53] Indeed, in his response to Shields, Whidden expressed something of that ignorance: "Probably the members of the Senate had never read a theological statement by Dr. Faunce. I myself had not seen any of his pamphlets."[54] Yet, for Shields the insult was too blatant to be missed. As Shields was the newly anointed president of the BBU, Faunce was the face of much of his opposition in the Northern Baptist Convention, and he epitomized Shields' angst against those who had infiltrated and "burglarized" many of the leading Baptist theological institutions in the Northern states.[55] Seeing the same perfidy at work now in his own back yard and realizing that through devious means the decision had been made behind his back in a way that skilfully excluded his interference, Shields determined to publish.

---

51. The quotations in this paragraph are from Shields, "A Regrettable Incident," *GW*, 29 November 1923, 10.

52. "Won't Break Bread with Foe of Christ Says Rev. Dr. Shields," *Toronto Telegram Clippings File* (hereafter *TTCF*), 4 December 1923, 11.

53. It should be noted that in the 1923 Atlantic City convention there had been a significant protest by fundamentalists led by Dr. Straton to prevent the keynote speaker, Dr. W. H. P. Faunce, from speaking because he was an avowed modernist. Delnay, "A History of the Baptist Bible Union," 67.

54. T. T. Shields, "A Regrettable Incident," *GW*, 29 November 1923, 11.

55. T. T. Shields, "The Baptist Bible Union At New York," *GW*, 13 December 1923, 3. Cf. Delnay, "A History of the Baptist Bible Union," 67.

Knowing full well the storm of protest that would come from disseminating his protest publicly, Shields justified his actions: "It is impossible for the Senate to rescind its action; the damage has already been done, and it has been done publicly; and I feel that I should be recreant to my trust as a minister of the gospel if I did not make my protest equally public."[56] Furthermore, since this action was openly taken by the authority of the Senate, Shields insisted on his right openly to "dissociate myself as a member of the Senate and Board of Governors from the Senate's action in conferring an honorary degree upon one whose teachings I regard as being absolutely anti-Christian."[57]

Perhaps it was Shields' growing awareness of the methods of his modernist foes, or perhaps it was his own growing paranoia following his war experiences and the 1921 Jarvis Street schism, but Shields immediately suspected an insidious plot to insinuate modernist influences into the school: "I cannot help asking myself what sinister influence seems ever to be seeking to commit the University to a course which one cannot approve without being guilty of treason to Christ and His Gospel."[58] That Shields took the action of the Senate as a personal insult was born out by his press release in New York a few days after the convocation ceremonies had occurred. On 5 December, in an Associated Press dispatch entitled "Shields Throws Down Gauntlet to Faunce," Shields "characterized the Brown University head, and all other Modernists, as 'religious cuckoos,' and asserted that the Fundamentalists 'throw down the gauntlet' to them." Shields broadcast in the same release that "he absented himself from the installation services of the new chancellor of McMaster University, Toronto, because Dr. Faunce was given an honorary degree."[59] A matter that most board members felt was a private institutional matter had now been inflated into an international incident. Worse yet, it had hurled them into the epicentre of the fundamentalist-modernist conflict. The Senate's extraordinary reactions to this series of events reflected its own chagrin at the unwanted publicity. Knowing now that it had 'poked' the BBU 'bear,' the Senate moved quickly to isolate Shields and protect itself from the deployment of BBU's resources.

---

56. T. T. Shields, "A Regrettable Incident," *GW*, 29 November 1923, 11.

57. T. T. Shields, "A Regrettable Incident," *GW*, 29 November 1923, 10.

58. T. T. Shields, "A Regrettable Incident," *GW*, 29 November 1923, 10.

59. Associated Press Dispatch, "Shields Throws Down Gauntlet to Faunce," *Toronto Daily Star*, 6 December 1923, 3.

On 14 January 1924, the Senate called an emergency meeting ostensibly to comply with Shields' request that his letters of protest to Whidden be read to the board. The meeting was "arranged to suit the convenience" of Shields. The board's resolution on that occasion indicated that this was their first meeting since the Montreal convention in October of 1923.[60] Nevertheless, the lengthy and detailed preamble to their resolution suggested that a certain measure of orchestration of their agenda had been engaged in prior to the meeting. Shields later complained that "It was evident from the beginning of the meeting on January 14th that every man had been assigned his part."[61] He also noted the judicial character of the meeting and the fact that the judiciary he faced consisted predominately of the disenchanted secessionists from his church who had finally discovered a convenient forum in which to wreak their revenge. At no point did the discussion include a consideration of the complaints that Shields had raised and for which the meeting had ostensibly been called. The four-hour meeting did, however, entertain a discussion of every conceivable objection to Shields' actions. The board's defensive reaction to Shields' public exposure of its actions consisted of a protracted personal attack on Shields. They accused him of intentionally missing the meetings in which this was proposed, even though they knew that he was half-way across the continent at the time. They accused him of deliberately damaging the credibility of both Chancellor Whidden and the university itself. They castigated him for embarrassing Faunce, "the honoured President of the oldest university in America, controlled by Baptists." Finally, they condemned him for dropping McMaster from Jarvis Street's budget. The Senate then passed three resolutions which were to be "communicated to the constituency through 'The Canadian Baptist.'" These resolutions expressed "unqualified disapproval of the conduct and methods of Dr. Shields," an expression of "confidence in Chancellor Whidden, Dean Farmer and Professor McCrimmon" and also their "deep resentment at the unwarranted reflections attempted to be cast on them by Dr. Shields." They concluded with an expression of their belief "that the actions and attitude of Dr. Shields make it obviously impossible to cooperate with him longer in any constructive work with any hope of success."[62]

60. "McMaster and Faunce Degree," *Canadian Baptist*, 17 January 1924, 5.

61. T. T. Shields, "McMaster's Approval of Dr. Faunce's Infidelity," *GW*, 31 January 1924, 23.

62. The quotations after footnote 61 are from T. T. Shields, "McMaster's Approval of

With *The Canadian Baptist*'s publication of the Senate's resolutions, Shields immediately retaliated. He announced to the press that on the evening of 24 January he intended to respond to the Senate's action in an address delivered at his church. The address, "McMaster' Approval of Dr. Faunces' Infidelity," was subsequently published as a 56-page special edition of *The Gospel Witness*. The demand for this issue was so heavy that it ran through four editions. The next day the public press announced: "Shields Proposes to Starve McMaster into Submission." Characterizing his response to the Senate's action the *Star* reporter quoted Shields in his defiant declaration, "It is war . . . It is war on McMaster as it is at present." The report's subtitle noted Shields' call for all "Baptists to Withdraw Financial Support from the University until 'McMaster behaves herself.'" [63]

With the wide publication of the controversy throughout the following months, both from the pages of *The Gospel Witness* and *The Canadian Baptist*, there was little doubt that the question of the Faunce degree would be the main focus of the 1924 London convention. Shields reflected: "We called it a 'blunder' in the beginning, but their [the Senate's] justification of the 'blunder' was little less than treason." He appealed the issue to the convention: "*We repeat, the one single issue at the Convention will be this, 'Does the Convention approve of the use of McMaster University's powers to honour a man who dishonours Christ?' Let the delegates come prepared to answer that question with their ballots!*"[64]

On the convention floor the matter erupted with the Chancellor's presentation of the report of the Senate and Board of Governors of McMaster University. Shields immediately rose to make an amendment. Noting the wide discussion of "the propriety of the action of McMaster University in conferring an Honorary degree upon one who is known as a leader among Modernist theologians," Shields moved the resolution "That this Convention, without intending any reflection upon the distinguished recipient of the degree, hereby declares that the action of the University must not be interpreted as an endorsement by this convention of the theological views of the Modernist theologian referred to; but reaffirms its adherence to the

---

Dr. Faunce's Infidelity," *GW*, 31 January 1924, 27.

63. "Shields Proposes to Starve McMaster into Submission," *Toronto Daily Star*, 25 January 1924, 11. Note: In April he published an article in *The Gospel Witness* entitled "The Necessity for Passive Resistance" in which he reiterated his appeal: "it becomes a military necessity to cut off supplies altogether." *GW*, 3 April 1924, 10.

64. T. T. Shields, "What is The Issue?" *GW*, 2 October 1924, 13–14. Italics are as they appear in the original article.

doctrinal standards incorporated in the Trust Deeds and Charter of McMaster University." To this Shields added a resolution forcing the board "to refrain, in the future, from conferring a degree upon any religious leader whose theological views are known to be opposed to the principles of Evangelical Christianity." An amendment to the amendment was moved which would essentially have replaced Shields' amendment with an expression of confidence in the Senate. When put to a vote, the amendment to the amendment was lost by two votes, 264 to 262. After hours of resolutions and counter resolutions, Shields suggested to the president that a committee of five be "appointed to retire" and to frame a resolution "that would be acceptable to the delegates."[65] This recommendation was accepted by the convention and a committee consisting of both sides of the argument, including both Whidden and Shields, withdrew to deliberate.

Upon their return, a resolution concerning honorary degrees was moved by Shields and seconded by Whidden: "That without implying any reflection upon the Senate, this Convention relies upon the Senate to exercise care that honorary degrees be not conferred upon religious leaders whose theological views are known to be out of harmony with the cardinal principles of evangelical Christianity."[66] The motion was carried unanimously. To the chagrin of the Senate, Shields' complaint had been heard and acted upon with a diminishment of their own powers. To add insult to injury, Shields was once again nominated and elected to the Board of Governors. As if rubbing salt in an open wound, Shields made much of the failed amendment to the amendment in the afternoon session. Since this was the only expression of confidence in the Senate placed on the floor of the convention throughout the whole discussion, Shields gloatingly noted that "for the first time in thirty-six years the Convention refused the University a vote of confidence." This, however, marked the high point of Shields' fundamentalist crusade in the Baptist Convention of Ontario and Quebec, and the critical vote was only won by two votes. Given Shields' penchant for publishing insult and innuendo, the next round was destined to go very differently.

---

65. The quotations in this paragraph are from "Proceedings," *Baptist Year Book* 1924, 40.

66. *Baptist Year Book*, 1924, 43.

PROFESSOR L. H. MARSHALL AND THE 1925 HAMILTON CONVENTION

The controversy that erupted with the appointment of Professor Marshall to the faculty of McMaster University was the most divisive and prolonged of all the fundamentalist-modernist battles waged within the Baptist Convention of Ontario and Quebec. The struggle between the warring factions entirely riveted the attention and drained the energies of the entire denomination for the next three annual conventions. Given the extensive character of the records from the period, only the most cursory treatment can be offered.[67]

Shields' fears for McMaster's orthodoxy were further exacerbated in July 1925 when he received notification of an emergency meeting of the Senate ostensibly to fill the "vacant professorships" in the Faculty of Theology after the deaths of professors Dr. Joseph L. Gilmour and Dr. Stuart S. Bates.[68] Shields, conveniently for the Senate, was across the continent in Los Angeles, California, at the time of the announcement. He immediately responded by telegram and warned the Senate that "an important action such as filling vacant professorships at emergency meeting called midsummer when some Convention—elected representatives known so far away make attendance impossible" would not be approved by the Convention.[69] Despite Shields' warning, the Senate went ahead with appointments. A formal announcement was made "by the Senate and Board of McMaster University that Rev. L. H. Marshall, of Coventry, England, had been appointed to the Chair of Practical Theology in succession to Dr. Gilmour."[70] Shortly after this action, unsolicited by himself, Shields received two second-hand communications from England concerning Marshall's appointment. The author of these missives was Rev. W. M. Robertson, minister of a Baptist church in Liverpool, the same city where Marshall for some time had pastored. Upon hearing of Marshall's appointment he wrote a warning letter: "Mr. Marshall is a Modernist and of entirely different stamp to Rev. Henry

---

67. For a fuller treatment of each of these battles see Adams, "War of the Worlds," 430–96.

68. Shields announced the passing of these men in: "Educational Vacancies," *GW*, 25 January 1925, 9.

69. T. T. Shields, "Will the Convention Approve the Appointment of McMaster's New Professor, Rev. H. T. Marshall?" *GW*, 15 October 1925, 14.

70. T. T. Shields, "Shall Modernism Capture McMaster?" *GW*, 29 October 1925, 1.

S. Curr whose place he is to take."⁷¹ Furthermore, noted Robertson, "The church of which he was pastor here is open membership. A few pointed questions on Inspiration, bodily Resurrection of Christ would reveal his position." He concluded: "I learn from Rev. Hughes of Toronto, now in this country, that a fight has already taken place over Modernism at McMaster; and if this appointment is confirmed, Modernism had gained a great victory."⁷² A second letter responding to an additional enquiry was a further delineation of the matter.

With both these letters in hand, and now thoroughly alarmed, on 24 September 1925, Shields sent a communication to the Senate. Acknowledging that "no word spoken or written by Mr. Marshall is quoted" and that this only represented "an opinion of a minister who laboured with Mr. Marshall in the same city," Shields asserted that it would be unfair to pass judgment on Marshall on the basis of the letters. However, he did feel that in light of the seriousness of the charges that "Mr Marshall should come before the Senate, and that permission should be given to all members to question him touching the subject represented by these letters; or, otherwise, that a committee of the Senate should be appointed to interview Mr. Marshall with the same end in view."⁷³

Not surprisingly, Shields met with serious resistance when the convened Senate met to discuss the matter. Most members of the board seemed to be quite perturbed at Shields for raising the matter at all. Although Shields was careful to avoid passing judgment on the basis of the letters, Dr. John McNeill insisted that "the submission of them here tends to prejudice the whole case." The consensus of the board was that "the Senate had already satisfied itself of Mr. Marshall's fitness." If he was still concerned, Shields was told to interview Marshall himself. Chancellor Whidden, showing remarkably little understanding of his opponent, suggested that Shields invite Marshall to preach in Jarvis Street "and sometime to play a game of golf with him!" Shields responded: "We need make no comment on the character of such a suggestion, except frankly to say to our readers that with great reluctance and disappointment we submitted our communication to the

---

71. The correspondent was incorrect at this point. Marshall was appointed to take the place of Gilmour, not Curr.

72. T. T. Shields, "Will the Convention Approve the Appointment of McMaster's New Professor, Rev. H. T. Marshall?" *GW*, 15 October 1925, 14.

73. The quotations in this paragraph are from T. T. Shields, "Will the Convention Approve the Appointment of McMaster's New Professor, Rev. H. T. Marshall?" *GW*, 15 October 1925, 15.

Senate as relating to matters of infinitely greater moment than the playing of golf."[74]

Over the following weeks the controversy over Marshall's actual theological position rapidly escalated. A Senate meeting called to try and defuse Shields' concerns largely backfired. Their discussions surrounded Marshall's view of "questions of authorship and dates of Old Testament Scriptures," and his view of "the resurrection of Christ" which he professed to interpret as a spiritual resurrection.[75] Shields went into the critical Senate meeting with concerns about unsubstantiated allegations regarding Marshall but came out with the conviction that everything of which Robertson had warned them was true. He was also horrified at the casual attitudes toward significant issues of modern critical thought taken by both Chancellor Whidden and Dean Farmer. No one on the Board seemed at all concerned that the charges might be true. In the end, the Senate refused to take any further action except to appoint a committee "to consider what action the Senate should take in view of our [Shields'] communication."[76]

Over the course of the following months and years, it became painfully evident that Shields' concerns were fully warranted. Waves of controversy crashed upon the denomination in regular succession as the fundamentalists exposed one after another of Marshall's theological deviations. The first struggle erupted in the 1925 Hamilton convention. For the McMaster faction, Stanley Avenue Baptist Church, Hamilton, was decidedly hostile territory. Along with Jarvis Street Baptist Church, Stanley Avenue was one of the largest and most fundamental Baptist churches in the convention. Pre-convention rallies of the BBU were held simultaneously in both Jarvis Street and Stanley Avenue Baptist Churches as the delegates were gathering.[77] McMaster officials were assured of a rocky reception.

As expected, the presentation of the McMaster University report generated a great deal of interest and opposition. The consequent debate featured bitter recriminations, grandstanding by Shields, and backlash from

---

74. The quotations in this paragraph are from T. T. Shields, "Will the Convention Approve the Appointment of McMaster's New Professor, Rev. H. T. Marshall?" *GW*, 15 October 1925, 16.

75. T. T. Shields, "Will the Convention Approve the Appointment of McMaster's New Professor, Rev. H. T. Marshall?" *GW*, 15 October 1925, 16.

76. T. T. Shields, "Will the Convention Approve the Appointment of McMaster's New Professor, Rev. H. T. Marshall?" *GW*, 15 October 1925, 16.

77. T. T. Shields, "A Great Pre-Convention, Baptist Bible Union Conference at Hamilton," *GW*, 17 September 1925, 7.

Marshall himself. Shields, armed with stenographic reports, published in *The Gospel Witness* a blow-by-blow account of the whole affair. The major issue was Farmer's revelation of Marshall's acceptance of the Samuel Rolles Driver view of the inspiration of Scripture, which was critical of the historicity of the Old Testament. Shields immediately published excerpts from Driver's books to demonstrate the author's wholesale attack on the Bible's historicity and his denial of supernaturalism, and by extension of Christ's infallibility.[78] In subsequent weeks Shields would further develop his analysis of the danger implicit in Driver's higher criticism. In a sermon preached Sunday evening, 8 November 1925, entitled "Will Baptists Consent to McMaster's Throwing over Redemption by Blood?" Shields demonstrated the ramifications of Driver's teaching for the New Testament understanding of Jesus Christ and his atonement. The traditional understanding of Christ's priesthood would be undermined since the whole section on Old Testament priesthood was part of the priestly code that higher critics like Driver took out of the Pentateuch and placed after the Babylonian exile. For Shields, the ramification of this manipulation of Old Testament dating was staggering: the whole ritual of Jewish worship did not come down from heaven at Sinai, but was copied from Babylonian influences.

Perhaps the most significant development of the convention was Shields' attempt to force a vote of confidence. Noting that such a vote would give the convention the "opportunity to express approval or disapproval" of his action in demanding of the Senate an investigation of Marshall's alleged modernism, Shields moved an amendment to the motion recommending the acceptance of the McMaster report: that "it is hereby resolved, that the position of the said Rev. T. T. Shields as a member of the Board of Governors be and is hereby declared vacant as from this date."[79] While on the surface it may have appeared that Shields was offering to resign his position on the Board of Governors, his opponents were quick to divine his intent.

---

78. Critical views of the Old Testament dismissed the historicity of the book of Jonah. However, Jesus Christ himself attested to the historicity of Jonah by using it as a type and symbol of his own death, burial, and resurrection (cf. Matt 12:40). Driver himself acknowledged that this would of course cast doubt on Christ's infallibility. In his preface to his "Introduction to the Literature of the Old Testament" he commented: "It does not seem requisite for the present purpose, as, indeed, within the limits of a Preface it would not be possible, to consider whether our Lord, as man, possessed all knowledge, or whether a limitation in this, as in other respects . . . was involved in that gracious act of condescension, in virtue of which he was willing 'in all things to be made like unto His brethren' (Heb. 2:17)." See Driver, *Introduction to the Literature of the Old Testament*, 12.

79. "McMaster University Report," *Baptist Year Book*, 1925, 40.

This was an immediate means to force the question of Marshall's employment to a vote of the convention. Had Shields been supported by a vote of confidence from the floor, a committee to reinvestigate Marshall would have been forced on the Senate.

Although the amendment was rejected on a technicality, it was later reintroduced in another form by A. P. Wilson of Pembroke, Ontario. Marshall, though a guest of the convention, was allowed to address the gathering to respond to Shields' criticisms. When the discussion of the report was resumed, Wilson's amendment was replaced by an amendment to the amendment. This was a compromise solution reiterating the doctrinal statement of the university as "endorsed by the Senate and approved by this convention in Bloor Street in 1910," with the additional provision "that this Convention commends the Senate and Board of Governors for their action in appointing to the Chair of Practical Theology a professor who, having considered that declaration, sincerely accepted it." When the vote was taken, the results suggested that neither side in the debate was comfortable with a test of strength, as the amendment to the amendment passed 399 to 159.[80]

Shields' opportunity had been lost. More importantly, a significant precedent had been set. The convention was willingly blind to the possibility that Marshall might have been less than honest in his "sincere acceptance" of the denomination's position. They couched their willing ignorance in the assumption of the basic honesty of the modernists' professions of orthodoxy, and also in the appeal to the basic baptistic principle of "reasonable liberty."[81] Despite Shields' conviction that there was mounting evidence to the contrary, most of the delegates showed themselves unwilling to believe that there was any kind of deliberate duplicity by either the Senate or Marshall.

Severely compromising the convention's ability to deal with the issues at stake was the very personal war of words that broke out between Shields and Marshall both in the convention and its aftermath. In his convention speech Marshall immediately attacked the methodology of "slander" and "whisper." He alleged: "That is the method of the common slanderer, who tells you some horrible tale about somebody and then whispers: of course, we don't know whether it is true or not. But it is too late when it is out. The poison gas is already on the breast of the breeze—and it is in this case, so

80. *Baptist Year Book*, 1925, 42.
81. *Baptist Year Book*, 1925, 42.

far as I am concerned."[82] Not satisfied with labelling Shields a slanderer and gossip, Marshall attacked Shields' theological incompetence. Although his convention speech made the incompetence charge by innuendo, Marshall was not so reserved in his interview with a *Toronto Star* reporter later. In that forum Marshall openly declared: "Rev. Dr. T. T. Shields uses scripture . . . inaccurately and ignorantly. . . . He does not yet understand the scriptures and would be well advised to devote himself carefully to Bible study. . . . a man who interprets scripture as Dr. Shields does . . . proves himself utterly incompetent as an exponent of the word of God."[83]

If Marshall learned any lessons from the resultant blast it might have been never to underestimate Shields. He might, as well, have considered the inadvisability of providing too much information. Shields, of course, had a heyday with the material Marshall provided in his impromptu Shields' bashing. Regarding the allegations of Shields' theological ineptitude, Shields erupted: "Notwithstanding our reduction to the ranks of the theological awkward squad by Mr. Marshall, I still believe . . . [what] Paul teaches by the Holy Spirit."[84] Throughout his retort, Shields adopted a condescending attitude with which to belittle Marshall's imagined expertise:

> As *The Gospel Witness* goes all over the world, and is read by about one thousand ministers besides thousands of lay readers, my readers, especially the readers of the sermons, ought to be informed of the Editor's ignorance and general incompetence. As the Editor has been in his present pulpit for nearly sixteen years, and Professor Marshall has been in Toronto only about as many days, the readers of *The Gospel Witness* ought to be advised of Prof. Marshall's great discovery at once.[85]

Shields' efforts over the course of the following year to prove Marshall's modernism demonstrated a growing desperation. His campaign increasingly appealed to insult and innuendo. Rather than proving his point he succeeded only in driving the majority of the convention into the enemy camp. When, for instance, Shields discovered an apparent discrepancy between Marshall's profession of closed membership before the convention

---

82. T. T. Shields, "Shall Modernism Capture McMaster?" *GW*, 29 October 1925, 19.

83. "Incompetent Exponent of Body, Mind and Spirit; Professor H. T. Marshall So Characterizes Dr. T. T. Shields of Jarvis Street in Controversy Over St. Paul's Psychology," *The Star Weekly*, 24 October 1925, 1.

84. T. T. Shields, "Shall Modernism Capture McMaster?" *GW*, 29 October 1925, 26.

85. T. T. Shields, "Shall Modernism Capture McMaster?" *GW*, 29 October 1925, 22.

and an earlier published statement defending open membership, he leapt to the attack. He immediately published the details of Marshall's apparent duplicity. Marshall quickly responded with a reasonable explanation.[86]

Shields refused to back down. Despite a perfectly logical explanation of the apparent contradiction, Shields was completely incapable of admitting he was wrong. As subsequent events unfolded it became clear that the denomination as a whole was unconvinced by Shields' reasoning, and that it was increasingly suspicious of the powers of his logic. In similar fashion Shields went on to accuse Marshall of disputing the idea of a literal six-day creation; the atoning efficacy of Christ's death; human depravity and the inspiration of Scripture.

Though Shields was able to publish numerous testimonials by other witnesses of the veracity of these charges, the manner of his denunciations tended to seriously undermine his credibility. Shields may have been quite right about the modernists' practice of using the terminology of evangelicalism with an entirely different meaning, but by repeatedly resorting to insult and innuendo, he lost his audience.[87] In the end he was preaching only to the choir. His ability to convince McMaster supporters of the threat of a modernist takeover was lost.

"THOU LIEST"; THE 1926 TORONTO CONVENTION

Some of the bitterest acrimony in the history of the Baptist Convention of Ontario and Quebec was recorded in the furious battle that raged on the convention floor at the 1926 annual meeting in Forward Baptist Church, Toronto. At its height Rev. A. J. Vining, in a comment that was lambasted in the secular press, shouted "I have more respect for a toad catching flies in the vapor of a dunghill than for some of you."[88] While Vining later apologized for his unfortunate remark, his sentiment well encapsulated the hostility that existed between the fundamentalist and modernist camps.

---

86. In an article published in England Marshall wrote: "To regard baptism as essential to salvation or *even to membership in the Christian Church* is to ascribe to the baptismal rite a crucial importance for which there is not warrant in the New Testament or in any truly spiritual interpretation of the Gospel or in common sense." (Emphasis added.) T. T. Shields, "Editorial: Professor Marshall's Pamphlet," *GW*, 7 January 1926, 7. Marshall responded that in that article he was referring to the church universal and not the local church.

87. T. T. Shields, "Will Baptists Consent to McMaster's Throwing over Redemption by Blood?" *GW*, 19 November 1925, 6.

88. "Oh, That These Columns were D. D.," *Toronto Telegram*, 23 October 1926, 26.

Critical theological issues were at stake. Discussion on the convention floor very clearly demonstrated the deep theological divide between Marshall and the fundamentalists' faith perspective on Scripture. Marshall himself openly confessed that they were poles apart.[89] He refused to denounce the Driver approach noting that in the light of modern thought "Driver's book gave the best methods of approach." He challenged Old Testament historicity and quoting James Orr argued that "nobody could study the Old Testament in the light of modern knowledge without becoming a higher critic."[90] Concerning the historicity of the book of Jonah and the related question of Christ's infallibility he observed that:

> In Britain, the normal view is the allegorical or the parabolical view. I have never been in a university where that view was not held. I have never had a text-book recommended to me that did not take that view. I didn't know a single eminent Biblical scholar who does not take that particular attitude. I find in Canada that the normal view is the historical view. I will go back to England any time before I surrender my view.[91]

He refused to address Shields' concerns about the Driver view and its ramifications for Christ's priesthood. Most serious of all for Shields and his followers was the fact that Marshall rejected "the idea that in the atonement of our Lord there was a penal element, the innocent for the guilty."[92] For the fundamentalists, Marshall's attack on the doctrine of substitutionary atonement was "the whole heart of the matter."[93] When he produced a vague quotation from Spurgeon he hoped would support his position, he earned a lengthy and furious retort from Shields.

However, in reality the whole matter had descended to the practical realities of what the fundamentalists called "machine rule"[94] and/or the issue of personality assassination. For most delegates, their rage at Shields'

---

89. "Shields as Apology is Asked Says it Highest Honor of Life," *Toronto Daily Star*, 20 October 1926, 13.

90. "Chancellor's Report," *TTCF*, 20 October 1926, 32.

91. "'Thou Liest,'– Prof. Marshall's Defiance to Dr. T. T. Shields," *TTCF*, 20 October 1926, 34.

92. "Dr. Shields Defies Baptist Convention When Apology is Demanded," *TDS*, 20 October 1926, 12.

93. T. T. Shields, "Ichabod, McMaster's New Name," *GW*, 4 November 1926, 127.

94. Throughout the years of its existence the Bible Baptist Union fought furiously against the "machinery" of the big conventions and what they came to call "machine rule."

methods dominated the day. MacNeill opened the charge by testifying that Shields had published accusations that:

> "S. J. Moore ... has never done anything worth-while"; that "Dr. Sanderson has unseated Ananias"; that "Dr Bowley-Green has a kangaroo logic"; that "Dr. Dayfoot is held up to ridicule and scorn"; that "E. O. Ford must be discredited before he goes to Lethbridge, not because he is unorthodox, but because he refuses to come to heel"; and of the Convention's resolution of appreciation for Dr. McCrimmon that "a certificate of sanity is a good thing for a man who has occupied a place in an asylum."[95]

It was, however, the direct interaction between Marshall and Shields that was the high point of the sordid affair. The mutual antagonism that had built up over the course of the year now exploded. According to media reports Marshall "turned toward Dr. Shields and in ringing tones, referring to the charges, declared: ' . . . I thrust them down Dr. Shields' throat and I say to him: 'Thou liest!'"[96] What followed was Marshall's response to accusations of modernistic perspectives on the historicity of the Old Testament, along with the modernistic depreciation of Christ's person and atonement. However, rather than making an unambiguous declaration of his orthodoxy on these critical issues, he further muddied the water. Perhaps sensing the momentum shifting his way and revelling overmuch in the warmth of his reception by convention delegates, he offered, instead, only a thinly veiled expression of modernistic principles.

DENOMINATIONAL SCHISM: SHIELDS AS OUTCAST AND SEPARATIST

The immediate upshot of the 1926 convention was two-fold. When Shields refused to apologize for his open attacks on the university and its officers, he was evicted from his role as member of the Board of Governors and rejected as an acceptable delegate to future meetings of the Baptist Convention of Ontario and Quebec. Furthermore, foreseeing the eventuality that Shields would call into question the legality of the attempt to remove him, the officials of the convention passed a resolution to make legal application

---

95. "Fight to Last Drop of Blood in Defence of McMaster Faculty: Attacked Ministers are Defended," *TTCF*, 20 October 1926, 31.

96. "Dr. Shields Defies Baptist Convention," *Toronto Daily Star*, 20 October 1926, 12.

for an amendment to their Act of Incorporation thus setting the scene for the 1927 convention.

Shields' response to this humiliating defeat was immediate. Plans were set in motion that evening for the establishment of an "Association of Regular Baptists within the Baptist Convention of Ontario and Quebec, to make possible the co-operation of such Regular Baptists in missionary and educational work," a move that would pave the way to the formation the following year of the Union of Regular Baptist Churches.[97] The initial result was the formation of a replacement missions board, "The Regular Baptist Missionary and Educational Society of Canada," which would collect funds within the convention for the support of conservative missions and the establishment of an alternate institution of higher learning.[98] The eventual outcome of the latter object was the opening of Toronto Baptist Seminary in the fall of 1927. In response to the convention's removal of Thomas Urquart, a former mayor of Toronto, from the Home Missions Board "after thirty-two years of service," Shields held a spontaneous vote to cut off all Home Missions funding from the Jarvis Street church.[99] The motion was carried unanimously. Finally, he published a complete record of the convention, replete with editorial comment in a 176-page issue of *The Gospel Witness* entitled: "Ichabod! McMaster's New Name."[100] He spent "forty-eight hours of continuous desk work" without breaks "for food or rest" in preparing it.[101] The circulation of this edition was so extensive that a staggering twelve tons of paper was used in its publication.[102] In 1953 he still regretted that he never produced it in "book form" to make it "available to Evangelicals throughout the world."[103]

---

97. T. T. Shields, "Ichabod, McMaster's New Name," *GW*, 4 November 1926, 15. Cf. T. T. Shields, "The Union of Regular Baptist Churches of Ontario and Quebec," *GW*, 27 October 1927, 3.

98. "Proceedings," *Baptist Year Book*, 1927, 51.

99. "Shields' Reply to Convention Will be Made by Instalments," *Toronto Telegram*, 21 October 1926, 18.

100. Ichabod is an Old Testament term meaning "The Glory Has Departed." Cf. 1 Sam 4:21.

101. Shields, *The Plot That Failed*, 350.

102. T. T. Shields, "Ichabod University," *GW*, 18 November 1926, 17; cf. T. T. Shields, "Last Weeks' Great Issue," and "We Must Say a Word About the Cost of Mailing," *GW*, 11 November 1926, 11.

103. T. T. Shields, "The Great Contention; Chapter XXXI," *GW*, 18 June 1953, 10.

With the convening of the 1927 convention, the Baptists moved a significant resolution:

> BE IT RESOLVED that, in the opinion of this convention, such churches as have, by resolution or otherwise, identified themselves with such campaign [of 'division and discord'] or support the aforesaid organization [The Regular Baptist Missionary and Educational Society of Canada], should therefore be considered as being not in harmony and co-operation with the work and objects of this Convention.[104]

The vote was carried by a large majority and the scene was set for the final act. Rev. W. C. Smalley of Ottawa moved: "Be it resolved that in the opinion of this Convention the conduct and attitude of the Jarvis Street Baptist church, Toronto, are not in harmony and co-operation with the work and objects of this Convention, and that the said church shall cease to be entitled to send any delegates to the said Convention."[105] Despite a last ditch effort to resolve the impasse with a compromise amendment, the motion eventually carried by a vote of 532 to 217.[106] On 14 October 1927, Jarvis Street Baptist Church was read out of the membership of the Baptist Convention which it had dominated for most of the convention's history.

Despite the fact that the second resolution had provided for the removal of all the churches that supported Shields, convention officials remained reluctant to move to judgment. Even after the reading of a letter from several of the offending churches demanding that they be dealt with in the same fashion as Jarvis Street, the convention refused to act. Clearly the action taken in adopting the three resolutions had one goal and that was the removal of Jarvis Street and its pastor. There still seemed to be hope that with Shields gone a full-scale schism could be avoided. The executive issued a recommendation that no further action be taken. They also invited "the churches to determine their course of action in light of the resolution of October 13th, and assures them that if they desire to maintain their proper status in the Convention their co-operation will be welcome."[107]

Any hope that some sort of reconciliation with dissidents could be achieved was quickly dashed. Even before the convention had concluded, a huge meeting of Regular Baptists convened in Jarvis Street. On Saturday

104. *Baptist Year Book*, 1927, 30.
105. *Baptist Year Book*, 1927, 32.
106. *Baptist Year Book*, 1927, 34.
107. *Baptist Year Book*, 1927, 52–53.

night, 15 October, a lengthy resolution was passed by those in attendance denouncing the actions of the Baptist Convention of Ontario and Quebec as an act of "tyranny" and resolving to stand together "in the principles of the faith once for all delivered to the saints."[108] An immediate call went out for the formation of a new convention. The following Wednesday "a great company" gathered in Jarvis Street for that purpose. Shields estimated that "the attendance at the morning session probably exceeded the attendance of the day sessions of the Old Convention after Jarvis Street had been excluded."[109] All of the delegates enrolled under the following statement:

> The undersigned, accepting the statement of faith of The Regular Baptist Missionary and Educational Society of Canada, and being in full sympathy with its work and objects, and being opposed to the action of the Convention of Ontario and Quebec in its endorsation [sic] of McMaster's Modernism, and its adoption of an amendment to its Constitution enabling it to silence evangelical testimony, approves of the formation of a Convention of Regular Baptists, and desires to be enrolled as a delegate thereto.[110]

The total registration for the inaugural meeting of the new Union of Regular Baptist Churches of Ontario and Quebec numbered 778. Shields further noted that the "total number of churches represented by these persons was exactly one hundred, of which about thirty churches, as such, have already declared themselves as approving of the new organization."[111] Shortly thereafter the Union chose Shields as their new president, a position he occupied for the next two decades.

Defections from what the fundamentalists now called the "Old Convention" quickly multiplied.[112] By 1930, Shields boasted of thousands who had left the convention over the Marshall issue. When Marshall announced that he was returning to England, Shields could not miss his opportunity to say 'I told you so.' Insisting that Marshall was forced out because he was the primary cause of the convention's declining fortunes, Shields noted: "Twelve thousand Baptist church members at least have left the Convention because of his [Marshall's] presence in it."[113] A few months later, with

---

108. T. T. Shields, "A Canadian 'Harmony Convention,'" *GW*, 20 October 1927, 7.
109. T. T. Shields, "A Canadian 'Harmony Convention,'" *GW*, 20 October 1927, 8.
110. T. T. Shields, "A Canadian 'Harmony Convention,'" *GW*, 20 October 1927, 7–8.
111. T. T. Shields, "A Canadian 'Harmony Convention,'" *GW*, 20 October 1927, 7–8.
112. T. T. Shields, "A Canadian 'Harmony Convention,'" *GW*, 20 October 1927, 7–8.
113. T. T. Shields, "Why is McMaster Sending Prof. Marshall?" *GW*, 19 June 1930, 4.

the reports being presented in the annual convention, Shields published in detail the declines in income across the various boards and the declining attendance figures in churches and Sunday Schools.[114] By 1930, many militant Canadian Baptist fundamentalists had moved from the Baptist Convention of Ontario and Quebec to take up residence in the fledgling Union of Regular Baptist Churches of Ontario and Quebec.

THE AFTERMATH

The legacy of the rupture in Baptist ranks of Ontario and Quebec was staggering. A schism was produced that in many ways has never been healed. Where Baptists once stood united in purpose and identity, they were hereafter divided by animosity and distrust. Thirty years after the outbreak of hostilities, the bitterness stirred up during those schismatic years was still poignant in the published sentiments of McDormand and Shields. The real tragedy, however, was in the countless ruined relationships and broken churches that littered the battlefield. Very few churches in the denomination escaped unscathed. In the inaugural meeting of the new Union of Regular Baptist Churches, Shields triumphantly noted that over 100 churches were represented by the individuals in attendance. While the number quickly grew, the sad note was that only 30 of those 100 churches were ready at that moment to commit to the Union's principles. While presumably many of the remaining seventy would eventually join, it is suggestive of the inner turmoil that each of these congregations faced as they wrestled with the question of where their ecclesiastical loyalties lay. In some cases legal battles ensued as congregants wrestled over which faction should control the properties and assets that had been accumulated by decades of sacrificially giving. Sadly, denominational officials contributed to the division with legal threats of lawsuit or injunction wherever opposition to the dissenters could be stirred up within the local communities.[115]

Where one denomination had stood there were now two. The course of the two Baptist denominations quickly diverged on matters of doctrine and polity. Theological modernism was entrenched in McMaster University, and the "Old Convention" was soon led by pastors educated under its

---

114. T. T. Shields, "Gray Hairs are Here and There Upon Him, Yet He Knoweth Not!" *GW*, 6 November 1930, 3–4.

115. Cf. for instance the documentation and discussion provided in T. T. Shields, "The Red Cross in Religious Warfare," *GW*, 1 December 1927, 1–6. Cf. also T. T. Shields, "News from the Front," *GW*, 22 December 1927, 14–16.

principles. The Union of Regular Baptist Churches quickly established a new educational resource: Toronto Baptist Seminary, which championed more traditional understandings of biblical orthodoxy. Perhaps reflecting his desire to maintain a Regular Baptist liberal arts university, in this same period Shields led the Baptist Bible Union in their efforts to purchase Des Moines University. The attempt was disastrous. The forced closure of Des Moines University after only two years was an embarrassment that the BBU could not overcome. Robert Delnay's study concluded that "The collapse of Des Moines University, with the flood of lurid publicity, ruined the Baptist Bible Union. There was little for the leaders to do but go back to their churches."[116] For his part, Shields admitted that "Since we decided to close Des Moines University we have declined all invitations but one to cross the Border, and have concentrated all our energy upon our own work in Canada."[117] Though Shields retired from the American front in humiliation and defeat, the fundamentalist work that had begun under the auspices of the BBU was carried on. In the Northern States a new organization gathered up the remnants of the BBU and organized itself as the General Association of Regular Baptist Churches. In Canada the BBU survived as the Union of Regular Baptist Churches with Shields serving as its president for the next twenty years.

From its first inception, it is clear that the new Union of Regular Baptist Churches was deliberately designed to stand against many of the perceived flaws of the "Old Convention." In the 15 October resolution condemning the action of the convention in excluding Jarvis Street, there was also expressed the intent of forming a new convention using Jarvis Street Baptist Church as its example and pattern: "That this mass meeting of Baptist hereby declare that we stand for the same principles as the delegates of Jarvis Street Baptist Church."[118] Thus, the new denomination of Baptists that emerged reflected a distinctive ecclesiastical polity learned by Jarvis Street through the years of spiritual warfare. Jarvis Street's stand against cultural liberalism within its own body and against theological liberalism in the convention was formative. At the critical point of their own struggle in 1921, with Shields winning the decisive victory against the liberal challenge, a new series of resolutions was made that shaped both his own church and the new denomination which he would mould over

---

116. Delnay, "A History of the Baptist Bible Union," 237.

117. T. T. Shields, "The Bible Baptist Union," *GW*, 13 February 1930, 5.

118. T. T. Shields, "A Canadian 'Harmony Convention,'" *GW*, 20 October 1927, 7.

the subsequent decades. At the conclusion of that pivotal meeting in 1921, the purged membership of Jarvis Street passed a series of declarations demonstrating their commitment to the kind of biblical ministry Shields practiced. These included resolutions affirming Jarvis Street's belief in the "inspiration, integrity and Divine authority of the Bible"; its insistence on "a pure and separated Church life"; its desire for "an active and continuing evangelism" and the spirituality characterized by . . . prayer meetings; [and] its determination that deacons "are the servants, not the masters of the Church."[119]

As the new denomination took shape these fundamental principles were woven into its fabric. Theological orthodoxy was its foundational principle, and its ultimate authority would be found in the divinely inspired Word of God. The purity of church life would be guarded both by the separatist mentality developed throughout the years of controversy and by the Regular Baptist principle embraced universally among the churches of the Union of *Regular* Baptist Churches. Separation first spoke to the purity of the life of the congregants. It was Shields' call for "entire separation" that first ignited the firestorm of controversy in his own church. This standard constituted a demand for self-denial in the face of the pleasure craze rampant in the ungodly pursuit of worldly amusements. For the wealthy and socially elite members of his congregation withdrawal from their social entanglements was unthinkable. Nevertheless, in the end a narrow majority within the church endorsed Shields' vision and embraced his call to wholehearted commitment to kingdom pursuits. Years of revival followed but unfortunately, the list of questionable activities soon morphed into legalistic standards imposed on officers and church members alike. However, years of exposure to war had taught Shields' the importance of using the rigour and self-sacrifice of a military service model in the churches' enlistment efforts. In his earlier efforts to build the BBU he commented: "We shall also endeavour to enlist churches as such to present a solid front to the enemy."[120] With the establishment of this new denomination it was at least in part a realization of his dream "to mobilize the conservative Baptist forces of the Continent."[121]

Ecclesiastical separation was ultimately the natural extension of personal separation from worldliness. Nevertheless, for Shields the realization

---

119. Jarvis Street Baptist Church Minutes, 21 September 1921. JSBC

120. T. T. Shields, "Creeping in Unawares," *GW*, 22 October 1925, 4.

121. T. T. Shields, "Creeping in Unawares," *GW*, 22 October 1925, 4.

was a long time coming. He had led the BBU on a non-separatist platform. His goal had been to purge the denomination of modernistic influences, but in the end had been forced to admit his error. By 1930, Shields was publicly acknowledging that his fundamentalist ally, Oliver Van Osdel, pastor of Wealthy Street Baptist Church in Grand Rapids, had been right and that they should have set about "the formation of another Convention in the beginning."[122]

It was only as he exited the convention under the ban of excommunication that he was enlightened with a new appreciation of the biblical injunction: "Wherefore come out from among them, and be ye separate, saith the Lord, and touch not the unclean thing; and I will receive you."[123] Hereafter, militant fundamentalists would become denominational separatists. However, an ecclesiastical separatism that was born in schism too often created the spectre of brother separating from brother over increasingly minor principles. In time second- and third-degree separation became the sad fallout of a mentality that was more schismatic than separatist.

The second guarantor of the purity of church life was the Regular Baptist principle that had been so pivotal in the McMaster controversy. The provision that parties baptized by immersion in the name of the Father, Son, and the Holy Spirit were alone entitled to communion at the Lord's Table,[124] protected the baptistic character of each church and exclusion from the table provided the means of spiritual discipline when members strayed into sin.

It was also Shields' expectation that the Union churches would follow his lead in aggressive evangelistic efforts. Evangelistic campaigns and Sunday morning Sunday-School programs became the norm. "The Baptist Bible Union Lesson Leaf," published weekly in *The Gospel Witness* provided the Sunday-School curriculum. For most churches one or more prayer meetings would be central to the life of the church. Regular news updates of spiritual awakenings and revival efforts would be circulated hereafter in *The Gospel Witness*. "The Union Baptist Witness," now a regular segment of *The Gospel Witness*, became "the Official organ of the Union of Regular Baptist Churches of Ontario and Quebec."[125]

---

122. T. T. Shields, "The Baptist Bible Union," *GW*, 13 February 1930, 6.
123. 2 Cor 6:17.
124. T. T. Shields, "How to Improve McMaster," *GW*, 12 October 1922, 1.
125. Cf. for instance, "The Union Baptist Witness," *GW*, 2 January 1930, 14–15.

Finally, Union churches were congregational in their polity. The 1921 revolt in Jarvis Street Baptist Church had been engineered on the strength of the tradition of diaconal rule. In its rejection of the leadership of the cultural liberals in its midst, Jarvis Street Baptist Church adopted a more clearly defined position on congregation rule, where "officers and deacons should take office on the understanding that they are the servants, not the masters of the Church."[126] This ideal, in contrast with the "Old Convention," became standard in Union churches.

Shields was undoubtedly correct in labelling the battles of these years "The Great Contention." From the perspective of Baptist orthodoxy there can be little doubt that he was completely justified in confronting the modernist incursions occurring within McMaster and the denomination at large. The survival of doctrinal orthodoxy within Ontario Baptist circles had much to do with his championing of the cause. However, Shields' polemic was the stuff of innuendo, imputed motive, exaggeration, and the inflation of minor issues into insurmountable obstacles, giving them significance that they did not deserve. He was too emotionally engaged in the process. Shields' message was often lost in the noise of his demagoguery. His agitation left him looking unbalanced and paranoid.

The question of whether, with less offensive tactics, Shields could ever have convinced the Baptist Convention of Ontario and Quebec of the truth of his allegations or overcome the dishonesty and covert machinations of his modernistic enemies, is open and unlikely to be resolved. Yet Shields was never one to acknowledge defeat or to admit that he was wrong. Instead, as he exited the convention under the ban of excommunication he had a new appreciation of the Biblical injunction: "Wherefore come out from among them, and be ye separate, saith the Lord, and touch not the unclean thing; and I will receive you."[127] Hereafter, the militant fundamentalist would be the denominational separatist. He was already envisioning a new organization purged of the modernist leaven and equipped with the tools to "earnestly contend for the faith which was once delivered unto the saints."[128] For better and for worse, his departure marked the dawn of a new era in Baptist identity in Ontario and Quebec.

---

126. Jarvis Street Baptist Church Minute Book, 1918–1938, 21 September 1921.
127. 2 Cor 6:17.
128. Jude 1:3

BIBLIOGRAPHY

Primary

NEWSPAPERS

Canadian Baptist (Toronto, ON), 1924.
Christian Fundamentalist (Minneapolis, MN), 1928.
Gospel Witness (Toronto, ON), 1922–1927, 1930, 1947.
Gospel Witness and Protestant Advocate (Toronto, ON), 1952–1953.
Star Weekly (Toronto, ON), 1925.
Toronto Daily Star (Toronto, ON), 1923–1924, 1926.
Toronto Telegraph (Toronto, ON), 1926–1927.

YEARBOOKS

Baptist Year Book of the Baptist Convention of Ontario and Quebec, 1924–1927.

OTHER

Driver, Samuel Rolles. *Introduction to the Literature of the Old Testament*. New York: Scribner, 1898.
"Inspiration and the Authority of Scripture." Printed in *The Plot That Failed* by T. T. Shields, 128. Toronto: The Gospel Witness, 1937.
Jarvis Street Baptist Church Minute Book, 1918–1938. Jarvis Street Baptist Church Archives.
"Shields Correspondence." Jarvis Street Baptist Church Archives, Toronto, ON.
Shields, T. T. *The Inside of the Cup*. Toronto: Jarvis Street Baptist Church, 1921.
———. "Letter Diary." 21 July 1915. Jarvis Street Baptist Church Archives.
———. *The Plot that Failed*. Toronto: The Gospel Witness, 1937.
———. "Sermons Preached." 1908. Jarvis Street Baptist Church Archives.
Strong, Augustus Hopkins. "Our Denominational Outlook." In *Miscellanies*. Philadelphia: Griffith & Rowland, 1912.
———. *Systematic Theology*. Philadelphia: Judson, 1947.
Toronto Telegram Clippings File. Western University Archives.

Secondary

Adams, Doug. "The War of the Worlds: The Militant Fundamentalism of Dr. Thomas Todhunter Shields and the Paradox of Modernity." PhD diss., The University of Western Ontario, 2015.
Bebbington, David. *Evangelicalism in Modern Britain: A History From the 1730s to the 1980s*. London: Unwin Hyman, 1989.
Burkinshaw, Robert K. *Pilgrims in Lotus Land: Conservative Protestantism in British Columbia, 1917–1981*. Montreal: McGill-Queen's University Press, 1995.
Dallimore, Arnold. *Thomas Todhunter Shields; Baptist Fundamentalist*. Leamington: unpublished manuscript, c. 2001.
Delnay, Robert George. "A History of the Baptist Bible Union." PhD diss., Dallas Theological Seminary, 1963.

Ellis, Walter. "What the Times Demand: Brandon College and Higher Education in the West." In *Canadian Baptists and Christian Higher Education*, edited by G. A. Rawlyk, 63–88. Kingston: McGill-Queen's University Press, 1988.

Hulse, Erroll. "Charles Haddon Spurgeon and the Downgrade Controversy." In *Acorns to Oaks: The Primacy and Practice of Biblical Theology*, edited by Michael A. G. Haykin, 169–86. Dundas, ON: Joshua Press, 2003.

Pinnock, Clark H. "The Modernist Impulse at McMaster University, 1887–1927." In *Baptists in Canada: Search for Identity Amidst Diversity*, edited by Jarold K. Zeman, 193–207. Burlington: Welch, 1980.

Rawlyk, G. A. "Whidden, T. T. Shields, Christian Higher Education, and McMaster University." In *Canadian Baptists and Christian Higher Education*, edited by G. A. Rawlyk, 31–62. Kingston: McGill-Queen's University Press, 1988.

———. *Wrapped up in God: A Study of Several Canadian Revivals and Revivalists*. Burlington: Welch, 1988.

———. *Champions of the Truth: Fundamentalism, Modernism, and the Maritime Baptists*. Montreal: McGill-Queen's University Press, 1990.

Richardson, Kurt A. "Augustus Hopkins Strong." *The Reformed Reader*. Online: http://www.reformedreader.org/strong.htm.

Straub, Jeffery Paul. *The Making of a Battle Royal: The Rise of Liberalism in Northern Baptist Life, 1870–1920*. Eugene, OR: Pickwick, 2018.

Wilson, Paul R. "Baptists and Business: Central Canadian Baptists and The Secularization of the Businessmen at Toronto's Jarvis Street Baptist Church, 1848–1921." PhD diss., University of Western Ontario, 1996.

5

Brandon College and the Regular Baptists of British Columbia

ROBERT BURKINSHAW

IN 1925 BRITISH COLUMBIA experienced the first organizational split in Baptist ranks in North America during the fundamentalist-modernist controversy.[1] Fundamentalist Baptists who rejected any toleration of theological liberalism in their midst formed their own quasi-denominational organization that year and two years later, in 1927, completed the split by withdrawing from the Baptist Convention of British Columbia (part of the Baptist Union of Western Canada) and forming a new denomination, the Convention of Regular Baptists of British Columbia.

The Vancouver region, with over 12,000 identifying themselves as Baptists on the census, was the focal point of the controversy and its Baptist population was split almost down the middle by it.[2] Slightly over half of the region's Baptist churches and missions—fifteen of twenty-nine, with 40 percent of the membership—left the old convention to form the new

---

1. T. T. Shields of Toronto did not establish the Regular Baptist Missionary and Education Society until 1927 and the General Association of Regular Baptist Churches (GARBC) in the US did not separate from the Northern Baptist Convention until 1932.

2. The figure of 12,000 is derived from the 1921 and 1931 census figures. In 1921 just over 11,000 identified as Baptist in what is now called Greater Vancouver, a region with a population of about 226,000. In 1931 census, the number identified as Baptist grew to 13,900 and the total population in the region to 324,000. Compiled from Census of Canada, 1921, Table 38 and Census of Canada, 1931, Volume II, Table 42.

Regular Baptist Convention. In the province as a whole, approximately one-third of the Baptist membership joined the new convention.

Why did such an early and numerically significant division occur among the Baptists of British Columbia, particularly in the Vancouver region? This chapter focuses primarily on answering that question after providing a brief summary of the controversy leading to the schism, the story of which has been told in more detail elsewhere.[3]

BRIEF OVERVIEW OF THE CONTROVERSY

Public complaints against Brandon College first surfaced in 1920 and concerns about the college remained central to the controversy that led to the formal schism in Baptist ranks. Between 1921 and 1925, a total of three investigations were undertaken of the college, none of which settled the matter, as theological divisions within the Baptist Union increased until the schism took place in 1925.

Earlier rumours about Brandon seemed to be confirmed in the minds of many conservatives when Rev. Arnold Bennett—a Brandon student from 1915 to 1917—reported to the Baptist Ministerial Association of Vancouver in 1920 that Dr. Harris L. MacNeill, Professor of New Testament and Greek, taught heretical views regarding the inspiration and infallibility of the Bible. When other former students of Brandon confirmed Bennett's account and added their own concerns about MacNeill, including his views of the deity of Christ and what they felt were the negative impacts of his teaching upon the faith of students,[4] the Ministerial Association demanded that the Brandon College board of governors investigate the charges. The board did so in 1921 and the Ministerial Association accepted its report, which basically exonerated the college. However, that acceptance was reported to be conditional and was "on [the] definite understanding that MacNeill was leaving at the end of the year and Vancouver Ministerial Association did not wish him to 'leave under a cloud.'"[5]

---

3. See Pousett, "The History of the Regular Baptists of British Columbia"; Pousett, "A History of the Convention of Baptist Churches of British Columbia"; Richards, *Baptists in British Columbia*; and Burkinshaw, *Pilgrims in Lotus Land*.

4. J. B. Rowell and J. Linton, unpublished statements in Baptist Historical College, Northwest Baptist Theological College (hereafter NBTC). See also Dunlop, "James B. Rowell, 1888–1973," 425–26.

5. Richards, *Baptists in British Columbia*, 74–76 and Pousett, "A History of the Convention," 138–41 both cite a penciled remark to this effect in the margin of G. R. S. Blackaby's copy of the *Brandon Commission*.

Contrary to that understanding, however, Professor MacNeill did not leave Brandon College in 1921, and the issue was kept burning by the circulation of a number of new pamphlets, which created a storm in the Vancouver area. The increasingly-strongly worded pamphleteering efforts of former-Brandon students were augmented by the publication of other pamphlets, one by retired missionary, Mrs. A. A. McLeod, and another by a small group of anonymous "interested laymen." These broadened the scope to include the orientation and structure of the Baptist Union of Western Canada, of which the Baptist Convention of British Columbia was a part. They argued that not only was the Baptist Union supportive of modernism, as expressed in Brandon College, but also that its fiscal policies were too centralized and did not allow conservatives to steer their donations away from Brandon to other denominational causes in which they had more confidence.[6]

The increasingly widespread agitation based in Vancouver led the Baptist Union to launch a second investigation of Brandon College, but that effort failed to calm the controversy for several reasons. The original composition of the investigating commission came under fire because nine of its eleven members were also members the Brandon board or otherwise had close ties to the college.[7] Two members of the Brandon board resigned from the commission, but many British Columbia Baptists were left with the impression that the Baptist Union had designed the commission to create a positive outcome for the college. In addition, the report sent a mixed message to the denomination. It criticized Dr. MacNeill's accusers as "false and unchristian" and exonerated the professor, but the report also noted that he did not hold traditional interpretations of a number of doctrines. It also acknowledged the difficulties that his teaching had created for students and recommended that he no longer teach English Bible classes to Arts students but that, instead, a professor of practical theology be hired whose teaching was expositional in nature "rather than a critical study."[8] That recommendation did not actually help solve the problem because the college could not afford to hire a new faculty member and it did not adjust Dr. MacNeill's teaching responsibilities as recommended. Perhaps most importantly for conservatives in Vancouver, the city's two members of the

---

6. Pousett, "A History of the Convention," 138–45 and Richards, *Baptists in British Columbia*, 74–78.

7. R. K. Knight, "Letter to the Editors," *Baptist Herald*, 1 July 1922, 2.

8. Baptist Union of Western Canada, *Report of the Brandon College Commission*, 22.

commission, Revs G. R. Maguire and A. F. Baker, pastors of its two largest Baptist churches, First and Mount Pleasant, refused to sign its report because they did not agree with its analysis of MacNeill's doctrinal positions, especially regarding Scripture, the virgin birth, and the resurrection.

Brandon College seemed to have survived the two investigations, but the institution was losing ground on the financial front. In early 1922, Ruth Morton Baptist Church in Vancouver voted to withhold funds to the Baptist Union because the Union's budget supported the college. While Ruth Morton was the first congregation known to have done so, it appears that other churches soon followed its lead.[9] In 1924, although the Baptist Union passed a vote of confidence in Brandon, it removed the college from its budget. The rationale was that the college would be able to gain far more by appealing directly to its constituency than it was receiving from the Baptist Union. The reality, however, appears to be that too many churches had begun to withhold funds from the denomination because of the inclusion of Brandon College in its budget.[10] Many conservatives were not satisfied that removing Brandon from the denominational budget went far enough, however, and they put forward a motion at the British Columbia Convention "disapproving the action of the Baptist Union of Western Canada in the endorsation of, and fellowship with, the unscriptural teaching of Brandon College."[11]

The British Columbia Convention responded by forming another investigative committee, the third, and what proved to be the final, investigation. That body issued a majority and a minority report and the reception of those at the British Columbia Convention led to the 1925 formation of the quasi-denominational organization by fundamentalists.

Discussions and voting at the 1925 convention revealed that the split among British Columbia Baptists was more than a matter of a simple division between liberals and conservatives. In fact, the largest group in opposition to the position of the more militant conservatives was comprised of those often called moderate conservatives.[12] That large block, comprising

---

9. Minutes of Congregation, 11 January 1922, Ruth Morton Memorial Baptist Church, Vancouver.

10. This is Richards' interpretation, *Baptists in British Columbia*, 86–87.

11. Cited in Richards, *Baptists in British Columbia*, 87.

12. The term "militant" does not necessarily imply the same degree of militancy and the ultra-separatist mentality which sometimes has characterized fundamentalists in North America. In this context it refers to conservatives who, unlike those termed "moderate" conservatives here, believed strongly that decisive action needed to be taken

just over 40 percent of the 144 delegates, indicated in several votes, on the one hand, that it agreed with the more militant conservatives on matters of theology but, on the other, that it did not believe that Baptist polity allowed for the imposition of binding statements of faith on Baptist churches and individuals.[13]

Just over one-third of the delegates were militant conservatives, or fundamentalists, who voted to accept the minority report which recommended that Brandon faculty be required to subscribe to a detailed conservative statement of faith and to resign if they could not agree with it. The majority report was far too weak for these conservatives because it only recommended that theology faculty belong to a "Regular Baptist Church" without defining such nor requiring actual agreement with any statement of faith. They also joined liberals to defeat an important amendment to the majority report which was proposed by moderate conservatives in an attempt to bridge the gap between positions. The amendment proposed to create a definition of a "Regular Baptist Church" by spelling out in considerable detail a conservative theological position. However, it did not go far enough for many fundamentalists because it did not actually require that Brandon faculty members formally signify their agreement with that statement.[14]

Theological liberals appear to have comprised just over 20 percent of the delegates. Because of their opposition to defining a Baptist church by a conservative theological statement, they joined militant conservatives to defeat the amendment proposing to define a "Regular Baptist Church." They then voted with the moderate conservatives to accept the majority report which did not specify particular doctrinal beliefs.[15]

Two factors appear to have weakened the fundamentalist numbers in Vancouver in the two years before the 1925 convention. In the spring of 1923, the massive Charles Price evangelistic and healing meetings in Vancouver had caused hundreds of Baptists, many of them radical

---

against the liberalism evident at Brandon. Dunlop makes the case that the British Columbia fundamentalists' approach was "moderated by a more discerning separatism" and cites the example of Rev. J. B. Rowell, pastor of the Kamloops church, who "maintained a steady moderate approach" during the controversy. Dunlop, "James B. Rowell, 1888–1973," 428–29.

13. I have found convincing the analysis of the voting in Richards, *Baptists in British Columbia*, 89–90.

14. Richards, *Baptists in British Columbia*, 89–90

15. Richards, *Baptists in British Columbia*, 89–90.

fundamentalists, to leave their churches for one of the burgeoning number of Pentecostal congregations in the city.[16] While it is impossible to know for certain, it is quite possible that such people might have weighted opinion in favour of the fundamentalist position in some congregations had they remained in Baptist churches. Also in 1923, Rev. G. R. Maguire, the most charismatic and highest profile critic of Brandon College, left First Baptist Vancouver for Westmount Baptist in Montreal. He was replaced at First Baptist by Rev. J. J. Ross, a moderate conservative who was elected president of the British Columbia Convention in 1925 and, significantly, did not support the attempt to remove liberalism from the denomination. It is tempting to speculate what effect that change of leadership in British Columbia's largest and wealthiest Baptist congregation might have had on the outcome of the 1925 convention.[17]

The rift between moderate conservatives and fundamentalists was confirmed when, at the 1925 convention, all fundamentalist candidates for denominational offices, including respected members who had served in their positions for many years, were defeated by a margin of nearly two to one.[18] Almost immediately after that June 1925 convention, fundamentalists formed the British Columbia Baptist Missionary Council, the purpose of which was to receive and disperse missions donations from churches and individuals that no longer supported the British Columbia Baptist Convention. Very quickly the Council began to look even more like a denomination as two auxiliary organizations formed under its umbrella, the Baptist Womens' Missionary Council, which began operating its own city mission in Vancouver, and a youth organization which drew 300 young people to its first rally. Within a few months, the Council also founded its own periodical, the *BC Baptist*.[19] It was technically not a denomination, and its affiliated churches still belonged to the British Columbia Baptist Convention; but the Council operated sufficiently independent in the important area of finances and womens' and youth ministry for its formation to be considered the first schism in Baptist ranks in North America over the issue of modernism.[20]

16. See Burkinshaw, *Pilgrims in Lotus Land*, 100–120 for a description of the Charles S. Price meetings in British Columbia.

17. The reasons for Maguire's departure from First Baptist are unknown but Pousett speculates that his brand of conservatism was not universally acceptable among members of the prestigious congregation. Pousett, "A History of the Convention," 153–54.

18. Pousett, "A History of the Convention," 157

19. Richards, "A History of the Convention," 159–60, 176.

20. Richards, *Baptists in British Columbia*, 73.

After two years of the British Columbia Council's tense existence within the ranks of the denomination, the split was formalized when the British Columbia Convention approved a new constitutional clause in June 1927 that would have allowed a 60 percent vote of constitutional delegates to deny a seat to the delegates from any church "not in harmony and cooperation with the work and objects of said convention."[21] Rather than face expulsion, the delegates from the Council withdrew from the convention and on 9 July 1927 formed a new denomination: The Convention of Regular Baptists of British Columbia. Having failed to eliminate theological liberalism from their denomination, they separated themselves from it and from any toleration of liberalism.

Within a year, the new Regular Baptist Convention of British Columbia claimed nearly one-third of the Baptist membership in the province, numbering 1,840 members in twenty-four churches and mission stations, leaving the old Baptist convention with approximately 4,000 members in thirty-four churches and mission stations.[22] The Vancouver region was clearly the centre of strength of the new Regular Baptist Convention with fully 80 percent of its provincial membership. Its 1,500 members in fifteen churches and mission stations nearly equaled the membership of the old convention in the Vancouver region.[23]

By way of contrast, no formal split in Baptist ranks occurred in Manitoba or Saskatchewan in that era and, in Alberta, only three churches affiliated with the fundamentalist Regular Baptist Missionary Fellowship, and that was not formed until 1930. In Ontario, T. T. Shields began the Regular Baptist Missionary and Education Society of Canada in 1927, nearly two years after the similar body was founded in British Columbia. In the Maritimes, fundamentalists failed to split the United Baptist Convention.[24]

WHY VANCOUVER?

The main focus of this chapter is to explain why the fundamentalist-modernist split among Baptists in British Columbia came earlier than elsewhere in North America and why the fundamentalists proportionately were so

---

21. Convention Report, 1927, 17, cited in Richards, *Baptists in British Columbia*, 93.

22. Pousett, "The History of the Regular Baptists," 151, table 1, and "A History of the Convention," 218.

23. Pousett, "The History of the Regular Baptists," 152, Table 2 and Baptist Union of Western Canada, *Year Book*, 1930, 151–53.

24. Rawlyk, *Champions of the Truth*, 39–75.

strong in Vancouver. Factors to be considered include American influences, socio-economic differences, theological issues, and certain events and organizations which were unique to Vancouver in the years immediately prior to the Brandon College controversy.

American influences?

The British Columbia Baptist (old) Convention board argued that the split was due to American influences. In a 1925 pamphlet condemning the new fundamentalist Baptist Council, the board stated, "The movement, resulting in the organization of the Council, is an importation from the United States. . . . It certainly is not justified in BC."[25] Since that time, a number of scholars have similarly explained the growth of fundamentalist churches and organizations in Canada as primarily due to American influences crossing the border to provide inspiration, leadership and support.[26] British Columbia Regular Baptist historian John B. Richards agrees, arguing that the conservative Baptists in the province were "more receptive to American than to English Baptist influences."[27]

Unquestionably some evidence points to American influences on the Baptist schism in British Columbia. French E. Oliver, whose large-scale evangelistic meetings in Vancouver in 1917 helped spark considerable concern among Baptists about the inroads of modernism into the churches, was an American Presbyterian.[28] In addition, the Baptist Bible Union, a continent-wide organization of Baptist fundamentalists, had held a rally in Vancouver immediately before the formation of the British Columbia Baptist Missionary Council and membership in that Council required subscription to the Baptist Bible Union statement of faith.[29]

On closer examination, however, the picture becomes less clear and the strong fundamentalist movement among British Columbia Baptists appears to have been inspired and shaped by a "North Atlantic triangle" of influences; British, American, and Canadian. While the Baptist Bible

---

25. *Information for British Columbia Baptists* (Vancouver, 1925), cited in Richards, *Baptists in British Columbia*, 91.

26. E.g., Kilbourn, *Religion in Canada*; Mann, *Sect, Cult and Church in Alberta*, 153; Moir, "Sectarian Tradition in Canada," 129.

27. Richards, *Baptists in British Columbia*, 83.

28. Burkinshaw, *Pilgrims in Lotus Land*, 41–54, devotes a chapter to the French E. Oliver meetings in BC.

29. Pousett, "A History of the Convention," 158, 161, 175–77.

Union was strong in the United States, its "leading spirit" was the English-born Toronto fundamentalist, T. T. Shields, who has been described as "a Britisher of the Britishers, and actually one of the last great Victorians."[30] He consciously modelled himself after Charles H. Spurgeon and travelled to London on several occasions to preach in the Metropolitan Tabernacle and reportedly hoped to receive a call to become its permanent preacher.[31]

Shields visited Vancouver twice in the first half of 1925, and he published in his *Gospel Witness* glowing first-hand accounts of the vigorous fundamentalist Baptist activity in the city and of the huge crowds which rallied to its cause.[32] It is more than likely that Shields' English orientation contributed to gaining him a positive hearing among the thousands of British-born Baptists in Vancouver. He once noticed with delight how many former members of Spurgeon's Metropolitan Tabernacle he met in Baptist Bible Union meetings on the West Coast.[33] In fact, it is clear that Metropolitan Tabernacle, which had broken with the British Baptist Union in 1891 in protest against liberalizing trends, served as an inspiration and model not only for Shields but also for many of the British Columbia fundamentalist Baptists.[34]

The local leadership of the fundamentalist Baptist churches in British Columbia likewise provided evidence of complex North Atlantic influences. No single leader rose to pre-eminence among them but a considerable number of ministers, along with some strong laymen, gave leadership.[35] The sixteen ministers who led in the founding the Convention of Regular Baptists certainly appeared to be open to influences from the United States and sometimes brought in American evangelists for a series of meetings.

30. Tarr, *Shields of Canada*, 11–25; Rennie, "Theological Education in Canada: Past and Present," and Rennie, "Fundamentalism and the Varieties of North Atlantic Evangelicalism, 1900–1939."

31. Russell, "Thomas Todhunter Shields, Canadian Fundamentalist," 264, 277 and Adams, "The War of the Worlds," 77.

32. See, for example, *Gospel Witness*, 26 February 1925; *Gospel Witness*, 5 March 1925; and *Gospel Witness*, 2 July 1925.

33. *Gospel Witness*, 5 March 1925, 11.

34. E.g., *BC Baptist*, 19 November 1925, 2–3 and Dunlop, "James B. Rowell, 1888–1973," 428–29.

35. Rev. G. R. Maguire of the Vancouver's largest Baptist church, First Baptist, may have come to play such a leading role but he left the city for Montreal in 1923. After his departure, Rev. A. F. Baker of the large Mount Pleasant church perhaps came closest to being the leading voice for fundamentalist Baptists but there is no sense that he dominated.

However, the make-up of the body of sixteen was decidedly British, as over half of them (nine of sixteen, or 56 percent) were British-born. Four were from central Canada and two from the Maritimes. Only one came from the United States, and his Broadway West congregation did not appreciate his brand of fundamentalism. He was asked to leave within two years of his appointment. About half of the ministers received college or university training in Britain and one at Acadia University in Nova Scotia. Two had received all or part of the training in American Bible schools.[36]

The orientation of the fundamentalists' flagship church, Mount Pleasant Baptist, was perhaps best expressed by a member's response when she was asked why her congregation called W. M. Robertson from Scotland in 1927 on the recommendation of T. T. Shields. She replied, "When you looked for 'men of God,' you looked to the Old Country—that seemed to be where they came from."[37]

If openness to American influences had been a critical factor in the stimulation of Baptist fundamentalism, one would have expected Alberta's Baptists to have been more divided than their British Columbia Baptist counterparts. The American orientation was much stronger and the British and central and eastern Canadian orientation weaker than on the West Coast. In 1931, the proportion of Alberta's Baptist population born in the United States was nearly double that in British Columbia (17 percent cf. 9 percent) and the British proportion much smaller (12 percent cf. 21 percent). Likewise the Maritime-born Baptist population in Alberta was small compared to British Columbia (5 percent cf. 11 percent) and even its proportion of Ontario-born was also somewhat smaller (10 percent cf. 12 percent). Yet Baptist fundamentalism was much weaker in Alberta than in British Columbia and only three churches affiliated with the Regular Baptist Missionary Society when it was formed in 1930.[38]

In fact, one could argue that American influences were responsible for introducing liberalism, more so than fundamentalism, to western Canada's Baptist population. It seems clear that in areas of western Canada where American influences were strongest among Baptists, the theological tenor was more likely to be more liberal than conservative. The Northern Baptist

---

36. Compiled from Pousett, "The History of the Regular Baptists," appendix E, and from interviews with professors J. B. Richards and D. Hills and Mr. A. Cockle.

37. Interview with Mrs. I. Pepper, 2 December 1980, cited in D. Morton, "The Rise of Metropolitan Tabernacle," 6.

38. Figures calculated from Canada, *1931 Census*, Vol 4, table 8.

Convention in the United States contained a stronger liberal element than did its Canadian counterparts and its three most influential seminaries at the time—Chicago, Rochester, and Crozer—produced many liberal leaders. In 1927 twenty ministers serving in the Baptist Union of Western Canada had studied at one of those three institutions but significantly all of those, except one, worked in the Prairie Provinces.[39]

Brandon College's liberal orientation stemmed in large part to its pronounced American orientation. Dr. Dores R. Sharpe, superintendent of the Baptist Union before the First World War and later a member of the faculty of Brandon, recalled decades later both the liberal and American orientation of Brandon. He stated, "Brandon College played a large part in developing a forward looking liberal spirit" and went on to list a number of its more prominent faculty who he described as liberal and noted that they were all trained at either Rochester Seminary or Chicago Divinity School.[40]

On the West Coast, the orientation of the British Columbia fundamentalist Baptists is perhaps best summed up as being somewhat cosmopolitan. On the one hand, the stronger British and eastern and central Canadian influences balanced the American Baptist influences, far more so than occurred among Baptists in the Prairie Provinces. On the other hand, unlike Maritime Baptists, there was very little localism. George Rawlyk stated that Maritime Baptists "did not like outsiders telling them what to do, especially Torontonians," because their sense of regional identity was so strong. Thus, fundamentalists such as Shields gained a very limited following in that region.[41] Settlement in British Columbia, however, was simply too recent for strong localism to have developed. Its fundamentalists were alienated from the leadership and direction of their own denomination in western Canada and they were not at all adverse to looking to outsiders for inspiration and leadership, whether from the United States, central and eastern Canada, or, especially, from Britain.

Socio-Economic Factors?

The predominance of fundamentalist Baptists in the working-class east side of Vancouver suggests a potential socio-economic explanation for the split in Baptist ranks in the city. A long-standing scholarly tradition, including

39. Baptist Union of Western Canada, *1927 Yearbook*, 171–75.

40. Dores R. Sharpe to W. E. Ellis, 16 November 1961, cited in Ellis, "Baptists and Radical Politics in Western Canada: 1920–1950," 180.

41. Rawlyk, *Champions of the Truth*, 88.

the works of Richard Niebuhr in the United States and S. D. Clark and W. E. Mann in Canada have explained the rise of fundamentalist groups as being due to protests of socially and economically marginal groups against modernist trends within the dominant society.[42]

In Vancouver, 90 percent of the 1928 Regular Baptist membership belonged to the churches located east of Cambie Street, usually seen as the dividing line between the largely upper-middle class west side of the city and its working-class east side. By way of contrast, 80 percent of the membership of the old convention's membership belonged to churches west of Cambie Street. British Columbia Baptist Convention historian Pousett notes that the old convention became a largely middle-class denomination after the split.[43]

At the same time, it needs to be noted that the working-class Baptists could not be considered a truly marginal group in that society. For example, skilled tradesmen comprised the largest group of the 240 members of Ruth Morton Memorial Baptist Church in the city's southeast. Most of those, and even some of the labourers and other unskilled workers, owned their own homes on the inexpensive lots typical of that area.[44] A high percentage were relatively-recent immigrants from Britain and appear to have been part of the quite respectable British working class.

In addition, enough exceptions to the east-west geographic divide existed to make clear that socio-economic factors were not determinative in the split. For example, nearly one-quarter, or four of seventeen, members of the Baptist Missionary Council's first board were members of the leading and most prestigious old convention congregation in Vancouver, First Baptist Church. The leading fundamentalist church, Mount Pleasant, was situated just east of Cambie Street but in close proximity to a wide range of different socio-economic residential areas, including some areas of considerable wealth. Further, Mount Pleasant became something of a magnet for fundamentalists in old convention churches and, in 1926 alone, over 100 fundamentalist members left churches on the west side of the city

---

42. E.g., Niebuhr, *The Social Sources of Denominationalism*; Clark, *The Developing Canadian Community*; and Mann, *Church and Sect in Alberta*.

43. Pousett, "A History of the Convention," 172

44. Compiled from Membership Rolls, Ruth Morton Memorial Baptist Church, 1918–26; Henderson, *Vancouver Directory*, 1918–19; Wrigley-Henderson, *British Columbia Directory*, 1924–26; City of Vancouver, District Lot Assessment Books, 1924, City of Vancouver Archives.

that remained within the old convention to join it.[45] Membership lists for it are not available, but an analysis of the 200 members that broke from it in 1928 to form Metropolitan Tabernacle indicate that Mount Pleasant's congregation was not socially homogenous but included members of the working and lower middle classes but also professionals, bankers, and a manufacturer.[46]

Perhaps the best conclusion to draw from the data is that the working and lower-middle class Baptists were strongly influenced in their separatist stand by their alienation from the trends of modern thought in that era. Lacking, for the most part, university education, the majority were not familiar with, nor had vested interest in, modernist ideas such as evolutionary progress and ecumenism, and sought to separate from them. To them such ideas were alien forces which, once gaining a foothold at Brandon, would destroy the work of the denomination. Indeed, they used even stronger language, viewing modernists as being deliberately destructive. The statement of purpose of the Baptist Missionary Council declared that modernist teaching was "*calculated* to pervert the faith of our young men and women who go to Brandon with a view to preparation for life work on our mission fields and in our churches."[47]

The refusal by the majority of the upper- and middle-class Baptists on the west side of the city, even those who held to a conservative theology, to follow the separatist path seems to reflect greater levels of accommodation to modern society. Paul R. Wilson's study of Baptist businessmen in Toronto is suggestive in this regard. He argues that trends towards social integration, respectability, and a commitment to cultural progress characterized numbers of the upper-middle-class Baptists in Toronto, many of whom clashed with T. T. Shields with his more traditional, otherworldly perspective.[48] Similarly, most upper and middle-class Baptists in western Canada demonstrated their commitments to respectability and progress, at least in part, by supporting Brandon College. Baptist historian W. E. Ellis argues that the purpose of Baptist institutions of higher education such as Brandon, Rochester, and Chicago was to "socialize students who, mellowed

---

45. Pousett, "The History of the Regular Baptists," 78–79.

46. Metropolitan Tabernacle, Membership Rolls, 1928 and Wrigley-Henderson, *British Columbia Directory*, 1928–29.

47. *The BC Baptist Missionary Council*, cited in Pousett, "A History of the Convention," 157–58. Italics added.

48. Wilson, "Baptists and Business."

by culture, refinement, social convention and ivy-covered institutions, would create an environment where sectarianism would diminish and ecumenical cooperation and progress would flourish."[49]

British Columbia's fundamentalist Baptists, although containing some members of the professional and business classes, were not particularly concerned with respectability and cultural accommodation, and reacted against such trends as dangerous to spirituality. Shields' concern about a drift among upper and middle-class Baptists towards cultural accommodation, including "worldly amusements," seemed to be widely shared among fundamentalist Baptists in Vancouver. Shields reported that approximately one thousand attending a packed 1925 Vancouver meeting responded positively to the call to abandon worldly amusement in his message on "The Christian Attitude Towards Amusements."[50]

Theological Issues

Social and cultural factors thus cannot be dismissed, but it is also difficult to escape the fact that significant theological issues were at stake in the Baptist schism in British Columbia. In contrast with the situation in Ontario, no fundamentalist Baptist leader in British Columbia dominated as did T. T. Shields in Toronto, where it was his personality that often became the focus of debate, thus obscuring at times the theological issues at stake.[51] Instead, the complaints raised against Brandon College focused to a large extent on theological issues of historic importance to Baptists.

The highest profile complaints against Prof. MacNeill of Brandon College centred on his views of the Bible and the nature of the divinity of Christ. According to the former students making the accusations, he taught that the "verbal inspiration and infallibility of the Bible" was "not tenable in the light of modern knowledge and research"[52] and that Christ's human

---

49. Ellis, "Baptist and Radical Politics in Western Canada," 165–66.

50. Both Wilson, "Baptists and Business" and Adams, "War of the Worlds" spend time dealing with this tension in Jarvis Street Baptist Church, Toronto. Shields reported on the Vancouver response in *The Gospel Witness*, 5 March 1925, 11.

51. E.g., this is the argument of Pinnock, "The Modernist Impulse at McMaster University," 193–207.

52. A. W. Bennett, unpublished statements, n.d., in Baptist Historical Collection, NBTC.

limitations meant that he was not aware that his death was to be a substitutionary atonement for the sins of the world.[53]

The report of the 1922 commission, the second which the Baptist Union appointed to investigate the charges against Prof. MacNeill, included among its findings three areas in which his beliefs differed considerably from traditional Baptist views. First, on the inspiration of the Bible, the commission concluded that "he does not hold to the traditional, verbal theory" of inspiration even while holding to "the great throbbing, vitalizing fact of inspiration"; second, on the virgin birth of Christ, the report stated that he believed in the incarnation but "concerning the Virgin Birth as the method of realizing the incarnation, he frankly states his uncertainty"; and third, on the bodily resurrection of Christ, the commission noted that he distinguished "between the great fact of the resurrection and the bodily form in which He appeared."[54] The dissenting British Columbia commission members, Revs. A. F. Baker and G. R. Maguire, cited these three areas of belief as their reason not to agree with the recommendation to retain MacNeill at Brandon.[55] The commission's report, although exonerating MacNeill, also seemed to lend at least some credence to the conservatives' view that significant theological issues were at stake by adding the recommendation that he no longer teach Bible to Arts students.

Such theological issues were the concern of not only the intellectual elites, but had become the subject of widespread discussion among the Baptist laity of Vancouver for several years before the Brandon College controversy became public. In 1917, evangelist French E. Oliver, a conservative Presbyterian minister from Los Angeles, held a nine-week series of meetings in Vancouver which sparked a theological controversy in the city described by a newspaper as "the biggest sensation of recent years in Vancouver religious circles."[56] Oliver's preaching drew crowds which frequently filled the 5,000 seat temporary wooden "tabernacle" constructed on the east side of the city's downtown core and the meetings attracted considerable newspaper coverage. In the last three weeks of his meetings, a full-scale public theological debate broke out in the city's pulpits and press

---

53. J. Linton, unpublished statements, n.d., in Baptist Historical Collection, NBTC.

54. The commission's report noted other differences but these three were the most important, according to the conservatives opposed to Brandon. The main points of the report of the commission were reprinted in *The Gospel Witness*, September 1932, 2–3.

55. Letter to T. T. Shields, 12 March 1924. Reprinted in *The Gospel Witness*, September 1932, 3.

56. *Daily Province*, 10 July 1917.

as criticism from liberals of Oliver's belief in a literal hell quickly escalated to cover a much wider range of issues. Prominent liberal ministers from several denominations publicly criticized Oliver from their pulpits and in the city newspapers, accusing him of being against modern scholarship and social reform and of focusing on "dogma" and divisiveness. In response, Oliver escalated his denunciations of liberalism, thundering against "scholastic infidels," "ecclesiastical buzzards," and "theological degenerates" and a number of conservative ministers, with Baptists being most prominent among them, took up his defense.[57] In the tense war-time atmosphere in the strongly-British city of Vancouver, the charges of Oliver and his defenders that German scholarship was responsible for much liberal theology carried particular weight with the public.[58]

By way of contrast, in the city of Victoria, BC, where Oliver held large-scale evangelistic meetings a few months later, his meetings were very widely attended and were extended in length several times due to the large response to the evangelist's message. However, they did not create the same theological stir at the public level and the Baptist population in that city did not experience nearly as much division as it did in Vancouver in subsequent years.[59] The difference seems to be the lack of significant and public criticism by liberal ministers. In Vancouver, Oliver's harshest critics included high profile liberal ministers such as Rev. A. E. Cooke of First Congregational Church and president of the Vancouver ministerial association, Dr. Ernest Thomas of Wesleyan Methodist Church, the largest Methodist church in the province, and Dr. John Mackay of the Presbyterian Westminster Hall. Their public denunciations unwittingly made Oliver's warnings against liberalism and its dangers far better known in Vancouver than they would have been otherwise and large numbers of Baptists in the city, in particular, became especially attuned to signs of any inroads into their denomination. Oliver had singled out the divinity school of the University of Chicago for special criticism, calling it a "disgrace to the Baptist church of America" and its graduates "pegged-legged infidels."[60] In so doing he more than likely helped create an antipathy towards that institution

---

57. The three city newspapers gave the controversy considerable coverage. For a more complete account of the French E. Oliver meetings in Vancouver, see Burkinshaw, *Pilgrims in Lotus Land*, 41–54.

58. E.g., Vancouver *Daily World*, 11 June 1917 and 7 July 1917.

59. Burkinshaw, *Pilgrims in Lotus Land*, 53–54, 91.

60. *Vancouver Daily World*, 7 July 1917.

among many Vancouver Baptists, which several years later bore directly on Brandon College with its close ties to the University of Chicago.

In addition, the Vancouver Bible Training School (VBTS), formed in 1918, in the aftermath of the French E. Oliver meetings, brought conservative theological education to large numbers of Vancouver's evangelical lay men and women, including many in the city's Baptist congregations.[61] Significantly, it was the first interdenominational Bible school founded in western Canada, pre-dating Prairie Bible Institute by four years and Winnipeg Bible Institute by seven years.[62] Its founding principal was Walter Ellis. Ellis was an English-born, ordained Anglican who eventually added the role of minister of the non-concurring Fairview Presbyterian Church on Vancouver's west side to his work as principal of VBTS. Ellis had been involved in the committee that brought Oliver to Vancouver, but his approach was vastly different than that of the American evangelist and he was known as scholarly and as non-contentious as possible in promoting conservative theology.[63] Despite this more moderate style, he won the respect of many militantly conservative Baptists and provided a thorough grounding in conservative theology for a number of Baptists who came to support the fundamentalists. Ellis never took sides in the developing Baptist dispute but, nevertheless, the Vancouver fundamentalist Baptist publication, the *Baptist Herald*, prominently lauded the work of VBTS in 1923 and highly recommended the evening public "Fundamentals" lecture series by Ellis. The lectures were valuable, the editor states, because they demonstrated "without doubt that the old orthodoxy is entirely and perennially up-to-date and in keeping with the most exacting investigations of scholarship."[64] VBTS was run on strictly interdenominational lines but much of its financial support came from fundamentalist Baptists, particularly members of the Mount Pleasant Baptist, and the largest group in its student body was consistently Baptist.[65]

---

61. For a full description and analysis of the role of VBTS see Burkinshaw, *Pilgrims in Lotus Land*, 55–75.

62. Bruce Guenther notes that some local Mennonite Bible schools had been founded in western Canada before this time. Guenther, "Bible School Movement," 136–37.

63. Ellis believed that his involvement in the Oliver campaign and his role in VBTS led him to losing both his teaching post at Latimer Hall, the low-church Anglican theological college in Vancouver and his ministerial license. Interview with Mrs. A. E. Ellis.

64. *Baptist Herald*, January 1923, 8.

65. For example, businessman Robert Sharpe, a prominent member of Mount Pleasant Baptist, was the first president of the VBTS Council and its chief financial benefactor.

The school played a significant role in providing doctrinal and evangelistic training for lay people—both men and women—that was not available in other western Canadian provinces for several years. Ellis' purpose was to raise a generation of lay evangelists "with a thorough and practical use of the English Bible, and to send forth workers with an extreme love of souls."[66] The primary role of Bible schools, he believed, was to be "hotbeds of evangelistic action"[67] and, for him, that applied equally to women as well as men. As was the case with most Bible schools in North America, VBTS enrolled significant numbers of women in its full and part-time student body.[68] In addition, Ellis provided instruction for large numbers of women in his Thursday evening lecture for Sunday school teachers, which drew crowds of upwards of 150 each week to hear his conservative interpretation of the International Uniform Lesson Series.[69] Ellis worked hard to encourage students of both sexes to take leadership in starting up various mission organizations working in evangelism in the Vancouver region, whether downtown or in outlying areas, and, under his tutelage, young women took significant leadership roles at several local missions.[70] Thus it is not surprising to note that almost immediately upon formation of the British Columbia Baptist Missionary Council in 1925, the women's Missionary Council began operating its own city mission in Vancouver.[71]

Explanations for the split in Vancouver Baptist ranks need to take into account the role of VBTS and Ellis in helping to shape the orientation of conservative Baptist laypeople in Vancouver in the years from 1918 to the 1925 schism. Unlike other western Canadians Baptists, they had access to theologically conservative, practical biblical and evangelistic training in their city, which contributed to both a strong conservative doctrinal orientation and inclined them to be "more enthusiastic and ready to proclaim their faith openly."[72] The evangelistic orientation of Vancouver Baptists

---

VBTS Council minutes 4 January 1919 and 5 February 1923.

66. VBTS, Council Minutes, 17 May 1918.

67. VBTS, Council Minutes, 8 March 1919.

68. Brereton, *Training God's Army*, 69, notes that women comprised a majority of the students in most Bible schools in the United States. The same seems to be true of VBTS.

69. For a discussion of the International Uniform Lesson series, see Knoff, *The World Sunday School Movement*, 2, 35, 41, 64–68, 103.

70. Kuhn, *By Searching*, 24–25, 126–60 and Burkinshaw, *Pilgrims in Lotus Land*, 71–72.

71. The details of this mission are not known.

72. Pousett, "A History of the Convention," 171.

seemed to have motivated much of their criticism of Brandon College as they frequently pointed out that institution's lack of success in producing evangelists and home missions workers. In their minds, the academic honours bestowed upon its faculty could not compensate for the failure of the college to produce graduates who "would take up the work in many needy places."[73] They believed that one of the chief dangers of Prof. MacNeill and his doctrinal views was their role in undercutting the evangelistic commitment of some of his students.[74]

The evangelistic zeal of fundamentalist Baptists continued after the rupture and led to more rapid growth than that experienced by the old, mainline Baptist Convention of British Columbia. By 1960 the number of congregations affiliated with it in the province had surpassed the number of congregations in the old Baptist Convention[75] and by 1980 its weekly attendance had also surpassed that of the old Baptist convention.[76] That growth occurred despite further divisions over issues such as missions' policy and denominational identity, which split the Regular Baptist ranks several times in the decades after 1925.[77]

CONCLUSION

In summary, the evidence makes clear that the reasons for such an early and numerically significant division among Baptists in British Columbia, specifically the Vancouver region, are complex. American influences were not insignificant, but British and eastern Canadian influences were even stronger. Charles H. Spurgeon of London and T. T. Shields of Toronto were chief among those providing inspiration for the British Columbia fundamentalists, but no single leader rose to dominance in Vancouver. Working class members were most numerous in their ranks, but the membership in the new Regular Baptist convention was heterogeneous enough in terms of class to discourage a simple socio-economic explanation. Social and

73. J. Thompson, "Letter to the Editors," *The Baptist Herald*, December 1922, 9.

74. E.g., J. B. Rowell, unpublished statements, December 1921 and J. Linton, unpublished statements, n.d.

75. Compiled from Pousett, "The History of the Regular Baptists," table 17, Convention of Regular Baptist Churches, Convention *Yearbook*, 1961

76. Burkinshaw, *Pilgrims in Lotus Land*, 208, Table 4.

77. These further schisms resulted in the creation of the large, independent Metropolitan Tabernacle, the affiliation of six Vancouver area churches and missions with the Baptist General Conference and five churches in British Columbia with the Southern Baptist Convention. See Burkinshaw, *Pilgrims in Lotus Land*, 124–31 and 155–69.

economic differences certainly contributed to a rejection of the commitment to progress, respectability, and cultural accommodation, which was becoming evident among elements of the denomination, but significant theological differences were also at stake as was acknowledged by those investigating Prof. MacNeill's teaching. A combination of the timing of the French E. Oliver evangelistic campaign in Vancouver in 1917, during a tense period in World War I, and the high-profile exchange between liberal critics and Oliver and his conservative defenders forcefully brought theological issues to the forefront among the city's Baptist population. The establishment of VBTS in the immediate aftermath of the Oliver campaign provided instruction in conservative doctrines for many Baptists laypeople in the city as well as encouragement and experience in vigorous evangelism.

All of these factors worked together to create a wide receptivity among Vancouver Baptists to the public criticisms of Brandon College when they began in 1920. Once aroused, large numbers of these fundamentalist Baptists proved willing to press the fight against modernism to the point of a major schism in their ranks in 1925, the first such division among Baptists in North America.

BIBLIOGRAPHY

Primary

NEWSPAPERS

Baptist Herald (Vancouver, BC), 1922–1923
BC Baptist (Vancouver, BC), 1925
Daily Province (Vancouver, BC), 1917
Gospel Witness (Toronto, ON), 1925, 1932
Vancouver Daily World (Vancouver, BC), 1917

YEARBOOKS

Baptist Union of Western Canada, *Year Book*, 1927, 1930.
Convention of Regular Baptist Churches of British Columbia, *Yearbook*, 1961.

OTHER

Baptist Union of Western Canada. *Report of the Brandon College Commission*. Calgary, 1923.
Bennett, A. W. Unpublished statements, n.d., in Baptist Historical Collection, Northwest Baptist Theological College at Trinity Western University, Langley, BC.
The Sixth Census of Canada, 1921. Ottawa: F. A. Acland, 1924.
The Seventh Census of Canada, 1931. Ottawa: J. O. Patenaude, 1934.

Linton, J. Unpublished statement, n.d., in Baptist Historical Collection, Northwest Baptist Theological College at Trinity Western University, Langley, BC.
Rowell, J. B. Unpublished statements, n.d., in Baptist Historical Collection, Northwest Baptist Theological College at Trinity Western University, Langley, BC
Ruth Morton Memorial Baptist Church, Vancouver. Minutes of Congregation, 11 January 1922.
Vancouver Bible Training School. Council Minutes. 4 January 1919 and 5 February 1923.

Secondary

Adams, Doug A. "The War of the Worlds: The Militant Fundamentalism of Dr. Thomas Todhunter Shields and the Paradox of Modernity." PhD diss., University of Western Ontario, 2015.
Brereton, Virginia. *Training God's Army: The American Bible School, 1880–1940.* Bloomington: Indiana University Press, 1990.
Burkinshaw, Robert. K. *Pilgrims in Lotus Land: Conservative Protestantism in British Columbia, 1917–1981.* Montreal and Kingston: McGill-Queen's University Press, 1995.
Clark, S. D. *Church and Sect in Canada.* Toronto: University of Toronto Press, 1948.
———. *The Developing Canadian Community.* Toronto: University of Toronto Press, 1968.
Cockle, Arthur. Interview. Vancouver, 2 February 1980.
Dunlop, Aaron. "James B. Rowell, 1888–1973." In *A Noble Company: Biographical Essays on Particular-Regular Baptists in America: The Canadians*, vol. 12, edited by Michael A. G. Haykin and Terry Wolever, 417–39. Springfield, MO: Regular Baptist Press, 2019.
Ellis, Mrs. A. E. Interviews. Vancouver, 11 and 22 January 1982, 20 March 1982.
Ellis, Walter E. "Baptists and Radical Politics in Western Canada: 1920–1950." In *Baptists in Canada: Search for Identity Amidst Diversity*, edited by Jarold K. Zeman, 161–82. Burlington: Welch, 1980.
Guenther, Bruce L. "The Origin of the Bible School Movement in Western Canada: An Ethnic Interpretation." *Historical Papers: Canadian Society of Church History* (1993) 135–73.
Hills, Don. Interview. Vancouver, 3 January 1980.
Kilbourn, William. *Religion in Canada: The Spiritual Development of a Nation.* Toronto: McClelland and Stewart, 1968.
Knoff, Gerald E. *The World Sunday School Movement.* New York: Seabury, 1979.
Kuhn, Isobel. *By Searching: My Journey Through Doubt into Faith.* Chicago: Moody, 1959.
Mann, W. E. *Sect, Cult and Church in Alberta.* Toronto: University of Toronto Press, 1955.
Moir, John S. "Sectarian Tradition in Canada." In *Churches in the Canadian Experience*, edited by John W. Grant, 119–32. Toronto: Ryerson, 1963.
Morton, Dennis. "The Rise of Metropolitan Tabernacle." Seminar paper, Regent College, 1980.
Niebuhr, H. Richard. *The Social Sources of Denominationalism.* New York: Henry Holt and Co, 1929.
Pinnock, Clark H. "The Modernist Impulse at McMaster University, 1887–1927." In *Baptists in Canada: Search for Identity Amidst Diversity*, edited by Jarold K. Zeman, 193–207. Burlington: Welch, 1980.

Pousett, Gordon H. "The History of the Regular Baptists of British Columbia." BD thesis, McMaster University, 1956.

———. "A History of the Convention of Baptist Churches of British Columbia." MTh thesis, Vancouver School of Theology, 1982.

Rawlyk, George A. *Champions of the Truth: Fundamentalism, Modernism, and the Maritime Baptists*. Montreal: McGill-Queen's University Press, 1990.

Rennie, Ian S. "Theological Education in Canada: Past and Present." Unpublished paper in author's possession.

———. "Fundamentalism and the Varieties of North Atlantic Evangelicalism." In *Evangelicalism: Comparative Studies of Popular Protestantism in North America, the British Isles and Beyond, 1770–1990*, edited by Mark A. Noll et al., 39–75. New York: Oxford University Press, 1994.

Richards, John B. *Baptists in British Columbia: A Struggle to Maintain Sectarianism*. Northwest Baptist Theological College and Seminary, 1977.

———. Interview. Vancouver, 7 December 1979.

Russell, C. Allyn. "Thomas Todhunter Shields, Canadian Fundamentalist." *Ontario History* 70.4 (1978) 261–80.

Tarr, Leslie K. *Shields of Canada*. Grand Rapids: Baker, 1967.

Wilson, Paul R. "Baptists and Business Central Canadian Baptists and the Secularization of the Businessman at Toronto's Jarvis Street Baptist Church, 1848–1921." PhD diss., University of Western Ontario, 1996.

6

From United Baptist to Independent Baptist

Fundamentalism and Baptist Identity in the Maritime Provinces of Canada in the 1930s

TAYLOR MURRAY

UNLIKE THEIR COUNTERPARTS IN central and western Canada, the United Baptist Convention of the Maritime Provinces escaped the fundamentalist-modernist controversy of the early twentieth century comparatively unscathed.[1] As George Rawlyk has explored, the fundamentalists' inability to split the convention stemmed from a number of factors, including the small size of their circle of support and the relatively inconsequential clout of the movement's leading figures. Perhaps most significantly, however, as Rawlyk has written, this experience was due largely to the fact that the Baptists in the region generally had an "open-minded evangelical theology" that dated back to their revivalist heritage, which conflicted with the "increasingly closed-minded theological fundamentalism" common elsewhere in Canada and in the United States. To many Baptists in the Maritimes in the 1920s and 1930s, fundamentalism was something of an alien intrusion.[2]

---

1. Sections of this chapter are reprinted from the *American Baptist Quarterly* XXXVII.3 (Fall 2017), 282–303 with permission of the American Baptist Historical Society, Atlanta, GA 30341.

2. Rawlyk, *Champions of the Truth*, 37. While Rawlyk's assessment raises certain other questions, the crux of his thesis has proven its historical longevity, as it has filtered into various other interpretations of the event. For example, see Murray, "From Exodus

Although these factors may have insulated the United Baptists from the kind of theological turbulence that fractured the central and western Canadian Baptist communities during the early twentieth century, this did not mean that the convention was entirely free from controversy. Beginning in 1934, a number of fundamentalist leaders departed (or were removed) from the convention. They hoped that their protests might incite further action; however, ultimately fewer than ten churches joined them in their effort. Instead of forming a new denominational body, those churches that departed decided to identify strictly as independent Baptists—which reflected their opposition to the United Baptist Convention—and determined instead to create a loose network of churches that cooperated in several shared ministries. In many respects, this is typical of independent Baptists in general, "who are distinguished for their opposition to mainstream Baptist organizations" but who frequently practice "selective associationalism."[3] By 1939, this growing network suffered a significant internal schism that saw the bifurcation of the independent Baptist movement into two distinct streams. In each of these schisms the determining issue was over what constituted "proper" Baptist thought. Differing views both inspired the fundamentalists' protests and eventually frustrated their influence in the region.

This chapter begins with an overview of the United Baptist Convention in the early twentieth century before looking at the rise of the key fundamentalist leaders, the development of their ministries, and their attempted schism in the early-1930s. It concludes by looking at the debilitating internal schism that saw the independent Baptist movement go in two different directions.[4]

---

to Exile," 83–84; Coops, "Shelter from the Storm," 214–15; Wilson, "The Changing Role," 62; and Renfree, *Heritage and Horizon*, 239.

3. For a brief typology, see Brackney, *Historical Dictionary of the Baptists*, 222.

4. I am indebted to a number of people who aided in my research for this project, including Jim Tomlinson at Jarvis Street Baptist Church; Beth Lennox and Brian Banks at Kingston Bible College and Academy; Pat Townsend at the Esther Clark Wright Archives of Acadia University; Terry Fraser of Saint John, New Brunswick; and Sharon Leighton of Central Bedeque, Prince Edward Island. Thanks also to Greg Pike of Nasonworth, New Brunswick, who sacrificed his time and willingly accommodated my writing schedule so I could meet my deadline.

THE UNITED BAPTIST CONVENTION

The Maritime Provinces have always boasted the largest number of Baptists out of any region in Canada. At the dawn of the twentieth century approximately 19 percent of the population of the three eastern provinces identified as Baptist.[5] Much of this stemmed from the significant religious revivals of the eighteenth and nineteenth centuries, of which Baptists were the primary benefactors. In 1905–1906, the three largest Baptist bodies in the region—the Baptist Convention of the Maritime Provinces, the Free Baptist Conference of New Brunswick, and the Free Baptist Conference of Nova Scotia—formed the United Baptist Convention of the Maritime Provinces. Their common revivalist heritage and their strong regional identity proved to be the strongest unifying factors.[6] They combined their corresponding pastorates and ministries, and began publishing a new newspaper, *The Maritime Baptist*. A larger denominational body also meant an increased circle of support for Acadia University, the Baptists' traditional training ground in Wolfville, Nova Scotia. Altogether, the new convention had a total membership of 64,189 people in 569 churches.[7]

In the early twentieth century, Baptists in the Maritimes "were more open-minded, more experiential, [and] less doctrinaire" than their counterparts elsewhere in the country.[8] While only a select few leaders could be identified as avowed modernists, the general constituency exhibited what various historians have accurately identified as an "accommodating" theology.[9] Hearkening to their revivalist roots, they were more concerned with one's personal conversion than with his or her theological positions. This extended to the various modern advances in thought that emerged in the nineteenth century, especially the relationship between faith and science. According to Barry Moody, among Baptists in the Maritimes,

---

5. *The Fourth Census of Canada, 1901*, 144–45. The "Maritimes" refers to the provinces of New Brunswick, Nova Scotia, and Prince Edward Island.

6. Goodwin, "The Meaning," 153–74.

7. Renfree, *Heritage and Horizon*, 210.

8. Rawlyk, "J. M. Cramp," 133. See also See Rawlyk, *Champions of the Truth*, 34–37; and Moody, "Breadth of Vision," 4–27.

9. For a selection of historians that have noted the "accommodating" view, see Coops, "Shelter from the Storm," 214–15; Rawlyk, "J. M. Cramp," 119–34; and Rawlyk, *Champions of the Truth*, 70–71. Barry Moody has given an important overview of how this position played out at the Maritime Baptist-controlled Acadia College in the nineteenth century. See Moody, "Breadth of Vision," 3–30.

"Science fascinated, perplexed and mystified, but it does not seem to have frightened."[10] It was, for example, surprisingly uncontroversial for a prominent New Brunswick Baptist leader to state from the pulpit at the turn of the century that "The cry ... today against the advance of science into the realm of the religious life is a false alarm. We have nothing to fear from science but everything to hope."[11] Against this backdrop, two significant changes took place in the 1920s that would eventually lead the fundamentalists to take action against the convention.

The first major change involved a shift in ordination policy in 1922. At the time of union, the convening Baptists had relegated theological differences to the periphery of their discussions, but questions of polity loomed large. The Regular and Free Baptist communities managed to balance any remaining differences in a well-crafted (if sometimes conspicuously ambiguous) *Basis of Union*. This was perhaps most visible in their statement on independence and interdependence: "Each church is independent, but the churches are interdependent. All the power the more general bodies have over the less general and the individual churches is to advise and to enforce advice with the strongest moral motives."[12] Counted among those matters that fell to the local congregation was the practice of ordination. The *Basis of Union* stipulated that if a church were to ordain their pastor, they would gather a committee of local pastors and laypersons to determine if the candidate was prepared for Baptist ministry.[13] In 1922, the convention replaced this structure with a convention-led, centralized examining council,[14] which appeared to some to clearly favour interdependence over independence.

The second major change took place when Acadia introduced its Bachelor of Divinity degree in 1923. Acadia, the denomination's intellectual capital and a favourite target of the later fundamentalists, reflected the United Baptists' accommodating theology. It was this position that led one student to proclaim that "The lecturer and the preacher will have a

10. Moody, "Breadth of Vision," 26.

11. W. C. Keirstead, "What is Truth?" Sermon preached in 1899 or 1900, reprinted in Rawlyk, "J. M. Cramp," 133.

12. *United Baptist Convention of the Maritime Provinces Basis of Union (Doctrinal Statement and Church Polity)*, 1906, Article I.

13. *United Baptist Convention of the Maritime Provinces Basis of Union (Doctrinal Statement and Church Polity)*, 1906, Article IV.

14. Beals, ed., *The United Baptist Year Book of the Maritime Provinces of Canada*, 1922, 125.

common aim, the Darwins and the Spurgeons mutually give and take."¹⁵ They celebrated various modern advances in thought and integrated them into the classroom, especially as they related to scientific evolution. Not only were the United Baptists generally open to these kinds of positions, but also many were willing to overlook those views with which they disagreed because of Acadia's traditional role as a hub of spiritual activity for the Baptists. Since Acadia's founding in 1838, intermittent revivals had swept across the campus, which the Baptists believed were "God's stamp of approval on both education and Acadia."¹⁶ To them, it did not matter that Acadia was, as Moody has described, "very open to the winds of change that were blowing through the field of higher education" at the turn of the century.¹⁷ When they began offering Bachelor of Divinity degrees, it meant that if a student wished to enter the ministry in the Maritimes, they could now complete their entire educational requirements at Acadia. While most remained content with Acadia's role in the convention, others raised questions with regard to its ability to remain orthodox. It was in this context that the fundamentalists found their footing.

EARLY FUNDAMENTALIST DEVELOPMENTS

Among the most important early fundamentalists in the region was J. B. Daggett (1869–1939). Daggett was born on the island of Grand Manan in New Brunswick in 1869 to a family that was very active in the Free Baptist Conference in that province. Later he claimed that he was "reared a Baptist, cradled, pursed, and nurtured upon Baptist doctrines and principles."¹⁸ He cherished his Baptist heritage and routinely looked back to his denomination's revivalist roots to gauge the effectiveness of his own ministry. He had a small frame and suffered from chronic ill-health, but he had a fiery spirit, and he was a natural debater. He entered the ministry in 1891 and was ordained in 1894, and thereafter served in various Free Baptist (United Baptist after 1905) churches throughout Charlotte, York, and Carleton Counties. In 1898, he married Elizabeth Jane Merrithew, with whom he

---

15. W. H. Newcomb, "The Problem of Life," *Christian Messenger*, 6 July 1870, 209–10, as cited in Moody, "Breadth of Vision," 26–27.

16. Wilson, "The Changing Role," 61. See also Wilson, "From Revivals to Evangelism," 268.

17. Moody, "Breadth of Vision," 21.

18. J. B. Daggett, "Baptists in the Maritime Provinces," *The Gospel Witness*, 20 August 1925, 11.

had two sons, Cecil Rhodes (1900)—who did not survive infancy—and Eldon Edmund (1903).

His health forced him to retire from active ministry in 1908, but—after a brief career in the agricultural industry—he became the Secretary of Agriculture for the Province of New Brunswick in 1912. When Daggett's Tories were voted out of office in 1917, he accepted the pulpit at Marysville United Baptist Church, outside of the province's capital. That same year he was implicated in what the press called "the patriotic potato scandal," wherein it was revealed that the government had accepted a bribe to remunerate monies lost in an ill-planned wartime relief effort. In the end, although he was not charged with a crime, his connection to the events sullied his reputation to the degree that when he tried to reinstate his ministerial credentials in 1918 several "prominent member[s] of the Convention" objected.[19] The convention ultimately restored Daggett to the list of ordained ministers; however, he increasingly found himself as an outsider in the convention. Perhaps in an effort to move away from his one-time allies, he left his home province and accepted a pastorate at Tryon United Baptist Church in rural Prince Edward Island in 1921.

As he returned to the ministry, he also began comparing the state of the convention in the twentieth century to that of the previous century, and he could only conclude that its spiritual footprint had become virtually nonexistent. Revivalism no longer characterized the Baptist experience in the Maritimes, and he believed modernism was to blame: "there are signs of a great spiritual drought; the heavens are being shut up; there are a few scattered showers of blessing; . . . Horse-racing, dancing, card-playing, theatre-going, pleasure-loving, church members are increasing in city and country." Ultimately, Daggett pointed toward "a change in the teaching in some of our pulpits" and suggested that modernism had taken root in the United Baptist Convention.[20]

In an effort to address this new development, in early 1925, he sought guidance from T. T. Shields, the pastor of the prestigious Jarvis Street Baptist Church in Toronto and the *de facto* Baptist fundamentalist leader in Canada.[21] Shields had led protests of the purported modernism at the

19. Unsigned Letter to H. W. Carpenter, 2 February 1935, Acadia University Archives (hereafter AUA), Gordon C. Warren Collection (hereafter WAR) 2004.007-WAR/11.

20. J. B. Daggett, "Baptists in the Maritime Provinces," *Gospel Witness*, 20 August 1925, 11–12.

21. In his important *Champions of the Truth*, George Rawlyk notes that Daggett reached out to Shields in 1924; however, it appears as though this is a typographical

Baptist-controlled McMaster University in Ontario and Brandon College in Manitoba—each of which would eventually lead to significant schisms in their respective denominational bodies. "I am afraid Acadia College [sic] is badly tainted," Daggett noted, "[and] I know some of our leading preachers are."[22] Prior to this contact, Shields had received only "one or two letters from Nova Scotia urging [him] to come."[23] The two fundamentalists developed an extensive correspondence and evidently shared a great deal of mutual respect. Shields saw Daggett as "a most delightful man"[24] and, as Rawlyk has noted, viewed him as the clear fundamentalist leader in the United Baptist Convention.[25]

While Daggett drew inspiration from Shields, his closest ally became the likeminded J. J. Sidey (1891–1966). Sidey was born in Portsmouth, England in 1891, but relocated to Windsor, Nova Scotia around the time of the First World War apparently in an effort to become a missionary to North America, like his father before him. Here he met his future wife, Edna Reynolds Carde, with whom he had two children, Isabel Sarah (1919) and John Donald (1921). Sidey relocated to Chicago, Illinois (later joined by Edna after they wed in 1918) so he could pursue theological training. He graduated with a Bachelor of Theology from Union Theological College in Chicago in 1921 and only a few months later also received a Master of Arts and a Doctor of Divinity from Oriental University—a correspondence school in Washington, DC that was exposed as a degree mill and closed only six years later.[26] He returned to Nova Scotia the same year he graduated and launched the Soul Winners' Association of Nova Scotia, for which he worked as a travelling evangelist. He was a gifted preacher and, despite his intimidating six-foot build, was surprisingly approachable and deeply relational. Although he had been raised as a Methodist and ordained in the Methodist Episcopal Church, he received believer's baptism in 1921 and accepted a pastoral charge over Central Bedeque Baptist Church in rural Prince Edward Island in 1925.

---

error. Letters between Daggett and Shields prior to early 1925 are not in the Jarvis Street Archives, and the earliest extant letters (from 1925) suggest that the two were not in contact before this exchange. Rawlyk, *Champions of the Truth*, 89.

22. J. B. Daggett to T. T. Shields, 14 March 1925, Jarvis Street Baptist Church Archives (hereafter JSBC).

23. T. T. Shields to J. B. Daggett, 25 March 1925, JSBC.

24. T. T. Shields to R. W. Bennett, 24 August 1925, JSBC.

25. Rawlyk, *Champions of the Truth*, 76–102.

26. Rawlyk, *Champions of the Truth*, 44.

Daggett and Sidey's theology was a militant conservative evangelicalism that favoured dispensational premillennialism, the inerrancy of Scripture, and the deity of Christ. They determined that the Bible must be read literally and that all forms of "modern thinking" must be opposed, especially evolution and higher criticism. For Daggett and Sidey, these conservative ideas were the "foundation stones of the Baptist faith," and the ones that "gave Baptists their supremacy in [the Maritime] provinces."[27] They found various likeminded allies, such as R. W. Bennett, the pastor at Immanuel Baptist Church in Truro, Nova Scotia; and Neil Herman, the pastor of Central Christian Church in Charlottetown, Prince Edward Island. There were some slight theological differences between several of the key players—especially Bennett and Herman, who disagreed over the frequency with which preachers should talk about the second coming[28]—but they were unified around a common purpose: to challenge the perceived growing threat of modernism in the United Baptist Convention, especially as it existed at Acadia.

In addition to what they viewed as the convention's pronounced modernism, they identified a second, perhaps more insidious threat: the convention's new centralized ordination council. The fundamentalists claimed that this new procedure violated traditional Baptist polity, but it soon became apparent that it would be problematic for another reason, as they feared it could be used as a backdoor for modernists to enter the convention and rise to prominence. As they came together in the 1920s, they criticized Acadia's Dean of Theology, Simeon Spidle, who served as chair of the council, for giving his favourite students a pass without adequately assessing their thought or ability: "Our churches have delegated their power to the higher authority in our ranks," wrote one early fundamentalist, "Instead of one Pope we have about ten of them. THEIR WORD IS LAW."[29]

---

27. J. B. Daggett, "Baptists in the Maritime Provinces," *The Gospel Witness*, 20 August 1925, 11–12.

28. See R. W. Bennett to T. T. Shields, 2 January 1926, JSBC. In this letter, Bennett was critical of other fundamentalists: "Our fundamentalist brethren . . . of small intellect," especially those who routinely chastised him because "I do not preach 'the second coming' every Sunday." Herman was his primary antagonist. He was an ardent premillennialist who regularly preached that they were living in "a corrupt age" akin to Sodom and Gomorrah. For example, see Neil Herman, "The World Upside Down," *The Challenge*, September 1923, 7–14.

29. R. W. Bennett to T. T. Shields, 9 September 1925, JSBC.

Despite the urgency with which they wrote their evaluations of the convention, Shields recommended that they wait to launch their full protest. The primary reasons he gave were their minimal finances and their relatively inconsequential number of supporters.[30] As a result, it meant that as Baptists in central and western Canada were dividing over the fundamentalist criticisms, the United Baptists remained untouched. While Daggett and Sidey both admired Shields and sought his advice on several occasions, they became increasingly less interested in working directly with him, which coincided with his loss of interest in them. Rawlyk speculates that the falling out was at least somewhat related to their eschatological differences, as Shields routinely downplayed the centrality of premillennialism to the fundamentalist cause.[31] They would later express their interest in joining the group that departed from Shields to form the Fellowship of Independent Baptist Churches in 1933,[32] but (in traditional Maritimer fashion) they determined to limit the number of "outside" influences and opted instead to forge their own path.

As the fundamentalists waited for their time to strike, Daggett resigned from his church in Tryon and answered a call from the Kingston and Melvern Square Baptist pastorate in the Annapolis Valley of Nova Scotia in 1926. During this period, the area was known primarily for its apple and lumber industries.[33] The substance of the Kingston circuit pastorate reflected the region's blue-collar identity. For example, in 1934, out of the forty-seven members listed at Melvern Square Baptist Church, all but two men listed "farmer" as their profession, totalling nineteen.[34] When Daggett's declining health forced him to step into the role of Associate Pastor for the Kingston pastorate in 1930, the church extended an invitation for Sidey to become the Senior Pastor. The fundamentalist leadership hierarchy reflected this change as well, as Daggett remained an influential figure but increasingly became a secondary figure to Sidey. Shortly after Sidey's arrival in Kingston, the pastorate expanded to include neighbouring Lower Alyesford Baptist Church. Now working together on a single

30. J. J. Sidey to T. T. Shields, 16 August 1927, JSBC.

31. Rawlyk, *Champions of the Truth*, 87.

32. E.g., J. J. Sidey to T. A. Meister, 7 February 1933, AUA, Meister Fonds (hereafter MF).

33. Cochrane, ed., *Echoes Across the Valley*, 218.

34. "Covenant Deed of the Melvern Square Baptist Church (Independent)," 6 December 1934, 2–3. Melvern Square Baptist Church (Ind.). Copy in the possession of the author.

field, the fundamentalists were also closer to Acadia—a perceived liberal stronghold and the acknowledged capital of the convention—which meant it was finally time for them to plan their attack.

THE FUNDAMENTALISTS ORGANIZE AND THE CONVENTION RESPONDS

From their new base of operation, these fundamentalists formed ministries that were unrepentantly in line with fundamentalist views. In 1929, Sidey and Daggett organized the first annual Baptist Evangelical Bible Conference, which they renamed the Bible and Evangelistic Conference, in Kingston; and the following year they launched their own newspaper, *The Gospel Light*. As an outgrowth of their evangelistic conference, the fundamentalists formed the Kingston Bible College, which opened in late fall 1930. They saw the college as an alternative to Acadia, wherefrom their students could reach the convention's minimum standards for ordination.[35] "We have got to face the fact with deep sorrow," reported Daggett at the time, "that Acadia is not doing the work she was called into being to do."[36] It functioned like many other institutions of its kind, as it taught the Bible as the ultimate truth over academic subjects and focused primarily on training individuals for Christian ministry.[37]

Initially the fundamentalists claimed that their desire was not "division or separation," but rather to "swing our people back to the faith and spirit of our Father."[38] On one occasion, Sidey even went as far as to comment publicly on Shields' divisive leadership in central Canada by remarking: "The noise of such a conflict in Ontario and Quebec is still ringing in our ears, and we sadly confess that the cause of Jesus Christ is not glorified by such methods."[39] With this spirit, they made a number of allies

---

35. The Kingston Bible College Pamphlet (Kingston, 1929), 2–3, AUA. Initially they operated in the basement of the church in Kingston, before relocating to a six-acre plot of land situated on the outskirts of the town that Sidey described as "a sand heap with half a dozen uncultivated apple trees." See Sidey, *The Widow's Mite*, 16.

36. J. B. Daggett to T. A. Meister, 1 August 1930, AUA, MF.

37. Burkinshaw, "Evangelical Bible Colleges in Twentieth-Century Canada," 373. Sidey plainly outlined the dual function of KBC when he wrote in 1931: "The College emphasizes two things. First, the absolute authority of the Scripture in all things, and secondly [sic], Evangelistic Work in all its varied forms." Mimeographed programme for KBC Closing, 28–30 June 1931, AUA, MF.

38. J. B. Daggett to T. A. Meister, 1 August 1930, AUA, MF.

39. "Mr. J. J. Sidey's Address," Chester Basin Baptist Church Minutes, 27 October

within the convention, including R. W. Lindsay, F. C. Haysmore, William B. Bezanson, and A. L. Tedford in Nova Scotia; Alexander G. Crowe and A. C. Vincent in Prince Edward Island; and A. K. Herman in New Brunswick. In private, however, it was clear that they believed they were unlikely to purge the convention and that it would be necessary eventually to come out from it. As Sidey quietly reflected, "I do not think for one minute that there is the slightest chance of doing anything inside."[40]

Among their most promising allies was T. A. Meister (1893–1993). Born in New Ross, Nova Scotia in 1893, Meister had served overseas during the First World War. When he returned, he enrolled at Acadia, where he graduated with a Bachelor of Arts in 1921 and a Master of Arts in 1922. Following his graduation, he served as pastor of United Baptist fields in Debert and Clark's Harbour, before he accepted the rural Westchester United Baptist circuit in Nova Scotia in December 1930, which included churches in Greenville, Wentworth, Millvale, and—after May 1931—New Annan, as well as Westchester. He was a talented, yet blunt preacher who balanced his time in the pulpit with a successful agrarian career, primarily working in the blueberry industry. He shared many of Sidey and Daggett's theological convictions, especially their emphases on biblical inerrancy and premillennial dispensationalism. He also shared many of their concerns about Acadia and the convention.

Significantly, it was Meister's association with the Kingston fundamentalists that triggered the first real confrontation between the fundamentalists and the convention. Since 1930, the Home Mission Board had provided an annual grant of $300.00 to help support the work in the Westchester field. In 1932, after seeing Meister's association with the emerging fundamentalist cohort, E. S. Mason, the superintendent of the Home Mission Board, asked Meister for "a statement of . . . [his] attitude toward our denominational life."[41] Meister refused and the Home Mission Board decided to suspend the grant until he complied with their request. Finally, Meister replied: "Being in the Lord's work after the historic Baptist manner

---

1933, AUA.

40. J. J. Sidey to T. A. Meister, 27 February 1933, AUA, MF.

41. E. S. Mason to T. A. Meister, 14 October 1932, AUA, MF. The executive's decision to initially target Meister rather than the Kingston fundamentalists is somewhat puzzling; however, it is possible that they had hoped to isolate the fundamentalist circle of influence by investigating and enquiring of potential allies.

... I do not recognize the right of yourself or your board to interfere with the work of myself or my churches."[42]

The fundamentalists were thrilled with Meister's response. Upon learning about the exchange between the Westchester pastor and the Home Mission Board, Sidey concluded: "the time has come for a definite stand."[43] As he reflected on Meister's reply even further, he conveyed that he believed it would "ever live as a historic document" as the first stroke in the fundamentalists' campaign. As Sidey concluded, he noted: "Personally, I am a Baptist, but I am sure that in order to be one, the less I have to do with the United Baptist Convention the better for my own principles."[44] They saw absolute separation as entirely necessary. Neil Herman likewise encouraged Meister to spread what had happened throughout the convention, as he believed it could function as a helpful propaganda tool. "Publicity will not only cripple denominational bandits," wrote Herman, "but [it] will strengthen the hands of those who are waging battle against the foe."[45]

Not everyone in their inner circle shared the fundamentalists' enthusiasm, however, as Meister received a rather lukewarm reception from various conservative pastors who had previously stood alongside the fundamentalists in their ministries. Arthur C. Vincent, the pastor at Charlottetown Baptist Church in Prince Edward Island, and A. K. Herman, the pastor at Highfield Street Baptist Church (Moncton) in New Brunswick, each wrote to Meister in an effort to smooth the relations between him and the convention.[46] Although both Vincent and Herman had been regular attendees and frequent speakers at the Kingston Bible Conferences, both saw the value in remaining within the convention. Likewise, Henry E. Allaby, the pastor at Woodstock United Baptist Church in New Brunswick, wrote to Meister with "sympathetic interest," but noted that he did not agree with Meister's actions. As he explained:

> It is a matter of regret to me that you did not comply with the request of the board to state your opinion with regard to our

---

42. T. A. Meister to E. S. Mason, 2 February 1933, AUA, MF.
43. J. J. Sidey to T. A. Meister, 7 February 1933, AUA, MF.
44. J. J. Sidey to T. A. Meister, 27 February 1933, AUA, MF.
45. Neil Herman to T. A. Meister, 4 February 1933, AUA, MF.
46. A. C. Vincent to T. A. Meister, 13 March 1933, AUA, MF; and A. K. Herman to T. A. Meister, 16 March 1933, AUA, MF. See also A. C. Vincent to T. A. Meister, 3 May 1933. Other responses were much more unsympathetic to Meister's actions. See R. W. Carpenter to T. A. Meister, 23 June 1933, AUA, MF.

> denominational work. *Had you done that, even supposing that you differed in some respects from our present policy, the question the board would have to determine would be how far one could differ from the policy of the denomination and still be eligible for support from the H. M. Board.*[47]

Allaby believed that the executive had presented the fundamentalists with a legitimate opportunity to protest to the convention, which he felt they had failed to grasp. As he concluded, "your refusal to state your position makes it impossible for any of us to do anything . . . I now am persuaded that the board through its executive took the only proper action left open to it."[48] The fundamentalists' approach had the opposite effect of what they had hoped, as many of their strongest supporters and sympathizers from within the convention increasingly wanted little to do with them.[49]

By summer 1933, the convention executive had determined that it was time for a full-scale response to the fundamentalists, and at the annual gathering of that year they laid out their plan of attack. At one of the first sessions, L. E. Ackland, the out-going president of convention, gave his presidential address on the topic of denominational discipline. In his address, Ackland advocated being less stringent in one's doctrinal opinions: "One may be as orthodox as the pope or as the most loyal fundamentalist among us, and yet have very little fitness for the ministry." Instead he suggested that they focus on "a clean upright moral life." Finally, he asked: "Why should we retain one who has no regard for the success of the denominational enterprises, or one who cherishes open and avowed hostility toward our denominational fellowship?" While affirming the independence of the local church, he offered a caveat: "we know by observation and by personal experience, that most churches are unable to deal with such a problem as here indicated." With this word, he called for the ordination

---

47. Henry E. Allaby to T. A. Meister, 19 April 1933, AUA, MF. Emphasis added.

48. Henry E. Allaby to T. A. Meister, 19 April 1933, AUA, MF. Other leaders in the Maritimes (lay and pastor) noted their sympathetic stance with Meister's theology. E.g., J. M. Blasedell to T. A. Meister, 2 June 1933, MF, AUA; and A. G. to T. A. Meister, 3 May 1933, AUA, MF.

49. It is of some note that a number of those who had shown sympathetic interest to the fundamentalist cause but determined to remain within the convention went on to play a determinative role in the convention's gradual shift toward the conservative end of the theological spectrum in the 1960s. See Wilson, "Baptists Confront the Turbulent Sixties," 149–69.

council to take a much more active role in disciplining ministers.[50] The *Year Book* recorded that Ackland's address "brought to the Convention certain important matters which caused much heart-searching on the part of all who heard him."[51] The day after Ackland's address, the convention passed a motion that echoed his words:

> Therefore, be it now Resolved that, for the protection of the innocent and for the sake of the reputation of the ministry in general, this Convention authorize the said [ordination] Council to summon before it for inquiry and action any minister of our body against whose character, integrity or loyalty there may be persistent rumor or definite charge; but any minister so charged shall have the right of appeal to the Convention at large.[52]

The statement was loud and unmistakable: if the fundamentalists wished to battle, the convention executive was prepared for war.

THE FUNDAMENTALISTS' COUNTER-PROTEST

The decision to allow the ordination council to discipline ordained preachers as they saw fit was yet another way in which the fundamentalists believed the convention had undermined the authority of the local church. As a way to protest this change, they formed an ordination council in Chester Basin, a rural community on the South Shore of Nova Scotia. The Nova Scotia Western Association of the United Baptist Convention had denied an Associational License (a preaching license) to the pastor of the Chester Basin United Baptist Church, H. B. Lindsay, for what they believed had been past financial impropriety that included a substantial unpaid debt. It is likely that upon learning of this outcome, Lindsay's stepbrother, R. W. Lindsay, the pastor at Upper Canard and a regular attendee of the Kingston conferences, connected him with Sidey and Daggett. On 19 September 1933, the Chester Basin United Baptist Church assembled an independent council to assess their pastor. Following the United Baptist's pre-1922 ordination procedure, the council featured a group of local pastors, including F. C. Haysmore from Kingston, Neil Herman from Halifax, W. R. MacWalker

---

50. All quotes from this address are from L. E. Ackland, "Denominational Discipline," *The Maritime Baptist*, 27 September 1933, 2–3.

51. Morse, ed., *The United Baptist Year Book of the Maritime Provinces of Canada, 1933*, 15.

52. Morse, ed., *The United Baptist Year Book of the Maritime Provinces of Canada, 1933*, 21.

from Barass Corner, as well as Sidey, Daggett, and Lindsay. In addition to these United Baptist ministers, the church invited thirteen deacons from various churches in the area.[53] After over three hours, the council accepted Lindsay's statements of conversion, faith, and call to ministry.

After determining that Lindsay was fit for the ministry, Sidey recommended contacting the clerk of the Western Association for an answer on why they had denied Lindsay a license.[54] The implication was clear: the convention had too tight of a grip on who was a suitable candidate for the ministry and who was not. The association supplied the requested report and appended substantial documentation to support their initial claim.[55] Sidey and Daggett each publicly defended Lindsay against the association's report, noting that "the story that he acted dishonorably [in his unpaid debts] . . . was given direct and unqualified contradiction."[56] In an effort to resolve the issue, the church called a meeting on 14 November 1933, but this time they invited members from the convention executive. The executive had no illusions about the purpose of the meeting, as Ackland noted that "all signs point to the fact that this is a SIDEY [sic] Engineered council . . . resembling of one called in defiance of Associational Action and of Convention Procedure."[57] The convention sent several representatives from the executive office to review the situation, who unanimously resolved to deny Chester Basin's request for ordination and uphold the association's recommendation to withhold a preaching license from Lindsay.[58] This response was the Kingston fundamentalists' desired result, as it provided a platform from which to challenge the convention's authority. Sidey had declared unequivocally: "the Convention has abrogated to itself the powers which

---

53. "Minutes of the Ordination Council," 19 September 1933, Aenon Baptist Church Records, AUA.

54. "Minutes of the Ordination Council," 19 September 1933, Aenon Baptist Church Records, AUA.

55. See "Minutes of the Ordination Council," 19 September 1933, Aenon Baptist Church Records, AUA; I. A. Corbett to G. C. Warren, 12 October 1933, AUA 2004.007-WAR/ 11; and Sinclair and MacDonald to G. C. Warren, 13 November 1933, AUA 2004.007-WAR/11.

56. "Chester Basin Baptist Church Meeting," 27 October 1933, Aenon Baptist Church Records, AUA.

57. L. E. Ackland to G. C. Warren, 13 November 1933, AUA 2004.007-WAR/11

58. "Finding of Council at Chester Basin," 14 November 1933, AUA 2004.007-WAR/11.

destroyed the liberty of the local church." In particular, he blamed this shift on Baptist leaders and their influence on the "average Baptist member."[59]

The day after the November meeting at Chester Basin, *The Maritime Baptist* began a series entitled, "Fundamental Baptist Beliefs." Written by prominent United Baptist pastors, it ran for seven articles, including: The Lordship of Christ,[60] Soul Competency,[61] Regenerate Church Membership,[62] The New Testament as the standard of faith and practice,[63] Democracy in Church Government,[64] Believers' Baptism,[65] and The Lord's Supper.[66] The purpose of these articles—which had conspicuously omitted the independence of the local church—was to emphasize that the Baptist position was more inclusive than the fundamentalists had portrayed it. The article on soul competency provides the clearest example of this position: "exclusiveness has at times manifested itself even within the Baptist fold. We have had those who would assume the position of a spiritual dictator ... Such a stand seemed to me a betrayal of our most precious Baptist heritage."[67]

THE ATTEMPTED SCHISM

In the wake of the turbulent events at Chester Basin and in the midst of the controversial series in *The Maritime Baptist* that had flagrantly employed the term "fundamental," Sidey submitted a letter of resignation to the secretary of convention. In it, he wrote: "By this action it must be clearly understood that I am simply withdrawing from the fellowship of the Convention, and not from the Baptist church of which I am a member, or from the ministry of churches of which I am a Pastor." It was his contention that one central

---

59. "Mr. J. J. Sidey's Address," 27 October 1933, Aenon Baptist Church Records, AUA.

60. William H. Elgee, "The Lordship of Christ," *The Maritime Baptist*, 15 November 1933, 2.

61. A. L. Huddleston, "The Competency of the Soul to Find God," *The Maritime Baptist*, 22 November 1933, 2.

62. George E. Levy, "Regenerate Church Membership," *The Maritime Baptist*, 29 November 1933, 2.

63. Harry Barber, "The New Testament as a Standard for Faith and Practice," *The Maritime Baptist*, 6 December 1933, 2.

64. M. H. Mason, "Democracy in Church Government," *The Maritime Baptist*, 13 December 1933, 2.

65. E. J. Barrass, "Baptism," *The Maritime Baptist*, 20 December 1933, 2.

66. P. R. Hayden, "The Lord's Supper," *The Maritime Baptist*, 27 December 1933, 2.

67. A. L. Huddleston, "The Competency of the Soul to Find God," *The Maritime Baptist*, 22 November 1933, 2.

governing body like the convention was at variance with "the old-fashioned and historic Baptist position [of congregational independence]."⁶⁸ Sidey's churches were divided on how best to respond: Melvern Square voted to leave the convention; Kingston effectively split into two warring factions; and Lower Aylesford remained a part of the convention.

Sidey's partial resignation was not enough for the ordination council, however, who proceeded to launch their investigation of him. In July 1934, they notified him that they had discovered enough evidence to effectively disqualify him from the ministry, including that he had "bogus" educational credentials, that he had incurred a sizable debt, that there were several unexplained and suspicious irregularities in the finances at the Kingston pastorate, and that he had "made unwarranted charges against the Convention's doctrines and polity."⁶⁹ By the time the ordination council brought the matter before the convention assembly, they had dropped the fourth offense; but it did not matter to them, for they believed they had enough material to discredit him. The convention publicly removed him from their list and, in Rawlyk's words, "Thus secession became expulsion."⁷⁰ In early September 1934, they sent the result "to every church in the convention."⁷¹ Sidey's closest associates, Daggett and Haysmore, likewise offered their resignations from convention, but in Daggett's case they added that he was deleted "for cause."⁷² In the public press, they later heavily implied that their decision on Daggett was related to his involvement in the Patriotic Potato Scandal, which they argued had raised too many questions with regard to the content of his character.⁷³

Using its newfound power, the convention began investigating several of Sidey and Daggett's allies and systematically stripped them of their ordination credentials. The fundamentalists criticized the convention's actions as "contrary to Baptist principles" because "the sole and final authority

---

68. Quotations in this paragraph are from J. J. Sidey to S. S. Poole, 22 November 1933, AUA 2004.007-WAR/11.

69. S. S. Poole to J. J. Sidey, 28 July 1934, AUA 2004.007-WAR/11.

70. Rawlyk, *Champions of the Truth*, 55.

71. L. E. Ackland to J. J. Sidey, 4 September 1934, AUA 2004.007-WAR/11; and Open Letter to the Churches of the United Baptist Convention of the Maritime Provinces of Canada by L. E. Ackland, 5 September 1934, AUA 2004.007-WAR/11.

72. Poole, ed., *Annual Yearbook of the United Baptist Convention of the Maritime Provinces, 1934*, 13.

73. Simeon Spidle, "A Self-Respecting Gentleman," *The Outlook*, 11 October 1934.

rests in the local Baptist Church."[74] Meister likewise raised an important question: was the convention a "voluntary assemblage of self-governing churches" or "a concentration of power . . . [that] seeks to rule over and function for all"?[75] His pointed question did not make a difference, as the convention charged him with associating "with a secessionist movement antagonistic to The United Baptist Convention" and removed him from their list of ordained ministers in 1936.[76] Despite what little effect it had on the outcome of the ordination council's review, Meister's question perfectly captures the fundamentalists' chief criticism of the convention: that it had effectively become an autocratic ecclesiastical structure that was entirely foreign to Baptist ideals and was actively working to undermine the authority of the local church.

The last major confrontation between the fundamentalists and the convention took place in May 1935, when the convention executive brought Sidey and Daggett before the Supreme Court of Nova Scotia over the question of the ownership of church properties.[77] Although the Kingston fundamentalists were no longer part of the United Baptist Convention, they refused to surrender the Kingston parsonage. The convention had the strongest legal claim to the property because of a clause in their Act of Legislature that stipulated that the Home Mission Board could claim the properties of a church that ceased "to exercise the usual functions of a [United Baptist] church, or [lost] visibility."[78] Again reaching out to T. T. Shields for advice, the fundamentalists built their case on the fact that although they had indeed departed from the convention, they—not the United Baptists—were the "true Baptists."[79]

Despite some truly provocative testimony from convention officials that appeared to confirm the fundamentalists' suspicions about the state

---

74. A. L. Tedford to L. E. Ackland, 18 September 1935. AUA 2004.007-WAR/13.

75. T. A. Meister to L. E. Ackland, 7 October 1935. AUA 2004.007-WAR/14.

76. L. E. Ackland to T. A. Meister, 26 September 1935. AUA 2004.007-WAR/14; and Eaton, ed., *The United Baptist Year Book of the Maritime Provinces of Canada*, 1936, 305.

77. The best analysis of the Kingston Parsonage Case is in Rawlyk, *Champions of the Truth*, 55–67, see also pp. 98–99.

78. E. S. Mason, "The Security of United Baptist Church Properties," *The Maritime Baptist*, 19 September 1934, 5.

79. T. T. Shields to J. B. Daggett, 11 May 1935, JSBC. Shields sent them copies of a number of "authoritative" documents from Baptist history to enter into evidence, including the *New Hampshire Confession of Faith* and writings by Charles H. Spurgeon. On Shields' involvement, see Rawlyk, *Champions of the Truth*, 98–99.

of the convention, the trial itself garnered only mild interest from outside parties. As one reporter perceptively noted in the closing days of the trial, "There were several in the room from Kentville and vicinity, but it was the Kingston people who closely followed every witness and hung on every word."[80] The court ruled ultimately and unsurprisingly in favour of the United Baptist Convention in September 1935, thus ordering the fundamentalists to relinquish control of all of the church's properties. The events stirred very little interest in convention circles. Even Shields remarked that their efforts might be characterized as "The Plot that Partially Succeeded," a play on his recent volume about his own struggle in central Canada, *The Plot that Failed*.[81]

Whatever moral or theological victory Sidey and Daggett believed they had won at the trial, the fundamentalist voices in the convention during this period did not ever reach critical mass, and only a few churches actually left the convention. As Rawlyk has argued, and as already noted, the convention's "accommodating" posture prevailed and created a theological climate that was inhospitable to fundamentalism during the early twentieth century, which effectively insulated the United Baptist Convention from theological controversy.[82] Even those who were suspicious of Acadia appear to have been satisfied by the university president's reassurances that "the moral and spiritual life of Acadia has never been saner, more healthy or on a higher level than it is today."[83]

Those that departed identified strictly as "independent Baptists." As they later explained, "We occupy the historic Baptist position. The word 'independent' is only used to distinguish from what is commonly called the United Baptist Convention."[84] This new title also reflected their fiercely independent ecclesiology. As Meister would eventually comment that "no Christian should support or patronize a denominational church of any sort, as things stand today."[85] In addition to the Kingston churches, the fundamentalist influence reached United Baptist congregations in Clark's Harbour (1935), Louis Head (1936), Coddles Harbour (1936), Westchester (1938), and Clementsvale (1939) in Nova Scotia; and Central Bedeque

80. C. M. Dodge, "Clerics Called in Rebuttal," *The Halifax Chronicle*, 27 May 1935, 2.
81. T. T. Shields to J. B. Daggett, 11 December 1937, JSBC.
82. See Rawlyk, *Champions of the Truth*, 34–37, 70, 73–74.
83. Patterson, "Supplement," 249.
84. Max V. Bolser, "Is there a Need?" *The Independent Baptist*, May 1939, 6.
85. "The Church," *The Independent Baptist*, January 1941, 3.

(1939/1940) in Prince Edward Island. Each of these churches was pastored by one of the fundamentalists' allies, including Maxwell Bolser at Clark's Harbour and Onden Stairs at Louis Head—each of whom was a recent graduate of the Kingston Bible College. One fundamentalist who departed from the convention stated their shared sentiment: "I am still a Baptist and hold to the Doctrinal statement of the Basis of Union of 1905,"[86] which had enshrined the emphasis on the independence of the local church.

THE BIFURCATION OF THE INDEPENDENT BAPTIST MOVEMENT

When fewer than ten Baptist churches joined Sidey and Daggett in their protest, they determined instead to focus on building their ministries as nondenominational bodies. Their annual Bible conference and the Kingston Bible College had technically both been nondenominational since 1931 and 1932 respectively, but in early 1935 they came under the umbrella of the International Christian Mission (ICM)—a body that Sidey formed with hopes of becoming a Canadian equivalent of the cross-denominational fundamentalist network, the Independent Fundamental Churches of America.[87] It was a nondenominational—or, as Sidey preferred to call it, "undenominational"—group that focused initially on planting churches in the local area and facilitating fellowship for all interested parties. As Sidey later reflected, "there was insufficient Baptist support for the principle of Independency [sic] in the Maritimes to make it possible that the Work [sic] would continue if confined wholly to Baptist people."[88] Moreover, as Daggett explained in a letter to Shields, "We are finding that not only is this [modernistic orientation] true of the Baptists, but we are meeting members of the United and Anglican Churches who are thoroughly dissatisfied, unhappy, and are starving for the Word of Life."[89] They saw their new ministry as a way to mobilize and create a network for fundamentalist churches in the Maritime Provinces, one that they believed would serve

---

86. Frederick C. Burnett to A. L. Ackland, 19 June 1938, AUA 2004.007-WAR/18.

87. J. J. Sidey to T. A. Meister, 7 February 1933, AUA, MF. On at least one occasion, Sidey actually explored the idea of creating a regional expression of the Independent Fundamental Churches of America. See Donald Wood to J. J. Sidey, 21 February 1933, AUA, MF.

88. Sidey, *The Widow's Mite*, 28.

89. J. B. Daggett to T. T. Shields, 1 October 1936, JSBC.

as a vehicle for combatting modernism throughout the region, across *all* denominations.

While Sidey and Daggett believed that they had satisfactory grounds upon which to concentrate on their nondenominational efforts, many of their allies believed that by focusing on these ministries they had relegated the independent Baptist cause to secondary importance. By early 1936, for example, it had become clear that the ICM's newsletter, *The Question*, had replaced their original newspaper, the Baptist-focused *Gospel Light*, which had been out-of-print for more than a year.[90] Evidently, confusion about their movement had reached even Shields in Ontario, as Sidey had to write him a letter clarifying that "there are two phases of our work here," and that the "Independent Baptist Churches are straight Baptist Churches, and are strictly independent."[91] Increasingly, the Kingston fundamentalists hosted events that featured non-Baptist guest speakers and participants.

By the late 1930s, the nondenominational orientation of the majority of the fundamentalists' ministries had become a major point of contention for those within the movement. In particular, the most significant concern was over Sidey's apparent waffling over the spiritual gifts. This friction forced the ICM to come out with a statement on 11 July 1938 clarifying its position: "we do not believe that the gift of tongues either at Pentecost or for the individual communion with God is the necessary sign of the Baptism of the Holy Ghost, but the Holy Spirit divideth to each one severally as He willeth according to the individual need."[92] While this view satisfied some in the fundamentalist circles, its failure to affirm the cessation of the spiritual gifts provided fodder for Sidey's critics. In August of that year, at the annual Bible conference in Kingston, Meister raised concerns with regard to "the Pentecostal influence" at the Kingston Bible College, namely speaking in tongues:

> Some kind of a thing has been discussed here tonight that comes upon people but can be controlled by the people it seizes, and which, if not so controlled, runs to such excesses and indecency in human conduct as has been suggested here tonight. To call that thing the Holy Ghost is the foulest blasphemy I have ever listened to.[93]

90. J. J. Sidey to T. A. Meister, 11 January 1936, AUA, MF.
91. J. J. Sidey to T. T. Shields, 5 November 1935, JSBC.
92. As cited by Palmer, *The Combatant*, 166.
93. T. A. Meister to J. B. Daggett, 17 September 1938, AUA, MF.

He concluded that if they had "even a tolerant attitude" toward speaking in tongues, "then I am definitely broken with you and glad to be."[94]

Meister was not alone in his protest of Sidey's position on the Holy Spirit, as several of the most prominent emerging leaders, such as Maxwell Bolser at Clark's Harbour and Douglass M. Fraser at Central Bedeque, soon joined him in his criticism. While Fraser, who had been converted under Meister, had a limited connection to the Kingston fundamentalists, Bolser's defection would have been a unique kind of pain for Sidey and Daggett, as he was one of their first students at the Kingston Bible College in 1930. Perhaps not sensing the severity of the situation, Sidey responded by writing, "as this thing has happened we can do nothing about it except to trust the Lord to work it out."[95]

The impending separation was made even more difficult for Sidey when Daggett suffered a fatal heart attack on 15 January 1939, which left Sidey alone to be the sole heir of the Kingston fundamentalist movement. The timing was especially problematic for Sidey, as many of the out-going fundamentalists had praised Daggett's commitment to Baptist principles. Whatever they felt about Sidey, they had held a deep respect for Daggett.[96] Without Daggett's steadying leadership to supplement what they perceived as Sidey's experiential and ambiguous ministry, the potential schism became inevitable. When Meister organized a competing Bible conference in September 1939, it effectively made the divide permanent.

The schism saw the independent Baptist movement split into two distinct camps. Sidey continued his ministry in Kingston with marginal success. The rupture had swept away a number of important and promising leaders and had limited his sphere of influence to his local context. The declaration of the Second World War significantly reduced the number of students at the college and forced its temporary closure. Sidey formed the Maritime Fellowship of Independent Baptists in 1940 (which limited membership to individuals, rather than congregations so as to avoid the appearance of becoming a new convention), but the damage was already done. As he attempted to expand throughout the region and even internationally, he was met with middling success. When he died in May 1966, the

---

94. T. A. Meister to J. B. Daggett, 17 September 1938, AUA, MF.

95. J. J. Sidey to T. A. Meister, 25 August 1938, AUA, MF.

96. E.g., T. A. Meister, "As to our Paper," *The Independent Baptist*, January 1939, 4. In his personal correspondence, it appears that Meister foremost credited Daggett for the 1933-1934 schism and specifically blamed Sidey for the 1938-1939 controversy. See T. A. Meister to W. F. Roadhouse, 14 August 1939, AUA, MF.

influence of his once-promising fundamentalist body was confined almost exclusively to the Kingston area and a few small pockets on the South Shore of Nova Scotia.

Meister formed a loose network of churches that each retained its absolute independence. He launched a new newspaper, *The Independent Baptist*, which he believed was necessary because "no one else is looking after certain phases of [the independent Baptist movement]."[97] In it, he provided a number of thinly-veiled criticisms of Sidey. On one occasion, he described a ministry that closely resembled Sidey's own, noting that the independent Baptists were threatened by "religious adventurers," after which he concluded with a battle call: "Go not astray after Modernism, nor any other '-ism.' Be Baptist. Be independent Baptist."[98] Yet, Meister's brand of independent Baptist was not above controversy, as his wing of the movement suffered yet another schism—again over cooperation with non-Baptists—in the early 1950s, when he began to believe that some of his associates, including Maxwell Bolser and Douglass M. Fraser, were co-operating too closely with the schismatic, defrocked Presbyterian, Perry F. Rockwood, and with the nondenominational, fundamentalist New Brunswick Bible Institute.[99] Bolser and Fraser eventually played a key role in spreading the independent Baptist movement into New Brunswick, and formed the nucleus of the Fundamental Baptist churches that populate the province today, while Meister laboured independently in Westchester well into the twentieth century and eventually died at the age of 99 in 1993.

CONCLUSION

The question of Baptist identity provides a helpful lens through which to view the independent Baptist movement's early development and eventual internal schism. In their confrontation with the United Baptist Convention, the emerging fundamentalists believed that the convention no longer honoured the delicate balance between independence and interdependence, and it had effectively prioritized the latter at cost to the former. From their perspective, the convention's decision to form a centralized

---

97. T. A. Meister, "Open Letter," *The Independent Baptist*, January 1939, 1.

98. T. A. Meister, "The Need of the Hour," *The Independent Baptist*, August 1939, 2. Emphasis added.

99. Edward Blanchard to D. M. Fraser, 20 June 1950; and D. M. Fraser and Haye Fraser to T. A. Meister and Westchester Baptist Church, 15 September 1950, copies in the possession of the author.

ordination council had effectively taken power away from the local church, which placed it outside of what it meant to be truly Baptist. Moreover, it meant, significantly, that when they were faced with modernism within the convention and at Acadia, fundamentalists felt that they had no voice with which to confront what they believed was rank heresy. This reached its zenith in the early 1930s, when the convention granted the ordination council the right to discipline its ministers and began periodically ejecting the fundamentalists from the convention.

Their experience with the convention engendered a strong sense of anti-denominationalism and led the fundamentalists to adopt a fiercely independent ecclesiology. As this feature became their defining principle for what it meant to be a Baptist, they inadvertently annexed themselves from many of their strongest supporters within the convention, who shared their theological concerns but had hoped to retain a stronger sense of interdependence and cooperation than the fundamentalists could comfortably offer.

While the independent Baptists unanimously acknowledged that the United Baptists had strayed from traditional Baptist polity, they were deeply divided on what constituted proper Baptist theology. Unable to inspire any significant change in the United Baptist Convention, the Kingston cohort adopted an "undenominational" posture and welcomed cooperation with non-Baptists. As a corollary to this new direction, they refused to acknowledge the cessation of the charismatic gifts—the failure of which was especially detestable to several prominent independent Baptist leaders, as they believed it clearly placed them outside of proper Baptist theology. These differences of opinion led to the bifurcation of the movement into two distinct streams. One, led by Sidey, was much more *inclusive* by its nature and was not strictly focused on Baptist work. The other, led by Meister, was much more *exclusive* by its nature, and usually did not tolerate working with those outside of the independent Baptist fold.

On either end of the 1939 schism, they demonstrated a fiercely independent ecclesiology but differed on the boundary lines of what a Baptist could believe while also remaining within the Baptist fold. Taken together, by the end of the decade these two features manifested in their inability to cohabit with one another and resulted in a strong tendency toward isolationism that has endured to this day.

BIBLIOGRAPHY

Primary

NEWSPAPERS

Challenge (Kentville, NS), 1923
Christian Messenger (Halifax, NS), 1870
Gospel Witness (Toronto, ON), 1925
Halifax Chronicle (Halifax, NS), 1935
Independent Baptist (Westchester, NS), 1939, 1941
Maritime Baptist (Saint John, NB), 1933–1934
Outlook (Halifax, NS), 1933

ARCHIVES

Acadia University Archives, Wolfville, Nova Scotia; Gordon C. Warren Collection 2004.007-WAR/11, 13, 14, 18; Terence A. Meister Fonds; and Aenon United Baptist Church Records.
Jarvis Street Baptist Church Archives, Toronto, Ontario; "Shields Correspondence," 1925–1927, 1935–1937.
Kingston Bible College & Academy Archives, Kingston, Nova Scotia.

OTHER

The Fourth Census of Canada, 1901. Ottawa: S. E. Dawson, 1902.
Keirstead, W. C. "What is Truth?" Sermon preached in 1899 or 1900, reprinted in G. A. Rawlyk, "J. M. Cramp and W. C. Keirstead: The Response of Two Late Nineteenth-Century Baptist Sermons to Science." In *Profiles of Science and Society in the Maritimes Prior to 1914*, edited by Paul A. Bogaard, 119–34. Fredericton, NB: Acadiensis, 1990.
Sidey, John James. *The Widow's Mite*. Unpublished MS, Kingston Bible College and Academy Archives (1961).
United Baptist Convention of the Maritime Provinces Basis of Union (Doctrinal Statement and Church Polity), 1906.
United Baptist Year Book of the Maritime Provinces of Canada, 1922, 1933–1934, 1936.

Secondary

Brackney, William H. *Historical Dictionary of the Baptists*. 2nd ed. Historical Dictionaries of Religions, Philosophies, and Movements Series. Lanham: Scarecrow, 2009.
Burkinshaw, Robert K. "Evangelical Bible Colleges in Twentieth-Century Canada." In *Aspects of the Canadian Evangelical Experience*, edited by George A. Rawlyk, 317–48. Montreal: McGill-Queen's University Press, 1997.
Coops, P. Lorraine. "'Shelter from the Storm': The Enduring Evangelical Impulse of Baptists in Canada, 1880s to 1990s." In *Aspects of the Canadian Evangelical Experience*, edited by George A. Rawlyk, 208–22. Montreal and Kingston: McGill-Queen's University Press, 1997.
Cochrane, Tony, ed. *Echoes Across the Valley: A History of Kingston and its Neighbors, Volumes I–II*. Hantsport, NS: Lancelot, 1994.

Goodwin, Daniel C. "The Meaning of 'Baptist Union' in Maritime Canada, 1846–1906." In *Baptist Identities: International Studies from the Seventeenth to the Twentieth Centuries*, edited by Ian M. Randall et al., 153–74. Studies in Baptist History and Thought. Eugene, OR: Wipf and Stock, 2006.

Moody, Barry M. "Breadth of Vision, Breadth of Mind: The Baptists and Acadia College." In *Canadian Baptists and Christian Higher Education*, edited by George Rawlyk, 3–30. Montreal and Kingston: McGill-Queen's University Press, 1988.

Murray, Taylor. "Exodus to Exile: Independent Baptists in Nova Scotia, 1934–1939." *American Baptist Quarterly* 37.2 (2017) 282–303.

———. "From Exodus to Exile: The Early Fundamentalist Movement Among Maritime Baptists, 1930–1939." MA thesis, Acadia University, 2016.

Palmer, Gertrude A. *The Combatant: Biography of John J. Sidey*. Middleton, NS: Black Printing, 1976.

Rawlyk, G. A. *Champions of the Truth: Fundamentalism, Modernism, and the Maritime Baptists*. Montreal and Kingston: McGill-Queen's University Press, 1990.

———. "J. M. Cramp and W. C. Keirstead: The Response of Two Late Nineteenth-Century Baptist Sermons to Science." In *Profiles of Science and Society in the Maritimes Prior to 1914*, edited by Paul A. Bogaard, 119–34. Fredericton, NB: Acadiensis, 1990.

Renfree, Henry A. *Heritage and Horizon: The Baptist Story in Canada*. Mississauga, ON: Canadian Baptist Federation, 1988.

Wilson, Robert S. "Atlantic Baptists Confront the Turbulent Sixties." In *A Fragile Stability: Definition and Redefinition of Maritime Baptist Identity*, edited by David T. Priestley, 149–69. Hantsport, NS: Lancelot, 1994.

———. "From Revivals to Evangelism: Changing Patterns of Growth among Maritime Regular Baptists, 1850–1900." In *You Will be my Witness: A Festschrift in Honor of the Reverend Dr. Allison A. Trites on the Occasion of His Retirement*, edited by R. Glenn Wooden et al., 261–78. Macon, GA: Mercer University Press, 2003.

———. "The Changing Role of Ecumenical and Trans-Denominational Maritime Baptist Youth Ministries in the Middle of the Twentieth Century." In *Roots and Resurgence: Atlantic Baptist Youth Ministry at the Turn of the Millennium*, edited by Bruce Fawcett and Dale Stairs, 55–80. Wolfville, NS: Acadia Divinity College, 2013.

7

Prairie Preachers and Educators

William "Bible Bill" Aberhart, L. E. Maxwell, and Baptist Fundamentalism in Alberta, 1922–1970

BRIAN FROESE

IN 1922 AND 1927, two Bible schools opened in Alberta that became highly influential in the development of North American evangelicalism in distinctly different ways.[1] Together they had roots that extended into southern Ontario Presbyterianism and American Midwestern holiness-Calvinist evangelicalism. Ultimately, each had its longevity. The Prairie Bible Institute (PBI) of L. E. Maxwell opened in 1922. William Aberhart launched the Calgary Prophetic Bible Institute (CPBI) in 1927. Both Aberhart and Maxwell, of independent Baptist stock, found their way to Alberta in the early decades of the twentieth century on religious errands. Their work overlapped in several significant ways: Bible schools and radio preaching. Yet for the most part they remained in their spheres with little to do with each other. Both possessed indomitable spirits, boundless energy, and tendencies to authoritarianism. As religious entrepreneurs, they were among the earliest to open Bible schools on the prairies, where they made the most of the vast expanse of geography and a long evangelical practice of embracing the latest technologies, communication strategies,

---

1. This article was supported by a grant from the Social Sciences and Research Council of Canada (SSHRC).

and marketing brio to make Alberta an internationally recognized centre of fundamentalist Christianity.[2]

L. E. MAXWELL

Leslie Earl Maxwell was born in central Kansas in 1895 and grew up on a farm. Though his home was not religious, his aunt led him to Christ in 1915. His father ran a pool hall in Kansas where Maxwell worked racking balls and illegally selling cigarettes or, as he put it, he "played pool and played ball and played the fool."[3] Maxwell knew upon his conversion, at age twenty-two, that he had to give it all up. Soon thereafter, he served as a corporal in France during World War One, and credited God for his stability during the war. After the war, in the fall of 1919, he began studies at the Midland Bible School in Kansas City. There, William Stevens, a Presbyterian minister and founder of Midland, introduced him to inductive Bible studies—the observation, interpretation, application method often with guiding questions using only the Bible for finding answers—which he brought to PBI.[4] Maxwell also embraced Stevens' "introspective" teaching of Scripture, as opposed to contextual historical study and his embrace of Keswick holiness, which Stevens acquired while attending A. B. Simpson's Missionary Training Institute in Nyack, New York.[5] Bruce Hindmarsh has described Maxwell's religion as "quietist spirituality with its pronounced emphasis upon the renunciation of the self, his mistrust of dispensational or systematic theology, and the commune-style economic life of the institution."[6]

Meanwhile, in Alberta, the J. Fergus Kirk family, Scottish Presbyterians, moved to Three Hills from Ontario, near the turn of the twentieth century. In 1921, Kirk wrote Stevens at Midland, whom he knew from their days in Ontario where both were from, asking if there was someone there who could come to Alberta to teach the Bible to eight local teenagers

2. Burkinshaw, *Pilgrims in Lotus Land*, 67.

3. "Hot Seat: Interview with L.E. Maxwell #581" Radio Broadcast, CD at PBI Archives Station: CJDV, 1970, PCA.

4. "Forum on Q" Radio Broadcast, 1970 Station CHQR, CD "Forum Program L.E. Maxell #390470" #582 CD, Three Hills, AB, T.S. Rendall Library and Archives, Prairie College, Three Hills, Alberta [PCA]; Elliott, "Three Faces of Baptist Fundamentalism in Canada," 175; and Callaway, *Training Disciplined Soldiers for Christ*, 213–20.

5. Elliott, "Three Faces of Baptist Fundamentalism in Canada," 175; and, Callaway, *Training Disciplined Soldiers for Christ*, 2–3.

6. Hindmarsh, "The Winnipeg Fundamentalist Network, 1910–1940," 318.

and adults. Stevens recommended Maxwell, who accepted the invitation. Maxwell's acceptance was the result of his Keswick-like sanctifying crisis at Midland that ended with him making a public confession. Despite not liking cold weather, he interpreted the invitation as a call from God.[7]

The subsequent classes led to the creation of PBI. The emphasis in these classes was fourfold: personal revival influenced by Keswick holiness, strict Biblicism, the necessity and primacy of evangelism, and diligent training for missions work. The school had, as David Elliott described, "cultural aspects of a military camp, a monastery, and a Hutterite colony."[8] When PBI opened its doors in 1922, though Maxwell was a Baptist, it was, according to John Webster Grant, "undenominational but fundamentalist."[9] During the first two years, classes were held in an old farmhouse that Kirk bequeathed to Maxwell as a school. Then, given a couple of lots of land by Kirk and a local man, in 1924 they began to build—cheaply, concerned that the country would likely soon be overrun by communists and Christ could return at any moment—incurring no debt.[10]

PBI grew in the 1930s. American students in particular were attracted by Maxwell's preaching, which, on one occasion when crisscrossing the United States, was described as piercing, clear, and easy to listen to.[11] The young school survived the Great Depression on its principle of "no debt." They were tough years, and Maxwell explained that the scriptural phrase, "hoping for nothing" was a verse God gave him when he prayed at the time whether to take a mission salary.[12] It became an informal motto for the

---

7. "Forum on Q" Radio Broadcast, 1970 Station CHQR, CD "Forum Program L. E. Maxwell #390470" #582 CD, Three Hills, AB, PBI Archives; "Hot Seat: Interview with L. E. Maxwell #581" Radio Broadcast, CD at PBI Archives Station: CJDV, 1970, T. S. Rendall Library and Archives, Prairie College, Three Hills, Alberta [PCA]; and Elliott, "Studies of Eight Canadian Fundamentalists," 260–62; and Enns, "Every Christian a Missionary," 42–43.

8. Elliott, "Three Faces of Baptist Fundamentalism in Canada," 175; and Callaway, *Training Disciplined Soldiers for Christ*, 306–12.

9. Grant, *The Church in Canadian Era*, 128; "Forum on Q"; "Hot Seat: Interview with L. E. Maxwell #581"; Elliott, "Studies of Eight Canadian Fundamentalists," 260–62; and, Elliott, "Three Faces of Baptist Fundamentalism in Canada," 175.

10. "Forum on Q"; "Hot Seat: Interview with L.E. Maxwell #581"; and, Elliott, "Studies of Eight Canadian Fundamentalists," 260–62.

11. Founder's Evening 11-17-85 PBI CD Recording T. S. Rendall Library and Archives, Prairie College, Three Hills, Alberta [PCA].

12. "Forum on Q" Radio Broadcast, 1970 Station CHQR, CD "Forum Program L. E. Maxwell #390470" #582 CD, Three Hills, AB, PBI Archives.

school as unsalaried staff received room and board, medical care, and possibly an allowance if funds were available. To pay for school, many students got summer jobs parking cars or as hotel workers in the tourist town of Banff.[13]

The Crucified Life

In a sermon Maxwell delivered at the Student Foreign Missions Fellowship in Toronto, 27–31 December 1946, he connected Christ's Great Commission to advance the gospel to all nations to the outpouring of the Holy Spirit at Pentecost, and the two post-resurrection commands from Jesus: go into the world; and gather in Jerusalem.[14] He described missions as "mystic might and divine administration" as numbers were added to the Church in the book of Acts, confirming the "effusion" of Pentecost as vital to missions: "if we stay within the Scriptures, we shall find *no fanaticism there* . . . In Acts there is no extravagance." Fanaticism occurs, he argued, when people "migrate to extreme groups, for the simple reason that we have left them unfilled and unfed [spiritually.] Many of our fine fundamental and orthodox teachers have so cleverly skirted the Book of Acts with their extreme dispensational detour, that any receiving of the Spirit in His fullness has been well-nigh filched from us."[15]

Borrowing from R. A. Torrey, who served at Moody Bible Institute and pastored its associated Moody Church, Maxwell underscored the crucial need for the messenger to be "spirit filled," and not of "the flesh."[16] He also worked off the writings of Kate Booth-Clibborn, the daughter of Salvation Army founders William and Catherine Booth. In her mission work, Booth-Clibborn was responsible for bringing the Salvation Army to France. She wrote that what France needed was Christ in the personality of his followers mixing Holy Spirit power and suffering. Booth-Clibborn described ministry as presenting the "face, the character, the life of Jesus . . . in men and women" where people observed their lives and saw Christ. She called this "the flame."[17] "Wherever we went," Booth-Clibborn explained, "we

---

13. "Forum on Q" Radio Broadcast, 1970 Station CHQR, CD "Forum Program L. E. Maxwell #390470" #582 CD, Three Hills, AB, PBI Archives.

14. Maxwell, *The Holy Spirit in Missions*, 3. Commands are found in Matthew and Acts.

15. Maxwell, *The Holy Spirit in Missions*, 6 (emphasis in original), 8.

16. Maxwell, *The Holy Spirit in Missions*, 13.

17. Maxwell, *The Holy Spirit in Missions*, 13–14.

brought the fire with us, we fanned it, we communicated it. We could not help doing so, because it was in us; that was what made us sufferers."[18] Her influence on Maxwell is suggested by how he quoted her more than anyone else in this sermon and in their shared belief in the primacy of suffering.

Maxwell also did battle with the forces of modernism. He preached that while higher critics dismantled the Scriptures, they could not remove the light of God from a believer's face.[19] Such believers, Maxwell maintained, had received the filling of the Holy Spirit through faith. Though typically an emotional experience, Maxwell emphasized the "fact" of the Holy Spirit filling the believer. The filling did not come immediately upon salvation, which was concerned with past sins and the need for Christ as saviour. The spirit was present at conversion, but as Maxwell put it, "He [the Holy Spirit] may be *resident* without being *president*."[20] This filling was the crisis that moved the believer to sanctification.

Maxwell's most popular book was *Born Crucified* (1945). Intended for believers who laboured in their faith yet struggled to find it rewarding, he summarized the key for the Christian life in Christ's death. Working initially from Rom 5–6, he located the identity of the Christian in the justification, being made right with God, brought forth by Christ's death. His death not only justified the Christian, but also, as a new creation inhabited by the Holy Spirit, one was enabled to live a sanctified life that put to death the sinful ways of the past.[21] Thus, in becoming a Christian, a person was "born crucified." In this construction, a person was "born all over again through death, the death of Jesus Christ." In Maxwell's view, this was the only way for a person to experience salvation. For Maxwell this regeneration was the "first principle of the Christian life."[22] He repeated this theme in a variety of ways and in many contexts over the twenty-five chapters, but he always

---

18. Maxwell, *The Holy Spirit in Missions*, 13–14.
19. Maxwell, *The Holy Spirit in Missions*, 18.
20. Maxwell, *The Holy Spirit in Missions*, 21–22.
21. Although there are many understandings and nuances of terms such as "justification" and "sanctification," in sum, justification refers to God removing the penalty of sin, removing guilt from the person, and making the unjust just through the work of Jesus Christ in his death and resurrection accepted by faith. Sanctification follows justification and refers to spiritual maturation, being made holy through the work of God in the Holy Spirit, often associated with immense struggle. Justification makes salvation possible upon faithful acceptance and sanctification flows from salvation to Christian maturity.
22. Maxwell, *Born Crucified*, 15–18, 21, 27. Quotes p. 27; and Callaway, *Training Disciplined Soldiers for Christ*, 229–32.

highlighted the role of the cross. For Maxwell, the cross was the focal point of the Christian life. And taking up one's cross included the ongoing process of self-renunciation and the rejection of the carnal impulses and the lure of worldly things. Living a victorious Christian life meant dying to self daily and walking in newness of life.[23]

Throughout this extended entreaty, Maxwell quoted liberally from a variety of writers. For example, he cited the seventeenth-century French catholic mystic, the quietist Madame Guyon, who taught total surrender to God, to be acted upon by God; Anglican non-juror and influential mystic, William Law; and prolific author and missionary to India, Amy Carmichael. At PBI, Maxwell made the interior crucified life its core ethos. This ethos was based on Guyon's mystical writings which emphasized the ongoing killing of the flesh through the suppression of the self and all things sensual, the empowering presence of Christ brought forth in the individual through reflection, introspection, and strict discipline.[24] In practical matters, this was clearly expressed at PBI in its pedagogy of inductive Bible study, unpaid student work, and non-salaried staff. Moreover, the role of the teaching staff was to model this lifestyle, a quality that Maxwell considered more important than credentials and teaching competence. Even Dorothy Ruth Miller, the first Bible Instructor hired, who held degrees from Columbia University and New York University, was expected to adopt Maxwell's model lifestyle. Maxwell also shared his vision of for all those in ministry. For him it was essential "that we sink ourselves afresh into the unplumbed power of the Cross to take the nonentities, the nothings, and the nobodies, and yet make them, even in this infidel and unbelieving age, a mighty host for God."[25]

The crucified life extended then to campus life where rules were established to encourage students to "live a 'crucified' life."[26] This was exemplified in PBI's rigid approach to sexuality and romantic relationships as Maxwell and his staff did all they could to discourage romantic entanglements, immodest dress, and fashionable attire of any kind. They also segregated

---

23. Maxwell, *Born Crucified*, 27–28, 32, 34, 36, 51, 59–63.

24. Maxwell, *Born Crucified*, 109, 116–25, 131, 138–39, 142, 153; and Elliott, "Three Faces of Baptist Fundamentalism in Canada," 175; Fuller, "The Legacy of Leslie E. Maxwell," 127–28; and Balsama, "Madame Guyon," 350–54.

25. Maxwell, *Born Crucified*, 191.

26. Elliott, "Three Faces of Baptist Fundamentalism in Canada," 175; Elliott, "Studies of Eight Canadian Fundamentalists," 262.

the sexes and prohibited dating.[27] Such proscriptions, including most of popular culture and more, while flowing naturally from the personal holiness animating Maxwell, is part and parcel of the larger fundamentalist culture. As Tim Callaway explains, such legalistic social codes were meant to be markers of separation from the world.[28] On the issue of alcohol consumption, Maxwell conceded that while one cannot argue abstinence from alcohol from the Bible, the point was to avoid the appearance of evil.[29] The appearance of evil rationale was also extended to games like baseball and billiards. For Maxwell, these activities were fine in themselves, but the problematic issue was in their popular associations with such morally suspect behaviour as smoking, gambling, and alcohol consumption. In his "Hot Seat" interview in 1970, Maxwell again described this relationship as the issue is not the game, but rather what one does with the game, referencing his youthful practice of illegally selling cigarettes at a pool hall.[30]

The pedagogy of PBI was centered on the lives and examples of the teaching faculty grounded in the character-driven ideals of a mystically influenced holiness Christianity. This educational methodology and philosophy was also part of a centuries-long tradition in church education. Even the medieval cathedral schools of Europe, for example, held that the charismatic teacher was, in fact, the curriculum. The "imitation of teacher" was a "most ancient form of pedagogy."[31] This approach made the inculcation of moral character the essential element in a student's development. While the medieval schools educated future nobility and clergy, in Three Hills future ambassadors of the gospel to the world were steeped in the ancient pedagogy of imitating the charismatic teacher.[32] As the North American university transformed over the latter decades of the nineteenth century, replacing tradition and character formation as the core of its mission with research and innovation, the pursuit of these newer academic markers of reputation changed the trajectory of higher education. In the

---

27. Elliott, "Studies of Eight Canadian Fundamentalists," 263–64; and Mann, *Sect, Cult and Church in Alberta*, 101.

28. Callaway, *Training Disciplined Soldiers for Christ*, 326–29.

29. "Forum on Q" Radio Broadcast, 1970 Station CHQR, CD "Forum Program L. E. Maxwell #390470" #582 CD, Three Hills, AB, PBI Archives.

30. "Forum on Q"; and, "Hot Seat: Interview with L.E. Maxwell #581."

31. Jaeger, *The Envy of Angels*, 76–83.

32. Jaeger, *The Envy of Angels*, 76–83.

evangelical context, as morals and character were sidelined in universities, they became a central feature of education in the emerging Bible schools.[33]

Bringing the themes of Christian education and missions together, in his second book, *Crowded to Christ* (1950), Maxwell used the early history of PBI to speak directly about God's providential direction of his Christian errand. Maxwell quoted one of the school's promotional brochures, "Hoping for Nothing," to underscore the extraordinary and improbable existence and nature of PBI. He described locating the school "in a country district" as something "contrary to nature," because such schools were typically in urban settings. Yet, as Maxwell and his staff obeyed God in all matters related to PBI's existence from its location to future plans, and financing, they experienced success. When questioned about why PBI had thrived, Maxwell gave his answer: "We are still following."[34]

Maxwell was critical of the tendency among fundamentalists to avoid self-reflection. He was particularly disturbed by the lukewarmness and selfishness that, in his view, were the results of extreme dispensationalism. He observed, "there are many middle-of-the-road ministers who may be excused for wishing that God would hang all the modernists, but there is first an Agag to be hanged in the fundamentalist. The sinful self-life in the fundamentalist is of all modernists the worst."[35] Then he concluded, "we are convinced from Scripture that if fighting, militant, and daring fundamentalists would only sink into a selfless, carefree contempt for their own lives, forgetting their reputation and position, their cause and kingdom, and be willing to expose themselves to every battery the devil can muster against them we have little doubt that God could and perhaps would burn up His enemies round about."[36] Flowing from his "born crucified" theology of justification and sanctification, Maxwell located a significant barrier to effective Christian witness in the failure of fundamentalists to be self-aware and spiritually reflective.

Among the greatest threats to the missionary responsibility of Christians was "ultra-dispensationalism" which "furnishes Christians with an

---

33. Noll, *The Scandal of the Evangelical Mind*, 110–14.

34. Maxwell, *Crowded to Christ*, 40.

35. Maxwell, *Crowded to Christ*, 77. Agag was the King of the Amalekites in 1 Samuel, whom King Saul of the Israelites was commanded by God to kill. Saul did not, and in addition to letting him live permitted him and his peoples to keep some of the spoils despite their defeat. Having disobeyed God, the prophet Samuel declared him unfit to be king.

36. Maxwell, *Crowded to Christ*, 77.

excuse from the obligations of obedience."[37] Maxwell insisted that preaching the gospel from a strong dispensationalist position violated the gospel itself. The "hair-splitting and cataloguing of the good news into a great variety of gospels" worked against the scriptural point that the gospel was preached to those in the Old Testament.[38]

Despite the otherworldly nature of Maxwell's theology and school, everyone at Three Hills still lived in the world. Maxwell argued that scientific advances provided further evidence of "the heavens declaring the work of God" (Ps 19:1). He confidently declared that even "true scientists" admit "we didn't make ourselves."[39] Human scientific achievements, such as the Apollo 13 mission, were exciting and when reflecting on the Apollo space program Maxwell called it "a great scientific achievement . . . a wonderful thing," and irrelevant to "scripture or God or prophecy."[40] Similarly, when considering evolution, he said that while atheists "hail evolution" because it eliminates the creator, one could be a Christian and an evolutionist. But Maxwell admitted that he found it difficult to understand how one would construct such a view.[41]

Maxwell also taught that church apathy goes back to the book of Judges. When asked if the church should be involved in social issues such as poverty, integration, and racism, Maxwell argued that the first priority of the church is to preach the gospel throughout the world. Christ goes to "root of the matter namely selfishness . . . Christ did not give us ground for having part in class wars or industrial disputes or political battles. He advocated a super citizenship and he takes us to the real root cause of the trouble."[42] Social causes were therefore "incidental" to the main purpose of the church, and since the church has left its main purpose for the

37. Maxwell, *Crowded to Christ*, 137–38.

38. Maxwell, *Crowded to Christ*, 156.

39. "Hot Seat: Interview with L. E. Maxwell #581" Radio Broadcast, CD at PBI Archives Station: CJDV, 1970, T. S. Rendall Library and Archives, Prairie College, Three Hills, Alberta [PCA].

40. "Hot Seat: Interview with L. E. Maxwell #581" Radio Broadcast, CD at PBI Archives Station: CJDV, 1970, T. S. Rendall Library and Archives, Prairie College, Three Hills, Alberta [PCA].

41. "Hot Seat: Interview with L. E. Maxwell #581" Radio Broadcast, CD at PBI Archives Station: CJDV, 1970, T. S. Rendall Library and Archives, Prairie College, Three Hills, Alberta [PCA].

42. "Hot Seat: Interview with L. E. Maxwell #581" Radio Broadcast, CD at PBI Archives Station: CJDV, 1970, T. S. Rendall Library and Archives, Prairie College, Three Hills, Alberta [PCA]; and Callaway, *Training Disciplined Soldiers for Christ*, 131.

incidental, the church has lost its influence. Asked about racial tensions in the United States, Maxwell responded: "All you have to do is come to Prairie Bible Institute and see them sitting there from Jamaica and from the south, and from the islands of the seas and we never think anything about racial issues because the common denominator when a person is born again . . . [is] then these issues take care of themselves." Activism for Maxwell was the pursuit of salvation for others.[43] Ultimately, he added that the grace of God should bring humility, for the one in Christ should not be a "Bible-thumping bigot" for God rescued humanity from sin and the Christian must remember that.[44]

Maxwell remained largely aloof from politics, though he kept an eye on international events. He rejected the League of Nations and was deeply suspicious of the United Nations when it was formed. During World War II he kept up to date, as best he could, on the situation of the Jews and Nazi persecution. Maxwell's otherworldly emphasis and strict understanding of the separation of church and state led him to support Karl Barth in his opposition to German Nazism and the church's growing acquiesence to the state and Nazi influence. As the Cold War began to take hold in the 1950s, Maxwell argued that communism was a manifestation of theological modernism.[45]

PBI may have been remotely located, but it was well-connected to a larger inter-continental fundamentalist network. *The Prairie Pastor*, like many other evangelical periodicals, borrowed and reprinted stories and articles from their co-religionists as part of a large trans-Atlantic network. This reach expanded in the 1940s as the number of common enemies increased to include modernists, fascists, communists, Darwinists, and societal decadence.[46]

The roots of PBI extended into southern Ontario Presbyterianism and an American Midwestern holiness-Calvinist evangelicalism that refracted French catholic quietist mysticism and English Keswick higher life spirituality. In Alberta, Maxwell and his school then promulgated a form

43. "Hot Seat: Interview with L. E. Maxwell #581" Radio Broadcast, CD at PBI Archives Station: CJDV, 1970, T. S. Rendall Library and Archives, Prairie College, Three Hills, Alberta [PCA]; and Callaway, *Training Disciplined Soldiers for Christ*, 131.

44. "Forum on Q" Radio Broadcast, 1970 Station CHQR, CD "Forum Program L. E. Maxwell #390470" #582 CD, Three Hills, AB, PBI Archives.

45. Elliott, "Studies of Eight Canadian Fundamentalists," 267–68, 270–71.

46. Enns, "Sustaining the Faithful and Proclaiming the Gospel in a Time of Crisis," 117–18, 122–27.

of Christian fundamentalism that was nondenominational and apolitical, preaching on radio and teaching in class an austere mystically-oriented conservative evangelicalism. Though PBI often filled an evangelical popular cultural space for its famous legalism—notably in male/female relationships—what is often missed is where such strictures came from. The ideals of the disciplined life that Maxwell appreciated, formed in monasteries and militaries, meshed with forms of spirituality that took shape in Ontario, New York, and Kansas first, that finally migrated west to the fertile soil of Three Hills, Alberta.

WILLIAM ABERHART

William Aberhart was born in 1878 and was raised in Huron County, Ontario near Seaforth. He completed Normal College in Hamilton and for two years taught near Wingham at Brantford Central School. In 1910, he moved to Calgary, Alberta as a principal. While growing up in southern Ontario, he attended Bible conferences at Zion Presbyterian Church in 1902 and 1903, where he became interested in dispensationalism and took a correspondence course by C. I. Scofield. Aberhart began preaching in 1905 as a layperson and in 1918 he joined the Calgary Prophetic Bible Conference (CPBC) for intensive Bible study "formed by a number of earnest men of different denominations" to contemplate the return of Jesus.[47] Having its roots in the Plymouth Brethren of Ireland, dispensationalism came to North America through the preaching of John Nelson Darby. In America such evangelical luminaries as C. I. Scofield and Dwight L. Moody further spread dispensationalism though the creation of correspondence courses and Bible schools. As a young man Aberhart took such a course from Scofield and drank deeply from the dispensational well.[48]

Aberhart considered himself a Calvinist to the end of his life and, having experienced revivalism as a young person, he was attracted to the energy of revival preaching. He held to the tension of a sovereign God and human agency in conversion. This doctrinal position enabled Aberhart to

47. "William Aberhart, B.A., Our President, Dean and Lecturer," *Radio News* (Calgary: Calgary Prophetic Bible Institute, [1930]), 4, Calgary Prophetic Bible Institute fonds, M1357, File 7: Radio Sunday School. - ca. 1930–1969, Glenbow Library and Archives, Calgary, Alberta (GLA). Quote from, "The Building of the Institute," *Bulletin of the Calgary Prophetic Bible Institute*, 1927, p. 7, Calgary Prophetic Bible Institute fonds M1357 File: 1 CPBI, GLA; Elliott and Miller, *Bible Bill*, 3, 13–14; and Schultz, "Portrait of a Premier," 186.

48. Elliott, "The Devil and William Aberhart," 325.

view evangelism as both necessary and worthwhile. Aberhart moved toward dispensationalism as a young man. He also jettisoned his reformed Presbyterian eschatology and ecclesiology. Although he was strongly against setting dates for prophecy, he maintained a strong futurist position regarding Revelation. Despite his claim to holding dear to Calvinism all his life, his fealty to the Reformed tradition was more a coming and going in relation to his Presbyterian roots as his doctrinal emphasis shifted over time. Aberhart crossed a number of theological lines in his youth. He moved from reformed Presbyterianism to the grace of Arminianism and on to the premillennialism of Scofield dispensationalism. Later, in the early 1930s, as Robert Wright argues, Aberhart's political turn to Social Credit made religious sense. He was able to hold onto his dispensationalism and the social teachings of his Presbyterian and Methodist roots. In the 1930s, he merged these two different perspectives in his sermons, charts, and speeches.[49]

In Calgary, Westbourne Baptist Church began as a mission of the First Baptist Church in 1905, and it was served by supply preachers into 1916. Aberhart was one such preacher, and he was particularly appreciated by the congregation who, on 19 April 1916, agreed to hold a social function in his honour. At this event, a presentation of gratitude was made to Aberhart.[50] The church applied to the Home Mission Board of the Baptist Union of Western Canada (BUWC) for financial assistance to hire a full-time pastor as their numbers were growing. They were informed that they had to remove Aberhart first. The church rejected the request and retained Aberhart. The BUWC, it appears, was opposed to Aberhart's selection as pastor for two reasons: he was not ordained and he was strongly dispensational.[51]

His church classes, now called "Prophetic Bible Conference," administered with an executive board comprised of people from a variety of occupations, continued to attract many people, Baptists and non-Baptists alike. Alberta in late-1917, early-1918, experienced great prophetic interest spurred, in part, by the British Empire's capturing of Jerusalem from the Ottoman Empire. Aberhart obliged the demand and offered a series of classes on Revelation at the public library in a bid to attract a general

---

49. Goertz, "The Development of a Bible Belt," 40–42, 44–47, 59; and Wright, "The Canadian Protestant Tradition 1914–1945," 183–85.

50. "History of Westbourne," Notes on Westbourne Church Minutes (1911–1919), p. 2 M-9646-93, Iris Miller's William Aberhart Collection, GLA.

51. Goertz, "The Development of a Bible Belt," 55–58.

audience. This course was so well-attended that he offered it again to the larger congregation at Westbourne Baptist Church. The popularity of his classes led to higher church attendance. This new reality prompted Westbourne to move their main service to the Grand Theatre in 1920. Aberhart was a master presenter, with lively lectures, songs, charts, diagrams, and questions from the audience. The crowds who came to hear him were impressed and captivated. Aberhart used his immense memory of Scripture to answer questions by quoting the Bible. This talent gave him an air of authority. He believed in the primacy of the King James Version of the Bible and he claimed that a cause of the French Revolution was too many Bible translations. In the true spirit of fundamentalism, he equated new versions of the Bible with modernism.[52]

In 1923, while holding classes and leading the Westbourne congregation, Aberhart drew attention to the Sunday school materials. He asked that various churches in the city go over the International Sunday School lessons "under expert guidance." Convinced there was a problem with the materials many Sunday schools in Calgary were using, Aberhart observed, "it is painfully evident to us that most of the international lessons helps [sic] are tainted with higher criticism. This [should] be counteracted."[53] It was noted in the minutes that higher criticism originated in nineteenth-century Germany, where theologians "set themselves up as critics of the Bible."[54] Though he was very suspicious of anything that may have had contact with higher criticism, Aberhart also initially had reservations with Pentecostalism when it came to Calgary.

When the Pentecostal evangelist Charles Price came to Calgary in the summer of 1923, Aberhart weighed in early: "They used to go into a trance," he noted, "Some people think everything supernatural is of God but it isn't."[55] In fact, Price's campaign in Calgary split the evangelical churches. Aberhart was not closed to Pentecostalism in general, or divine healing, but he was "as those people practiced it."[56] The claim from Aberhart's quarter

---

52. Goertz, "The Development of a Bible Belt," 55–58; and, Mann, *Sect, Cult and Church in Alberta*, 22–23.

53. "Notes on Minutes of A's Bible Classes-1916–1929," 18 January 1923, 2, M-9646-92, Iris Miller's William Aberhart Collection, GLA. The page numbering on the document is off by one, in the footnotes here I give the actual page number, not the one printed on the document.

54. "Notes on Minutes of A's Bible Classes-1916–1929," 18 January 1923, 3.

55. "Notes on Minutes of A's Bible Classes-1916–1929," 21 August 1923, 4.

56. "Notes on Minutes of A's Bible Classes-1916–1929," 21 August 1923, 4.

was that the Price campaign based their healing ministry on a verse in Isaiah, "'He bore our diseases'" to justify faith healing "even with unbelievers." Aberhart and his cohort were convinced that Price was using hypnotism. He attended some of Price's meetings, though the deacons of his church remained split on the value of attending themselves.[57]

Within Westbourne itself, disagreements and questions about the church's doctrinal beliefs began to surface. It was moved that everyone on the executive board should be in "absolute accord with each statement of belief" and if there was disagreement then discussion was to follow with an "open bible." The assumption was if that a member could not find a way back into harmony with the statement of belief then they must resign. The process was to go through the Conference creed stating outright that "the matter of the Baptism of the Holy Spirit being distinctive and separate from ordination (?) [sic]."[58] There were some resignations at that meeting. That the baptism of the Holy Spirit was controversial was clear, though the details in the minutes are thin, there seems to be a separation of doctrine and polity that was necessary in the context of coming to agreement regarding a response to Price and the presence of higher criticism in teaching materials. Without further explanation, the issue was separated out as distinctive in nature and unrelated to the practice of ordination. This may have been the committee simply returning to their purpose of overseeing Bible study at an upcoming conference and since ordination already established a baseline of doctrinal faithfulness, perhaps the question of the baptism of the Holy Spirit did not need deeper exploration at the time.

Nevertheless, his conference lectures were very popular, and in 1925, he began airing them on the radio. At its peak, Aberhart's radio audience numbered up to 350,000 listeners. While on the air he emphasized a literal reading of the Bible, the second coming of Jesus, and eventually brought Social Credit theory into the mix. As the number of people attending his conferences grew, they were held at increasingly larger venues. To address this, he raised $60,000 to build the Calgary Prophetic Bible Institute (CPBI) building, with construction completed in 1927.[59]

57. "Notes on Minutes of A's Bible Classes-1916-1929," 21 August 1923, 4.
58. "Notes on Minutes of A's Bible Classes-1916-1929," 21 August 1923, 4.
59. "William Aberhart, B.A., Our President, Dean and Lecturer," *Radio News* (Calgary: Calgary Prophetic Bible Institute, [1930]), 4, Calgary Prophetic Bible Institute fonds, M1357, File 7: Radio Sunday School. - ca. 1930-1969, GLA; and, "The Building of the Institute," *Bulletin of the Calgary Prophetic Bible Institute*, 7, Calgary Prophetic Bible Institute fonds, M1357 File: 1 CPBI, GLA; and Friesen, *The Canadian Prairies*, 411-12;

When he opened CPBI in 1927, he moved it and Westbourne Baptist Church into the building. About two years later, on 18 April 1929, the Bible Institute Baptist Church (BIBC) was formed by supporters of Aberhart after a large number of people withdrew from the Westbourne congregation. BIBC was distinct from CPBI, though it was comprised of supporters of Aberhart and "the fundamentalist Baptist faith."[60] The split occurred after tensions developed at Westbourne over theology and finances. Westbourne had difficulties finding ministers on account of Aberhart's theology, and they begrudged the high rent paid to CPBI. They also objected to Aberhart's sole control over the church's financial decisions.[61] After the church split, about half of the congregants returned to the old building with Morley Hall as the pastor. Five years later, in 1932, this congregation began a rival Bible institute to CPBI, named the Western Baptist Bible College (WBBC). It was under the control of the Regular Baptist Missionary Fellowship of the Prairie Provinces. It closed at the start of World War II and then re-opened after the war in Port Coquitlam, British Columbia under the new name of Northwest Baptist Bible College.[62]

Some of the continued opposition to Aberhart was the result of his "Jesus only" formula of baptism (as opposed to a trinitarian formula), his adoption of the title "apostle," and the introduction of charismatic practices in the 1920s.[63] Even in his time at Westbourne, not only did he move his followers towards fundamentalism, but also, he adopted some Pentecostal views that divided his congregation. He was friends with Pentecostal pastor Harvey McAlister in Calgary from whom he adopted the teaching that it was at the point of baptism (instead of conversion) when a Christian received the Holy Spirit. Consequently, baptism could only be performed in the name of Jesus and not the orthodox trinitarian formula of the Father,

---

and Laycock, *Populism and Democratic Thought in the Canadian Prairies*, 216.

60. "Kent" [n.a., n.d.] draft of newspaper article], p. 1, Fred Kennedy fonds, M1621 File 12: *Calgary Herald*, newspaper Calgary Prophetic Bible Institute, 1934–39, GLA at UCA.

61. Brennan, *The Good Steward*, 11, 13.

62. Renfree, *Heritage and Horizon*, 229; "Notes on Minutes of A's Bible Classes-1916–1929," 28 May 1916, p. 1, M-9646-92, Iris Miller's William Aberhart Collection, GLA; and Goertz, "The Development of a Bible Belt," 48–49, 54–55; and Burkinshaw, *Pilgrims in Lotus Land*, 166.

63. "A Baptist for the Old Gospel," letter to the editor, *Calgary Albertan*, 29 October 1926, p. 4, reprinted in Elliott, ed., *Aberhart*, 2; and Elliott, "Three Faces of Baptist Fundamentalism in Canada," 173.

Son, and Holy Spirit. He emphasized gifts of prophecy, faith, and teaching, but not those of tongues and healing.[64]

Aberhart's deft touch with media certainly set him apart. He was already publishing a magazine, *The Prophetic Voice*, launched in October 1924. Its purpose was clearly explained: "It is true, that the days of John the Baptist are over, and yet the need of a voice in the present wilderness is as great NOW as it was THEN. People to-day want to know that God has to say about the future."[65] It was clearly identified as fundamentalist: "We are fundamentalists in the actual sense of the word, not in the popular sense. We are not funny-mentalists, but Pauline Heretics," based on Acts 24:14. To ensure clarity, they emphasized the primary point of fundamentalism: they worked from the principle of the infallible, verbally-inspired Scriptures.[66] In the early issues of *The Prophetic Voice*, readers encountered screeds supporting creationism, reports on visions people experienced regarding Christ's second coming, Pentecostal youth in Ohio dancing the "shimmy" during a church service, poems and exegetical study of the prologue of Gospel of John, and amusing anecdotes.[67]

Through *The Prophetic Voice* we have a window into Aberhart's pre-radio theological imagination. He argued that history repeated itself, and he went back to both Old Testament prophecy and Christ's incarnation claiming that social and political conditions then would recur again at the time of Christ's return. Modernism was a regular concern, and he criticized modernist biblical interpretations that rejected literal interpretations of the Bible. Aberhart's revulsion at modernism was strong. He recounted, "I met one of these modernists a few years ago and he was a bird (a real fowl of the air in the Scriptural sense), a religious Bolshevist." As the conversation progressed, Aberhart recalled, "a dark scowl crept over his face." The modernist spoke against literal readings of the Bible and the nature of apocalyptic literature. Aberhart then called his readers "to a higher life" where they believed in Christ's return and allowed this truth to influence their lives.[68]

---

64. Elliott, "Antithetical Elements in William Aberhart's Theology and Political Ideology," 42; and Stackhouse, *Canadian Evangelicalism in the Twentieth Century*, 40.

65. "Editorial," *The Prophetic Voice* 1.1, Published by the Calgary Prophetic Bible Conference, October 1924, PR 1982, William Aberhart Fonds, Box 1, File: PR 1970.0239/31 Booklet, *The Prophetic Voice*, 1.1, Published by the Calgary Prophetic Bible Conference, October 1924, PAA.

66. "Editorial," *The Prophetic Voice*, 1.1.

67. "Editorial," *The Prophetic Voice*, 1.1:3.

68. William Aberhart, "Is Christ's Coming Again a Reality or a Mere Fancy?" Address

In addition to print media, Aberhart also took full advantage of the airwaves. The impact of radio on fundamentalist growth can hardly be overstated. It helped make numerous small groups recognizable as a larger movement, and it provided relief from the isolation experienced by rural populations with minimal entertainment options. In Alberta, the Rocky Mountains were a barrier to BC radio. So many areas had no access to radio. This reality provided an opportunity for local stations to open. They sprang up quickly and widely on the prairies. These stations reached virtually every corner in Alberta, Saskatchewan, and northern states, such as Montana. Fundamentalists viewed other new media technologies associated with entertainment, such as movies, as dangerous sources of temptation. In contrast, radio carried no such stigma, and it was quickly adopted by fundamentalists as an instrument that could be used to spread God's truth. Starting as an adjunct to a church service, it soon became a tool of evangelism. Both Aberhart and Maxwell were early adopters of radio and excited about its potential for ministry. The first radio broadcast of any kind from Calgary was made in 1922 and in November 1925 Aberhart began his radio ministry—the most effective at fundamentalist radio. In fact, the 1930s nearly killed off station CFCN but revenue from Aberhart's ministry kept it afloat.[69]

Though Aberhart's audience was broad, mostly evangelicals tuned in. He had oratorical skills and an instinct for communicating complex ideas simply—from answering questions in listener's letters to holding mock debates with other religious groups (such as Jehovah Witnesses or Seventh Day Adventists) or unpacking ancient biblical prophecies in current events, he kept listeners excited.[70] Radio was ideally suited for fundamentalist broadcasting styles, and it became a significant revenue stream for Bible schools thriving in a milieu that mixed religion and entertainment. As media attention and coverage of evangelicalism abated after the mid-1920s, radio was also an effective way to creatively reach audiences without media filters.[71]

---

at Opening of Prophetic Conference, Calgary, Fall 1924, p. 15–21. *The Prophetic Voice*, Vol. 1.1, Published by the Calgary Prophetic Bible Conference, October 1924, PR 1982, William Aberhart Fonds, Box 1, File: PR 1970.0239/31 Booklet, *The Prophetic Voice*, Vol. 1.1, Published by the Calgary Prophetic Bible Conference, October 1924, PAA.

69. Mann, *Sect, Cult and Church in Alberta*, 118–19.

70. Mann, *Sect, Cult and Church in Alberta*, 121.

71. Mann, *Sect, Cult and Church in Alberta*, 128–32; and Opp, "The New Age of Evangelism," 100, 103, 110–11.

Bible Institute Baptist Church & School Curriculum

Aberhart's new church was incorporated on 19 April 1927. This new church community was one result of the split earlier that same year at Westbourne Baptist Church. This entity was part of what the lawyer George Hobson Steer described in a memo as a "fundamentalist branch of the Baptist denomination."[72] Its mandate was to bring souls to Christ, edify believers, spread the word of God, and "use every legitimate Christian means of combating and resisting Modernism, Higher Criticism and Skepticism in all its forms." To these ends, Aberhart and his congregation would teach Christian "fundamental doctrine" and "broadcast as often as we can . . . the exact literal interpretation of the verbally inspired Word of God."[73]

The nerve centre of Aberhart's religious operation was CPBI, or as he called it, "The Great Prairie Monument to the Faith." The doctrinal statement of CPBI not only summarized their belief but also offered twelve doctrinal position statements about current doctrinal and cultural controversies. "Divine Verbal Inspiration" of the Bible and its "absolute supremacy, infallibility and efficiency in all matters of faith and practice" led the dozen statements. Other positions were taken on, such as "the Immaculate Conception of the Lord Jesus Christ," the creation of humanity "by the direct act of God, and not by an evolutionary process," and the final resurrection at the conclusion of the coming millennium.[74] The aims of CPBI were to blunt the influence the "Modernists, Evolutionists, and skeptics of every kind."[75]

Working toward the goals described, Aberhart developed various curricula. His first lesson, *The Euodia Bible Course*, dealt with "Dispensational Truth." For, "Without a knowledge of the Dispensations," Aberhart claimed,

---

72. N.a., "Memo for Mr. Steer: RE-Calgary Prophetic Bible Institute Church," 18 May 1939, 1, Fred Kennedy fonds, M1621 File 12: *Calgary Herald*, newspaper Calgary Prophetic Bible Institute, 1934–39, Glenbow Library and Archives at the University of Calgary Archives. At the time of research for this chapter the Glenbow Library and Archives were in the midst of moving their materials to the University of Calgary Archives. Therefore, some material is simply GLA, and others are GLA at UCA.

73. "Memo for Mr. Steer: RE-Calgary Prophetic Bible Institute Church," 18 May 1939, 2, Fred Kennedy fonds, M1621 File 12: *Calgary Herald*, newspaper Calgary Prophetic Bible Institute, 1934–39, GLA at UCA.

74. "Doctrinal Basis of the Institute," *Bulletin of the Calgary Prophetic Bible Institute*, 1, 5, Calgary Prophetic Bible Institute fonds, M1357 File: 1 CPBI, GLA.

75. "The Aims and Purposes of the Calgary Prophetic Bible Institute," 9, *Bulletin of the Calgary Prophetic Bible Institute*, 7, Calgary Prophetic Bible Institute fonds, M1357 File: 1 CPBI, GLA.

"the Bible will remain a closed book."[76] Aberhart produced *The Euodia Bible Course* while he worked at Trinity Methodist Church. He went through a series of churches in his early years in Calgary, leaving each when working relationships became tense. The list of churches he left includes Grace Presbyterian, Wesley Methodist, and Trinity Methodist. In his course, Aberhart began by naming several Bible reading strategies and interpretations that were false. These false teachings included using the Bible as a "charm to keep away spirits or disease," skepticism, Christian Science, Mormonism, Pastor Russell, or the "pick and choose method," the "Holus-bolus Acceptance" which was his term for the approach used by Seventh Day Adventism, and Religious Vegetarianism. The last section of Aberhart's course offered an apologetic for the veracity of dispensationalism and a lesson in proper dispensational Bible reading methodology which meant "rightly-dividing" the Scriptures according to time periods.[77]

Aberhart also created a correspondence course entitled, "Systematic Theology," with a strong dispensational component to it. Clearly, Scofield's earlier Systematics course served as a model for Aberhart's course. In fact, Aberhart adopted and adapted Scofield's course tag and his claim of "rightly dividing the word." He wrote of "dispensational distinctions," "dividing the Word dispensationally," and of people possessing "dispensational knowledge" in an effort to show how the Bible does not contain contradictions, but rather differences for different eras. Aberhart explained, for example, the reasons for dietary injunctions and the contrast between the vegetarian state of Eden and the fully-stocked meat-filled final banquet in the eschaton.[78]

He also taught biblical exegesis with an emphasis on various literary styles in the Bible. In Aberhart's view, the biblical authors utilized historical narrative, poetry, epistles, and prophecy to communicate God's revelation. While all biblical authors spoke God's truth, they did so by using a variety

76. "Lesson 1," *The Euodia Bible Course*, p. 1, PR 1982, William Aberhart Fonds, Box 1, File: PR 1970.0239/38 Booklet Containing *Euodia Bible Courses*, Published, Prepared by William Aberhart, B.A., Calgary [19??], PAA.

77. "Lesson 1," *The Euodia Bible Course*, p. 1, PR 1982, William Aberhart Fonds, Box 1, File: PR 1970.0239/38 Booklet Containing *Euodia Bible Courses*, Published, Prepared by William Aberhart, B.A., Calgary [19??], PAA; and Hiller, "A Critical Analysis of the Role of Religion in a Canadian Populist Movement," 50.

78. William Aberhart, "Lesson Eleven: A General View of God's Great Plan," *Systematic Theology 'A' Course* (Calgary: Calgary Prophetic Bible Institute, n.d.), 2–7, Calgary Prophetic Bible Institute fonds, M1357 File 5: Rightly Dividing the Word of Truth Course. - n.d. and 1945–1949, GLA.

of different literary genres.[79] Unsurprisingly, prophetic Scripture was Aberhart's favourite genre. For him, these Scriptures were "declarative, often highly symbolic and objective presenting truth in a definite detailed fashion often as though it were actually taking place."[80] He particularly enjoyed Revelation for its rich language, though conceded its difficulty to understand on account of its highly symbolic language, leading many to miss that its main theme is Jesus Christ, not human history. Aberhart also described the beauty of Revelation:

> It's grandeur, its sublimity of thought, its imposing scenery, its gorgeous similitude, its pregnant maxims, its significant dialogues, its stirring exhortations, its evangelic songs, its gracious doxologies not only stamp it as inspired but give to it all the majesty of the mighty revelation of the consummation of the greatest theme the world ever knew, as it opens out before our eyes the plans, purposes of a great God.[81]

Aberhart's deep appreciation for biblical prophecy, and Revelation in particular, profoundly informed his theology and his perception of history and geopolitics.

Aberhart's mixing of Revelation, history, and geopolitics is manifested in a play he wrote. In their pre-Social Credit days, in 1931, Aberhart and Ernest Manning, his right-hand man at CPBI and in the Social Credit Party and his successor in both organizations, wrote and performed their play entitled, "The Branding Irons of Antichrist." Set in a post-rapture world, this didactic play—based on the end-times novels of Sydney Watson—depicted three siblings navigating the hellish time as the Antichrist ascends to global domination. Throughout this play the audience was told that a range

---

79. William Aberhart, "Teaching Forms of Literary Style in Bible," Booklet: *Bible Exegesis B*, p. 1, PR 1982 William Aberhart Fonds, Box 2, File: PR 1970.0239/41 Seven Booklets Containing Aberhart's Handwritten Lecture Notes re: Bible Exegesis [Probably Used at the Prophetic Bible Institute, Calgary] Booklet: *Outline for Year* "Lesson I—General Arrangement of Bible as a Whole," PAA.

80. William Aberhart, "Epistles," Booklet: *Bible Exegesis B*, p. 3, PR 1982 William Aberhart Fonds, Box 2, File: PR 1970.0239/41 Seven Booklets Containing Aberhart's' Handwritten Lecture Notes re: Bible Exegesis [Probably Used at the Prophetic Bible Institute, Calgary] Booklet: *Outline for Year* "Lesson I—General Arrangement of Bible as a Whole," PAA.

81. William Aberhart, Handwritten Lecture Notes re: Revelation, 1-3, quote on p.1, PR 1982 William Aberhart Fonds, Box 2, File: PR 1970.0239/44 Booklet containing Aberhart's Handwritten Lecture Notes re: Revelation [Probably Used at the Prophetic Bible Institute, Calgary] 1930-35, PAA.

of people will not be spared the tribulation. In fact, the main protagonists, a pair of reprobate brothers and a deeply religious yet unregenerate sister, Mary, discovered that their mother disappeared while they were left behind. Saddened and despairing Mary asked mournfully, "Why didn't our minister tell us about the Rapture?"[82] As the siblings attempted to understand what was happening around them, Mary explained to her brothers, John and Howard, that their mother was raptured because she was born again. Mary also noted that she had asked her pastor about the rapture, and he told her that taking such Scriptures seriously was "old fashioned and unscholarly."[83]

Throughout the short drama several religious points were raised. For example, the infernal legacy of liberal ministers, the inadequacy of a merit or works-based salvation, and the apocalyptic roles played by Russia and the Jewish people were highlighted. As the newly-born again were executed at play's end, a question was posed: will you be the saintly mother, unrepentant brother, or martyred sister?[84] For Aberhart, at the time of writing the play in 1931, the recent ascension of dictatorships in Germany, Russia, and Italy, appeared to fulfill biblical prophecy. This conclusion was of considerable importance to his religious thought, and soon the Great Depression would add to his concerns.[85]

Social Credit and Conflict

In July 1932, Aberhart, now principal of Crescent View High School in Calgary, arrived in Edmonton, as he did every July, to mark exams. At these annual grading sessions, Aberhart regularly met with a chemistry teacher, Charles Morton Scarborough of Edmonton. During this summer Aberhart read a book entitled, *Unemployment and War*, by British stage actor Maurice Dale Colbourne. This book provided a simplified explanation of English engineer C. H. Douglas' system of Social Credit. In Canada, Social Credit was a form of western Canadian political utopianism that promised prosperity and ease in the near future. It was a technocratic philosophy premised upon two pillars: technology would rescue humanity from toil

82. William Aberhart and E. C. Manning, "The Branding Irons of the Antichrist," [1931] reprinted in Elliott, ed., *Aberhart*, 2.

83. William Aberhart and E. C. Manning, "The Branding Irons of the Antichrist," 3.

84. William Aberhart and E. C. Manning, "The Branding Irons of the Antichrist," 2–9.

85. Sutton, "Was FDR the Antichrist?" 1053–54.

and drudgery, and experts would solve society's problems in a technocratic bureaucracy. Prosperity, it was claimed, would be perpetual.[86] Scarborough was an avid reader of Douglas' Social Credit theories, and while he was grading exams, he would extol the virtues of Social Credit attempting in vain to attract Aberhart to his view. However, summer in 1932 was different than other summers. That July, Aberhart arrived in Edmonton in an unusually sullen mood as the economic depression and severe drought was seriously grinding on the Albertan economy. He watched helplessly as the graduates of his school could not find work. Aberhart's pain deepened further when he learned that one of his graduating students had committed suicide that spring.[87]

While he was in residence at St. Stephen's College at the University of Alberta, Aberhart embraced Social Credit, and a month later he began the work of establishing a Social Credit presence in Calgary. He then started to lay the foundation for a movement that would become a political dynamo running Alberta from 1935 to 1972.[88] Aberhart himself would be Premier and Minister of Education until his death in 1943. Aberhart took Douglas' ideas and recast them for Alberta. He proposed that without interfering with the structures of private enterprise, ownership, and responsibility, adjustments could be made to monetary policy that would facilitate a mandatory distribution of a society's "cultural heritage" to ensure a baseline of purchasing power. In Aberhart's view, Albertans were deprived of their rightful "cultural heritage" which included their fair share of the province's resources and abundance. The blame for this state of affairs lay at the feet of rapacious bankers and a corrupt financial sector based in eastern Canada.[89]

Social Credit rallies took on the trappings of evangelical revival meetings. Often opening with the hymn, "Our God in Ages Past," these "monster meetings" had singing, speakers, and enthusiasm. Combined with Sunday picnics, these rallies were complimented by a growing network

---

86. Laycock, *Populism and Democratic Thought*, 218, 224, 252–53, 265–66; and Friesen, *The Canadian Prairies*, 412.

87. Bob Gilmour, "Unsung Teacher Changed the History of Alberta," *Edmonton Journal*, 9 January 1995 n.p. Available online: www.aberhartfoundation.ca; and Brennan, *The Good Steward*, 13–14, 16.

88. Bob Gilmour, "Unsung Teacher Changed the History of Alberta," *Edmonton Journal*, 9 January 1995 n.p.; and Laycock, *Populism and Democratic Thought*, 204.

89. Friesen, *The Canadian Prairies*, 412; and Laycock, *Populism and Democratic Thought*, 204.

of study groups that gathered weekly.[90] The early Social Credit movement was characterized by its anti-large-scale economic views. In a similar vein, dispensationalists, like Aberhart, shared these views. Central to dispensationalism was the belief that big finance, big banks, and centralized state power were the bedrock of a satanic system. Aberhart sought redemption for Alberta through an economic system that guaranteed social justice and prosperity.[91]

In the months leading up to the 1935 election, Aberhart spent his radio time mixing his dispensationalist theology with Social Credit ideology. He addressed listener questions, and he repeatedly reiterated how well dispensational theology and Social Credit's political ideology complimented each other. It is important to note, however, that not all fundamentalists or evangelicals agreed with Aberhart's position. In fact, Aberhart engaged in a few public disputes with leading Canadian fundamentalists, most notably, J. Fergus Kirk, the president of PBI, concerning the proper place for fundamental Christians in the worldly political order. Although Aberhart's mixing of theology and political ideology strained his relationships with other evangelicals and fundamentalists, his political turn brought in a wider audience, and his theological horizons broadened. Aberhart became more tolerant of other religious worldviews that were well outside dispensationalist circles. He interacted more frequently with mainstream Protestants, Pentecostals, Catholics, and Mormons.[92] Though Aberhart did not place the Great Depression solidly in the interpretive dispensationalist framework, he did see it as the work of the Devil. This view raised another firestorm of criticism from his fellow fundamentalists who interpreted the Depression as a manifestation of God's judgment.[93]

The social democracy that Aberhart advocated was needed to address distinct challenges of the Depression. In addition, Aberhart's application of his political philosophy enhanced individual freedom and offered a pathway to his brand of Christian conversion. As Clark Banack has demonstrated, Aberhart's ideology was anti-collectivist in its objective to free the individual from the bondage of poverty. Unlike collectivism, socialism,

---

90. Friesen, *The Canadian Prairies*, 414; and Laycock, *Populism and Democratic Thought*, 205–206, 208–209, 216–17.

91. Laycock, *Populism and Democratic Thought*, 262.

92. Radio Broadcasts by William Aberhart, Glenbow M6840 File 941; and Elliott, "Antithetical Elements in William Aberhart's Theology and Political Ideology," 39–57.

93. Elliott, "Antithetical Elements in William Aberhart's Theology and Political Ideology," 45, 47.

and the social gospel that relied heavily on state-imposed solutions to fix social ills, Social Credit relied on individual effort and entrepreneurship as the means to provide opportunity and eliminate poverty. Social Credit also fit well with Aberhart's dispensationalism, for it aimed to create a sociocultural and religious environment that Aberhart hoped would lead people to Christ. This political agenda was not, however, intended to impose a Christian theocracy on Alberta. In fact, Aberhart and Manning strongly opposed this political agenda. Above all, individual freedom was the supreme value that had to be established and maintained. Hopefully, such freedom would lead many individuals to choose to be guided by God.[94]

In his broadcasts, after addressing questions from listeners about Social Credit, he typically preached a sermon that included political themes and content. Even Easter was an occasion to offer a Social Credit message. Aberhart expounded on the resurrection of Jesus: "I think the movement which we represent is in perfect accord with the spirit of Easter." After asserting that the conditions in 1935 Alberta were as "distorted, dull, discouraging, and hopeless" as in early first century Judea, he proclaimed: "The Easter message is a message of hope. There is deliverance. There is salvation. God can and will work even a miracle to bring his people into the place of joy and prosperity. Is that not a message for all believers in Social Credit?"[95]

Kirk wrote a ten-page mimeographed and circulated essay entitled, "Social Credit and the Word of God," in response to Aberhart's political involvement and the looming 1935 election. He opposed what he saw as the materialist thinking of Social Credit and how Aberhart's mixing of it with Christianity was similar to the "great mistake" of the Catholic Church of assuming political authority where no such purpose exists.[96] Most seriously, he accused Aberhart of attempting "to eliminate the cross," acting like the Devil tempting Jesus in the wilderness. Social Credit appealed to worldliness for its promise of material benefit and comfort with little effort, contrary to scriptural entreaties of giving to the poor, of avoiding suffering. It

---

94. Banack, *God's Province*, 118–33.

95. "Under the Auspices of the Alberta Social Credit League Broadcast by William Aberhart, 19 April [1935], at 8:30," p. 1, J. McKinley Cameron fonds, M6840 File 941: William Aberhart radio broadcasts.—March-July 1935, GLA.

96. Kirk, "Social Credit and the Word of God," reprinted in Elliott, ed., *Aberhart*, 109–11. Quotes from p. 111; and, Banack, *God's Province*, 112–13, 118.

was the stuff of communism and the principle of jubilee debt relief in the Old Testament.[97]

Aberhart responded to Kirk, who proved to be one of his loudest critics. He soundly rejected Kirk's claim that the Great Depression was a judgment of God against nations that had once professed Christian faith but had fallen away. Aberhart also rejected Kirk's accusation that he had abandoned dispensationalism when he embarked on his political work. In response to Kirk, Aberhart, on 21 April 1935, went on the offensive in his sermon. He took on Kirk's accusation that Social Credit attempted "to avoid paying the cost" of their proposed reforms, as flowing from the logic from what he saw as Kirk's heterodox theology. Since eternal security was not taught at PBI, Aberhart argued that it implied that in Kirk's view the grace of God was not sufficient for salvation and similarly his political critique was framed by human struggle. While a seeming non sequitur, Aberhart's intuitive mixing of theology and politics seems to have interpreted Kirk's political critique as simultaneously a theological statement when it appears that Kirk saw the Social Credit long on promises and short on planning. Then Aberhart heightened his rhetoric and expressed his righteous indignation by firing back: "children are still crying from hunger. Mothers are suffering, not because God has failed to give but because the selfish greedy ungodly worshippers of the Golden god and their henchmen have stolen the bounties from them . . . Children are crying for bread. This man [Kirk] says you shouldn't try to relieve them. You shouldn't try to stop them from doing it."[98]

Aberhart also sparred with L. E. Maxwell. Maxwell did, at times, fill the pulpit at Westbourne for Aberhart, but he could not countenance his theology, calling Aberhart's strong dispensationalism "antinomian" and

---

97. Kirk, "Social Credit and the Word of God," 114–20, 122. Kirk does make allowance for political activity for the Christian to include praying for the government and voting, although voting ultimately does not count for much as many end up voting for the loser and the winner often is not what was presenting during a campaign. The true Christian form of government is an autocracy under God, not a democracy nor an autocracy without God.

On the matter of Communism, Maxwell argued that this worldview was atheistic and consequently unacceptable. "Hot Seat: Interview with L. E. Maxwell #581" Radio Broadcast, CD at PBI Archives Station: CJDV, 1970, T. S. Rendall Library and Archives, Prairie College, Three Hills, Alberta [PCA].

98. Elliott, "Studies of Eight Canadian Fundamentalists," 268–269; and, Wm. Aberhart's sermon, 21 April 1935 W. Norman Smith Papers, File No. 57, Glenbow-Alberta Institute, Calgary reprinted in Thomas, *William Aberhart*, 66.

compared his move into politics to Lot sitting at the gates of Sodom. Aberhart, in kind, described Maxwell as the Levite ignoring the man in the ditch, and denounced Maxwell's mystical faith and legalism. Maxwell called Aberhart's doctrine of eternal security something "straight out of hell."[99] The two men also had conflict over the curriculum of the PBI high school. Maxwell assigned Madame Guyon's writings in English classes instead of Shakespeare and other literary classics. In his role as Minister of Education, Aberhart used Maxwell's literary selections as grounds to reject PBI's accreditation. Though Maxwell was trained in dispensationalism, and it influenced his eschatology, he rejected much of it and described himself as a "partial dispensationalist." He accepted the basic contours of dispensationalism and its Christian triumphalism. However, Maxwell rejected the binary view of salvation held by Scofield. Scofield believed in salvation by works for the Jews and salvation by faith for the Gentiles. In contrast, Maxwell held that in both testaments the key efficacious element in salvation was grace. He followed Calvin in believing that the laws of the Bible do not save a person but are needed to live a righteous life.[100]

CONCLUSIONS

Later, in 1970, in an interview Maxwell was asked about CPBI and Aberhart and Manning. He said he was friends with Manning, and that Manning saw PBI as a self-contained municipality that hauled its ashes, built its own streets, maintained its sidewalks, and granted tax exemptions. Though a friendship developed, there had been no organizational attachment between the two men. However, in Maxwell's view their religious orientations were "quite the same," and "we would be reckoned old fashioned fundamentalists."[101] Despite their shared old-fashioned Baptist fundamentalist tradition, Maxwell and Aberhart were remarkably different. Through their differences in biblical interpretation, how they created and administered their Bible schools, and the form and content of their radio

---

99. "Hot Seat: Interview with L. E. Maxwell #581" Radio Broadcast, CD at PBI Archives Station: CJDV, 1970, T. S. Rendall Library and Archives, Prairie College, Three Hills, Alberta [PCA].

100. "Hot Seat: Interview with L. E. Maxwell #581" Radio Broadcast, CD at PBI Archives Station: CJDV, 1970, T. S. Rendall Library and Archives, Prairie College, Three Hills, Alberta [PCA]; Elliott, "Three Faces of Baptist Fundamentalism in Canada," 176; and Elliott, "Studies of Eight Canadian Fundamentalists," 269-70.

101. "Forum on Q" Radio Broadcast, CD "Forum Program L. E. Maxwell #390470" #582 CD at PBI Archives, Station: CHQR, 1970, PCA.

preaching, these men demonstrated that diversity and nuance were often present in expressions of Baptist fundamentalism.

In fact, Aberhart and Maxwell represented two significant streams of fundamentalism. There was Aberhart, who fused dispensational millennialism with social democratic political inclinations and, by the end of his life, held together an *inchoate pastiche* of theological and political odds and ends. In contrast, Maxwell brought together a quietist, monastic form of community formation centered on the crucifixion of the self that mixed mystical influences, holiness sanctification, and a Calvinist understanding of law and grace. As Mark Noll has suggested in his analysis, these strands of conservative Protestantism shared some common views, but they "never entirely aligned."[102]

Ironically, the decentralized congregational principles of Baptist polity, theology, and ecclesiology were manifested here through two autocratic leaning individuals who employed their ambition, energy, and suave use of communication technology to construct religious operations. Both found the other deeply wanting in their biblical interpretations and engagement with the wider world. These men migrated to Alberta from southern Ontario and the American mid-west and brought with them dispensational eschatology, evangelical errand, and religious entrepreneurship. On the one hand, Aberhart's camp pursued political objectives and eventually formed government. On the other hand, Maxwell's camp rejected politics as the means to achieve personal piety and sociocultural regeneration. Instead, Maxwell's followers saw self-sacrifice as the pathway that would lead to personal and social transformation. Both Maxwell and Aberhart then sought to transform society as they waited for Christ to return. They pursued their objectives through fundamentalist utopian visions that were rooted in long-running Christian traditions. Their dispensationalism was a form of commonsense realism that was applied to biblical interpretation. The mystical experience of crucifying the self in Christ that was based on English higher life spirituality and the quietism of French mysticism informed the pursuit of personal piety. There were spirited conflicts at times, but by the 1970s, these dominant personalities of Albertan fundamentalist Christianity, formed in the interwar period, had become simply a couple of old-fashioned fundamentalists. Nevertheless, their legacies made Calgary,

---

102. Noll, *The Scandal of the Evangelical Mind*, 120; Mann, *Sect, Cult and Church in Alberta*, 27–28; and Banack, *God's Province*, 149.

Edmonton, and Three Hills vibrant and long-lasting sources of global fundamentalist and evangelical influence.

BIBLIOGRAPHY

Primary

NEWSPAPERS

Radio News (Calgary, AB), 1930
Bulletin of the Calgary Prophetic Bible Institute (Calgary, AB), 1927
Calgary Albertan (Calgary, AB), 1926
The Prophetic Voice (Calgary, AB), 1924
Edmonton Journal (Edmonton, AB), 1995

RADIO BROADCASTS

"Forum on Q" Radio Broadcast, 1970 Station CHQR, CD "Forum Program L.E. Maxell #390470" #582 CD, Three Hills, AB, T. S. Rendall Library and Archives, Prairie College, Three Hills, Alberta.

"Hot Seat: Interview with L. E. Maxwell #581" Radio Broadcast, CD at PBI Archives Station: CJDV, 1970, Three Hills, AB, T. S. Rendall Library and Archives, Prairie College, Three Hills, Alberta.

OTHER

Aberhart, William. "Lesson Eleven: A General View of God's Great Plan." *Systematic Theology 'A' Course*. Calgary: Calgary Prophetic Bible Institute, n.d.

Aberhart, William, and E. C. Manning, "The Branding Irons of the Antichrist," [1931] reprinted in, *Aberhart: Outpourings and Replies*, edited by David R. Elliott, 2. Calgary: Historical Society of Alberta, 1991.

Kirk, J. Fergus. "Social Credit and the Word of God," Three Hills, Alta., n.p., 1935, reprinted in *Aberhart: Outpourings and Replies*, edited by David R. Elliott, 109–11. Calgary: Historical Society of Alberta, 1991.

Maxwell, L. E. *Born Crucified*. Chicago: Moody, 1945.

———. *Crowded to Christ*. Grand Rapids: Eerdmans, 1950.

———. *The Holy Spirit in Missions*. Three Hills, AB: Prairie Book Room, 1946.

T. S. Rendall Library and Archives, Prairie College, Three Hills, Alberta.

William Aberhart Collection, Glenbow Library and Archives at the University of Calgary Archives, Calgary, Alberta.

Secondary

Balsama, George. "Madame Guyon, Heterodox." *Church History* 42.3 (September 1973) 350–65.

Banack, Clark. *God's Province: Evangelical Christianity, Political Thought, and Conservatism in Alberta*. Montreal: McGill-Queen's University Press, 2016.

Brennan, Brian. *The Good Steward: The Ernest Manning Story*. Brighton, MA: Fitzhenry and Whiteside, 2008.
Burkinshaw, Robert. *Pilgrims in Lotus Land: Conservative Protestantism in British Columbia 1917–1981*. Montreal: McGill-Queen's University Press, 1995.
Callaway, Tim W. *Training Disciplined Soldiers for Christ: The Influence of American Fundamentalism on Prairie Bible Institute (1922–1980)*. Bloomington, IN: WestBow, 2013.
Elliott, David R., ed. *Aberhart: Outpourings and Replies*. Calgary: Historical Society of Alberta, 1991.
———. "Antithetical Elements in William Aberhart's Theology and Political Ideology." *Canadian Historical Review* 59.1 (March 1978) 38–58.
———. "Studies of Eight Canadian Fundamentalists." PhD diss., University of British Columbia, 1989.
———. "The Devil and William Aberhart: The Nature and Function of His Eschatology." *Studies in Religion* 9.3 (September 1980) 325–37,
———. "Three Faces of Baptist Fundamentalism in Canada: Aberhart, Maxwell, and Shields." In *Memory and Hope: Strands of Canadian Baptist History*, edited by David T. Priestley, 171–82. Waterloo, ON: Wilfrid Laurier University Press, 1996.
Elliott, David R., and Iris Miller. *Bible Bill: A Biography of William Aberhart*. Edmonton: Reidmore Books, 1987.
Enns, James. "Sustaining the Faithful and Proclaiming the Gospel in a Time of Crisis: The Voice of Popular Evangelical Periodicals During World War Two." *Historical Papers 2004: Canadian Society of Church History* (2004) 113–32.
———. "Every Christian a Missionary: Fundamentalist Education at Prairie Bible Institute, 1922–1947." MA thesis, University of Calgary, 2000.
Friesen, Gerald. *The Canadian Prairies: A History*. Toronto: University of Toronto Press, 1987.
Fuller, W. Harold. "The Legacy of Leslie E. Maxwell." *International Bulletin of Missionary Research* 28.3 (2004) 126–31.
Goertz, Donald Aaron. "The Development of a Bible Belt: The Socio-Religious Interaction in Alberta Between 1925 and 1938." MCS thesis, Regent College, Vancouver, BC, 1980.
Grant, John Webster. *The Church in Canadian Era*. Burlington, ON: Welch, 1988.
Henry, Daryn. *A. B. Simpson and the Making of Modern Evangelicalism*. Montreal: McGill-Queen's University Press, 2019.
Hiller, Harry H. "A Critical Analysis of the Role of Religion in a Canadian Populist Movement: The Emergence and Dominance of the Social Credit Party in Alberta," PhD diss., McMaster University, 1972.
Hindmarsh, D. Bruce. "The Winnipeg Fundamentalist Network, 1910–1940: The Roots of Transdenominational Evangelicalism in Manitoba and Saskatchewan." In *Aspects of the Canadian Evangelical Experience*, edited by G. A. Rawlyk, 304–19. Montreal: McGill-Queen's University Press, 1997.
Jaeger, C. Stephen. *The Envy of Angels: Cathedral Schools and Social Ideals in Medieval Europe, 950–1200*. Philadelphia: University of Pennsylvania Press, 1994.
Laycock, David. *Populism and Democratic Thought in the Canadian Prairies, 1910 to 1945*. Toronto: University of Toronto Press, 1990.
Mann, W. E. *Sect, Cult and Church in Alberta*. Reprint, Toronto: University of Toronto Press, 1972.

Noll, Mark A. *The Scandal of the Evangelical Mind*. Grand Rapids: Eerdmans, 1994.

Opp, James W. "The New Age of Evangelism: Fundamentalism and Radio on the Canadian Prairies, 1925–1945." *Historical Papers 1994: Canadian Society of Church History* (1994) 99–119.

Renfree, Henry A. *Heritage and Horizon: The Baptist Story in Canada*. Mississauga, ON: Canadian Baptist Federation, 1988.

Schultz, Harold J. "Portrait of a Premier: William Aberhart." *Canadian Historical Review* 45.3 (1964) 185–211.

Stackhouse Jr., John G. *Canadian Evangelicalism in the Twentieth Century*. Toronto: University of Toronto Press, 1993.

Sutton, Matthew Avery. "Was FDR the Antichrist? The Birth of Fundamentalist Antiliberalism in a Global Age." *The Journal of American History* (2012) 1052–74.

Thomas, Lewis H. *William Aberhart and Social Credit in Alberta*. Vancouver: Copp Clark, 1977.

Wright, Robert A. "The Canadian Protestant Tradition 1914–1945." *The Canadian Protestant Experience, 1760–1990*, edited by George A. Rawlyk, 139–97. Montreal: McGill-Queen's University Press, 1990.

8

Imports and Exports

Cross-Border Fundamentalism in the Early Twentieth Century

JEFFREY P. STRAUB

BY THE BEGINNING OF the twentieth century, Canadian Baptists were a theologically diverse lot—from extreme conservatives who came to be known as fundamentalists to extreme progressives who were called modernists.[1] The struggle between these two extremes was particularly intense with battles enjoined in newspaper articles and at denominational gatherings. Problems were heightened, because Baptists had no mechanism, such as a common creed, with which to rein in wayward ministers.

No church serves as a better exemplar of early-Canadian Baptist conservativism than Jarvis Street Baptist Church of Toronto.[2] Since 1818, the

---

1. A precise taxonomy of participants in these conflicts is well beyond the scope of this essay. One should note that the Protestant religious landscape of the period was not binary with two simple, polar opposite views but is best seen as a continuum of positions from one extreme to the other. At the end of the day, when the battle lines were drawn, particular individuals aligned themselves with one side of an issue or the another. But simply choosing a side on an issue did not imply lock step agreement across the board. One segment on the conservative end of the continuum were the fundamentalists who ultimately sought to separate from their opponents—either by driving them out of their movements or by their own withdrawal when things were perceived to be hopelessly irredeemable to justify remaining within. For a taxonomy of the views of the time, see Rawlyk, *Champions of the Truth*, 70.

2. For a recent history, see *Set for the Defense of the Gospel*.

church in the heart of Canada's largest city has stood as a bastion of historic Christianity. From the pastorate of Thomas Todhunter Shields (1873–1955, p. 1910–1955), "The Canadian Spurgeon,"[3] it has been deeply associated with a Canadian iteration of fundamentalism. Shields' brand of fundamentalism was forged in a world of theological turmoil on both sides of the border. Baptists had been expressing concerns about a new theological ethos that had taken root in Baptist life since at least the 1870s.[4] The conflicts that arose over diverse views saw several denominational splits among various Baptist groups and the birthing of new fellowships in the wake of these ruptures.

While Baptists on both sides of the border faced unique challenges close to home, many were cognizant of larger issues among their cousins north and south. This chapter focuses on the cross-border influences among Baptists which contributed to Canadian Baptist fundamentalism. While it deals primarily with the Ontario experience and Shields, it includes evidence from across Canada to demonstrate significant cross-border influences experienced from coast to coast.

A HISTORY OF CROSS-BORDER RELATIONS

Relationships among Baptists worked in both directions and existed before and after the fundamentalist-modernist controversy. Baptists of both Canada and the United States, while appreciating their theological kin to the south or to the north, had their own national identities, fellowships, and agencies. Nevertheless, as the need arose, Canadian Baptists happily travelled to the United States for education and pastoral ministry, while Americans returned the favour, filling Canadian pulpits and teaching in their schools with regularity.

Evidence of the cross-border nature of North American Baptist life may be seen in many Baptist journals of the nineteenth and twentieth centuries. Baptists were prolific writers and kept abreast of the denominational affairs far and wide, regularly informing one another of activities at home and abroad through weekly newspapers. The papers were typically regional in orientation, with a primary focus on issues within the geographical reach of the papers, such as marriages, deaths, and local events, but they

---

3. On Shields as "The Canadian Spurgeon," see Straub, "Thomas Todhunter Shields, Jr." and Adams, "The War of the Worlds." Adams is the best full-length treatment of Shields to date. Also, Stackhouse, "Shields," 23–34.

4. For a chronicle of this turmoil, see Straub, *The Making of a Battle Royal*.

also included clergy news on ordinations, pastoral changes, special meetings like revivals, educational efforts, regional mission projects, and church plants or buildings dedicated. At the same time, the papers followed important denominational affairs farther away.

Canadian Baptists figured into American Baptist journals and American Baptists into Canadian denominational papers. Sermons of prominent pastors among the global Baptist witness received coverage on a regular basis. Baptists on both sides of the border were keenly aware of the major pulpit voices. They knew the names of prominent preachers such as Robert Stuart MacArthur of New York and T. T. Shields as well as being introduced to an assortment of other regional Baptist pastors and laymen. Cross-border pulpit affiliation kept Baptists aware of the wider Baptist work. Thus, the cross-border influences were already strong at the time of the fundamentalist-modernist controversy. Baptists saw themselves as a global family and appreciated one another's ministries from afar.

T. T. SHIELDS AND HIS AMERICAN ALLIES IN THE BATTLE FOR THE BIBLE

While the details of Shields' conflict with McMaster University and the Baptist Convention of Ontario and Quebec are rehearsed elsewhere in the book, what needs to be added to the story is the cross-border influences that contributed to this conflict.[5] Shields was not a lone voice of protest in the debates of the hour. He was joined by a cadre of co-belligerents, some who were students or former students at McMaster, others who studied at Shields' Toronto Baptist Seminary, plus a company of Americans who

---

5. The Canadian conflict did not take place in a vacuum. The focus of this chapter is primarily on the cross-border influences in the direction of fundamentalism, but it should be noted that cross-border influences in the other direction were equally prominent, such as Matthews of McMaster who studied at the University of Chicago. For details, see Straub, *The Making of a Battle Royal*, 165–226. The university represented the cutting edge of North American liberal thinking, which Matthews imported back to Canada, though doubtless he may have been attracted to those ideas before going south. For details of this chapter in McMaster University's story, see Johnston, *McMaster University*, 1:90; for Elmore Harris' charges against Matthews, see Harris, *Concerning the Attacks of Prof. Matthews*. Many Baptists traveled to the United States for education, returning with progressive ideas further leavening Baptist thought.

This story is not about the progressive cross-border influences but about the conservative ones. Travel between the countries was relatively easy at the beginning of the twentieth century, so it is little wonder that American preachers were welcomed to Canada to hold meetings in churches and public halls, importing their conservative views.

affirmed his convictions and who could be counted on to echo views similar to his own.[6]

One of the earliest American fundamentalist voices in Canada was Reuben Archer Torrey (1856–1928), who came to Toronto's Massey Hall in 1906. The campaign had significant success, including the conversion of a young Oswald J. Smith (1889–1986), who went on to become a Canadian fundamentalist in his own right.[7] Torrey came at a time when a theological crisis was brewing and his dogmatic preaching was "proto-fundamentalist."[8] Late in the meetings, Torrey denounced German higher criticism. "The vital question of to-day is whether we believe Jesus or the consensus of German scholarship."[9] By late 1909, a series of pamphlets, *The Fundamentals*, was issued with Torrey as one of the principal editors. These booklets were mailed to ministers around the world by the hundreds of thousands.[10] *The Fundamentals* were intended as a restatement of conservative Christianity in an age of progressive thought. The essays were written by a wide array of conservative Christians across Protestant denominations and were distributed widely thanks to the funding of the California oil magnates Lyman and Milton Stewart.[11]

Torrey was among a long list of fundamentalists whose voices were heard in churches and public meetings in Canada during the first quarter of the twentieth century.[12] To the west, French E. Oliver, a Presbyterian from Los Angeles and a Torrey colleague, held evangelistic meetings in Vancouver

---

6. Men like John Linton of Montreal and Clifford J. Loney of Hamilton, Ontario.

7. Kee, *Revivalists*, 55. Smith was among a small but influential number of Canadian fundamentalists whose influence was felt south of the border long after the fundamentalist-modernist battles had been fought. See Elliott, "Knowing No Borders."

8. Close, *Revival in the City*, 149.

9. Torrey, cited in "Believes Christ Against the World," *The Globe*, 20 January 1906. For more on Torrey, see Gloege, *Consumed*.

10. On *The Fundamentals* and A. C. Dixon, see Priest, "A. C. Dixon, Chicago Liberals."

11. On Lyman Stewart, see Pietsch, "Lyman Stewart and Early Fundamentalism," and Sandeen, "Fundamentals."

12. Torrey's influence was felt elsewhere in Canada. In 1906, he also held a month-long campaign in Ottawa. See "The Living Gospel to Be Preached," *The Evening Journal*, 26 May 1906, 11. He spoke in Montreal the following year. See "Torrey Evangelistic Campaign," *The Gazette*, 20 Apr 1907, 9. In 1910, he held meetings in Fredericton, NB, 12 May to 9 June. See "Personalia," *A Record of Christian Work*, May 1910, 332. Torrey was a periodic visitor to Canada in the early twentieth century.

in 1917 in which he addressed liberal theology that caught the attention of Baptists there.[13]

When Torrey came to Toronto on that first visit, Shields was still in London, Ontario, at the Adelaide Street Baptist Church, having become its pastor the year before at the age of thirty-two. Shields' star was on the rise in Baptist circles. Adelaide Street opened a balcony to increase its seating capacity due to the demand of ever-increasing crowds who wished to sit under Shields' preaching. He brought the Canadian-born Baptist Robert Stuart MacArthur to preach at the dedication service.[14] MacArthur was born in Dalesville, Quebec, in 1841, and after studies at Woodstock College he finished at the University of Rochester in New York, graduating with a BA in 1867. He also attended the nearby seminary, graduating in 1870. MacArthur became the first pastor of Calvary Baptist Church of New York City in May. While MacArthur spent his entire pastoral career at Calvary, he periodically preached in Canadian pulpits such as Adelaide Street.[15] He was elected president of the Baptist World Alliance in June 1911 at their second congress and left the Calvary pulpit to devote his time to the global Baptist witness.[16] MacArthur, esteemed in Canada, delivered the 1911 baccalaureate sermon for McMaster University, held at Jarvis Street.

Shields did not arrive on the Toronto scene until 1910, and he was soon introduced into the larger world of Baptist denominational life. Soon, he brought the force of his rhetoric and influence into the conflict over the direction of Canadian Baptists. He became the champion of the conservative views among the Baptists in central Canada and beyond. He may even have

13. See Burkinshaw, *Pilgrims in Lotus Land*, 41–54. French E. Oliver was an outspoken fundamentalist. His campaign in Vancouver in 1917 warned Baptists of troubles at Brandon College. Oliver held meetings across western Canada in a variety of churches including Baptist ones. He also had a hand in the collapse of Des Moines University (see below) as a member of the BBU board. See a photo of the board of the university in *Arizona Daily Star*, 21 May 1929, 4. Eventually Oliver started First Fundamental Church of Los Angeles, preaching its opening meeting on "The Great Apostacy." The church was interdenominational in character and followed "strict principles of the fundamentalists." See "New Church Hears Oliver," *Los Angeles Evening Express*, 7 Jul 1928, 4.

14. Adams, "The War of The Worlds," 74.

15. On MacArthur, see *Rochester Theological Seminary General Catalogue*, 88. On MacArthur at Adelaide Street, see "Adelaide St, London," *CB*, 22 February 1906, 9. Also "Dr. R. S. MacArthur, Noted Baptist Dead," *NYT*, 25 February 1923, 16. Just what Shields' opinion was of this message in 1911 is uncertain. He mentions his "intimate" acquaintance with MacArthur but offers no comment on this particular message. Cf. Shields, *The Plot that Failed*, 62.

16. Briggs, "From 1905 to the End of the First World War," 35.

been displeased with MacArthur's address in his new pulpit. MacArthur affirmed the compatibility of evolution with religion: "Evolution is simply God's method of accomplishing determined results."[17] Shields repeatedly and publicly spoke out against evolution as time went on and he could not have been happy with MacArthur's comments.[18] Others joined him in identifying evolution as a key marker of rising theological liberalism.

A few years later, Shields hosted another significant American preacher at Jarvis Street. Russell H. Conwell was long-time pastor of Grace Baptist Church of Philadelphia, Pennsylvania, and founder of Temple University.[19] On Conwell's visit to Toronto in 1917, he brought with him an honorary doctorate from the Temple board to be conferred on Shields. Shields, knowing that the honour was pending, determined to refuse the degree, but Conwell surprised him with the presentation in a Jarvis Street service.[20] With men like MacArthur and Conwell, Jarvis Street hosted some of the most well-known Baptists from south of the border. As time went on, Shields' choice of pulpit allies became decidedly more conservative, especially after the fundamentalist-modernist controversy was fully enjoined.

EARLY FUNDAMENTALIST ALLIES

Now as the pastor of the great church, Shields began to shape Jarvis Street in his own image.[21] He took firm control over its administration during his

17. "No Conflict Between Science and Religion," *The Globe*, 10 May 1911, 8.

18. For Shields' later views on evolution, see "Contending for the Faith," *GW*, 31 May 1923, 3. It was "absolutely antichristian" and "ought not to be permitted in any Christian school." He lamented that evolution was being taught at McMaster.

19. Conwell was an extraordinary preacher in his own right. His famous lecture, "Acre of Diamonds," was delivered more than six thousand times to countless masses in person, on the radio, and in print. See "Russell H. Conwell," Temple University website. For more on Conwell, see Burr, *Russell H. Conwell*; Bjork, *Victorian Flight*; Nelson, "Russell H. Conwell" and Hall, "Conwell, Russell Herman."

20. See *The Plot that Failed*, 64–65.

21. It is my belief that if Shields' predecessor, H. Francis Perry, had remained for a lengthy stay at Jarvis Street (he was there only five and a half years), the church may well have moved into progressive Christianity. Perry's uncle was the American Baptist Daniel W. Faunce, father of William Herbert Perry Faunce, President of Brown University, who became the object of a Shields attack in 1923 when McMaster awarded the noted liberal an honorary doctorate. Both Perry and the younger Faunce studied at Newton Theological Institution about the time that Alvah Hovey forced Ezra P. Gould off the faculty over liberal theological views, although Faunce had graduated by the time Perry commenced his education there. The Faunces and the Perrys knew each other. Daniel performed Francis' wedding. On Faunce and Hovey, see Straub, *The Making of a Battle Royal*.

first decade[22] and brought into the pulpit a number of well-known conservative Baptist leaders on whom he could count to ratify his dogmatic positions. At the same time, he joined hands with American colleagues to build a geographically broad coalition to stem the tide of advancing progressive theology. The most important effort in this regard was Shields' participation in the Baptist Bible Union (BBU). While the BBU initially showed promise, a series of public-relations fiascos (one of which Shields himself presided over) in the late 1920s caused it to lose momentum before it eventually terminated in 1932. The decline of the BBU will be covered in greater detail below; however, first it is necessary to look at some of Shields' key allies that contributed to this growing alliance.

A. C. Dixon

One early like-minded confederate to enter the Jarvis Street pulpit was the well-known Amzi Clarence Dixon. Dixon came to Jarvis Street in 1914 while pastor of the Metropolitan Tabernacle (p. 1911–1919) of London, England, former home to Charles Haddon Spurgeon. Dixon established his fundamentalist *bona fides* at his Chicago pastorate, the Moody Church (1906–1911), during the controversial days of George Burman Foster (1858–1918), the noted Baptist liberal of the University of Chicago Divinity School. Both Foster and Dixon participated in the Chicago Baptist ministerial fellowship. The group became embroiled over Foster's radical views with Dixon publishing against Foster's troubling opinions.[23] Given Foster's extreme ideas, many questioned the validity of Foster's standing as a member of a Baptist fellowship.[24]

Dixon left Chicago, accepting a call to the Metropolitan Tabernacle, but did not remain solely in London during his Tabernacle days, returning periodically to North America. Shields preached for Dixon in London on several occasions beginning in 1913, and arranged to have Dixon preach at Jarvis Street the following summer. Dixon returned the favour, inviting

---

22. The first issue addressed was a deficit budget despite the church's size and the wealth of its members. See *The Plot that Failed*, 35. A few years later, Shields had a conflict with the church's choir and director which resulted in his assuming control over the music portion of the services. See Straub, "T. T. Shields Against the World."

23. Dixon, *"Destructive Criticism."*

24. For details on Dixon's role in the Foster controversy, see Straub, *The Making of a Battle Royal*, 201–5. For more on Dixon, see Meehan, "A. C. Dixon, Early Fundamentalist"; Priest, "Apologetical Ministry of Amzi Clarence Dixon"; Lewis, "The Thought of Amzi Clarence Dixon"; and Mayfield, "Striving for Souls."

Shields to fill the famous pulpit again in his absence. They exchanged pulpits during the decade four times.[25]

The Shields-Dixon confederation occurred before the beginning of the fundamentalist-modernist controversy. Shields' use of Dixon demonstrated the kind of ally to whom Shields gravitated wherever he went. On Dixon's 1920 visit, he joined with American Baptist conservative pastors William Bell Riley of Minneapolis and Jasper Cortenus Massee of Boston for an eight-day campaign that ran concurrently with the Forward Movement,[26] though not as a formal part of it. Clearly the things Dixon stood for were indicative of the coming fundamentalism. At Massey Hall in January 1920, Dixon railed against evolution: "If ever there was a thing that smelt of the pit ... it was this, and back of the war was the infernal theory that the strong and the fit have the right to destroy the weak and the unfit, and if that is scientifically right then Germany was right in all she did."[27]

Dixon was back at Jarvis Street again as discussions were underway for the formation of the BBU. He again denounced evolution which when "pressed to its logical conclusion had caused the late war." This "jungle theory" was a destroyer of homes, the sanctity of marriage and "filled the divorce courts."[28] The Dixon-Shields alliance soon passed as Dixon died in 1925. Other men arose to fill the Jarvis Street pulpit, strengthening the views of its prominent pastor.

William Bell Riley

William Bell Riley, a Dixon ally, became a Shields ally in the Canadian fight for fundamentalism. Riley, pastor of First Baptist Church, Minneapolis and "the dominant figure in American fundamentalism in the 1920s,"[29] made his first visit to Toronto by 1904 and became a regular speaker in churches

---

25. Shields, *Plot that Failed*, 35. Also Adams, "The War of the Worlds," 138.

26. On the Forward Movement, see Goertz, "A Missed Opportunity."

27. Cited in *The Globe*, 16 January 1920, 9. Not all Torontonians appreciated Dixon's preaching. *The Globe*'s "The Voice of the People" ran several letters from those who took exception to Dixon's strong rhetoric. See Dorothy Glen, "Evolution on Religion," *The Globe*, 20 January 1920, 6 and John J. Phillimore, "Reply to Dr. Dixon," *The Globe*, 29 January 1920, 6.

28. "Slashing Attack Upon Modernism by Able Preacher," *The Globe*, 12 September 1923, 12. This may have been Dixon's final visit to Jarvis Street. He died in 1925 in Baltimore, having been in poor health for some time. See his death notice in *The Globe*, 4 July 1925, 17.

29. Trollinger, Jr., *God's Empire*, 33.

and public halls in Canada.[30] He established his fundamentalist credentials early in the twentieth century, joining the attack on Foster. In opposing Foster's *Finality of the Christian Religion* (1906), he suggested that it would be better to simply burn the Bible rather than retain "a book whose claims of heavenly birth are false, whose commands are only the invention of men, whose supposed historical records are simply myths, or at the most a combination of fact and fancy and whose plan of salvation, culminating in a Christ—the sinner's substitute—is purely a delusion."[31]

Riley questioned the soundness of the Northern Baptist Convention's schools. The schools were a hot-button issue on both sides of the border, with Riley leading the charge from his pulpit, in his paper, and in other writings. Of particular concern was the effect that modernism had on evangelical schools. Evangelical Christianity builds on three important truths: "an inerrant book," "an infallible Christ," and a "spiritual experience." In view of this definition, he concluded, "The Critics are capturing denominational colleges."[32]

Riley also led in the formation of the World's Christian Fundamentals Association (WCFA). When the WCFA held its first meeting in Philadelphia in June 1919, Canadians were alerted to the meeting with a summary of the conference as well as one held at Buffalo, New York, a few days following. Riley figured heavily in the movement and was present at its annual meeting in Toronto held at Jarvis Street and at Massey Hall in 1926.[33] Riley's presence was felt often on the Canadian scene before and after his association with Shields.[34]

Riley preached in 1920, alongside Dixon, at a Toronto Association of Baptist Churches sponsored meeting.[35] On the closing night, Riley attacked Darwinism, higher criticism, and their effects on the recent war. These were

---

30. The first reference to a Riley visit to Toronto that could be discovered came in 1904 to Walmer Road Baptist, pastored by W. W. Weeks. See *The Globe*, 29 Aug 1904, 12. Riley was back in Toronto in 1916 for the dedication of the Boon Ave Baptist Church, Earlscourt, holding a five-day mission. See *The Globe*, 2 December 1916, 14.

31. Riley, *The Finality of Higher Criticism*, 124.

32. Riley, *The Menace of Modernism*, 107, 115.

33. "City Church Services," *The Globe*, 21 April 1926, 21.

34. See "To Reassert Basic Belief," *The Globe*, 2 June 1919, 11 and "Basic Points of Doctrine," *The Globe*, 7 June 1919, 3.

35. Campaign advertisement, *The Globe*, 27 December 1919, 18.

themes on which Riley preached regularly and were hallmarks of fundamentalism, north and south.³⁶

Through the 1920s, Shields and Riley were comrades in the fundamentalist-modernist conflict raging in the Baptist denominations. Shields made journeys to the United States to speak before large gatherings on critical issues and Riley returned the favour, coming to Canada and particularly to Jarvis Street to join Shields in attacking modernism.³⁷ Common subjects during the conflict were evolution and the effect of liberalism on the schools.³⁸ In 1923, Riley made two trips to Toronto, speaking in March and September. His coming was announced in *The Gospel Witness* with great fanfare:

> Dr. Riley is one of the outstanding preachers of America. About twenty years ago, he passed through an experience similar to our own. But he stood his ground, and God honored [sic] his faith....
> He is known all over the United States as a stalwart defender of the faith, and is one of the chiefs of the Fundamentalist Movement.³⁹

On this first visit to Jarvis Street, Riley attacked evolution—it was without foundation. Charles Darwin had used the phrase "we may well suppose" or the like over eight hundred times in *On the Origin of the Species* (1859), yet there was not one clear example of evolutionary change which, if one could be produced, would end the debate completely.⁴⁰ Riley and Shields collaborated in the formation the BBU. At the first meeting, a resolution was passed against evolution.⁴¹ In September, Riley, back in Toronto, stated

---

36. Shields raised the spectre of evolution at McMaster in 1923. "Contending for the Faith," sermon delivered at Jarvis Street, Sunday morning 20 May 1923 in *GW*, 31 May 1923, 2.

37. For instance, in May 1923, Shields joined Riley in Kansas City for the first conference of the Baptist Bible Union. See *Word and Way*, 24 May 1923, 7-8. It was at this conference that Shields was elected president.

38. Riley used his own paper, *School and Church* (later *The Christian Fundamentals in School and Church*) to address these issues repeatedly during this decade. Eg, Riley, "Seminaries and a Statement of Faith," *School and Church*, Jan-Mar 1919, 114-15 and Riley, "Undenominational Bible Training Schools," *Christian Fundamental in School and Church*, Jul-Sep 1923, 24-26.

39. *GW*, 22 February 1923, 7.

40. "Decries Evolution as Speculatory and Non-Scientific," *The Globe*, 12 March 1923, 11.

41. Shields read the resolution from the pulpit at Jarvis Street shortly after it was passed on 15 May 1923 in Kansas City. For the resolution, see Shields, "Contending for the Faith," *GW*, 31 May 1923, 5-6.

he would rather send his children to state schools than into denominational ones that were dominated by error, funded largely by noted liberal Baptist philanthropist John D. Rockefeller, Jr.[42]

Riley came often to Jarvis Street in the mid-1920s. At the end of 1926, as Shields prepared to open a new seminary, a conservative alternative to McMaster, *The Gospel Witness* announced that Riley would open the new school. Riley would doubtless answer negative comments made at the recent convention and it was hoped that John MacNeill, pastor of Walmer Road Baptist Church in Toronto and opponent of Shields, would attend. "Special seats" would be reserved for him or other McMaster representatives.[43] Riley addressed "Modernism, the Enemy of Evangelism" to a packed crowd. Liberalism "can only live and flourish as a parasite. It has got to bore into the evangelical flesh in order to exist at all." Later, Riley spoke about "The Blight of Unitarianism."[44] Riley returned to Jarvis Street in April of 1929. He warned about the dangers of Darwinism and cautioned against dancing, smoking, "murderous movies, salacious theatre, and the plethoric purse."[45] The Riley-Shields alliance disintegrated in the late 1920s. Two factors contributed to the collapse of their collaboration—Riley's alliance with H. C. Wayman, president of Des Moines University (DMU),[46] and Shields' relationship with Edith Rebman, a major contributing factor in the DMU collapse.

Harry Clifford Wayman is a man about whom little is known today. He taught Old Testament courses at the Southern Baptist Theological Seminary from 1914–1923. He accepted the presidency of William Jewell College of Liberty, Missouri. Wayman left William Jewell under a cloud

---

42. "Verities of the Faith Not Being Taught," *The Globe*, 13 September 1923, 13. John D. Rockefeller, Jr., son of J. D. Rockefeller, Sr., had attended Fifth Avenue Baptist Church during the ministry of William H. P. Faunce, the pastor who first led the church into liberalism. Rockefeller, Jr., went to Brown University, where Faunce had become its president, and continued on a committed path into liberalism. For the Rockefeller story, see Schenkel, *Rich Man and the Kingdom*.

43. "Dr. W. B. Riley is Coming," *GW*, 20 Dec 1926, 16.

44. "Modernist Parasite Flourishes on Flesh of Evangelical Body," *The Globe*, 6 January 1927, 1.

45. "Women Smoking, Modern Dancing Scored by Pastor," *The Globe*, 12 April 1929, 18.

46. See Shields to Riley, 4 April 1930. Wayman enlisted Riley's help to stop Shields domination of DMU. Copy in possession of author. I am indebted to author David R. Elliott, "Eight Canadian Fundamentalists," for supplying me copies of letters he found in the files of T.T. Shields in the Jarvis Street archives.

of suspicion over the genuineness of his academic *bona fides*.[47] Wayman, who periodically travelled in fundamentalist circles, was hired by Shields to assume the presidency of DMU in June 1928. The matter of Wayman's credentials soon became an issue at the university. Shields found out about the bogus degrees and moved to oust Wayman, but the faculty rallied to him. Shields also believed that the faculty was infested with liberalism. He proposed to fire the entire faculty and staff, submitting them all to a re-hiring process whereby he could vet their orthodoxy. Wayman defended himself and the faculty, and directed the attention of all who would listen toward T. T. Shields and Edith Rebman. They were the problems at DMU. At this time, Wayman gained the ear of W. B. Riley who sided with him in his dispute with Shields.[48]

The hiring and firing of Wayman and the faculty at DMU created much of the chaos that resulted in the closure of DMU.[49] Another significant factor was the dominant presence of Edith Rebman on campus. Edith had been a member of Shields' Toronto church. When the BBU formed in 1923, she relocated to Chicago to run its office. After the Union gained control of DMU and placed Shields at its helm, Rebman became the secretary-treasurer and went to Des Moines to be the point person to ensure that the BBU's agenda was carried out. Rebman was both efficient and tyrannical. Historian Robert Delnay, who corresponded with some of the living participants at Des Moines, concluded that Rebman "fit a rigid pattern: those who worked over her felt she was magnificent, those who worked under her felt she was intolerable."[50]

47. On Wayman's bogus degrees, see Hinman et. al., "Academic Freedom and Tenure." The particular degree in question was a DLitt from Oxford University in 1921, a school that Wayman had apparently never attended. The 1926 William Jewell yearbook, *The Tatler*, dedicated to Wayman, has the suspect degree listed under his picture, but in the 1928 yearbook, the degree is omitted. Also missing from the degrees listed in 1928 is a ThD supposedly earned at the Southern Baptist Theological Seminary in 1912. This degree is listed in *The Tatler* for 1926.

48. In a letter to O. W. Van Osdel, a pastor from Grand Rapids, MI and a DMU board member, Wayman sent a three-page defense of his position in which he set forth the problems with Shields and Rebman among the students, faculty, and area pastors. See H. C. Wayman, "The Trouble at Des Moines University," undated, attached to a letter from Wayman to Van Osdel, 15 May 1929. He likely sent the same letter to Riley. I am indebted to my former colleague Kevin T. Bauder for his collection of Van Osdel correspondence gathered as he prepared to write "O. W. Van Osdel." Copy in the author's collection.

49. For a recent discussion of the collapse, see Douglas, "The Serious Nature of the Division."

50. Delnay, "Baptist Bible Union," 193–94.

Edith Rebman's demeanour on campus and a questionable relationship to Shields became a source of concern for Riley. An accusation of "moral turpitude" against Shields was raised at a DMU board meeting in May 1929.[51] It became the largest single issue to arise between he and Riley as the latter expressed his belief that there was credence to the charge. The allegation itself was made at a board meeting Sunday, 12 May.[52] The board met for sixteen hours during which students and faculty were "grilled." At the end of the meeting, the board fully and completely exonerated Shields and Rebman of wrongdoing.[53] Apparently Shields and Rebman, by mere coincidence, had been booked in a Waterloo hotel in rooms that were adjoining. News of the story hit the Iowa papers the next day. The hotel issued a statement that the room assignments were "entirely accidental and not by request." Had such a request been made, they (Shields and Rebman) would have been told that no such rooms were available.[54]

The papers in Iowa seemed satisfied that the liaison never took place as the story died in the press.[55] Nevertheless, Riley thought the story had merit. In a letter to Shields the following year, Riley declared, "The basis of my conviction in the Des Moines matter is not at all that of hearsay, but what I myself saw and feared for some years."[56] In a letter to O. W. Van Osdel, Riley reminded Van Osdel, "I do not need to tell you, and you know

51. "Shields and Two Trustees Reveal Probe," *Des Moines Register*, 13 May 1929, 1.

52. In point of fact, Riley was opposed to the whole Des Moines proposal and especially of the role Edith Rebman was to play in it. He therefore refused to support the effort. Riley's assessment of Rebman was that "his [Shields'] view of Miss Rebman's fitness for her position I have never been able to share . . . she was difficult to work with and under certain conditions might become impossible." See, Riley to Wayman, 10 May 1929, copy in author's possession, from the Elliott letters.

53. "Shields and Two Trustees Reveal Probe," *Des Moines Register*, 13 May 1929, 1.

54. "Waterloo Hotel in Spotlight on Shields Charges," *Waterloo Evening Courier*, 13 May 1929, 2.

55. The best explanation for this seems to be a statement from Dean Calloway in *Waterloo Evening Courier*. The paper reported "that the principal point of attack he and Stevens would make to the bible union would be against continued control of school administration by Dr. Shields and Miss Rebman. He said the deans were willing to sign the trustees' resolution adopted Saturday [Sunday], clearing Dr. Shields and Miss Rebman of charges of indiscretions, but that they had been given no opportunity to do so." "Trustee Carries Story of Shields Fight to Buffalo" subtitled "Faculty Satisfied Charge of 'Indiscretions' Were Not Well Founded," *Waterloo Evening Courier*, 14 May 1929, 2.

56. Riley to Shields, 10 Apr 1930, from David Elliott's file. Copy in the possession of the author. This letter is the most important statement that I have read to date to explain why Riley did not support the work of DMU.

perfectly well, as well as any body living why I did not, and why I could not back Shields in the Des Moines affair, and down in your secret soul you admired me for refusing to put myself in the breech that would have required falsification on my part." Van Osdel responded to Riley's accusation about a week later: "I must disagree with the last paragraph of your letter. I have been with Dr. Shields and Miss Rebman a great deal, and know them both very intimately. I cannot feel that you are justified in your attitude toward Dr. Shields."[57]

In assessing the end of the relationship, Doug Adams delves into the fracturing of the BBU leadership team. Both men lived long after 1930 and remained active pastors but their working together did not extend into the next decade. The DMU affair was tense and ugly. It marked the nadir of the BBU. Additionally, Shields was unhappy that Riley refused to break with the Northern Baptist Convention.[58]

Yet Riley's Canadian presence was felt beyond his relationship with Shields. Riley had laboured among Winnipeg fundamentalists through his preaching at Elim Chapel in 1915 and again in 1930. He also preached in Winnipeg at Central United Church in 1928.[59] Riley revisited Toronto in 1928, though not at Jarvis Street, to debate Joseph McCabe, an ex-Catholic priest and a supporter of evolution.[60] McCabe challenged Rev. Dr. John Inkster of Knox Presbyterian Church to a debate, but when Inkster refused Oswald Smith of Cosmopolitan Tabernacle telegraphed Riley asking for assistance. Riley accepted the challenge.[61] The debate, held at Massey Hall on

---

57. Riley to Van Osdel, 10 Sep 1930 and Van Osdel to Riley, 18 Sep 1930, both in the Bauder collection, copies in author's possession.

58. Adams, *Shields*, 422–26. Little can be said of Shields' comments to Riley during these days as few of Riley's personal papers are extant. The former archivist at Northwestern College (today the University of Northwestern) suggested to me that the papers were likely destroyed due to flooding issues when construction was being undertaken. Conversation with Mary Lou Hoveda, circa 2003. While it cannot be said for certain that Riley was not in Toronto with Shields after the Des Moines University debacle, a search of the *Toronto Daily Star*, *The Globe*, and *The Gospel Witness* yielded only two references to Riley in Toronto after 1929, neither of which were with Shields.

59. *Winnipeg Evening Tribune*, (*WET*) 4 Sep 1915, 13. Also meeting advertisement, *WET*, 29 Mar 1930, 29. "Dr. W. B. Riley to Preach Sunday at Central Church," *WET*, 24 Mar 1928, 16.

60. On McCabe, see Cooke, *A Rebel to His Last Breath*.

61. "Evolution Question Will Be Debated," *The Globe*, 17 October 1928, 14.

19 October with Oswald Smith moderating, resulted in a Riley "win" with approximately three-fourths of the audience standing to affirm his victory.[62]

Early in the 1930s, Riley had occasion to address the Fundamentalist Baptist Youth Association at Stratford, Ontario. More than one thousand young people from Ontario and Quebec gathered for preaching and for fellowship. He again decried evolution.[63] He returned to Toronto again in 1936, at another meeting of the WCFA, working with Oswald J. Smith of the Peoples Church.[64] He preached on Sunday, 3 May, in the morning at Peoples and then in the evening at Massey Hall.[65]

FUNDAMENTALIST ALLIES IN THE HEAT OF THE BATTLE

With the death of Dixon and the distance between Riley and Shields, Shields needed other fundamentalist confederates to fill his pulpit. Among these were the flamboyant New York fundamentalist John Roach Straton (1875–1929) and the highly controversial John Franklin Norris (1877–1952), the "Texas tornado." Both men had sensational ministries and both represented the extreme edges of fundamentalism. Shields found kindred spirits in them both. Shields also depended on the veteran fundamentalist pastor, O. W. Van Osdel of Grand Rapids, Michigan.

John Roach Straton

J. R. Straton earned his fundamentalist stripes in the city of Chicago, like Dixon and Riley, during the George Burman Foster affair. Straton was pastor of the Second Baptist Church when Foster wrote his first book. Straton wrote a critique and offered a resolution against the views expressed at a meeting of the Chicago Baptist ministerial fellowship.[66] He had a mind to fight the rising liberalism and the will to do so.

---

62. "Evolution Theory Suffers Defeat as Audience Votes," *The Globe*, 20 October 1928, 17.

63. "1,000 Young People Attend Conference," *The Globe*, 25 May 1932, 2.

64. Riley also preached at WFCA meeting in Vancouver in 1935. See "Fundamentals Conference," *The Daily Province*, 5 June 1935.

65. "Services in Toronto Churches on Sunday," *TDS*, 2 May 1936, 11.

66. For details, see Straub, *The Making of a Battle Royal*, 198–205. For Straton's critique, see John Roach Straton, "False Culture a Foe of Christianity: A Review of Prof. George Foster's book on *The Finality of the Christian Religion*," *Journal and Messenger*, 1 Mar 1906, 9.

In 1918, on the cusp of the fundamentalist-modernist controversy that was about to erupt in the Northern Baptist Convention, Straton moved to New York City to the prestigious Calvary Baptist Church, former home of Robert Stuart MacArthur, its pastor emeritus. Straton was no stranger to controversy in New York and brought his temperament to bear on Canadian fundamentalism through his ministry at Jarvis Street during the days of Shields.

His first visit to Toronto seems to have been in 1920 at St. James Methodist Church. The subject of his message was one that would make him attractive the next year for Shields—dancing.[67] In 1921, shortly after Shields took control of Jarvis Street, he charged the leadership of the church with worldliness: church members attended dances. Shields invited Straton to assist him in his frontal assault on worldliness. Straton was a master at confronting worldliness as he perceived it and his message fit well with that of Shields. Shields promoted Straton as a fiery preacher who would advance his recent opinions.[68] Straton certainly did not disappoint. He attacked liquor, worldliness, and especially dancing. He also excoriated preachers who either failed to warn their people of indulging in these behaviours, or worse, who participated in them themselves.[69] Straton garnered attention for Shields and Jarvis Street with his provocative style.

A few months later, Torontonians were treated to an article in their local paper discussing a debate that Straton had in New York City with a theatrical producer, William A. Brady. The debate resulted in a near riot.[70]

67. "Says Dancing Today is a Dance of Death," *TDS*, 17 November 1920, 10.

68. "Straton to Assist Pastor Shields in Worldly War," *TDS*, 17 August 1921, 9. In the lead up to these meetings, announcements ran in the papers to prepare for what would prove to be a real show. Shields preached his controversial sermon, "Christian Attitude toward Amusements," in February of that year and Straton echoed many of his themes later that year August 19–31. Cf. Shields, *The Plot that Failed*, 209–29 with "The Spotlight," *TDS*, 29 Aug 1921, 4. Sermon titles proposed in advance included, "Fighting the Devil in Modern Babylon" and "The Dance of Death—Should Christians Indulge?" See *TDS*, 13 August 1921, 20. Dancing had been a major issue in the Shields sermon six months earlier.

69. "Pities Anglican Padre for Company He Keeps," *TDS*, 25 August 1921.

70. "Preacher and Actor Debate in a Church," *TDS*, 14 February 1922, 3. Also, "Straton and Brady Clash in Church over Stage Morals," *NYT*, 13 February 1922, 41. The New York papers had much to say about this debate with prominent celebrities weighing in. A week after the debate, Lillian Gish added her thoughts. "Lillian Gish Speaks for Stage in Pulpit," *NYT*, February 20, 1922, 5. The stir finally drove the church's former pastor Robert Stuart MacArthur from its membership. MacArthur had been the pastor emeritus alongside Straton until 1922. He resigned his membership over Straton's antics

In late 1922, Straton went on record opposing the Ku Klux Klan after a man named Haywood, associated with the church as a general evangelist, went public supporting it. Again, the story made the Toronto papers.[71] Straton made for good copy from afar and when in town.[72]

It is little wonder that he and Shields were such good companions. They were both actively involved in the work of the BBU and other efforts. At the invitation of Straton, Shields travelled to New York to preach an evangelistic campaign at Calvary.[73] He may have travelled there at just this particular occasion because Straton was embroiled in his own fundamentalist problems in the city. At the May Anniversaries of the Northern Baptist Convention, Straton objected to the preaching of William H. P. Faunce, standing on a chair at the convention, attempting to shout down the liberal clergyman.[74] Then Straton learned that the foreign mission board supported outright liberals—he had a member of his church who brought him news from inside the agency. Straton and his New York allies formed the Baptist Fundamentalist League of Greater New York and Vicinity to meet the enemy aggressively. Shields' visit seems hardly coincidental. The two men were allies and the meetings would have had the effect of strengthening one another's hands in the battle.[75] Straton returned the favour, preaching at Jarvis Street on 29 July, with a planned stay until at least 16 August.[76] *The Gospel Witness* summarized Shields' assessment of Straton's ministry.

> We remember with joy and gratitude his former visit of two years ago, when he met us under entirely different conditions. Dr. Straton's visit on that occasion was fraught with great blessing and

---

and joined Old Cambridge Baptist where his son was pastor. See "Dr. MacArthur Quits Dr. Straton's Church as Too Sensational," *NYT*, 8 March 1922. The "stage debate" was the last straw.

71. "Ku Klux Klan Opens Headquarters in New York," *TDS*, 24 November 1922, 28.

72. Straton had little direct ministry in Canada outside his preaching at Jarvis Street. However, Straton likely had some indirect influence in Canada as Canadian newspapers across the country carried hundreds of stories about him, following his flamboyant career through the 1920s and noting his final illness and death.

73. "Pastor's Out of Town Engagements," *GW*, 22 May 1923, 8. Shields preached April 8–18. Later that month, he attended the WCFA in Texas and in May he was at the inaugural meeting of the BBU.

74. Shields was also a vocal opponent of Faunce. When McMaster conferred upon him an honorary degree, Shields objected loudly. "Shields Throws Down Gauntlet to Faunce," *TDS*, 3 December 1923, 3.

75. For details, see Straub, *The Making of a Battle Royal*, 26.

76. "Church Announcements," *GW*, 26 July 1923, 8.

far-reaching results. Since then he has been waging a noble warfare for the faith in New York; and in what is probably one of the most difficult places in the world for the Gospel to get a hearing.[77]

Shields also carried news of Straton's debate with Charles Francis Potter, who left the Baptists to become a Unitarian. As pastor of Westside Unitarian Church (1920–1925), Potter became a pronounced liberal. The debates took place in 1923–1924 between the two men and were covered in many news agencies. Shields carried news of these contests in *The Gospel Witness*.[78] Also, Straton, like his friend Shields, did not hesitate to go after politicians as well as preachers for their misdeeds. In 1928, Straton challenged New York Governor Al Smith to appear before the Calvary Baptist congregation where Straton would repeat public criticisms of Smith calling him "the deadliest foe in America today."[79] Straton died on 2 November 1929, ending Shields' relationship with his American co-belligerent. Together and separately, they were constantly on the offense against perceived theological error wherever it reared its ugly head. Together, through the work of the BBU, they made formidable allies in the cause of fundamentalism on both sides of the border.

J. Frank Norris

The most controversial fundamentalist that Shields brought to the Jarvis Street pulpit was J. Frank Norris. Norris represented the Southern Baptist wing of fundamentalism. In 1909, he became the pastor of First Baptist Church of Fort Worth, Texas. He made a name for himself as the leader of southern fundamentalism, attacking liberalism at Baylor University, his *alma mater*, charging professors with teaching evolution.[80]

77. "Dr. John Roach Straton," *GW*, 5 August 1923, 12.

78. On these debates, see *Fundamentalist vs. Modernist*. Cf. "From a Southern Contemporary," *GW*, 27 March 1924, 6.

79. "Smith's Challenge Accepted by Pastor," *The Globe*, 10 August 1928, 2. T. T. Shields was well-known for his antagonism of Ontario Premier Mitchell Hepburn and Canadian Prime Minister Mackenzie King. For details, see Adams, "Fighting Fire with Fire," 53–104.

80. Recent studies of Norris include Stokes, *The Shooting Salvationist*; Hankins, *God's Rascal*; and Tatum, *Conquest or Failure*. Hankins marks Norris's shift towards fundamentalism in 1917 when he began having men like A. C. Dixon, W. B. Riley, and others into FBC to speak. In the early 1920s, Norris set his sights on Baylor and evolutionary teaching by some professors. He was censured by the Baptist General Conference of Texas for his efforts. See Hankins, *God's Rascal*, 26.

Norris' first visit to the great church in Toronto was 1923. Shields began to work with this American colleague through the newly formed BBU, beginning with the conference in which he brought six of the leading figures in the budding movement into his pulpit—Dixon, Riley, R. E. Neighbour, O. W. Van Osdel, William Pettingill, and Norris. All came to Toronto to attend an executive meeting of the BBU. Shields boasted of Norris' fundamentalist qualifications. He "is the terror of evolutionists . . . and is denounced and vilified by modernists everywhere." Shields found in Norris another strong ally with whom to stand in his own battle for truth.[81]

Norris was a sensational preacher, pummeling his opponents from his pulpit or any other platform that gave him an audience. Norris and Shields shared many pulpits over the next three years, especially through the work of the BBU. Norris returned to Toronto to preach at Jarvis Street when time permitted. Shields was quick to defend Norris when he came under fire from his Southern Baptist contemporaries. In late 1925, First Baptist's delegates were denied seats at the Texas Baptist convention. *The Canadian Baptist* ran an article on the dust-up, siding with Norris' opponents. Shields rose to his friend's defense in *The Gospel Witness* supporting Norris and the church.[82] The men were confederates who made common cause in the battle and could count on one another for support. Norris also joined Shields at a BBU meeting in Vancouver in 1925.[83]

There was, however, a limitation to Shields' relationship with Norris. In 1926, Norris was angered with the Fort Worth mayor, H. C. Meacham, over the firing of six of his church members who refused to leave First Baptist Church as a condition of further employment. Dexter Edward Chipps, a local lumberman and ally of the mayor, went to Norris' office. The events going forward are contested. What is clear is that Norris pulled a revolver from his desk, shot and killed Chipps. Norris was charged with murder but exonerated at trial, claiming self-defense. Members of Norris' staff testified

---

81. "City Church Services," *The Globe*, 8 March 1923, 18. Also, "Great News," *GW*, 6 September 1923, 11–12. He returned to the Jarvis Street pulpit and at Massey Hall through most of August 1924 and into September to hold a revival campaign. *The Globe* carried numerous articles on Norris sermons during his lengthy stay. In 1925, Norris and Pettingill were back in Canada again at a meeting of the BBU held concurrently at St. James Baptist Church of Hamilton and Jarvis Street. See "City Church Services," *The Globe*, 10 October 1925, 20.

82. "*The Canadian Baptist* and Dr. J. Frank Norris," *GW*, 14 Jan 1926, 10–11.

83. See advertisement for the "Baptist Meetings," *The Province*, 13 Jun 1925, 14.

that Chipps had threatened the preacher.[84] Still, the incident hurt the work of the BBU. Coupled with the collapse of Des Moines University two years later, the BBU reached its nadir, putting a strain on the relationship between Norris, Riley, and Shields. Norris did not return to Jarvis Street for the next six years.[85]

O. W. Van Osdel

Oliver Willis Van Osdel was an ardent fundamentalist and became a staunch confederate of Shields during the formation of the BBU. Van Osdel, pastor of Wealthy Street Baptist Church in Grand Rapids, Michigan, was an early fundamentalist who demonstrated a willingness to withdraw from denominational affairs when theological drift became too severe.[86] He was a natural ally of Shields in the work of the BBU, attending an early board meeting at Jarvis Street and preaching at the church.[87] Van Osdel was back in Canada in 1925 at another BBU meeting and conference held at James Street Baptist Church in Hamilton, Ontario.[88] Van Osdel's influence with the BBU was felt throughout its stormy history. He returned to Jarvis Street for its sixth annual conference giving Shields' the occasion to express his personal appreciation for another esteemed friend.

> The presence of the veteran warrior, Dr. O. W. Van Osdel, was a benediction to all his brethren as it always is. What a man he is! [sic] quiet, unassuming, strong and able, an invaluable counsellor, a gracious friend and companion—indeed, it seems to us, all that a minister of Christ should be. It is impossible to estimate the contribution of this great man, who, though no longer belonging to the younger generation, seems every year to renew his youth, and is as keen and vigorous as ever.[89]

---

84. Hankins, *God's Rascal*, 119–20.

85. The next visit Norris made was in December 1934. "Dr. J. Frank Norris," *GW*, 20 December 1934, 7. Norris returned to Jarvis Street in 1937. See "Dr. Norris in Jarvis Street," *GW*, 24 1937, 6. The last reference to a Norris trip to Canada in the *GW* came in 1939 when he visited Briscoe Street Baptist in London on February 28. See "News of Union Churches," *GW*, 26 January 1939, 7.

86. For a study of Van Osdel, see Bauder, "O. W. Van Osdel."

87. "Great News," *GW*, 6 Sep 1923, 11.

88. "The Hamilton Baptist Bible Union Conference," *GW*, 24 Sep 1925, 15.

89. "Baptist Bible Union Annual Meeting," *GW*, 21 Jun 1928, 2.

Shields also used Van Osdel's paper, *The Baptist Temple News*, as a periodic source for content to publish in *The Gospel Witness*.[90]

Lesser-Known American Fundamentalists at Jarvis Street

Jarvis Street was not the lone Toronto platform for fundamentalist voices during the 1920s. From time to time, other lesser-known figures, important in their own right but men who did not carry the same sensational draw as Riley, Straton, and Norris, appeared in Toronto pulpits but seldom at Jarvis Street. R. E. Neighbour visited the city on several occasions. In 1923, Oswald J. Smith of Alliance Tabernacle brought Neighbour in to preach, although his subject was more focused on missions than on fundamentalism.[91] In 1925, he and fellow fundamentalist Paul Rader, an evangelist and former pastor of Moody Church of Chicago, were also featured by Smith at the Tabernacle.[92] Later that year, Neighbour filled the Jarvis Street pulpit for Shields, speaking on Sunday twice and during the evenings through the week.[93]

William L. Pettingill, Dean of the Philadelphia School of the Bible, preached at Jarvis Street on occasion. In 1925, as part of a Bible conference with other fundamentalist leaders Riley and Norris, Pettingill spoke on Sunday morning on "The Christ of Fundamentalism vs. the Christ of Modernism." Pettingill was back at Jarvis Street in 1929, preaching on Sunday morning.[94]

Shields' preference for pulpit men was clearly weighted toward the grand leaders of American fundamentalism. W. B. Riley and J. Frank Norris, with Shields, formed the triumvirate of power behind the BBU. Straton and Norris were active participants in the movement and sensationalists in their own right. Shields knew on whom he could count to draw a crowd and to expound the issues of the day from his pulpit. He had a steady parade of these fellows into Jarvis Street during the heat of his battle with Canadian Baptists.[95]

---

90. "Are Baptists Done?" *GW*, 20 Sep 1928, 5.
91. The theme of Neighbour's message was Russia. See *TDS*, 3 November 1923, 7.
92. "Alliance," *TDS*, 25 March 1925, 9.
93. "Jarvis Street Baptist," *TDS*, 20 June 1925, 10.
94. "Dr. Shields in Jarvis Street," *TDS*, 10 November 1928, 29.
95. This story is recounted elsewhere in this volume.

THE INFLUENCES OF AMERICAN BAPTIST FUNDAMENTALISTS OUTSIDE TORONTO

It has already been demonstrated how men like R. A. Torrey and W. B. Riley had a wider ministry in Canada besides in Toronto. From coast to coast, prominent American preachers held meetings in churches or public halls championing a fundamentalist brand of Christianity. A few representative examples will be helpful to demonstrate this point.

Jasper Cortenus Massee

J. C. Massee was a well-known pastor with an extensive Canadian ministry. He served southern churches before moving to a series of northern churches that placed him in the centre of the fundamentalist-modernist controversy. He pastored First Baptist of Dayton, Ohio (1913–1919), Baptist Temple in Brooklyn, New York (1920–1922), and Tremont Temple Baptist Church of Boston, Massachusetts, during the height of the controversy.[96]

During these days, Massee was a periodic visitor to Canada, speaking at fundamentalist-type churches and gatherings, Baptist or otherwise, though not particularly as a close ally to Shields. In 1915, Massee joined Riley at the Interdenominational Bible Conference at Winnipeg's Elim Chapel mentioned above. In 1917, he participated in a Bible Conference at Boon Avenue Baptist Church of Toronto.[97] In 1919, he was in Calgary at the inauguration of First Baptist Church at a "Fundamentals of the Christian Religion" conference. Then it was on to Moosomin, Saskatchewan, east of Regina, to another interdenominational Bible conference before heading to Edmonton, Alberta, to another "Conference on Christian Fundamentals" at McDougall Methodist Church.[98] Massee's influence in Canada was not confined to the western region. Churches in the east also heard the American

---

96. Russell, *Voices of American Fundamentalism*.

97. See advertisement for the meetings in *The Globe*, 6 August 1917, 8. In 1920, he preached for the Toronto Baptist Association. He was at Knox Presbyterian Church in 1922. See "Says Bible Embodies God's Will to Man," *TDS*, 20 April 1922, 5. In 1925, he was at High Park Baptist Church. See *TDS*, 4 July 1925, 10. No evidence from the *TDS*, *The Globe*, or *GW* indicates that Massee preached from the famous pulpit. While he began the decade of the 1920s allied with the fundamentalists, he proved in the end to be a moderate when he called for a truce in the fighting within the Northern Baptist Convention.

98. "Big Gathering at Bible Rally," *Calgary Daily Herald*, 10 Sep 1919, 13. "Bible Conference in Moosomin," *The Leader*, 8 Sep 1919, 8. *Edmonton Journal*, 9 Sep 1919, 8.

preacher.[99] Massee was a moderate fundamentalist who had little relationship with Shields during conflict, likely due in part to Shields' assessment that Massee had hurt the fundamentalist cause in failing to press the issues and secure a victory.[100]

Other fundamentalists who had supported Shields also had a wider Canadian ministry. In 1919, plans were announced for an undenominational Bible conference on Christian fundamentals in Calgary, either in First Baptist Church or in Grace Presbyterian Church. Riley, Dixon, Pettingill, and Massee would be preaching.[101] A few years later, Pettingill held meetings in Winnipeg at Metropolitan Theatre and at the undenominational Elim Chapel, a favourite western Canadian church for fundamentalist preachers. He was back the next year for a ten-day meeting at the Chapel.[102]

American fundamentalists had a wide representation across Canada during the first third of the twentieth century. From east to west, Canadian churches platformed a wide array of Americans suggesting a sympathy of ideas on pertinent religious issues of the day. At the same time, their Canadian brethren, some less prominent but no less committed, returned the favour.

CANADIAN CONTRIBUTIONS TO AMERICAN FUNDAMENTALISM

A brief sketch of the involvement south of the border by Shields and other lesser-known Canadian fundamentalists like John Linton is in order. While Shields was not the only Canadian to join the battle in the United States, he was certainly the most prominent. The most important aspect of his Canadian contributions are his numerous activities as part of the BBU. However, even before Shields went south, other Canadians contributed to the American conflict. An early and under-appreciated aspect of Canadian fundamentalism or "proto-fundamentalism" which influenced American

---

99. "Deep Interest Shown in Meetings in Centenary," *Telegraph-Journal*, 21 Nov 1929, 14.

100. See comments on Massee by Shields, cited in Adams, "Shields," 421.

101. "World Famous Exponents of the Bible Coming Here," *Calgary Daily Herald*, 22 Aug 1919, 14.

102. Advertisement for the meetings, *WET*, 29 Mar 1924, 16 and *WET*, 29 Aug 1925, 7. For a discussion on the nature of Elim Chapel fundamentalism, consult Hindmarsh, "Winnipeg Fundamentalism," 304–8.

Christianity were the five contributors to *The Fundamentals* who called Canada home. Four men came from Ontario and one was from Quebec. Some historians mark the publication of these essays as the formal beginning of the fundamentalist-modernist controversy. At minimum, they represent a "proto-fundamentalism" that existed in denominations worldwide including Canada. They also served as a harbinger of things to come. Conservatives such as E. J. Stobo of Smith Falls, Ontario, a Canadian Baptist contributor, and others were determined to show a version of Christianity that had not succumbed to modernity. The Canadians represented preceded Shields' influence and demonstrate that Shields was not a solitary voice of fundamentalist views below the forty-ninth parallel.[103]

Shields was clearly "Canada's best known and most influential fundamentalist"[104] and by far Canada's most frequent representative in the battles south of the border. From 1923 forward, he was tireless in the work of the BBU, serving as its president as well as a regular conference speaker at meetings across the United States. In late 1924, the BBU meetings were in New York City and featured Shields, Norris, and Canadian John Linton of Montreal.[105] The following year, Shields was in Chicago at a BBU meeting with Riley, Norris, Straton, Pettingill, and others. Shields' brother, E. E. Shields, of Oshawa, Ontario, participated at this meeting. Shields was back in New York at Calvary Baptist Church for another BBU meeting. On this occasion, Shields attacked S. Parkes Cadman, liberal pastor of Central Congregational Church in Brooklyn, New York, and Harry Emerson Fosdick.[106]

In 1928, Shields was in Los Angeles, speaking at Old First Congregational Church, promoting fundamentalism and Des Moines University.[107] Shields occasionally supported the work of the WCFA in the United States. Riley was its founder and main organizer, but Shields lent a hand when he could for the greater good of the movement. The WCFA met once at Jarvis Street in Toronto in 1926, during which Riley spoke on "The Menace of Corporate Control of Education" and "Will Our Colleges Destroy the Baptist Denomination?"[108] Shields spoke the following year at a WCFA-

---

103. As the other four contributors to *The Fundamentals* were not Baptist, they need not be discussed here. Stobo is treated elsewhere in this volume.

104. Stackhouse, *Canadian Evangelicalism in the Twentieth Century*, 23.

105. "Baptist Bible Union Meeting in New York," *GW*, 24 November 1924, 10–11.

106. "Baptist Bible Union Meets in New York," *The Globe*, 9 March 1927, 2.

107. "Minister Will Explain Stand," *Los Angeles Evening Express*, 5 May 1928, 5.

108. "Dr. Shields," *TDS*, 17 April 1926, 20.

sponsored meeting in Iowa, no doubt in conjunction with his role at Des Moines University.[109]

Shields' work with the BBU eventually led to Des Moines University in 1927. Des Moines was a Baptist school that had fallen on hard times. The BBU took control of the school, intent on rescuing it from modernism. Shields served as its president and chairman of the board with Edith Rebman, the secretary of the BBU, as his lieutenant who looked after the school in his absence. The school became the only fundamentalist university "in the northern half of the continent."[110] To gain control, the BBU agreed to assume the school's debt of $330,000. In return it received a million dollars in assets.[111] Periodically, Shields made the long journey south via rail to look after the transition of the school from a broad institution into a fundamentalist one. He was also joined by Riley and Norris to fundraise for the institution across the United States and Canada.[112] At the sixth annual meeting of the BBU held at Jarvis Street, Shields dedicated one full day to promote the university.[113]

In assuming the helm of Des Moines, Shields set about to ensure the school was aligned fully with the fundamentalist cause. Problems soon arose with the man Shields hired to run the institution, H. C. Wayman, formerly of William Jewell College. As discussed above, early in their relationship, Shields and Wayman had difficulties. Wayman accused Shields of trying to dominate the school. Questions arose over Wayman's academic pedigree. Rumours swirled over Shields' relationship with Rebman. When the board exonerated Shields, Shields demanded Wayman's resignation. A campus revolt ensued. Chaos reigned and the students rioted, terrorizing the board when they met to sort things out. The police were called but refused to intervene. Shields and company snuck away, fearing for their lives. The board voted to close the university after the riot but before graduation in 1929.[114] With this calamity following on the heels of the Chipps incident,

109. "Fundamentalists Host of Iowa is Here for Parley," *Waterloo Evening Courier*, 9 November 1927, 18.

110. "Fundamentalists Control Des Moines University," *TDS*, 15 June 1927, 4.

111. "Fundamentalists Control Des Moines University," *TDS*, 15 June 1927, 4.

112. "Shields Strong for Old Time Religion," *The Seminole Morning News*, 4 December 1927, 3. Also, "Baptists Seek Support for College," *Salt Lake Tribune*, 31 December 1927, 3 and "New Reformation is Prepared by Fundamentalists," *Bridgeport Telegram*, 9 December 1927, 7.

113. "Sixth Annual Meeting of the Baptist Bible Union," *TDS*, 16 June 1928, 23.

114. For further information on Des Moines University and Shields's role, see

the BBU had collapsed. Soon a new Baptist group, the General Association of Regular Baptists, was formed without Shields' involvement.[115]

Other Canadian Baptists played a role south of the border, promoting the fundamentalist cause. John Linton (1888–1965), a Scotsman who came to Canada as a boy, and graduated from McMaster in 1917. He pastored Parkdale Baptist Church of Toronto until being called to Point St. Charles Baptist Church of Montreal in 1920.[116] In early 1925, Linton assumed the pastorate of High Park Baptist Church of Toronto to Shields' satisfaction.[117] He was among those men who joined Shields as an outspoken critic against the modernism of McMaster.[118] As a Toronto pastor, Linton was a regular participant with Shields in the work, especially that of the BBU. He was also a featured speaker in the United States at fundamentalist gatherings. Also participating in the American struggle was Hamilton pastor Clifford J. Loney. Loney, pastor of Immanuel Baptist Church of Hamilton, Ontario, was another regular participant in the BBU, serving on its board during the fateful experience of the rise and fall of Des Moines University.[119]

T. T. Shields' brother Ernest Edgar Shields (d. 1952) also had a presence among American fundamentalists. After pastorates in Brantford and Oshawa, he became associated with William Fetler and the Russian Missionary Society of Chicago, serving as its agent. He also was featured at a BBU meeting in its early years.[120] He periodically spoke for his brother at Jarvis Street throughout his life and was a periodic contributor to his brother's fundamentalist cause.

Wiggins, *An Iowa Tragedy*, and May, "Des Moines University."

115. For a recent discussion on these issues, see Bauder, *One in Hope and Doctrine*, 147–83.

116. "Rev. J. Linton Coming," *The Gazette*, 4 Oct 1920, 7.

117. "Fenelon Falls and High Park," *GW*, 9 Apr 1925, 13.

118. C. S. Wallace, "Montreal Letter," *The Baptist*, 2 April 1921, 280. See also Linton, *Camel's Nose* and Linton, *The McMaster Controversy*.

119. The Des Moines University collapse was big news across the United States with newspapers carrying pieces of the conflict and collapse and the BBU meeting at Buffalo which dealt with the failure. E.g. see a photo of the board of the university including Loney in *The Arizona Daily Star*, 21 May 1929, 4.

120. "Rev. E. E. Shields Called," *The Globe*, 12 Sep 1917, 10 and Donald Day, "Seek $1,000,000 in America for Soviet Missions," *Chicago Sunday Tribune*, 26 Aug 1928, 26. For E. E. Shields' obituary, see "Rev. Edgar Shields," *GW*, 8 May 1952, 6.

ASSESSMENT AND CONCLUSION

What is clear from this chapter is the degree that Baptists north and south supported each other in their battles within their respective denominations. Cross-border preaching was a regular occurrence from the early years of the twentieth century and continued apace through the fundamentalist-modernist controversy into the 1930s. Canadian Baptist fundamentalism did not ripen in a vacuum. While the struggles Canadian Baptists faced were local, the ideas over which they fought had larger implications. Like their Baptist forebearers and successors, Canadian Baptist fundamentalists saw themselves as a part of the larger Baptist family and looked for allies wherever they could be found. Canadian Baptist fundamentalists were also willing to join their American cousins at the time of their need and raise their voices in support of their local challenges. They were grateful when their American allies returned the favour. Truly fundamentalism, at least at the end of the 1920s, had become a North American issue.

Assessing contributions made by these cross-border relationships is difficult. Clearly the participants valued the relationships as there were so many incidents on either side of the border. Across North America, fundamentalist Baptists looked to each other for encouragement in their struggles. The issues were common ones: evolution, worldliness among the church members, theological liberalism in denominational schools, even political adversaries. At the same time, they also suffered with each other's embarrassments. When Norris shot Chipps or when Des Moines failed, both American and Canadian Baptists reassessed alignments. Coalitions were formed and broken. Battles were fought and lost. The cross-border nature of Baptist fundamentalism in the early twentieth century adds to the complexity of a very interesting story.

BIBLIOGRAPHY

Primary

NEWSPAPERS

A Record of Christian Work (Northfield, MA), 1910
Arizona Daily Star (Tuscan, AZ), 1929
Baptist (Chicago, IL), 1921
Bridgeport Telegram (Bridgeport, CT), 1927
Canadian Baptist (Toronto, ON), 1906
Calgary Daily Herald (Calgary, AB), 1919
Christian Fundamentals in Church and School (Minneapolis, MN)

Des Moines Register (Des Moines, IA), 1929
Des Moines Tribune (Des Moines, IA), 1929
Evening Daily Journal, (Ottawa, ON), 1906
Edmonton Journal (Edmonton, AB), 1919
Gazette, (Montreal, QC), 1907, 1920
The Globe (Toronto, ON), 1904, 1906, 1911, 1916, 1917,1919, 1920, 1923, 1925–1929, 1932
Gospel Witness (Toronto, ON), 1923–1928, 1937, 1939
Journal and Messenger (Cincinnati, OH), 1906
Leader-Post (Regina, SK), 1919
Los Angeles Evening Express (Los Angeles, CA), 1928
New York Times (New York, NY), 1923
The Province (also *Daily Province,* Vancouver, BC), 1925, 1935
Salt Lake Tribune (Salt Lake City, UT), 1927
Seminole Morning News (Seminole, OK), 1927
Telegraph-Journal (Saint John, NB), 1929
Toronto Daily Star (Toronto, ON), 1918, 1920–1923, 1925–1928, 1936
Watchman-Examiner (New York, NY),
Winnipeg Evening Tribune (Winnipeg, MB), 1915, 1924, 1925, 1928, 1930
Word and the Way (Kansas City, MO), 1923
Waterloo Evening Courier (Waterloo, ON), 1927, 1929

Other

Dixon, A. C. *"Destructive Criticism" vs. Christianity.* Np: nd.
Harris, Elmore. *Concerning the Attacks of Prof. Matthews on the Bible: Open Letter to the Baptists of Ontario and Quebec.* Toronto: n.p., 1910.
Lewis, Frank Grant, and Rittenhouse Neisser, eds. *Alphabetic Biographical Catalog, The Crozer Theological Seminary, 1855–1933.* Chester, PA: The Crozer Theological Seminary, 1933.
Riley, William Bell. *The Finality of Higher Criticism: The Theory of Evolution and False Theology.* Minneapolis, MN: n.p., 1909.
———. *The Menace of Modernism.* New York: Christian Alliance, 1917.
Rochester Theological Seminary General Catalogue, 1850–1900. Rochester, NY: Andrews, 1900.
Shields, T. T. *The Plot that Failed.* Toronto: The Gospel Witness, 1937.
The Tatler, yearbooks of William Jewell College, 1926, 1928.

Secondary

Adams, Douglas Allan. "The War of The Worlds: The Militant Fundamentalism of Dr. Thomas Todhunter Shields and the Paradox of Modernity." PhD diss., The University of Western Ontario, 2015.
Bauder, Kevin T. "Biography of O. W. Van Osdel." ThM thesis, Denver Baptist Theological Seminary, 1983.
Bauder, Kevin T., and Robert Delnay. *One in Hope and Doctrine: Origins of Baptist Fundamentalism, 1870–1950.* Schaumburg, IL: Regular Baptist Press, 2014.

Bjork, Daniel. *Victorian Flight: Russell H. Conwell and the Crisis of American Individualism.* Washington, DC: University Press of America, 1978.

Burkinshaw, Robert K. *Pilgrims in Lotus Land: Conservative Protestantism in British Columbia, 1917–1981.* Montreal and Kingston: McGill-Queen's University Press, 1995.

Burr, Agnes Ruth. *Russell H. Conwell and His Work.* Philadelphia: John C. Winton, 1917.

Carpenter, Joel A., ed. *Fundamentalist vs. Modernist: The Debates Between John Roach Straton and Charles Francis Potter.* New York: Garland, 1988.

Close, Eric. *Revival in the City: The Impact of American Evangelists in Canada, 1884–1914.* Montreal and Kingston: McGill-Queen's University Press, 2005.

Cooke, Bill. *A Rebel to His Last Breath: Joseph McCabe and Rationalism.* Amherst, NY: Prometheus, 2001.

Delnay, Robert G. "History of the Baptist Bible Union." ThD diss., Dallas Theological Seminary, 1963.

Douglas, Bill R. "'The Serious Nature of the Division': Calvary Baptist Church of Des Moines and the Fundamentalist Challenge of the 1920s." *Baptist History and Heritage* 52 (2017) 32–48.

Elliott, David R. "Eight Canadian Fundamentalists." PhD diss., University of British Columbia, 1989.

———. "Knowing No Borders: Canadian Contributions to American Fundamentalism." In *Amazing Grace: Evangelicalism in Australia, Britain, Canada, and the United States,* edited by George A. Rawlyk and Mark A. Noll, 349–74. Montreal: McGill-Queen's University Press, 1994.

Gloege, Timothy. "Consumed: Reuben A. Torrey and the Construction of Corporate Fundamentalism." PhD diss., University of Notre Dame, 2007.

Goertz, Donald A. "A Missed Opportunity: Central Canadian Baptists and the Forward Movement, 1919–1920." In *Baptists and Public Life in Canada,* edited by Gordon L. Heath and Paul R. Wilson, 304–40. McMaster General Series 2. Canadian Baptist Historical Society Series 1. Eugene, OR: Pickwick, 2012.

Hall, Timothy L. "Conwell, Russell Herman." In *American Religious Leaders,* 77–78. New York: Facts on File, 2003.

Hankins, Barry. *God's Rascal: J. Frank Norris and the Beginnings of Southern Fundamentalism.* Lexington, KY: University of Kentucky Press, 1996.

Haykin, Michael A. G. with Roy M. Paul, eds. *Set for the Defense of the Gospel: A Bicentennial History of Jarvis Street Baptist Church, 1818–2018.* Toronto: Jarvis Street Baptist Church, 2018.

Heath, Gordon L., and Paul R. Wilson, eds. *Baptists and Public Life in Canada.* McMaster General Series 2. Canadian Baptist Historical Society Series 1. Eugene, OR: Pickwick, 2012.

Hindmarsh, D. Bruce. "The Winnipeg Fundamentalist Network, 1910–1940: The Roots of Transdenominational Evangelicalism in Manitoba and Saskatchewan." In *Aspects of the Canadian Evangelical Experience,* edited by G. A. Rawlyk, 303–19. Montreal: McGill-Queens's University Press, 1997.

Hinman, Edgar L., et al. "Academic Freedom and Tenure, Committee A: Report of the Sub-Committee of Inquiry for William Jewell College." *Bulletin of the American Association of University Professors* 16 (1930) 226–44.

Johnston, Charles M. *McMaster University: The Toronto Years.* Toronto: University of Toronto Press, 1976.

Kee, Kevin. *Revivalists: Marketing the Gospel in English Canada, 1884–1957*. Montreal: McGill-Queen's University Press, 2005.
Lewis, Jr., Donald Martin. "The Thought of Amzi Clarence Dixon." PhD diss., Baylor University, 1989.
Longfield, Bradley. *The Presbyterian Controversy*. New York: Oxford University Press, 1991.
Marsden, George. *Fundamentalism and the American Culture*. New York: Oxford University Press, 1980.
May, George S. "Des Moines University and T. T. Shields." *Journal of Iowa History* 54 (1956) 193–232.
Mayfield, Jeffrey. "Striving for Souls by the Power of God: The Life of Amzi Clarence Dixon." PhD diss., The Southern Baptist Theological Seminary, 2010.
Meehan, Brenda M. "A. C. Dixon, Early Fundamentalist." *Foundations* (1967) 51–63.
Nelson, Clyde K., and Russell H. Conwell. "The Gospel of Wealth." *Foundations* (1962) 39–51.
Pierard, Richard V., ed. *Baptists Together in Christ, 1905–2005: A Hundred Year History of the Baptist World Alliance*. Falls Church, VA: Baptist World Alliance, 2005.
Pietsch, B. D. "Lyman Stewart and Early Fundamentalism." *Church History* 82 (2013) 617–46.
Priest, Gerald. "A. C. Dixon, Chicago Liberals, and *The Fundamentals*." *Detroit Baptist Seminary Journal* 1 (Spring 1996) 113–34.
———. "An Examination of the Apologetical Ministry of Amzi Clarence Dixon." PhD diss., Bob Jones University, 1988.
Russell, C. Allyn. *Voices of American Fundamentalism: Seven Biographical Studies*. Philadelphia: Westminster, 1976.
Sandeen, Ernest. "Fundamentals: The Last Flowering of the Millenarian-Conservative Alliance." *Journal of Presbyterian History* 47 (Mar 1969) 55–73.
Schenkel, Albert. *Rich Man and the Kingdom*. Minneapolis: Fortress, 1995.
Stackhouse, John G., Jr. *Canadian Evangelicalism in the Twentieth Century: An Introduction to Its Character*. Toronto: University of Toronto Press, 1993.
Stokes, David R. *The Shooting Salvationist*. Hanover, NH: Steerforth, 2011.
Straub, Jeffrey P. *The Making of a Battle Royal: The Rise of Religious Liberalism in Baptist Life, 1870–1920*. Eugene, OR: Pickwick, 2018.
———. "T. T. Shields Against the World: One Pastor's Struggle for a Pure Church," a paper delivered at the 8th International Conference on Baptist Studies, Baylor University, Waco, TX, July 2018.
———. "Thomas Todhunter Shields, Jr.: The Canadian Spurgeon." *Detroit Baptist Seminary Journal* 24 (2019) 97–117.
Tatum, B. Ray. *Conquest or Failure?* Dallas: Baptist Historical Foundation, 1966.
Trinier, Harold. *A Century of Service*. Toronto: The Board of Publication of the Baptist Convention of Ontario and Quebec, 1954.
Trollinger, Jr., William Vance. *God's Empire: William Bell Riley and Midwestern Fundamentalism*. Madison, WI: University of Wisconsin Press, 1990.
Wiggins, David. *An Iowa Tragedy: The Fall of Old Des Moines University*. Mt. Horeb, WI: Midwest Historical Books, 1988.

9

"Wider Than This One Church"

The Fellowship of Evangelical Baptist Churches in Canada, 1953–1970

Ian Hugh Clary

A SURVEY OF THE landscape of twentieth-century Canadian Baptist fundamentalism reveals a number of Baptist denominations and various independent Baptist churches that shared the same basic commitments to evangelical Christian orthodoxy. Despite their theological commonalities, however, these groups remained relatively isolated from one another. There is no doubt that geographical limitations contributed to Baptist isolationism, but a number were regionally close enough to raise the question of why there was such separation. Considering that Baptists comprised an already-small portion of the Canadian population throughout this era, the division was especially unfortunate.[1] This disunity elicits the same consternation felt by Augustine of Hippo (354–430), who once said: "How unfortunate those who hate unity and form parties among men! Let them listen to the one who wished to lead men to unity in One alone and for One alone, let them hear him say: You do not multiply!"[2]

---

1. Robert Wright provides census information by decade from 1911 to 1941 indicating that Baptists made up no more than five percent of the population throughout those years. Wright, "The Canadian Protestant Tradition 1914–1945," 141.

2. Augustine, "Twelfth Homily on the Gospel of St. John," 288.

The first half of the twentieth century was marked by battles over questions of doctrine, but as history moved through the 1930s and into the 1940s, disputes amongst Baptists were less about theology and more about personalities. This is what makes the year 1953 an important milestone in Canadian Baptist life. That year marked the beginning not only of what would become a new trans-Canadian Baptist denomination, but also it signaled that moderate fundamentalist Baptists in Canada were seeking to move beyond past divisions and experience a new season of unity and cooperation that would facilitate evangelization of the entire country. As one leader put it, Canada was a large enough nation and what was needed was not division, but "a firm and solid front of Evangelical Baptist effort."[3] To sustain the argument that some Baptists actively pursued unity and cooperation, this chapter will examine not only the shift away from division for Baptists in Canada and the forming of a new and broadly unified denomination that now numbers at over 500 churches, but also the move away from militant Baptist fundamentalism into the burgeoning and more moderate Baptist fundamentalism that characterized many Baptists who supported the resurgence of North American evangelicalism in the mid-twentieth century.[4]

BACKGROUND TO A DENOMINATION

The Fight Against Modernism

Details about the background of the 1953 formation of the Fellowship of Evangelical Baptist Churches of Canada (FEBC) have been given in other chapters by Paul Wilson and Doug Adams. For the sake of immediate context, however, this section will offer a brief account of the major formative events with a particular focus on a key debate that directly led to the Fellowship's creation.[5] This context was marked primarily by controversy between the fundamentalists and modernists that wracked American and Canadian Protestantism throughout the early part of the twentieth century. As Robert A. Wright has observed, "In Canada the impact of the fundamentalist movement was felt most dramatically among Baptists."[6] The di-

---

3. W. H. MacBain, "To the Work!" *The Union Baptist*, November 1952, 1. Cited in Haykin with Song, *"To Yield My Will, My Hopes, My All,"* 89.

4. www.fellowship.ca/AbouttheFellowship (accessed 25 July 2020).

5. See Doug Adams' chapter in this volume.

6. Wright, "Canadian Protestant Tradition," 159. For the nature of Canadian

rect precursor to the founding of the Fellowship occurred when the initial controversy of the 1920s was finished and things turned inward as certain factions continued to fight against former comrades in the 1940s.[7]

In Canada, the focal point of the original controversy surrounded the fundamentalist T. T. Shields (1873–1955), a British immigrant who was pastor of Jarvis Street Baptist Church (hereafter JSBC) in Toronto, arguably one of the most important churches in Canada at that time.[8] By the late nineteenth and early twentieth centuries, when it found its home at the corner of Jarvis and Gerrard streets, JSBC was a leading church in both in the city of Toronto and in the Baptist Convention of Ontario and Quebec (BCOQ), under the powerful ministries of men like Robert Alexander Fyfe (1816–1878) or the Welshman B. D. Thomas (1843–1917).[9] Shields was elected as pastor of the church in 1910, succeeding Henry Francis Perry (1861–1942), and soon held important leadership positions within the denomination including memberships on the Board of Home Missions and, significantly, on the Board of Governors of McMaster University.[10] In the early twentieth century, McMaster was housed in what is now the Royal Conservatory of Music on Bloor Street, Toronto, and included ministerial training for would-be pastors in the BCOQ.[11] The university courted controversy with Shields in the 1920s when it underwent changes both in governance and faculty, bringing along with it changes in theological direction.

Shields had long been involved with fundamentalist groups. For example, he was an early supporter of the World Christian Fundamentals Association, which he spoke at in Toronto in 1916.[12] He was also associated with fundamentalists like A. C. Dixon (1854–1925), an American who had a significant ministry at Spurgeon's church in London, England, William Bell Riley (1861–1947) of Minneapolis, and the infamous J. Frank Norris

---

Protestantism in Canada during the time covered in this chapter see Flatt, "A Century of Change," 31–65.

7. For American Fundamentalism, see Marsden, *Fundamentalism and American Culture*; Straub, *The Making of a Battle Royal*.

8. The standard study of Shields is now Adams, "The War of the Worlds."

9. For Fyfe see Gibson, *Robert Alexander Fyfe*; Yuille, "Robert A. Fyfe (1816–1878)," 243–67.

10. He was elected twice, once in 1920 and again in 1924. Wright, "Canadian Protestant Experience," 159.

11. Johnston, *McMaster University*.

12. Renfree, *Heritage and Horizon*, 219.

(1877–1952) of Texas.¹³ The fundamentalist controversy of which he was a conservative protagonist largely had to do with the perceived modernism that was making inroads at McMaster in the 1920s.¹⁴ Shields had already seen conflict at McMaster in 1910, the year he became pastor of Jarvis Street. Fundamentalist Elmore Harris (1855–1911), president of what was then called Toronto Bible Training School (now Tyndale University), moved to have the university's Old Testament Professor Isaac G. Matthews (1871–1959) removed due to questions over the latter's higher critical views of the bible.¹⁵ Shields seconded the motion to accept McMaster's report on Matthews, who was exonerated but ultimately left McMaster in 1919 for Crozer Theological Seminary in Pennsylvania.¹⁶

To give voice to his ongoing concerns with the school, Shields founded *The Gospel Witness* magazine in 1922. Early issues set about decrying the re-election of three members to McMaster's board whom Shields suspected of heterodoxy. His efforts were to no avail, as the three were elected.¹⁷ The dispute over McMaster's governance was heightened in the following year when H. P. Whidden (1870–1952) was selected as chancellor of the university.¹⁸ As part of the inauguration celebrations, McMaster attempted to

13. For each see Trollinger, *God's Empire*; Hankins, *God's Rascal*; Mehan, "A. C. Dixon," 50–63. For Shields as Fundamentalist see Tarr, "Another Perspective on T. T. Shields and Fundamentalism," 209–24; and the chapter on Shields in Elliott, "Studies of Eight Canadian Fundamentalists," 138–69. For a more hagiographic account see Tarr, *Shields of Canada*.

14. For detailed examination of the McMaster controversy see the chapter in this volume by Doug Adams, entitled, "The Great Contention." See also Pinnock, "The Modernist Impulse at McMaster University, 1887–1927," 193–207. Pinnock argues that theological liberalism had been a present reality in Baptist education in Ontario for some time, seen most notably with the professorship of William Newton Clarke (1841–1912), the "Schleiermacher of American theology," at Toronto Bible College. See Pinnock, "Modernist Impulse," 197.

15. Harris, the son of wealthy farmers, was also founding pastor of Walmer Road Baptist Church in Toronto. See Goertz, *A Century for the City*, 5–37. Goertz notes a certain irony in that Harris supported Oliver Horsman for the pastorate of Walmer Road, though the latter shared similar views on the bible as Matthews. See Goertz, *Century for the City*, 31–35. See also Perin, *The Many Rooms of This House*, 116. For a brief description of Harris and his role at what became Toronto Bible College see Austin, "'Hotbed of Missions,'" 134–35.

16. See Priest, "T. T. Shields the Fundamentalist," 73–74. See also Johnston, *McMaster University*, 1:90–117 and Horn, *Academic Freedom in Canada*, 30–32, for details of the controversy.

17. Renfree, *Heritage and Horizon*, 220.

18. Rawlyk, "A. L. McCrimmon, H. P. Whidden, T. T. Shields, Christian Higher

honour Brown University's president, W. H. P. Faunce (1859–1930), with an honorary degree.[19] Shields took to the pages of *The Gospel Witness* and charged Faunce with liberalism, sparking a dispute that ended with the university backing down and not conferring the degree. This would not end matters. In 1925, McMaster made the fateful decision to hire Laurence Henry Marshall (1882–1953), a theologian and renowned preacher from England, to be Professor of Practical Theology.[20] Shields was in California at the time of Marshall's appointment and while there he heard of the latter's liberalism. Marshall affirmed the theory of evolution and denied key evangelical doctrines like penal substitutionary atonement, human depravity, aspects of the bodily resurrection of Christ, and the inerrancy of the Bible.[21] As a result of Marshall's hiring, Shields pulled his support from McMaster and in 1927 founded The Toronto Baptist Seminary and Bible College (TBS).[22]

The same year, Shields and Jarvis Street, along with thirteen other congregations who supported him, were expelled by an act of the convention. By 1928, some 65 other supporting churches left the convention and with Shields founded the Union of Regular Baptist Churches of Ontario and Quebec with a membership of 8500 people; nearly a seventh of the convention had left. By 1930, the number of Union churches had risen to 90. There would soon be decline, however, as 27 churches and six mission churches would secede either from the convention or the Union to form the Fellowship of Independent Baptist Churches of Canada in 1933. The Independents were conservative and evangelical, but also more broad-minded than the Union. Under the leadership of Norman W. Pipe (1909–2000), they saw themselves as a loose fellowship of churches without a centralized denominational structure. This ecclesiological perspective and approach grew out of the distrust that had been engendered as a result of the debates over McMaster and the convention. While it existed, the Independent movement experienced many challenges. A lack of resources, no central coordination of effort, and both cooperation and competition with Union churches were a few of the struggles that Independent churches faced in

---

Education, and McMaster University," 31–62.

19. Sillen, "William H. P. Faunce," 235–49.

20. For a memoir of Marshall see Bonser, "A Memoir of the Author," 1–15.

21. L. H. Marshall, "Religious Controversy in Canada," *The Fraternal and Remembrancer*, January 1931, 6–11.

22. *By His Grace To His Glory*.

the 1930s and 1940s.²³ Yet, despite these difficulties, Independent numbers grew steadily. By 1950, there were 150 member churches.²⁴

Disputes within the Union centred on its relationship with the Fundamentalist Baptist Young Peoples Association and the Women's Missionary Society of Regular Baptists of Canada (WMS). Both operated independently from the denomination, and the WMS was led by Caroline Holman (d. 1962).²⁵ Holman is notable not only as a strong supporter of missions and a prolific essayist, but also as one of the few women at the time to publicly take a stand against Shields. The Union, through the WMS, had started a mission in Liberia in 1928, and by 1937, had sent ten missionaries. The financial pressures wrought by the Depression led the denomination to the conclusion that it could no longer support the work. This decision caused internal consternation, conflict, and division. The independent-minded WMS fought to preserve its work under Holman's leadership.²⁶ When challenged by Shields for insubordination, Holman is recorded to have replied: "All I can say is this: I feel the Lord gave me a commission four years ago to begin the Women's Missionary Society of Regular Baptists of Canada, and He has not withdrawn that commission. I must obey God rather than man."²⁷

The Shield(s) of War is Broke: Personality and Polemic in Ontario Baptist Life

Divisions continued to dog Shields, TBS, and the Union well into the 1940s and until Shields' death in 1955. This continuous infighting and conflict would have great significance for Baptists in Canada. The controversy at TBS in the late 1940s was not waged against theological liberals who—following J. Gresham Machen's (1881–1937) dictum that Christianity and liberalism were two different religions—could be viewed as part of a different tribe.²⁸ While this dispute was in many ways over Baptist identity, it was

---

23. Tarr, *This Dominion His Dominion*, 107; and Davis, "The Struggle for a United Evangelical Baptist Fellowship," 242.

24. Watt, *The Fellowship Story*, 34.

25. For a short statement of her life see *The Regular Baptist Call: A Testimony*, September 1962, 5–6. Cf. Haykin and Clary, "Rivers of Living Waters," 72. For Holman's role in women's missions see Cullen, "Debating and Dividing," n.p.

26. Renfree, *Heritage and Horizon*, 278.

27. Recorded in *The Gospel Witness*, 5 November 1931, 12.

28. Machen, *Christianity and Liberalism*. Machen had gone through significant

also largely about personality, and it involved one of Shields most trusted colleagues.

W. Gordon Brown (1904–1979), along with other Shields allies, such as W. S. Whitcombe (1905–1990), was a student at McMaster during the controversy over modernist teaching and views in the late 1920s, and he played a key role in bringing Professor Marshall's teaching to light. Theologically conservative, Brown provided first-hand accounts of Marshall's classroom lectures. He expanded and published his shorthand notes from Marshall's classes in his own magazine, *The Prophet*, which would often be reprinted by Shields in *The Gospel Witness*. When Shields formed TBS in 1927, Brown was engaged initially as a part-time lecturer in biblical languages and pastoral theology. Eventually he became a full-time professor in 1931. By 1945, not long before the split at TBS, Brown took on the role of Dean. Whitcombe would join the seminary in 1932 to teach English literature and systematic theology and would also have a significant impact on Baptist missions to French Canada.[29] The new seminary was founded to counter the influence of McMaster on Baptist churches and became the training ground for fundamentalist ministers in the Union, many of whom would later join the Fellowship. "Dean" Brown was well-positioned to exert a significant influence on his Baptist community.

Brown brought serious scholarship to the seminary classroom. He had a BA from McMaster and an MA from the University of Toronto. He also studied theology at The Southern Baptist Theological Seminary in Louisville, Kentucky, and at Winona Lake School of Theology in Indiana. He was part of the translation committee for the New International Version of the Bible (1978), and he contributed to commentaries such as the Holman Bible Commentary. He served the academy and the church in a number of capacities, particularly as a founder of the Evangelical Theological Society and the Evangelical Fellowship of Canada. He passed away in 1979 while he was overseas studying at Oxford University. His scholarly efforts were recognized by Northwest Baptist Theological Seminary in Vancouver, British Columbia, a Fellowship seminary, who awarded him an honorary Doctor

---

turmoil within his own Presbyterian Church (USA) and Princeton Theological Seminary over issues of modernism. This controversy resulted in the founding of the Orthodox Presbyterian Church and Westminster Theological Seminary. For Machen's life see Hart, *Defending the Faith*. For a survey of his classic work see Gatiss, *Christianity and the Tolerance of Liberalism*.

29. Wilson, "A Mission Transformed," 193. For more on Baptist missions to Quebec see Fath, "The Other American Dream," 243–63.

of Divinity in 1963.[30] It could be argued that the dispute between he and Shields had to do with jealousies over Brown's gifts and accomplishments. At the very least, as Paul Wilson argues, "their personalities, leadership styles, and ever-changing relationship lay at the root of the schism."[31] Both Shields and Brown had strong personalities and could be over-bearing as leaders. Shields expected "unreserved and complete support and loyalty" from the men under him, like Brown. When there was perceived subversion of Shields' over-bearing management style, serious consequences would follow.[32] Likewise, Brown's leadership style was described by others as "autocratic." As Wilson comments about each man: "Brown and Shields were cast from the same mold."[33]

The particulars of the disagreement between Brown and Shields had to do not with theological disagreements, but with personality differences and fundamentalist separatism. Both men were committed to the fundamentals of the faith. As Wilson astutely notes, the impact of World War II on the seminary negatively affected the friendship between Shields and Brown. As a British imperialist, Shields wanted to throw as much of his support behind the Allied cause as he could, much as he did in the Great War.[34] To do so, Shields opted to close the seminary, a decision which Brown opposed both for professional and personal reasons. The result was a three-year break from studies between 1940 and 1943. This left Brown without a job. He had to work for meagre and what he deemed unfair wages for Shields at Jarvis Street. He was eventually hired as interim pastor at Forward Baptist Church in Toronto, which was part of the Independent Fellowship, while its pastor Jack Scott (1914–1981) served as a military chaplain.[35] Also, in 1940, Brown had opted to take a Bachelor of Divinity degree, initially with the support of Shields, though that was eventually revoked, a move that hurt

---

30. For a brief survey of Brown's life see Tarr, "Dr. W. Gordon Brown," 33–38. See also "Memorials," 91. D. A. Carson, who taught at Northwestern before becoming a New Testament scholar at Trinity Evangelical Divinity School in Chicago, dedicated his book *Exegetical Fallacies* to Brown. See Carson, *Exegetical Fallacies*, 5.

31. Wilson, "Torn Asunder," 37. This section is heavily indebted to Wilson's excellent article.

32. Wilson, "Torn Asunder," 38.

33. Wilson, "Torn Asunder," 39.

34. Wilson, "Torn Asunder," 40–41. For Shields and World War I, see Haykin and Clary, "'O God of Battles,'" 170–96.

35. Wilson, "Torn Asunder," 42. For Scott, see Dallimore, *Only One Life*.

Brown personally.[36] D. A. Carson adds that Shields later "ordered" Brown to leave his pastorate at Runnymede Baptist Church in Toronto—a ministry that he had commenced in 1946 and continued with until 1972—to join him at Jarvis Street. This was part of Shields' plan to have the seminary and its students under the influence of his ministry.

The growing tension between the two men, and Brown's experiences working at Jarvis Street during the war, kept him from wanting to return.[37] When the seminary was in session, it was Brown's broad vision that TBS's influence would expand beyond the borders of the Union, especially with the like-minded Independents, of whom he was now intimately acquainted, and from whom they could pull students and to whom they could send graduates.[38] Shields, however, wanted seminary graduates to stay within the Union and under his control. Many students, especially after the war, grew close to Dean Brown, as he intentionally cultivated personal relationships with them, something that Shields failed to do. When things came to a head between the two leaders, most of the students sided with Dean Brown.[39]

After a declaration by the seminary's trustees in 1945 that attempted to consolidate control of the school under the auspices of Jarvis Street Baptist Church, the tensions at TBS and particularly between Shields and Brown, deepened. The implication of the trustees' pronouncement, though not clearly stated, was that there was a rift between the church and the seminary and that Brown and a number of his fellow faculty were untrustworthy and disloyal. These veiled charges left a pall hanging over TBS for the next number of years. As Wilson notes, the academic year for 1947–1948 was tense, and the conflict between the two leaders became more acute. Whitcombe sided with Shields thus making academic life all the more difficult, especially as Brown and Whitcombe would publicly disagree over the direction and curriculum of the school.[40]

36. Wilson, "Torn Asunder," 42.

37. Carson, *Memoirs of an Ordinary Pastor*, 52. Carson's biography of his father, who had trained under Shields, and pastored in Quebec, indicates the lengths that Shields would go to in order to preserve power. When the senior Carson was asked about Shields' controversy with Brown, Carson diplomatically sided with the latter. Shields then set on undermining Carson's work in Drummondville, by refusing to finance it through Union coffers. Carson, *Memoirs of an Ordinary Pastor*, 52–53.

38. Davis, "The Struggle for a United Evangelical Baptist Fellowship," 243.

39. Wilson, "Torn Asunder," 43.

40. Whitcombe would leave TBS in 1954 under duress due to his own conflict with Shields—largely to do with his request of a car—to plant a church that would join FEBC

The ongoing tension and turmoil at TBS came to a head in 1948, when in December of that year Shields called a faculty meeting and voiced his concerns about the seminary. In it he said, "I feel sometimes that the Seminary is a parasite, draining our life, and yet making no contribution." He noted that he preferred when the school was smaller and closer in its relationship with Jarvis Street, and indicated that if there were no seminary, the church would survive.[41] He accused the school of not producing what he deemed as "real Baptists," likely a reference to closed communion, which was a classic Baptist distinctive and was what made the Regular Baptists "regular."[42] The meeting further deteriorated as Shields questioned Brown's ties with the Independent Baptists and accused him of disloyalty to Jarvis Street, an accusation that Brown declared unjust. Wilson records Brown's reply: "To me the Seminary is not a branch of Jarvis Street Church, but it is the Baptist Seminary of Canada. I think that our views must be wider than this one church, even than the Union. We must have a vision of doing something in the whole country. If we are to confine it to our group of sixty-seven churches, what are we going to do in the future?"[43] As Wilson rightly notes, "Such statements illustrate the ecclesiological and philosophical divide that had developed between Brown and Shields. It was a breach that could not be reconciled."[44]

It should be noted that for the Baptist fundamentalist movement in Canada the breakdown in the relationship between Brown and Shields signaled the beginning of a new phase and the emergence of a new more moderate form of Baptist fundamentalism. Brown's broader and bolder evangelistic and educational vision, his more inclusive ecclesiological outlook, and his willingness to work with others outside of the Regular Baptist fold, were indicative of a more open, expansive, and moderate fundamentalism. In Brown's view, Baptist fundamentalists needed to break free from the confines, controls, and conflict that characterized militant fundamentalists like Shields. Only then would Baptist fundamentalists be free to do

---

in 1961. He would also serve on the board of Central Baptist Seminary in Toronto. Cf. Whitcombe, "Dr. W. S. Whitcombe," 370. For Shields and TBS's response to Whitcombe and the car, see *An Authoritative Statement of Facts Respecting the Resignation of Rev. W. S. Whitcombe*.

41. Cited in Wilson, "Torn Asunder," 48–49.

42. For Baptists and the issue of open versus closed communion see Clary, "Throwing Away the Guns," 84–101.

43. Cited in Wilson, "Torn Asunder," 50.

44. Wilson, "Torn Asunder," 50.

"something in the whole country."⁴⁵ Of course, there would be many more rounds of conflict and controversy at TBS and within the Union before Brown and his allies could pursue their fundamentalist vision and agenda.

A week after the first TBS faculty meeting in December of 1948, another faculty meeting was held. This time Shields came armed with accusations that he claimed he could support with factual evidence about student agitation against his church, their support of the Independents, and their lackluster Baptist credentials.⁴⁶ He presented to the meeting a letter of recommendation that he drafted for the seminary trustees that attempted to scale back the influence of the seminary, including a statement that no faculty member could accept financial remuneration from any outside organization—the latter restriction was an obvious reference to Brown. At the close of the meeting Shields said, "We are not going to make this [seminary] a convenience . . . for interdenominationalists to come here and cut our throat . . . We are training Independents. When they go out to the Independent churches some of them are the worst enemies this church has."⁴⁷ Brown wrote a defense of himself entitled "An Account of My Stewardship."⁴⁸ This tract was addressed to the TBS trustees, which they read along with Shields' letter recommending action. In the opinion of some trustees, faculty divisions and student disloyalty were cause enough to close TBS. Other members of the board opposed this view and instead made a motion to request Brown's resignation, as he was "no longer in harmony with the principles and purposes of Toronto Baptist seminary [sic] as originally conceived."⁴⁹ The motion carried unanimously.

Brown was chagrined that he was not allowed to defend himself in person to his employers, and consequently, he refused to sign a letter of resignation. He also went public with a statement entitled, "The Truth Is . . ."⁵⁰ This statement articulated Brown's intentions for the seminary, and it included the minutes of the trustees' meeting. Brown sent this publication

45. Cited in Wilson, "Torn Asunder," 51.
46. Wilson, "Torn Asunder," 52.
47. Cited in Wilson, "Torn Asunder," 53.
48. W. Gordon Brown, "An Account of My Stewardship," 10 December 1948, copy in Box 6, File "Account of my Stewardship," W. Gordon Brown Papers, Canadian Baptist Archives, McMaster Divinity College, McMaster University, Hamilton, Ontario. Cited in Wilson, "Torn Asunder," 54.
49. Brown, "An Account," cited in Wilson, "Torn Asunder," 54.
50. W. Gordon Brown, "The Truth Is . . ." (Toronto: Canadian Baptist Seminary, 1949), copy from Marina Coldwell, cited in Wilson, "Torn Asunder," 66.

to all Union pastors and to TBS students. Given Shields' notoriety and his public role in Canadian life, the controversy with Brown made it into the media including *The Globe and Mail* and *Toronto Star* newspapers.[51] The TBS alumni were alarmed at what was happening and sent a letter in support of Brown to the seminary trustees, stating his loyalty and his commitment to Baptist principles. They requested that the board revoke their request to have Brown resign and to reinstate him.[52] The trustees ignored the letter and pushed forward to have Brown removed, effective 31 December 1948. As a result, the students responded with a letter of support for their Dean, requesting that the board's decision to have him resign be rescinded. Brown never undermined Shields or Jarvis Street, they said, rather the indignation that students had long felt was a result of Shields' heavy-handedness. They suggested that a meeting be held between them and Shields to sort matters amicably. The trustees again ignored their letter. The result of such mishandling of the situation by Shields and the trustees was a split within the seminary with Brown finally leaving, and a large number of TBS students resigning their education.

Geoffrey Adams (d. 2006), one-time Principal of Toronto Baptist Seminary and Professor of Old Testament, noted: "Looking back it is easy to see that on both sides many things said and done did not advance the cause of Christ."[53] Though surely one side bore the greater weight of responsibility. The question for Brown and the students now was, where would he teach and where would they be taught?

The schism at TBS in 1948 was a turning point for the Canadian Baptist fundamentalist movement. A new more moderate form of fundamentalism, led by Brown and supported by his Independent and Union allies, emerged from the conflict. The militant fundamentalists under Shields' leadership were left to continue their attacks on all who opposed their version and view of Baptist polity and practice. For Baptists who longed for an end to controversy, conflict, and strife and instead sought unity and cooperation with their fellow Baptist fundamentalists, the moderates offered a new vision of what the fundamentalist Baptist presence in Canada could be.

---

51. For newspaper accounts, see, for example, "90 PC Students," *Toronto Daily Telegram*, December 1948; "Take Recorded Student Vote," *Toronto Globe and Mail*, December 1948; "Seminary Dean," *Toronto Daily Telegram*, December 1948; "Overflow Crowd," *Toronto Daily Star*, December 1948; "Talk," *Toronto Daily Star*, December 1948.

52. Wilson, "Torn Asunder," 56.

53. Cited in Haykin, "'Jesus, Wondrous Saviour,'" 142. For a life of Adams, see Haykin, *From Acorns to Oaks*.

The push to make this new more moderate Baptist fundamentalist vision a reality would now move to the Regular Baptist denominational arena.

THE FORMING OF THE FELLOWSHIP

Denominational Split

During this time of tension between Shields and Brown in the late 1940s, there was stagnation within the broader reaches of the Union as its membership slowly declined while Independent Baptist churches continued to grow in strength and numbers. A document addressed to Shields and circulated among Union pastors in 1949, put the matter plainly: "under your leadership we have not grown."[54] An important cause of this stagnation was Shields' authoritarianism. It had a chilling effect across the denomination. A reflection on Shields' control and intimidation tactics by W. Hal MacBain (1916–2016), one of the key leaders in the Union, reveals how Shields operated: "there were a whole series of issues where we were told either you (the Union) back down or else Jarvis Street will pull out."[55] As Kenneth R. Davis comments, "MacBain and others began to see the Union as being under the complete control of the Jarvis Street Church. The only permitted journal was *The Gospel Witness*, and the only authorized school was the Toronto Baptist Seminary, both totally controlled by Jarvis Street Church."[56] Many Union pastors were increasingly discouraged and frustrated by this reality.

MacBain had trained at TBS, joining the fledgling seminary as a student in 1934. After two years there he took a one-year hiatus to plant Temple Baptist Church in Sarnia, Ontario, eventually completing his schooling by traveling back and forth between the small town and Toronto by train, finally graduating in 1939.[57] A year later he was ordained at Temple. MacBain recognized the influence that Shields had on him as a student, both in terms of the "strong Biblical and evangelical foundation in doctrine" Shields' teaching provided and the training in "how to build strong evangelical Baptist churches."[58] Temple Baptist would join the Union in 1940, and it would become a leading church in the denomination. Yet, with the growing concerns about the direction of the Union, and upset

---

54. Davis, "Struggle for a United Evangelical Baptist Fellowship," 242.
55. Davis, "Struggle for a United Evangelical Baptist Fellowship," 241.
56. Davis, "Struggle for a United Evangelical Baptist Fellowship," 240.
57. Haykin and Song, *"To Yield My Will,"* 48.
58. Haykin and Song, *"To Yield My Will,"* 49.

over the treatment of Brown, MacBain went to Shields to try and quell the controversy and reconcile Shields with the former Dean. Michael Haykin, quoting an interview he conducted with MacBain, has noted that MacBain thought he had convinced Shields, who was threatening to publicly defend his actions, to back down. But, as MacBain stated, "he was wrong."[59] Jack Scott, who had hired Brown as interim at Forward Baptist during the war, also tried to dissuade Shields but to no avail. It was Scott's view that "There should be a spirit among the churches of evangelical Baptists that we should go out and preach the gospel, build churches, get souls saved, get involved in missions and not spend our time wrangling."[60]

Shields refused to heed the counsel of MacBain and Scott. Arnold Dallimore, the noteworthy biographer of the transatlantic revivalist George Whitefield (1714–1770), was a close friend of MacBain as the two had trained together at TBS and pastored in Union churches. While Dallimore was in upstate New York for mental health reasons, the Brown-Shields controversy raged in his denomination. In an undated letter from that time, Dallimore shared his thoughts on Shields with his friend: "Your Union news—well I was glad to learn of it—yet it makes me sick . . . Dr. [Shields], with all his matchless gifts, is none better than a spoiled child,—a good spanking is in order. I can but feel sorry for your men, who are forced to soil your hands by dealing with so sordid a situation."[61]

The efforts of MacBain and Scott, and the views expressed by Dallimore, show that some key Baptist fundamentalist leaders had, by 1949, come to three key conclusions. First, they had lost confidence in Shields, his brand of militant fundamentalism, and his ability to lead the Union. Second, such leaders longed for an end to infighting and the damage to the cause of Christ that came out of endless "wrangling." Finally, the actions and attitudes of these leaders reveal a deep desire for a new more positive fundamentalist identity and a new vision where unity, cooperation, and kingdom work would be the hallmarks of Baptist endeavours. Some Baptists, like Hal McBain and Jack Scott, would now turn their attention to actively pursuing their vision and creating structures that would allow a more moderate Baptist fundamentalist identity to flourish.

---

59. Cited in Haykin and Song, "To Yield My Will," 86.

60. Cited in Haykin and Song, "To Yield My Will," 86.

61. Cited in Haykin and Song, "To Yield My Will," 86–87. For Dallimore's life and writing see Clary, *Reformed Evangelicalism and the Search for a Usable Past*. For his writings on Whitefield in particular see Clary, "Arnold Dallimore," 170–93.

From its early days MacBain had sat on the board of the Union, and later became its president, and had earned the respect of many in the denomination. According to Dallimore, writing to MacBain's mother in 1951, her son bore "much of the responsibility of the Union" for "the men continually look to him for leadership and expect his wise and steady counsel on all matters of policy."[62] Part of his leadership vision was to see greater cooperation between his denomination and the Independents. This marks a significant contrast between the moderate fundamentalists, who stressed cooperation, and the isolationism of the militant fundamentalists like Shields. As relationships deteriorated with Shields and Jarvis Street, MacBain reached out to Norman Pipe of the Independents to see about a potential merger between the two groups. MacBain, along with his Union colleague Robert Brackstone (b. 1909), met with Pipe and Donald Loveday (b. 1915) of the Independents to explore possibilities. In MacBain's words, "In a very short while it became obvious that there should be an amalgamation and that it should be as soon as possible. These two groups of Baptist churches represented about 200 churches in Ontario and Quebec."[63] The Independent's magazine, *The Fellowship Evangel*, ran an editorial by John F. Holliday (b. 1902) noting the historic cooperation between the two groups, and their common doctrine, stating that, "The probable outcome of these trends is obvious."[64]

That outcome came on 11 March 1952, when 90 pastors from both the Union and the Independents met at High Park Baptist Church in Toronto, an Independent church that is now called Westminster Chapel, in order to pray about a merger. From there they struck a liaison committee to explore what an "eventual fusion" could look like.[65] The committee suggested time for further prayer, mutual meetings between the two groups for conferences, a joint pastor's conference for the autumn of 1952, the promotion of the Independent's summer camp in Muskoka, pulpit exchanges, and a due consideration of reorganization and merger at a future date.[66] They recog-

---

62. Cited in Haykin and Song, "To Yield My Will," 13.
63. MacBain, "Dr. Hal MacBain," 195.
64. *The Fellowship Evangel*, 1949, 3. Cited in Tarr, *This Dominion His Dominion*, 127.
65. Tarr, *This Dominion*, 128.
66. Listed in Tarr, *This Dominion*, 128. For Muskoka Baptist Conference (now Muskoka Bible Centre), see Haykin and Clary, "*Rivers of Living Water*," 42–47; Holliday, *Muskoka Miracles*.

nized that such a merger would be a positive testimony of Christian unity to a watching world. As MacBain stated,

> Wise statesmen of government and industry do not plan a few months at a time but survey the broad vistas of the future and develop a long range programme which will build up and accumulate in the years to come. We believe that we would do well to emulate their far-sightedness and sit down to plan with earnest prayer for the next twenty-five years. A country the size of Canada demands a carefully developed design for establishing new churches . . . We are not discounting the leading and power of the Holy Spirit in suggesting this but merely make the observation that God uses men and consecrated methods to accomplish His purposes.

Speaking of the need to follow the Spirit's leading to develop a "blueprint of future action," MacBain said, "We owe it to Canada and to our Lord and Master to seize the initiative in these progressive and formative years in our great Dominion."[67] Pipe shared these sentiments stating in the *Fellowship Evangel* that "the merger of these two bodies of Bible-believing Baptists would also present a solid-front Evangelical Baptist testimony in Canada."[68] These two leaders saw clearly that their respective denominations shared the same basic evangelical convictions and that to provide a clear gospel testimony to Canadian society, they needed to work together. The vision was to move this testimony from just Ontario and Quebec to include the whole country, including "our newest province, Newfoundland" that as yet did not have a Baptist church in its borders.[69]

On 20–21 October 1953, the Union and the Independents held separate gatherings of their ministers in Toronto. On the last day of the meetings they joined one another at Cooke's Presbyterian Church to hold a joint session that had 108 representatives from the Union and 217 from the Independents while hundreds of others looked on. The decision was made to merge and form the Fellowship of Evangelical Baptist Churches in Canada. It began with roughly 200 churches and some 15,000 in membership. Hal MacBain was elected to be the first Fellowship President. In his address at the 21 October meeting he observed that this was a significant move forward in Canadian Baptist history. The new denomination should not be

67. *The Union Baptist*, July–August 1952, 2. Cited in Tarr, *This Dominion*, 129.

68. *The Fellowship Evangel*, December 1952, 5. Cited in Tarr, *This Dominion*, 130.

69. W. H. MacBain, *The Union Baptist*, November 1952, 2. Cited in Tarr, *This Dominion*, 131.

a "stagnant pool" but rather "a swift moving stream, blessing and refreshing all who may come in contact with it."[70] To the question of where they were going, it was not towards the BCOQ. Maintaining their stand with Shields from the 1920s, they were committed to evangelical orthodoxy. They recognized, said MacBain, that mere formal union between groups was useless if it was not grounded in classical theology. Instead, the Fellowship was headed "along a God-directed path of untainted fundamentalism."[71] Not only would the fledgling Fellowship be committed to the fundamentals of the faith, they would be distinctly Baptist. Though they recognized the work that other Protestant denominations were doing, "Our doctrinal statement . . . makes it very clear that we are a body of Baptist Churches holding forth the precious New Testament truths."[72] The President's stated aim was to "see a true Biblical Baptist Church in every community in Canada," that would be done in a "spirit of co-operation" and not a "spirit of competition."[73]

The creation of the Fellowship provided a venue for the expression of a more moderate Baptist fundamentalism in Canada. With unity, co-operation, and evangelism, as its core values, the Fellowship was well-positioned to become a moderate and evangelical expression of Canadian Baptist fundamentalism. Of course, success would depend on the ability of the Fellowship to remain united, increase its evangelistic efforts across the country, form new partnerships, and put in place the administrative and educational infrastructure required to run the denomination and train pastors who shared the Fellowship's ethos. It should be noted that not all churches or pastors who joined the Fellowship were enthusiastic about its moderate approach and vision. Militancy died hard. Nevertheless, in its early years, Central Baptist Seminary under the leadership of Dean W. Gordon Brown would be pivotal in furthering the realization of the Fellowship's new vision.

Central Baptist Seminary

When Brown was in the midst of the controversy and conflict at TBS he began contingency plans with ministers in the Union and the Independents, including Scott and Holliday, as well as some TBS faculty, for another seminary in case there was a split. When he had finally been dismissed

70. Cited in Tarr, *This Dominion*, 133.
71. Cited in Tarr, *This Dominion*, 134.
72. Cited in Tarr, *This Dominion*, 134.
73. Cited in Tarr, *This Dominion*, 135.

in December 1948, Brown and the students who followed him immediately began classes in January 1949 at Forward Baptist Church in Toronto. The pastor, Jack Scott, assumed the position as first President of the newly founded Central Baptist Seminary (CBS), and Brown resumed his role as Dean, which he maintained until 1973.[74] The seniors graduated on 5 May 1949, at Toronto's famed Massey Hall. CBS never took on formal affiliation with the Fellowship after 1953, though the two groups were deeply connected. The one stipulation was that trustees had to be a member of an evangelical Baptist church, thus at the time cementing its relationship with the Fellowship.[75] Wilson refers to the founding of Central as the most "profound consequence" of Brown's dismissal.[76] Jack Watt, the first chronicler of the Fellowship, and one of its key pastors, would concur:

> Of all the problems and crises which the Union had experienced in its relatively short history, this one, which was precipitated by the affairs of Toronto Baptist Seminary, which Dr. Shields handled, proved to be a most important one, for, instead of leading to further splits or separations, it was to be used to heal some old wounds and to reunite the Union and the Independent Fellowship.[77]

Thus, the founding of CBS had an important role to play in the bringing of the two denominations together to form FEBC.

Central would continue to train moderate fundamentalist Baptists into the 1980s, maintaining formal independence from the Fellowship, though graduating ministers who would serve in the denomination. Probably its most well-known graduate is the New Testament scholar, D. A. Carson. Its independence did not help when the school experienced financial difficulties in the late 1980s. In 1993, in order to continue its education program, CBS merged with London Baptist Bible College (LBBC), a fundamentalist school located in London, Ontario, to form what is now Heritage College and Seminary. A potential roadblock to a merger might have been less to do with personalities and more with theology. LBBC was both strongly fundamentalist and dispensational in its eschatological outlook, meaning that it held to a future premillennial reign of Christ immediately preceded by a pre-tribulational rapture of the church. CBS, on the other hand, tended towards Reformed theology and its faculty generally held to an amillennial

74. McHale, *The History of Central Baptist Seminary*.
75. Watt, *The Fellowship Story*, 42.
76. Wilson, "Torn Asunder," 58.
77. Watt, *Fellowship Story*, 42–43.

eschatology. In other denominations in North America, eschatology had become a test-point for whether one was theologically conservative or liberal.[78] Within Fellowship ranks there had been a push from a vocal minority to make dispensationalism part of their confession that could have led to further division.[79] Thankfully this did not pose a threat to unification of the two seminaries, and has not been an issue at Heritage, which adopted the broad and inclusive article on eschatology found in the Fellowship's doctrinal statement.[80]

Having learned from the past history of CBS's struggles and eventual merger, the Fellowship entered into a partnership with Heritage in order to strengthen their relationship and provide stronger support, such that in turn, the college and seminary still trains leaders to strengthen and grow the denomination. Their website notes that Heritage currently has some 2300 alumni ministering around the world.[81]

The efforts to create a more moderate Baptist fundamentalist identity and vision in Canada and an educational institution that supported these objectives aligned well with the broader North American resurgence of evangelicalism in 1940s and 1950s. Attention now turns to looking at how Canadian Fellowship Baptists fit within the larger North American evangelical context.

Fundamentalism, Evangelicalism, and Church Unity

While the crisis that hit the Ontario Baptists raged in the 1940s, there were similar fights and divisions occurring south of the border. In response, the National Association of Evangelicals (NAE) was founded in the United States in 1942, that in part would signal a move away from the sectarianism of the fundamentalist movement.[82] As George Marsden notes, the term "evangelical" was not common at that time, with those espousing that theology preferring the term they were most comfortable with, namely "fundamentalist." However, as many Protestants became battle-weary, they also

---

78. Mangum, *The Dispensational-Covenant Rift*.
79. Lockey and Haykin, "Polemic, Polity, and Piety," 146.
80. See www.fellowship.ca/WhatWeBelieve (accessed 25 July 2020).
81. www.discoverheritage.ca/about/history/ (accessed 25 July 2020).
82. It had originally been founded to bring fundamentalists together in response to the ecumenical movement in America, but the fundamentalists within the NAE eventually separated, leaving the movement with more of a neo-evangelical identity. See George Marsden, "Fundamentalism and American Evangelicalism," 22.

came to eschew the fundamentalist moniker, opting to be called evangelical instead. In many ways, this marks the birth of twentieth-century evangelicalism.[83] When Billy Graham (1918–2018) came to national prominence in 1949, he gave this new movement a public face.[84] As Graham moved more and more away from his fundamentalist roots, so too did evangelicalism. Thus, the evangelicals tended towards a broad-mindedness in relation to various Protestant distinctives, while maintaining a generally conservative theology.

The new Fellowship Baptists in Canada, with their more moderate fundamentalism, open ecclesiology, and emphasis on evangelism, fit well within the mainstream of this emerging brand of evangelicalism. By contrast, militant Baptist fundamentalists, like those who remained in the Union of Regular Baptists, become more isolated and entrenched in their hardline position. Militants demanded separation from any church or denomination that tolerated what they deemed to be liberalizing tendencies.

With the rise of parachurch ministries, such as Campus Crusade for Christ or the magazine *Christianity Today*, evangelicalism gained wider acceptance in the public at large, and thus to be a conservative Protestant likely meant one was an evangelical. The movement was so significant that *Newsweek* declared 1976 "the year of the Evangelical." Under the leadership of people like Graham and Carl F. H. Henry (1913–2003), the evangelicals developed international alliances through big-tent organizations such as the International Congress on World Evangelization that was founded by Graham and others in 1974.[85]

As broad as the movement was, it was nevertheless concerned to maintain boundaries, as hard as they were to determine at times.[86] Though the term "evangelical" is notoriously hard to define, one of its hallmarks in the late twentieth century was its desire for unity. This can be seen by the different groups that have identified themselves as evangelical, including "black Pentecostals" on the one hand, and separatist fundamentalists like Bob Jones Sr. (1883–1968) on the other. In light of this, Marsden observes, "Once we recognize the wide diversity within evangelicalism and the dangers of generalization, we may properly speak of evangelicalism as a single phenomenon." Marsden then goes on to highlight three "distinct,

---

83. Marsden, "The Evangelical Denomination," 17.
84. For Graham see Wacker, *America's Pastor*.
85. For Henry see Thornbury, *Recovering Classic Evangelicalism*.
86. Marsden, "Evangelical Denomination," 18.

though overlapping, senses in which evangelicalism may be thought of as a unity."[87] These are: the conceptual unity that seeks to define terms that will bring groups together in a single framework, which for Protestants were Reformational doctrines like the authority of Scripture, and salvation in Christ alone; the organic unity, such that groups with common traditions and beliefs can join together, bound to one another often in resistance to cultural trends; the transdenominational unity, which is a unity "with complicated infrastructures of institutions and persons who identify with 'evangelicalism.'"[88]

The founding of the Fellowship in 1953, which was the result of a merger between two like-minded Baptist groups, fits well with Marsden's description of what constitutes an evangelical of this period. Conceptually, the early leaders of the Fellowship like Hal MacBain identified themselves as "evangelical Baptists," even adopting that as part of their denomination's new name. The Union and the Independents were organically connected as both had, in one way or another, removed themselves from the mainline BCOQ. They maintained their own evangelical Baptist identity and beliefs as they struggled to make their way in this new context. The two denominations came together into a unity wherein institutions like Central Baptist Seminary, their various publications, and even Muskoka Baptist Conference, were brought together to serve the broader denomination and eventually other groups. Even newer institutions like Heritage College could navigate this unity, as CBS and LBBS came together in spite of significant differences over doctrine. This unity continued to grow and expand as the Fellowship brought in other Baptist groups across Canada under the aegis of its own denomination framework.[89]

The process of the Fellowship becoming a "trans-Canadian" entity was not easily achieved. In the Maritimes, progress was slow indeed. The United Baptist Convention of the Maritime Provinces ("of Atlantic Provinces" after 1963) was unified and dominated in the region. The best opportunities for the Fellowship to make inroads were through church-planting and attracting Independent Baptist churches that had no denominational affiliations. The first Atlantic church to join the Fellowship was Faith Baptist Church in

---

87. Marsden, "Evangelical Denomination," 22.

88. Marsden, "Evangelical Denomination," 22.

89. The story of these groups that stretched from the Maritimes to British Columbia and includes the northern provinces and territories of Canada are told in standard histories like that of Watt, Tarr, and Haykin and Lockey.

Sydney, Nova Scotia. This church became a member of the Fellowship on 17 May 1957. This was good first step. But as Rob Lockey has noted, "it was another twelve years before another church was added in the Maritimes."[90] Eventually, the members of Melvern Square Baptist Church in Nova Scotia, one of the churches to depart from convention under J. J. Sidey in the 1930s, renamed their church "Fellowship Baptist Church" and voted to join the Fellowship in 1969. When Malcolm Jennings, a key member of the church, was asked what motivated this Independent church to join the Fellowship he stated: "We were tired of being alone."[91]

In western Canada, the Fellowship presence took considerable time and effort to take root. On the prairies, in 1963, after almost two years of interaction and negotiations, the Prairie Fellowship of Regular Baptists was absorbed into the Fellowship of Evangelical Churches in Canada.[92] In British Columbia, after a serious flirtation with the idea of joining the American Southern Baptists ended in the mid-1950s, Regular Baptists entered into discussions with the Fellowship in 1956.[93] These discussions and negotiations took nine years to complete. The main sticking points included internal disagreements in both Ontario and British Columbia over timing, structure, and approach. The turning point towards merger finally came at a two-day meeting of the Eastern Executive Committee and two representatives from British Columbia in 1964. Three recommendations were put forward. The key deadlock-breaking recommendation allowed British Columbia's Convention "to be," as Davis notes, "'perpetuated as an autonomous Convention,' responsible for local activities and cooperation with the FEBC in areas of national concern."[94] The recommendations were subsequently approved at a special joint convention held in June of 1965. A formal reception of the British Columbia churches happened at the FEBC's regular convention in October 1965.[95] At this point, the vision of the Fellowship as a "trans-Canada" entity that was able to unify fundamentalist

---

90. Lockey, "Fishing for Men," 45–49.

91. The quotation and information in this paragraph is found in Lockey, "Fishing for Men," 45–49.

92. For an account of this development and the tensions it caused see, Davis, "The Struggle for a United Evangelical Baptist Fellowship," 253–55.

93. Burkinshaw, *Pilgrims in Lotus Land*, 167–68.

94. Davis, "The Struggle for a United Evangelical Baptist Fellowship," 257.

95. Davis, "The Struggle for a United Evangelical Baptist Fellowship," 257.

Baptists and bring them into the evangelical mainstream took a major step forward.

Thus, in a very real way, the Fellowship marked a significant step away from the militant fundamentalism of Shields in the 1920s and 1930s and into a more moderate fundamentalism that fit well within the new and broader evangelicalism that was taking shape in 1940s America. While the Fellowship remained self-consciously Baptist, its leaders recognized the good work done in different denominations, as demonstrated by Brown's role in the early days of the Evangelical Theological Society and the Evangelical Fellowship of Canada. Though MacBain would speak of maintaining a "fundamentalist" identity, he did so in the original use of the term as way of signaling fidelity to the fundamentals of the faith, without a turn back to the perceived modernism of the convention. Yet clearly MacBain and the Fellowship were staking out a new moderate fundamentalist identity that would become part of the evangelical mainstream. This broader identity would stay with the Fellowship well into the early twenty-first century. In fact, the Fellowship retains the name "evangelical" today.

CONCLUSION

This chapter has argued that the Fellowship of Evangelical Baptist Churches in Canada represented a new more moderate form of Baptist fundamentalism that rejected the infighting, conflict, and confrontation that so often characterized militant Baptist fundamentalists. Instead the more moderate FEBC emphasized the values of unity, cooperation, and evangelism. This repositioning and redefinition of both fundamentalist identity and vision allowed the FEBC to participate in the burgeoning and broader post-war North American evangelical movement.

Of course, the FEBC certainly faced its share of controversy and challenges in the late twentieth century. Tensions and disagreements over legalism, the role of women in ministry, the Charismatic movement, and eschatology would put a strain on the unity of the FEBC at times. Nevertheless, the ethos of the FEBC challenged the all too prevalent stereotypical view that all fundamentalist Baptists were militant, angry, combative people who relished conflict and shunned cooperation. The FEBC, through its emphasis on unity and cooperation, offered Canadians a moderate and more nuanced alternative form of Baptist fundamentalism. The new approach and vison put forward by the FEBC reshaped Baptist fundamentalist identity and countered the misperceptions and oversimplifications that so often dominated the twentieth century public discourse about Canadian Baptist fundamentalists.

BIBLIOGRAPHY

Primary Sources

NEWSPAPERS

Fellowship Evangel, 1949, 1952
Fraternal and Remembrancer, 1931
Gospel Witness, 1931
Union Baptist, 1952

OTHER

An Authoritative Statement of Facts Respecting the Resignation of Rev. W. S. Whitcombe, M. A., from Toronto Baptist Seminary and The Gospel Witness. Toronto: Toronto Baptist Seminary, n.d.

Carson, D. A. *Memoirs of an Ordinary Pastor: The Life and Reflections of Tom Carson*. Wheaton, IL: Crossway, 2008.

Dallimore, Arnold. *Only One Life: The Story of Dr. Jack Scott*. Hamilton, ON: Image, 1984.

Holliday, John F. *Muskoka Miracles: A Record of Forty-Five Years of Blessings—Commemorating the Forty-Fifth Anniversary of Muskoka Baptist Conference*. Toronto: The Fellowship of Evangelical Baptist Churches in Canada, 1975.

Machen, J. Gresham. *Christianity and Liberalism*. New York: Macmillan, 1923.

Whitcombe, Leila. "Dr. W. S. Whitcombe." In *Fellowship Baptist Trailblazers, Book One: Life Stories of Pastors and Missionaries*, edited by Fred Vaughan, 369–72. Belleville, ON: Guardian, 2001.

Secondary

Adams, Doug A. "The War of the Worlds: The Militant Fundamentalism of Dr. Thomas Todhunter Shields and the Paradox of Modernity." PhD diss., University of Western Ontario, 2015.

Augustine of Hippo. "Twelfth Homily on the Gospel of St. John." In *Augustine of Hippo: Selected Writings*. Translated by Mary T. Clark. Classics of Western Spirituality. Mahwah, NJ: Paulist, 1984.

Austin, Alvyn. "'Hotbed of Missions': The China Inland Mission, Toronto Bible College, and the Faith Missions-Bible School Connection." In *The Foreign Missionary Enterprise at Home: Explorations in North American Cultural History*, edited by Daniel H. Hays and Grant Wacker, 134–51. Tuscaloosa, AL: University of Alabama Press, 2003.

Bedard, Stephen. "Alexander Stewart (1774–1840)." In *A Noble Company: Biographical Essays on Notable Particular-Regular Baptists in America: The Canadians*, edited by Michael A. G. Haykin and Terry Wolever, 12:43–53. Springfield, MO: Particular Baptist Press, 2019.

Bonser, Henry. "A Memoir of the Author: Laurance Henry Marshall 1882-1953." In *Rivals of the Christian Faith*, by L. H. Marshall, 1-15. London: Carey Kingsgate, 1954.

By His Grace To His Glory: 60 Years of Ministry: Toronto Baptist Seminary and Bible College, 1927-1987. Toronto: Toronto Baptist Seminary, 1987.

Carson, D. A. *Exegetical Fallacies*. 2nd ed. Grand Rapids: Baker, 1996.

Clary, Ian Hugh. *Reformed Evangelicalism and the Search for a Usable Past: The Historiography of Arnold Dallimore, Pastor-Historian*. Reformed Historical Theology 61. Göttingen: Vandenhoeck & Ruprecht, 2020.

———. "Arnold Dallimore: Whitefield's Champion." In *Making Evangelical History: Faith, Scholarship and the Evangelical Past*, edited by Andrew Atherstone and David Ceri Jones, 170-93. Routledge Studies in Evangelicalism. Abingdon, UK: Routledge, 2019.

———. "Throwing Away the Guns: Andrew Fuller, William Ward, and the Communion Controversy in the Baptist Missionary Society." *Foundations* 68 (2015) 84-101.

Cullen, Pamela. "Debating and Dividing: The Women's Baptist Home Missionary Society of Ontario West 1925-1927." *McMaster Journal of Theology and Ministry* 4.2 (2001) online: https://www.mcmaster.ca/mjtm/4-2.htm.

Davis, Kenneth R. "The Struggle for a United Evangelical Baptist Fellowship, 1953-1965." In *Baptists in Canada: Search for Identity Amidst Diversity*, edited by Jarold K. Zeman, 237-65. Burlington, ON: Welch, 1980.

Elliott, David Raymond. "Studies of Eight Canadian Fundamentalists." PhD diss., University of British Columbia, 1989.

Fath, Sébastien. "The Other American Dream: French Baptists and Canada in the 19th and 20th Centuries." In *French-Speaking Protestants in Canada: Historical Essays*, edited by Jason Zuidema, 243-63. Religion in the Americas 11. Leiden: Brill, 2011.

Flatt, Kevin N. "A Century of Change: Protestantism in Canada in the Twentieth Century." In *Desiring a Better Country: 150 Years of Christian Witness in Canada: Legacy and Relevance*, edited by Chance Faulkner et al., 31-65. Peterborough, ON: H&E Publishing, 2018.

Gatiss, Lee. *Christianity and the Tolerance of Liberalism: J. Gresham Machen and the Presbyterian Controversy of 1922-1937*. London: Latimer Trust, 2008.

Gibson, Theo T. *Robert Alexander Fyfe: His Contemporaries and His Influence*. Burlington, ON: Welch, 1988.

Goertz, Donald. *A Century for the City: Walmer Road Baptist Church, 1889-1989*. Toronto: Walmer Road Baptist Church, 1989.

Hankins, Barry. *God's Rascal: J. Frank Norris and the Beginnings of Southern Fundamentalism*, Religion in the South. Lexington: University Press of Kentucky, 2010.

Hart, D. G. *Defending the Faith: J. Gresham Machen and the Crisis of Conservative in America*. Phillipsburg, NJ: P&R Publishing, 2003.

Haykin, Michael A. G. "'Jesus, Wondrous Saviour': Ontario Baptist Roots in the Nineteenth Century." In *A Glorious Fellowship of Churches: Celebrating the History of the Fellowship of Evangelical Baptist Churches in Canada, 1953-2003*, edited by Michael A. G. Haykin and Robert B. Lockey, 115-44. Guelph, ON: The Fellowship of Evangelical Baptist Churches in Canada, 2003.

Haykin, Michael A. G., ed. *From Acorns to Oaks: The Primacy and Practice of Biblical Theology: A Festschrift for Dr. Geoff Adams*. Guelph, ON: Joshua Press, 2003.

Haykin, Michael A. G., and Ian Hugh Clary. "'O God of Battles': The Canadian Baptist Experience of the Great War." In *Canadian Churches and the First World War*, edited by Gordon L. Heath, 170–96. McMaster General Series 4. Eugene, OR: Pickwick, 2014.

———. "*Rivers of Living Waters*": Celebrating 125 Years of Hughson Street Baptist Church, Hamilton, Ontario, 1887-2012. Hamilton, ON: Hughson Street Baptist Church, 2012.

Haykin, Michael A. G., with Baiyu A. Song. *"To Yield My Will, My Hopes, My All": A Portrait of the Life and Ministry of W. Hal MacBain*. Guelph: ON: The Fellowship of Evangelical Baptist Churches in Canada, 2016.

Johnston, Charles M. *McMaster University: Volume 1: The Toronto Years*. Toronto: University of Toronto Press, 1976.

Lockey, Robert B. "Fishing for Men: Fellowship Atlantic." In *A Glorious Fellowship of Churches: Celebrating the History of the Fellowship of Evangelical Baptist Churches in Canada, 1953-2003*, edited by Michael A. G. Haykin and Robert B. Lockey, 33–60. Guelph, ON: The Fellowship of Evangelical Baptist Churches in Canada, 2003.

Lockey, Robert B., and Michael A. G. Haykin, "Polemic, Polity, and Piety: Some Themes in the Story of FEB Central." In *A Glorious Fellowship of Churches: Celebrating the History of the Fellowship of Evangelical Baptist Churches in Canada, 1953-2003*, edited by Michael A. G. Haykin and Robert B. Lockey, 145–74. Guelph, ON: The Fellowship of Evangelical Baptist Churches in Canada, 2003.

MacBain, Hal. "Dr. Hal MacBain." In *Fellowship Baptist Trailblazers, Book One: Life Stories of Pastors and Missionaries*, edited by Fred Vaughan, 189–99. Belleville, ON: Guardian, 2001.

Mangum, R. Todd. *The Dispensational-Covenant Rift: The Fissuring of American Evangelical Theology from 1936 to 1944*. Studies in Evangelical History and Thought. Eugene, OR: Wipf and Stock, 2007.

Marsden, George M. "The Evangelical Denomination." In *Evangelicals: Who They Have Been, Are Now, and Could Be*, edited by Mark A. Noll et al., 17–30. Grand Rapids: Eerdmans, 2019.

———. *Fundamentalism and American Culture*. Oxford: Oxford University Press, 2006.

———. "Fundamentalism and American Evangelicalism." In *The Variety of American Evangelicalism*, edited by Donald W. Dayton and Robert K. Johnston, 22–35. Knoxville: University of Tennessee Press, 1991.

McHale, Gary W. *The History of Central Baptist Seminary*. Gromley, ON: Central Baptist Seminary, 1993.

Mehan, Brenda M. "A. C. Dixon: An Early Fundamentalist." *Foundations* 10.1 (1967) 50–63.

"Memorials: W. Gordon Brown." *Journal of the Evangelical Theological Society* 23.1 (March 1980) 91.

Perin, Roberto. *The Many Rooms of This House: Diversity and Toronto's Places of Worship Since 1840*. Toronto: University of Toronto Press, 2017.

Pinnock, Clark H. "The Modernist Impulse at McMaster University, 1887–1927." In *Baptists in Canada: Search for Identity Amidst Diversity*, edited by Jarold K. Zeman, 193–207. Burlington, ON: Welch, 1980.

Priest, Gerald L. "T. T. Shields the Fundamentalist: Man of Controversy." *Detroit Baptist Seminary Journal* 10.1 (2005) 69–101.

Rawlyk, G. A. "A. L. McCrimmon, H. P. Whidden, T. T. Shields, Christian Higher Education, and McMaster University." In *Canadian Baptists and Christian Higher*

Education, edited by George A. Rawlyk, 31–62. Montreal: McGill-Queen's University Press, 1988.

Renfree, Harry A. *Heritage and Horizon: The Baptist Story in Canada*. Mississauga, ON: Canadian Baptist Federation, 1988.

Sillen, J. Walter. "William H. P. Faunce: A Representative Religious Liberal." *Foundations* 2 (1959) 235–49.

Straub, Jeffrey Paul. *The Making of a Battle Royal: The Rise of Liberalism in Northern Baptist Life, 1870–1920*. Monographs in Baptist History 8. Eugene, OR: Pickwick, 2018.

Tarr, Leslie K. "Dr. W. Gordon Brown." In *Fellowship Baptist Trailblazers, Book One: Life Stories of Pastors and Missionaries*, edited by Fred Vaughan, 33–38. Belleville, ON: Guardian, 2001.

———. "Another Perspective on T. T. Shields and Fundamentalism." In *Baptists in Canada: Search for Identity Amidst Diversity*, edited by Jarold K. Zeman, 209–24. Burlington, ON: Welch, 1980.

———. *This Dominion His Dominion: The Story of Evangelical Baptist Endeavour in Canada*. Willowdale, ON: Fellowship of Evangelical Baptist Churches in Canada, 1968.

———. *Shields of Canada: T. T. Shields (1873–1955)*. Grand Rapids: Baker, 1967.

Thornbury, Gregory Alan. *Recovering Classic Evangelicalism: Applying the Wisdom and Vision of Carl F. H. Henry*. Wheaton, IL: Crossway, 2013.

Tomlinson, Glenn. "A Hard Beginning, 1818–1844." In *Set for the Defense of the Gospel: A Bicentennial History of Jarvis Street Baptist Church, 1818–2018*, edited by Michael A. G. Haykin and Roy M. Paul, 11–40. Toronto: Jarvis Street Baptist Church, 2018.

Trollinger, Jr., William Vance. *God's Empire: William Bell Riley and Midwestern Fundamentalism*, History of American Thought and Culture. Madison, WI: University of Wisconsin Press, 1991.

Wacker, Grant. *America's Pastor: Billy Graham and the Shaping of a Nation*. Cambridge, MA: The Belknap Press, an Imprint of Harvard University Press, 2014.

Watt, J. H. *The Fellowship Story: Our First 25 Years*. Willowdale, ON: The Fellowship of Evangelical Baptist Churches in Canada, 1978.

Wilson, Paul R. "Torn Asunder: T. T. Shields, W. Gordon Brown, and the Schisms at Toronto Baptist Seminary and Within the Union of Regular Baptist Churches of Ontario and Quebec, 1948–1949." *McMaster Journal of Theology and Ministry* 19 (2017–2018) 34–80.

———. "A Mission Transformed: Fellowship Baptist Outreach in Quebec, 1953–1986." In *Baptists and Missions: Papers from the Fourth International Conference on Baptist Studies*, edited by Ian M. Randall and Anthony R. Cross, 189–204. Studies in Baptist History and Thought 29. Milton Keynes, UK: Paternoster, 2007.

Wright, Robert A. "The Canadian Protestant Tradition 1914–1945." In *The Canadian Protestant Experience 1760 to 1990*, edited by George A. Rawlyk, 139–97. Montreal: McGill-Queen's University Press, 1990.

Yuille, J. Stephen. "Robert A. Fyfe (1816–1878)." In *A Noble Company: Biographical Essays on Notable Particular-Regular Baptists in America: The Canadians*, edited by Michael A. G. Haykin and Terry Wolever, 12:243–67. Springfield, MO: Particular Baptist Press, 2019.

Canadian Baptist Fundamentalism Since 1978

An Epilogue

Taylor Murray and Paul R. Wilson

The period covered in this book is not the end of the story, nor do the individual chapters provide the final word on the events or people examined. This epilogue serves two purposes: first, it briefly traces the contours of Baptist fundamentalism in Canada since 1978; and second, it suggests a few possible areas for future study.

CHANGES IN THE RECENT PAST

Fundamentalism did not suddenly disappear among Baptists in Canada after 1978; yet, the new forms and features, and the context in which they were born, resulted in a movement that was quite different from that which existed a century ago. By the second half of the twentieth century, it became increasingly clear that the militant breed of fundamentalism that had launched effective campaigns against Convention Baptist bodies in the 1920s had become a minority voice in the Canadian Baptist world.

By 1978, the majority of the prominent fundamentalists that had been involved in the militant campaigns against theological liberalism earlier in the century had died, including J. B. Daggett, William Aberhart, T. T. Shields, J. J. Sidey, and James B. Rowell. There were several exceptions, of course, such as L. E. Maxwell and T. A. Meister, but for the most part the mantle of leadership had fallen to the second—and in some cases the third—generation. While these new leaders were usually influential and competent in their own right, the political and social capital so expertly wielded by the likes of Shields and Aberhart in the early twentieth century was gone and those who remained were unable to obtain the same kind of clout as their theological ancestors.

As the face of the fundamentalist movement changed, so too did the operational structures that sustained the movement. Shields' Association of Regular Baptist Churches survived for a time "to provide a vehicle of fellowship and cooperation to local churches who love sound doctrine" and "promote and maintain the autonomy of the local churches."[1] In 1983, William E. Payne, pastor at Trinity Baptist Church in Burlington and Professor at Toronto Baptist Seminary, formed the Sovereign Grace Fellowship of Baptist Churches (SGF) as a network of Calvinistic Baptist churches that allowed for dual affiliation with other denominational bodies.[2] At the turn of the century, the SGF more formally organized. Their constitution stated their purpose:

> promoting joint activities and cooperation between member churches; assisting churches in maintaining and propagating sound biblical doctrine; working together in world missions, church planting and evangelization; assisting in the education, recognition and support of biblically qualified ministers.[3]

As of 2020, the SGF had fourteen Baptist churches (including Jarvis Street Baptist Church) in Ontario and one in New Brunswick.[4] Attempts at creating other formal structures in the west and in the Maritimes had middling success at best and generally faded into obscurity.[5]

---

1. Tom Rush, "Vision and Purpose of the Association of Regular Baptist Churches (Canada)," *The Gospel Witness*, 19 November 1987, 14. They safeguarded the independence of the local church by having the larger Association function more as a coordinating body that would provide organizational and financial support for other churches while also maintaining that "Each member church is involved in only those projects in which it desires to participate."

2. Fellows, "William E. Payne," 556.

3. Sovereign Grace Fellowship, "The Constitution of the Sovereign Grace Fellowship" (2001).

4. These churches are listed on the Sovereign Grace website: sgfcanada.com.

5. In the case of the latter region, the inheritance of these formal groups is the various "Fundamental Baptist" churches that populate New Brunswick. The two most visible

While some fundamentalist Baptist churches have opted to come together in formal structures to encourage shared ministries and fellowship, independent Baptist congregations are also quite prominent throughout Canada. A 2014 database listed 307 different independent Baptist "Churches/Works" across the country: 98 in the Western Provinces; 126 in the Central Provinces; 75 in the Atlantic Provinces; and 8 in the Territories.[6] While the independent ecclesiology of these churches obviously precludes them from joining together in any official capacity, as a single unit their number of churches rivals that of some of the larger Baptist bodies in Canada. Of course, this does not take into account the size of each congregation, but some (such as the Fundamental Baptist Church in Saint John, New Brunswick) are quite large and still occupy a significant place in the community.

One area where Baptist fundamentalists in Canada have remained active is in the field of higher education. Toronto Baptist Seminary, which, aside from a few periods of turbulence,[7] remains an important training ground for conservative Baptists in southern Ontario. On the Prairies, the Prairie Bible Institute (PBI; Prairie College since 2015) has functioned as an important location for conservatives across the denominational spectrum. By the mid-1970s, PBI had graduated approximately 1800 foreign missionaries and 1200 domestic missionaries.[8] In Nova Scotia, after Sidey's death in 1966, William Moorehead was appointed President of the Kingston Bible College. Moorehead—who had also succeeded Sidey as pastor at Bible Baptist Church (later renamed Faith Baptist Church) in Kingston—remained in this role until his death in 2014, after which he was not replaced and the college froze its academic operations. As of writing, the Kingston Bible College Academy in Nova Scotia remains operational, though it does so in a much-reduced form as a private day school with a small student body.

These institutions remained largely uncompromised in their founding principles. In 1978, for example, Paul Maxwell succeeded his father, L. E. Maxwell, as President of PBI and was, according to one contemporary,

---

Maritime fundamentalist Baptist groups were led by those who had split from Sidey, including Douglass M. Fraser and Maxwell V. Bolser. They were the Maritime Fellowship of Regular Baptist Churches (1953), and the Fellowship of Fundamental Baptist Churches in the Maritime Provinces (1961).

6. Stastny, "Canadian Independent Baptist Churches by Province," 2.

7. For example, it suffered a significant schism in 1949 in the wake of Shields' unexpected decision to dismiss the dean. On the schism, see Wilson, "Torn Asunder." The dean was W. Gordon Brown, who went on to form Central Baptist Seminary.

8. Elliott, "Three Faces," 175.

"similar to the fundamentalists of days gone by" in the sense that "he did not shrink from sounding a prophetic warning concerning the social ills of the day" including "gospel rock" and alcohol.[9] This changed somewhat, notes historian David R. Elliott, after the death of the elder Maxwell in 1984, when "many of [PBI's] rigid social rules and emphases began to change" and they raised the educational standards.[10] Yet it, like the others, remains a centre for conservatism in its region.

In addition to those educational efforts discussed above and elsewhere throughout this volume, a number of other, smaller Baptist fundamentalist training schools have opened across Canada since 1978. They include Baptist Bible College Canada and Theological Seminary in Simcoe, Ontario (1978); FaithWay Baptist College in Scarborough, Ontario (1983); Canadian Baptist Bible College in Winkler, Manitoba (1996); Emmanuel Baptist Bible Institute in Moncton, New Brunswick (2001); and Golden Plains Baptist Bible Institute in Portage La Prairie, Manitoba (2002). Many of these schools focus on training missionaries and are based out of a single church. Others, such as the New Brunswick Bible Institute in Victoria Corner, are technically nondenominational but are closely associated with one or more Baptist church and generally demonstrate a Baptist-leaning theology.

There are other bodies that are baptistic in nature, though they do not identify as Baptists. One such group is the Associated Gospel Churches, which spans the entire country. This group of independent churches was founded originally as the Christian Workers' Church of Canada in 1895. Centred initially in Ontario's Toronto-Hamilton corridor, this church community gradually expanded its reach over time. By 1922, the desire to strengthen the existing bonds of fellowship and preserve doctrinal orthodoxy prompted Peter W. Philpott (1866–1957) of the Gospel Tabernacle in Hamilton and H. E. Irwin of the Missionary Tabernacle in Toronto to pursue a union of like-minded churches. The resulting union was renamed the Associated Gospel Churches (AGC) in 1925. Some church members who were dismayed by the doctrinal drift within their own denomination found refuge in this expression of fundamentalism. The AGC continued to expand to the west in 1940, to Quebec (English ministry) in 1944, the Maritimes in 1962, and in Quebec (French ministry) in 1969. The AGC has experienced structural change over the years. The latest was in 2018. Today,

---

9. Callaway, "Training Disciplined Soldiers for Christ," 335.
10. Elliott, "Three Faces," 177.

the AGC extends across Canada, serves eleven language groups, and has over 150 churches.[11]

Yet, these new forms and commitment to the "old time religion" have not guaranteed smooth sailing. For example, in 1978, the Kingston movement experienced yet another minor schism, when the principal of the Kingston Bible College Academy (KBCA), Richard Jones, resigned to begin a new, competing Christian day school in nearby Meadowvale,[12] for which he took nine members of the teaching staff. Gertrude "Addie" Palmer became the acting Principal at KBCA (which she justified by noting that "the school was merely an extension of the home" and that she would remain only "until there was a man to take the leadership of the school"[13]) until 1983, during which time she rebuilt the teaching staff.

Of course, any discussion of the Canadian Baptist fundamentalist experience in the second-half of the twentieth century requires some discussion of the Fellowship of Evangelical Baptist Churches in Canada (FEBCC), arguably the most significant legacy of the fundamentalist controversies in Canada. Despite their roots in the 1927 schism, few in that body today would identify as "fundamentalist." Elsewhere Paul R. Wilson has argued that the creation of this new denominational body symbolized that the militancy of earlier fundamentalists had largely been replaced by "a less strident, more cooperative, more inclusive and less tightly organized expression of conservative evangelicalism."[14] In more recent years, this attitude has manifested in unexpectedly irenic relations between FEBCC and Convention Baptists. As early as the 1980s, FEBCC pastor Bruce Woods was prepared to say publicly that he saw "no reason why relations between Fellowship and Convention cannot improve," before adding: "There are many reasons why we should challenge it: obedience to our Lord's call to spiritual oneness, love among the brethren, justice in our treatment of one another,

---

11. The material in this paragraph is taken from two denominational sources. Associated Gospel Churches, "A Brief History of the AGC," n.p. For the over-150 churches referenced, see Alan, "Transformed," 1. For a detailed history of the AGC see Redinger, *A Tree Well Planted*.

12. See Jones, "The History," 198–203. The fracture resulted in a split within Faith Baptist Church and saw the creation of the competing Charity Baptist Church. Recently, however, Faith Baptist—the last church in the independent Baptist fold with direct uninterrupted ties to Sidey—dissolved and the remaining members joined Charity Baptist in neighboring Meadowvale.

13. Palmer, *Addie's Pilgrimage*, 108, 113.

14. Wilson, "Torn Asunder," 72.

and greater effectiveness in mission."[15] While Woods was something of a rarity at the time, it appears as though relations between the two large Baptist groups have been steadily improving. Perhaps the clearest example of this is visible in the FEBCC's invitation to the Executive Minister of the Canadian Baptists of Ontario and Quebec to open their annual gathering in prayer in 2015—nearly 90 years after the schism in 1927.

POSSIBILITIES FOR FUTURE STUDY

Where does this leave the study of Baptist fundamentalism in Canada? Historians have focused on various aspects of the movement, but there remain numerous other areas in need of exploration. Among the most promising and largely-unexplored areas of investigation relate to the proto- and early-fundamentalist movement. As this volume has shown, there were influential figures that predate Shields who have been virtually ignored. While the current historiography of fundamentalism among Baptists in Canada is primarily Shields-focused, these studies suggest that future historians should not so briskly move past these earlier figures. Although Baptists in the west were in their infancy during these years, one wonders if there were parallel figures elsewhere in the country that we have missed entirely.

In a similar way, very little has been written on the development of the Canadian Baptist fundamentalist movement after the controversies of the 1920s and 1930s. This epilogue has shown that each of the bodies explored by the various authors in this book continued in some form long after the events described. There is ample space to explore the second- and third-generation leaders and the turbulent legacies they inherited. Such studies would provide insight into how each group evolved and adapted, even as the Canadian socio-religious landscape changed so significantly in the mid-twentieth century.

There has likewise been a tendency among historians to focus on one or two prominent individuals in each region. Who were the other figures involved? Moreover, if these "secondary" players have been overshadowed, the people in the pew have been entirely neglected. Identifying which particular aspects the average church-goer found most appealing or where they disagreed with their pastor would add depth and texture to our understating of the movement overall.

---

15. Woods, "Theological Directions and Cooperation," 185.

Perhaps the most egregious omission in the historiography relates to the absence of women. Upon a quick overview of the literature, it becomes clear that historians have afforded women very little attention. (In fact, judging from some writings, the casual reader might be forgiven for thinking that several prominent Baptist fundamentalists never even met a woman aside from his own wife!) Further exacerbating this oversight is the fact that not all Baptist fundamentalists in Canada were opposed to women in ministry.[16] It could very well be, in the words of Margaret Bendroth, that "Adding women to the master narrative will inevitably change its meaning."[17]

There is also room to expand the conversation on fundamentalists and conservative evangelicals that remained in the various convention bodies even after the events of the 1920s. After reading this book, for example, one might be left with the impression that all those who remained in the Baptist Convention of Ontario and Quebec were not as faithful to Baptist orthodoxy as those who left in 1927; however, that was certainly not the case. Many conservative evangelical Baptists—who also held the doctrinal views espoused by T. T. Shields—chose to remain within the denomination. Their experience after 1927 certainly needs a more fulsome examination by historians.

The opportunities in study are not limited to these few examples. Historians have focused primarily on Canadian Baptist fundamentalism as a white and English-speaking phenomenon. Widening the scope of investigation may reveal some as-yet-unknown details or additional questions. Likewise, little research has been done on the legal consequences of the fundamentalist controversies. There are numerous avenues available in this area for future study.

The purpose of this volume was to provide a foundation for the future study of Baptist fundamentalism in Canada. Each chapter has underscored the fact that fundamentalism is not a monolith—it is a diverse, complex, and dynamic movement. The scholarship offered here has addressed old themes in new ways and, in the process, raised a variety of questions and possibilities for exciting new avenues of study. The above questions and

---

16. One thinks of L. E. Maxwell of PBI, who was publicly in favour of women in ministry for his entire career and even published a book on the topic (co-authored by Ruth C. Dearing). See Maxwell and Dearing, *Women in Ministry*.

17. Bendroth, "Angry Women and the History of American Evangelicalism," 119.

possible areas for additional study reflect the breadth of opportunities that remain for future historians to explore.

BIBLIOGRAPHY

Alan, Bill. "Transformed." *Connect Magazine* (2020) 1.
Associated Gospel Churches. "A Brief History of the AGC." n.p. Online: https://agcofcanada.com/history.
Bendroth, Margaret. "Angry Women and the History of American Evangelicalism." *Fides et Historia* 34.2 (2002) 113–19.
Callaway, Timothy Wray. "Training Disciplined Soldiers for Christ: The Influence of American Fundamentalism on Prairie Bible Institute During the L. E. Maxwell Era (1922–1980)." DTh diss., University of South Africa, 2010.
Elliott, David R. "Three Faces of Baptist Fundamentalism in Canada: Aberhart, Maxwell, and Shields." In *Memory and Hope: Strands of Canadian Baptist History*, edited by David T. Priestley, 171–82. Waterloo, ON: Wilfrid Laurier University Press, 1996.
Fellows, Roger. "William E. Payne (1938–1997)." In *A Noble Company 12: The Canadians*, edited by Michael A. G. Haykin and Terry Wolever, 535–58. Springfield, MO: Particular Baptist Press, 2019.
The Gospel Witness (Toronto, ON), 1987.
Jones, Richard. "The History of the Calvary Baptist Church (Ind.) Meadowvale, Annapolis County." In *Echoes Across the Valley: A History of Kingston and its Neighbors*, vol. 1, edited by Tony Cochrane, 198–203. Hantsport, NS: Lancelot, 1994.
Maxwell, L. E., and Ruth C. Dearing. *Women in Ministry: An Historical and Biblical Look at the Role of Women in Christian Leadership*. Camp Hill, PA: Christian Publications, 1987.
Palmer, Gertrude A. *Addie's Pilgrimage*. Kingston, NS: International Christian Mission, n.d.
Redinger, Lauren. *A Tree Well Planted: The Official History of the Christian Workers' Churches of Canada and the Associated Gospel Churches, 1892–1993*. Burlington, ON: Associated Gospel Churches, 1995.
Reimer, Sam, and Michael Wilkinson. *A Culture of Faith: Evangelical Congregations in Canada*. Montreal: McGill-Queen's University Press, 2015.
Sovereign Grace Fellowship. "The Constitution of the Sovereign Grace Fellowship." 2001. n.p. Online: https://www.sgfcanada.com.
Stastny, Thomas. "Canadian Independent Baptist Churches by Province." 2014. n.p. Online: http://www.valleyviewbc.org.
Wilson, Paul R. "Torn Asunder: T. T. Shields, W. Gordon Brown and the Schisms at Toronto Baptist Seminary and within the Union of Regular Baptist Churches of Ontario and Quebec, 1948–1949." *McMaster Journal of Theology and Ministry* 19 (2017–2018) 34–80.

Index of Names

Aberhart, William, 8, 21, 96, 205, 215–32, 292–93
Ackland, L. E., 191–92, 193
Adams, Doug, 25, 27, 248, 266
Adams, Geoffrey, 276
Allaby, Henry E., 190–91
Alline, Henry, 32
Appleby, R. Scott, 2
Augustine of Hippo, 265

Baker, A. F., 160, 171
Ban, Joseph, 21–22
Banack, Clark, 227–28
Barth, Karl, 214
Bates, Stuart S., 138
Bauder, Robert, 18
Bebbington, David, 3, 125
Bendroth, Margaret, 298
Bennett, Arnold, 158
Bennett, R. W., 186
Bezanson, William B., 189
Bolser, Maxwell, 198, 200, 201, 293n5
Booth, Catherine, 208
Booth, William, 208
Booth-Clibborn, Kate, 208–209
Brady, William A., 250
Broadman, George, 85
Brookman, William, 70–84
Brown, W. Gordon, 271–77, 281–82, 294n7
Burkinshaw, Robert, 21, 30–31

Cadman, S. Parkes, 258

Callaway, Tim, 11, 211
Campbell, Alexander, 89
Campbell, Peter Sinclair, 108
Carson, D. A., 272n30, 273, 282
Case, Shirley Jackson, 33
Castle, John Harvard, 74–79, 81–82
Caven, William, 95
Chipps, Dexter Edward, 253–54, 259, 261
Clark, S. D., 168
Clarke, Brian, 2
Clarke, William Newton, 122
Cooke, A. E., 172
Colbourne, Maurice Dale, 225
Conwell, Russell H., 240
Cross, Anthony, 6
Crowe, A. G., 41
Curr, H. S., 124, 137–38

Daggett, Elizabeth Jane (née Merrithew), 183
Daggett, John Bolton, 33, 128n42, 183–202, 292
Dales, John Nelson, 96
Dallimore, Arnold, 35, 278–79
Darby, John Nelson, 215
Darwin, Charles, 94, 244
Davies, William, 52, 58–59
Davis, Kenneth, 35, 37, 277, 286
Delnay, Robert, 18, 121–22, 246
Denovan, Joshua, 8, 19, 49–91
Denovan, Jane (née Macnab), 51

Index of Names

Dixon, A. C., 241–42, 243, 249, 253, 257, 267
Douglas, C. H., 225–26
Douglas, Tommy, 7
Driver, Samuel Rolles, 141, 145
Dyke, Samuel A., 77–82

Elliott, David R., 207, 295
Ellis, Walter E., 20, 30, 169–70
Ellis, Walter, 173

Faunce, W. H. P., 27, 132–37, 240n21, 251, 269
Fea, John, 18
Felter, William, 260
Ford, Murray J. S., 17
Fosdick, Harry Emerson, 27, 258
Foster, George Burman, 241, 243, 249
Fowler, Stan, 5
Fraser, Douglass M., 200, 201, 293n5
Fyfe, Robert A., 59, 267

Garrettson, Freeborn, 32
Gilmour, Joseph L., 138
Gould, Ezra P., 240
Graham, Billy, 284
Grant, John Webster, 207
Guenther, Bruce, 173n62

Hague, Dyson, 95, 110
Hague, George, 95–96
Hall, James Masson, 112
Harris, Elmore, 19–20, 91, 95–96, 107, 120, 237n5, 268
Haykin, Michael, 39, 278
Haysmore, F. C., 189, 192, 195
Henderson, Quartus B., 26
Henry, Carl F. H., 284
Hepburn, Mitchell, 28–29
Herman, A. K., 190
Herman, Neil, 23–24, 33, 186, 190, 192
Hill, J. W., 33
Hindmarsh, Bruce, 23
Hogg, James, 53, 55
Holliday, J. F., 35, 279, 281
Holman, Caroline (née Haigh), 270
Holman, Charles J., 20, 25, 105, 125
Hovey, Alvah, 240n21

Inkster, John, 248
Irwin, H. E., 295
Ivison, Stuart, 7

Jennings, Malcolm, 286
Jones, Sr., Bob, 284
Jones, Callum, 31
Jones, Richard, 296

King, William Lyon Mackenzie, 29
Kirk, J. Fergus, 206, 227, 228–29

Lager, Carl H., 30
Lailey, Thomas, 83
Law, William, 210
Laws, Curtis Lee, 9
Lesslie, James, 83
Lindsay, H. B., 192–94
Lindsay, R. W., 189, 192
Linton, John, 30, 257, 260
Loisy, Alfred Firmin, 111
Loney, Clifford J., 260
Loveday, Donald, 279

MacArthur, Robert Stuart, 237, 239–40
MacBain, W. Hal, 277–81, 285, 287
Macdonald, Stuart, 2
Machen, J. Gresham, 270
Mackay, John, 172
Macnab, Alan, 51
MacNeill, Harris Lachlan, 30, 158–59, 170, 171, 176
MacNeill, John, 121, 139, 245
MacWalker, W. R., 192
Maguire G. R., 160, 162, 171
Mann, W. E., 168
Manning, Ernest, 22, 224, 230
Marty, Martin, 2
Marsden, George, 9, 283–84
Marshall, L. H., 27, 132, 138–46, 149, 269, 271
Mason, E. S., 189
Mason, Rex, 5
Masse, J. C., 256–57
Mathews, Shailer, 122
Matthews, I. G., 96, 100, 106, 120, 237n5, 268
Maxwell, Leslie E., 11, 205–215, 229–30, 293, 294–95

Index of Names

Maxwell, Paul, 294–95
McAlister, Harvey, 219
McCabe, Joseph, 248
McCrimmon, Abraham Lincoln, 96, 107
McDiarmid, Archibald P., 74
McDormand, T. B., 119, 150
McEwen, J. P., 87
McGregor, Daniel Arthur, 80–81, 86–87, 91
McKay, Alexander, 84
McLeod, A. A., 159
McNicol, John, 95
McMaster, William, 59, 130
McMaster, William Wardley, 100
Meacham, H. C., 253
Miller, Dorothy, Ruth, 210
Milton, John, 111
Meister, T. A., 33, 189–92, 195–96, 199–200, 293
Moody, Barry, 181–82
Moody, Dwight L., 215
Moorehead, William, 294
Muir William, 72
Murray, Taylor, 23–24, 33

Niebuhr, Richard, 168
Neighbour, R. E., 253, 255
Noll, Mark, 231
Norris, J. Frank, 93, 252–54, 255, 258, 261, 267

Oliver, French, 21, 164, 171–73, 176, 238–39
Orr, James, 110, 145

Palmer, Gertrude, 296
Parson, Francis T., 58–59
Payne, William E., 293
Perry, H. Francis, 240n21, 267
Pettingil, William, 253, 255, 257, 258
Philpott, Peter W., 295
Pinnock, Clark H., 40
Pipe, Norman W., 269, 279–81
Porter, Stanley, 6
Potter, Charles Francis, 252
Price, Charles, 161–62, 217–18
Priestley, David, 32

Quarrier, William, 98

Rader, Paul, 255
Raikes, Robert, 114
Rauschenbusch, Walter, 122
Rawlyk, George A., 4, 32–33, 94, 167, 179, 184n21, 195, 197
Rebman, Edith, 246–48, 259
Reed, D. W., 37
Reeve, James Josiah, 97, 102, 109, 110
Reilly, Brent, 49, 52, 53
Reimer, Sam, 1
Renfree, Harry, 20
Richards, John B., 164
Richardson, George, 70–71
Riley, W. B., 124, 242–249, 253, 255, 256, 257, 267
Robertson, W. M., 138–39, 166
Rockefeller, Jr., John D., 245
Rockwood, Perry F., 201
Ross, J. J., 162
Rosser, Fred, 7
Rowell, James B., 292
Ryrie, James, 25

Sawatsky, Ronald, 19, 58, 61, 63
Scarborough, Charles Morton, 225–26
Schmidt, Nathaniel, 122
Scofield, C. I., 215, 223, 230
Scott, Jack, 272, 278, 281–82
Sharpe, Dores R., 167
Sharpe, Robert, 173n65
Shenstone, Joseph N., 20
Shields, T. T., 25–30, 34, 36–37, 90, 93, 97, 101–102, 106, 108–109, 119–54, 157n1, 163, 165, 166, 169, 170, 175, 184–85, 188, 196, 198, 236–61, 267–79, 287, 292–93, 298
Shields, E. E., 258, 260
Sidey, Edna Reynolds (née Carde), 185
Sidey, J. J., 33, 128n42, 185–202, 286, 292, 294, 296n12
Simpson, A. B., 206
Smalley, W. C., 148
Smith, Al, 252
Smith, Huston, 10
Smith, Ira, 87–88
Smith, Oswald J., 238, 249

Index of Names

Spidle, Simeon, 186
Spurgeon, Charles H., 52, 90, 124, 125–26, 165, 175, 236
Stairs, Onden, 198
Stackhouse, Jr., John G., 1, 9, 25
Steer, George Hobson, 222
Stevens, William, 206
Stewart, William, 87
Stobo, Dorothy Macklem, 112
Stobo, Jr., Edward John, 91, 93–117, 258
Stobo, Sr., Edward John, 98
Stobo, Elizabeth Stuart (née Lindsay), 98
Stobo, Catherine Edwards, 99
Stobo, W. Q., 99
Straton, John Roach, 249–52, 255
Strong, Augustus Hopkins, 121–22

Tarr, Leslie, 35
Tedford, A. L., 189
Thomas, B. D., 267
Thomas, Ernest, 172
Thomas, William Henry Griffith, 95
Thomson, D. E., 25
Torrey, Reuben Archer, 110, 208, 238–39, 256
Troop, George Osborne, 95

Urquart, Thomas, 147

Van Osdel, Oliver, 153, 246n48, 247–48, 249, 253, 254–55
Vincent, Arthur C., 190
Vining, A. J., 144

Watson, Sydney, 224
Watt, Jack, 282
Wayman, H. C., 245–46, 259
Weeks, W. W., 243n30
Welch, George Russell, 100, 107
Wellinger, Frederick William, 83
Wesley, Cindy, 31–32
Whidden, Howard P., 30, 123n19, 132–37, 139, 268
Whitcombe, W. S., 271, 273
Whitefield, George, 278
Wilkinson, Michael, 1
Wilson, A. P., 142
Wilson, Paul R., 122n14, 169, 266, 272, 273, 274, 282, 296
Wilson, Robert S., 41–43
Wilson, Robert W., 38–39
Woods, Bruce, 40, 296–97
Wordsworth, William, 111
Wright, Robert, 216, 265n1, 266

Index of Subjects

Acadia University, 33, 42, 166, 181, 182–83, 186
Amillennialism, 282–83
Arminianism, 53–55, 57, 216
Associated Gospel Churches, 295–96
Atlantic Baptist College (see United Baptist Bible Training School)
Atlantic Baptist Fellowship, 43
Atonement, 145, 170–71

Baptism (see Ordinances)
Baptist, definition of, 2–8; "distinctives," 5–8, 85–86, 194; Identity, 32, 70–84, 90, 180–202, 274
Baptist Bible College Canada and Theological Seminary, 295
Baptist Federation of Canada, 107–108
Baptist Temple News, The, 255
BC Baptist, 162
Bebbington Quadrilateral, 3
Bible (see Scriptures)
Bible and Evangelistic Conference, 188
Bible Baptist Union, 26, 121–22, 127–29, 132, 140, 151–52, 164–65, 241, 244–49, 251, 258–60
Biblical criticism (see higher criticism)
Biblical Inerrancy, 25, 186, 189, 243
Biblical Infallibility, 97, 170
Born Crucified, 209–10
Brandon College, 22–23, 30–31, 123n19, 128n42, 132, 157–76, 185
British Columbia Baptist Missionary Council, 162–63, 168–69

Brookman Controversy, 70–84

Calgary Prophetic Bible Institute, 205, 218–19, 222
Calvinism, 53–54, 57, 90, 214, 215, 230
Canadian Baptist Bible College, 295
Canadian Baptist Seminary, 35
Canadian Baptists (name), 1n3
Canadian Council of Churches, 42
Catholicism, criticism of, 28–29, 115, 228
Central Baptist Seminary, 281–83, 285
Christianity Today, 284
Church, doctrine of, 67–68
Church and State, Baptist relation to, 7
Church Membership, 5, 6, 23–24, 143–44; Regenerate, 86–87
Concerned Pastors (Atlantic Baptists), 42–43
Convention of Regular Baptists of British Columbia, 157–76
Creationism, 116, 186, 213, 222, 244, 252
Crowded to Christ, 212

Darwinian Evolution, 4, 94
Des Moines University, 151, 245–248, 254, 259, 260n119
Dispensationalism, 9, 42, 60–63, 66–67, 186, 189, 212–13, 215–16, 222–23, 227, 229–30, 231
Downgrade Controversy, 125–26, 165

Index of Subjects

Emmanuel Baptist Bible Institute, 295
Eschatology, 7–8, 9, 60–63, 216–17, 220, 224, 282–83; see also amillennialism, dispensationalism, premillennialism, and postmillennialism
Euodia Bible Course, The, 222–23
Evangelical Fellowship of Canada, 271
Evangelical Theological Society, 271
Evangelicalism, definition of, 3; 265–88

FaithWay Baptist College, 295
Feller Institute, 106–107
Fellowship Evangel, The, 279
Fellowship of Evangelical Baptist Churches in Canada, 36–40, 265–88, 296–97
Fellowship of Fundamental Baptist Churches in the Maritime Provinces, 293n5
Fellowship of Independent Baptist Churches of Canada, 30, 35–36, 187, 269–70, 273–81
Fundamentalism, definition of, 1, 8–11; Militant, 10, 24–34, 38–39, 49–92, 153, 160–61, 276–77, 281, 284; Moderate, 10, 34–44, 93–117, 160–61, 265–88; Rebel, 10, 38, 40, 296–97
Fundamentalist Baptist Young People's Association, 29, 270
Fundamentals, The, 20, 93–97, 107, 109–12, 238, 258

General Association of Regular Baptist Churches, 37, 260
General Conference of German Baptist Churches in North America, 31–32
Golden Plains Baptist Bible Institute, 295
Gospel Light, 199
Gospel Witness, The, 26, 119, 129, 131, 136, 165, 253, 255, 268
Grand Ligne Mission, 99, 106
Great Depression, 207, 225, 227, 270

Hell, doctrine of, 72, 74

Heresy, 68, 87, 90, 133
Heritage College and Seminary, 282–83, 285
Higher Criticism, 20, 94, 141, 186, 209, 222
Historicity of the Bible, 110–112, 113, 141n78, 146
Holy Spirit, 209, 218; see also Spiritual gifts

Independence of the Local Church, 6, 85, 86–87, 154, 180–202, 231, 293
Independent Baptist, The, 201
International Christian Mission, 198–200
International Standard Bible Encyclopedia, 97
"Inspiration and Authority of Scripture" (series in *The Canadian Baptist*), 124

Jarvis Street Baptist Church (Toronto), 25–26, 28, 53, 59, 86, 108, 122n14, 134, 235–36, 240, 242, 267, 272–73; removal from convention, 148
Jehovah's Witnesses, 84, 221
Justification, 209, 212

King James Version of the Bible, 217
Kingston Bible College and Academy, 188, 199–200, 294, 296
Kingston Parsonage Case, 33, 196–97
Ku Klux Klan, 251

Legalism, 38–39
London Baptist Bible College, 282, 285
Lord's Supper (see Ordinances)

Maritime Fellowship of Independent Baptists, 200
Maritime Fellowship of Regular Baptist Churches, 293n5
McMaster Divinity College, 40
McMaster University, 20, 27–28, 96, 97, 99–103, 103, 107, 108, 111, 116, 119–54, 185, 237, 239, 245, 260, 267–69, 271
Midland Bible School, 206

Index of Subjects

Miracles, 110, 122
Missionary Training School, 206
Moody Bible Institute, 208
Moral Reform Committee, 106
Moulton College, 130
Mysticism, 210, 214

National Association of Evangelicals, 283
New Brunswick Bible Institute, 41–42, 295
New International Version of the Bible, 271
Northern Baptist Convention, 18, 121–22, 128–29, 133, 166–67, 243, 248, 250
Northwest Baptist Theological Seminary, 271

Ordinances, 5–6, 37, 42–43, 51, 74, 84, 85, 86, 122, 130, 153, 218, 274; "Jesus only" baptism, 219
Ordination, 82, 180, 186, 188, 191–92, 195, 218
Oriental University, 185
Oxford University, 271

Pacificism, 113
Pastor, office of, 60, 103
Pentecost, 208
Pentecostalism, 199–200, 217
Post-Christendom, 2
Postmillennialism, 105
Prairie Bible Institute (Prairie Bible College), 11, 205–215, 294
Prairie Fellowship of Regular Baptists, 286
Prairie Pastor, The, 214
Predestination, 64
Premillennialism, 8, 60–63, 66–67, 186, 189, 216, 282
Prophet, The, 271
Prophetic Bible Conference, 216–17
Prophetic Voice, The, 220
Proto-Fundamentalism, 19–24, 49–91, 93–117, 257–58

Question, The, 199

Racial Issues, 214
Radio ministry, 215, 218, 221, 227–28, 230–31
Regular Baptist Missionary and Educational Society of Canada, 147, 149, 163
Regular Baptist Missionary Fellowship of the Prairie Provinces, 219
Resurrection of Christ, 94, 110, 112, 122, 140, 171
Rochester Seminary, 167

Salvation, 5, 114, 209, 212, 230
Salvation Army, 208
Schism of 1927, 146–50
Scripture, 6, 50, 56–57, 68–69, 209; authority of, 66, 285; Inspiration of, 90, 122, 130, 141, 144, 170–71, 222, 224; literal reading of, 218, 220; see also Biblical Inerrancy, Biblical Infallibility, and "Inspiration and Authority of Scripture" (series in *The Canadian Baptist*)
School and Church, 244n38
Scopes Monkey Trial, 116
Séminaire Baptiste Évangélique du Québec, 41
Separationism, 7–8, 152–53
Shields-Rebman Affair, 246–48
Social Credit, 216, 218–19, 224, 225–29
Social Gospel, 33, 227–28
Soul Liberty, 85, 87
Soul Winners' Association of Nova Scotia, 185
Southern Baptist Theological Seminary, 271
Southern Baptists, 18, 37, 252
Sovereign Grace Fellowship of Baptist Churches, 293
Spiritual gifts, 199–200
Spurgeon's Metropolitan Tabernacle, 126–27, 165, 241–42

Toronto Baptist Seminary, 28, 237, 269, 270–78, 293, 294
Toronto Bible Training School, 19, 95–96, 268

Index of Subjects

Union of Regular Baptist Churches of Ontario and Quebec, 28, 34–37, 120, 147, 149, 150–51, 269–81
Union Theological College, 185
United Baptist Bible Training School, 41–43
University of Chicago, 123n19; Divinity School, 167, 241
University of Toronto, 271

Vancouver Bible Training School, 173–74

Wentworth Statement, 43
Winona Lake School of Theology, 271
Women, views of, 56, 88–89, 298; involvement of, 174, 296
Women's Missionary Society of the Regular Baptists of Canada, 29–30, 270
Woodstock College, 130
World's Christian Fundamentals Association, 243, 258–59, 267
Worldliness, 87, 89, 90, 170, 210–11, 250

CPSIA information can be obtained
at www.ICGtesting.com
Printed in the USA
BVHW091136060522
636033BV00006B/9